DAY FINES IN EUROPE

Day fines, as a pecuniary sanction, have a great potential to reduce inequality in the criminal sentencing system, as they impose the same relative punishment on all offenders irrespective of their income. Furthermore, with correct implementation, they can constitute an alternative sanction to the more repressive and not always efficient short-term prison sentences. Finally, by independently expressing in the sentence the severity and the income of the offender, day fines can increase uniformity and transparency of sentencing. Having this in mind, almost half of the European Union countries have adopted day fines in their criminal justice system. For the first time, this book makes their findings accessible to a wider international audience. Aimed at scholars, policy makers and criminal law practitioners, it provides an opportunity to learn about the theoretical advantages, the practical challenges, the successes and failures, and ways to improve.

Elena Kantorowicz-Reznichenko is a Professor of Quantitative Empirical Legal Studies at the Rotterdam Institute of Law and Economics, Erasmus School of Law, Erasmus University Rotterdam. As an expert on day fines, she has published widely on the topic in international journals and served as an expert advisor to Ministries in different countries that considered the implementation of day fines.

Michael Faure is a Professor of Comparative and International Environmental Law at Maastricht University and Professor of Comparative Private Law and Economics at Erasmus School of Law. He is member of the board of the European Centre of Tort and Insurance Law (Vienna) and a member of the Royal Netherlands Academy of Arts and Sciences.

Day Fines in Europe

ASSESSING INCOME-BASED SANCTIONS
IN CRIMINAL JUSTICE SYSTEMS

Edited by

ELENA KANTOROWICZ-REZNICHENKO

Erasmus University Rotterdam

MICHAEL FAURE

Maastricht University

With the cooperation of

MARIANNE BREIJER

Erasmus University Rotterdam

CAMBRIDGE
UNIVERSITY PRESS

CAMBRIDGE
UNIVERSITY PRESS

University Printing House, Cambridge CB2 8BS, United Kingdom

One Liberty Plaza, 20th Floor, New York, NY 10006, USA

477 Williamstown Road, Port Melbourne, VIC 3207, Australia

314–321, 3rd Floor, Plot 3, Splendor Forum, Jasola District Centre,
New Delhi – 110025, India

79 Anson Road, #06–04/06, Singapore 079906

Cambridge University Press is part of the University of Cambridge.

It furthers the University's mission by disseminating knowledge in the pursuit of
education, learning, and research at the highest international levels of excellence.

www.cambridge.org
Information on this title: www.cambridge.org/9781108490832
DOI: 10.1017/9781108855020

© Cambridge University Press 2021

First published 2021

A catalogue record for this publication is available from the British Library.

ISBN 978-1-108-49083-2 Hardback
ISBN 978-1-108-79643-9 Paperback

Contents

Figures

Tables

Contributors

HANS-JÖRG ALBRECHT, (emeritus) Max Planck Institute for the Study of Crime, Security and Law, Freiburg, as well as University of Freiburg, Germany.

JESÚS BARQUÍN SANZ, University of Granada, Spain.

LORENZ BIBERSTEIN, Zurich University of Applied Sciences, Switzerland.

BRUNO DEFFAINS, University Paris 2 Pantheon Assas, France.

THOMAS ELHOLM, University of Copenhagen, Denmark.

MICHAEL FAURE, Maastricht University and Erasmus University Rotterdam, the Netherlands.

CSABA GYŐRY, Hungarian Academy of Sciences, Centre for Social Sciences, Institute of Legal Studies, Budapest, Hungary.

CHRISTOPHER KAHL, Vienna University of Business and Economics, Austria, under the direction of Robert Kert.

ELENA KANTOROWICZ-REZNICHENKO, Erasmus University Rotterdam, the Netherlands.

MARTIN KILLIAS, (emeritus) Universities of Zurich, Lausanne and St. Gallen, Switzerland.

JIŘÍ KINDL, Skils s.r.o. law firm, as well as Charles University, Prague, Czech Republic.

MITJA KOVAC, University of Ljubljana, Slovenia.

JAN KUPČÍK, Skils s.r.o. law firm, as well as Masaryk University, Brno, Czech Republic.

RAIMO LAHTI, (emeritus) University of Helsinki, Finland.

DAWID MARKO, University of Gdansk, Poland.

HELENA MORÃO, University of Lisbon (Universidade de Lisboa), Research Centre of Criminal Law and Criminal Sciences (CIDPCC, supported by FCT), Portugal.

VALSAMIS MITSILEGAS, Queen Mary University of London, United Kingdom.

FOIVI SOFIA MOUZAKITI, Royal Holloway, University of London, United Kingdom.

MAJA MUNIVRANA VAJDA, University of Zagreb, Croatia.

JACOB ÖBERG, Örebro University, Sweden.

MARIA FERNANDA PALMA, University of Lisbon (Universidade de Lisboa), Research Centre of Criminal Law and Criminal Sciences (CIDPCC, supported by FCT), Portugal.

SLAWOMIR STEINBORN, University of Gdansk, Poland.

JEAN-BAPTISTE THIERRY, University of Lorraine, France.

MIHAIL UDROIU, Court of Appel Oradea, Romania.

VERENA WEINBERGER, Vienna University of Business and Economics, Austria, under the direction of Robert Kert.

Acknowledgements

This book is the result of a collaboration with reporters from many countries. They were asked to draft chapters according to a particular format in order to guarantee the comparability of the chapters. Drafts of the chapters were presented at an international conference organised at Erasmus School of Law Rotterdam on 26 June 2019. We acknowledge financial support for the organisation of that conference from the research programme Behavioural Approaches to Contract and Tort; the Erasmus University Rotterdam Innovation Programme Dynamics of Inclusive Prosperity and the Erasmus Trustfund. We are especially grateful to all authors of the country reports for their willingness to draft chapters under a tight schedule and for their agreement to incorporate comments received during the conference and from the editors.

As editors of this book, we are equally grateful to Marianne Breijer who, as a project manager, supported the entire research project. Marianne also critically examined all chapters and provided invaluable editorial support. We are also grateful to Vera Breijer for her help in harmonising texts, footnotes and references in preparation of the publication of this volume.

Abbreviations

BCCRC	Basis Criminal Code of the Republic of Croatia
CC	Criminal Code
CCP	Code of Criminal Procedure
CEC	Criminal Enforcement Code
CEO	Chief executive officer
CFC	Criminal Fiscal Code
CJA	Criminal Justice Act
CP	Código Penal (Spanish Penal Code)
CPC	Code of Civil Procedure
CSK	zechoslovak koruna (Czechoslovak koruna)
CZK	Czech koruna (Czech koruna)
DKK	Dansk krone (Danish krone)
ECLI	European Case Law Identifier
FINA	Financijska Agencija (Financial Agency)
FinStrG	Finanzstrafgesetz (Act on Fiscal Offences)
HC Deb	House of Commons Debates
HL Deb	House of Lords Debates
HRD	Hrvatski dinar (Croatian dinar)
HRK	Hrvatska kuna (Croatian kuna)
IAS	Indexante dos Apoios Sociais (Indexing reference of social support)
ICS	International Crime Survey
ICVS	International Crime Victims Survey
INE	Instituto Nacional de Estadística (Spanish Statistical Office)
LEC	Ley de Enjuiciamiento Civil (Civil Procedure Act)
LECr	Ley de Enjuiciamiento Criminal (Criminal Procedure Act)
NIP	Taxpayer Identification Number (Poland)
NJA	Nytt Juridiskt Arkiv (Cases from the Swedish Supreme Court)

OIB	Osobni identifikacijski broj (personal identification number) (Croatia)
OLG	Oberlandesgericht (Higher Regional Court of Appeal)
PC	Penal Code
PLN	Polski złoty (Polish Złoty)
RON	Romanian new leu / lei (Romanian currency)
SAN	Sentencia de la Audiencia Nacional (Decision of the National Court)
SAP	Sentencia de la Audiencia Provincial (Decision of the Provincial Court)
SCC	Swiss Criminal Code
SFRY	Socialist Federal Republic of Yugoslavia
SIT	Slovenian tolar
SORS	Statistical Office of the Republic of Slovenia
STS	Sentencia del Tribunal Supremo (Decision of the Supreme Court)
StG	Strafgesetz (Criminal Statute)
StGB	Strafgesetzbuch (Criminal Code)
StPO	Strafprozessordnung (Code of Criminal Procedure)
StVG	Strafvollzugsgesetz (Criminal Executive Code)
VbVG	Verbandsverantwortlichkeitsgesetz (Act on the Responsibility of Legal Entities)
VStG	Verwaltungsstrafgesetz (Act on Administrative Offences)

Introduction

Elena Kantorowicz-Reznichenko and Michael Faure

1.1 INTRODUCTION

A pecuniary sanction is a widespread criminal penalty and it is hard to think of a jurisdiction that does not have some form of such punishment. The most common pecuniary penalty is undoubtedly the fine. However, when we think about fines, we normally think about the most standard model where the size of the fine mainly depends on the severity of the offence. We refer to those fines as fixed fines, even though they might have other names in different criminal justice systems (for example summary fines, lump sum fines). A common feature of this type of fines is that the financial state of the offender does not play a systematic role in its calculation. This is not to say that the financial information is completely irrelevant. Some jurisdictions require accounting for the offender's income or wealth and more particularly his or her capacity to pay the fine when deciding on its size. However, there is no requirement to account for it systematically and usually there are no guidelines on how the financial capacity should be considered.[1]

In contrast, some countries around the world have introduced a different model of a pecuniary sanction – termed 'day fines'. This model can be regarded as a wealth- (or at least income-) dependent fine. It offers a unique calculation system, which enables the fine to reflect independently the severity of the crime, as well as the financial state of the offender. A day fine is meant to be imposed in two stages. First, the sentencer determines a number of days that will be used to calculate the fine based on the severity of the offence (and potentially other relevant factors such as the criminal record of the offender). In the next stage, the sentencer sets the daily unit of the fine, that is the amount the offender needs to pay per day. This unit depends on the income (or wealth)

---

[1]   See Chapter 2.

of the offender. For instance, some jurisdictions set the daily unit to around 50 per cent of the offender's daily income (Finland). The total fine is then the outcome of multiplying the number of days with the daily unit and constitutes the amount the convicted offender has to pay. Consequently, two offenders who committed the same crime but differ in their wealth will receive the same number of days but a different total amount of the fine.

There are multiple advantages of this fine system. First, day fines can increase the fairness of the sanctioning system. Many of the countries, which eventually adopted the wealth-dependent fines, were driven by the perceived inequality created by fixed fines. When fines reflect the severity of the crime and disregard the financial capacity of the offender, low-income offenders bear a heavier burden of punishment than high-income offenders. Moreover, if a country uses imprisonment for fine defaulters, the criminal justice system creates de facto two different sanctions for the rich and the poor: the rich can pay the fixed fine and the poor end up in prison. By reflecting independently the severity of the crime and the financial state of the offender, the day fine has the potential to mitigate the inequality problem. Two offenders who committed the same crime will face the same number of days. However, the amount by which the number of days will be multiplied will differ depending on the income of the offender thus, potentially equalising the relative burden imposed by the fine across offenders with different levels of income.

Second, day fines are also believed to improve deterrence. Fixed fines are often perceived as too low for high-income offenders. They can even simply be regarded as prices wealthy offenders can pay for committing crimes. As a result, fines are usually used only for minor offences. The ability of day fines to be adjusted to the wealth of the offenders opens up an opportunity to tailor the penalty more closely to the income of the offender. Consequently, it can impose a heavier burden of punishment than one size-fits-all fines. This aspect is especially relevant for criminal justice systems which over-utilise short-term imprisonment and search for potential reliable alternatives for the mid-range offences.

Third, day fines can improve uniformity in sentencing. This model of fines offers a clear and straightforward method to calculate the fine. Therefore, different sentencers are expected to impose similar fines in comparable cases and the offender (and public) can clearly see the factors that affected the size of the fine. This is different from the vague obligation not to disregard the financial capacity of the offender in fixed fine systems. Without a structured way of accounting for the wealth, judges are expected to give different weights to the financial aspect. This will result in lack of uniformity in sentencing.

Fourth, day fines can improve transparency in sentencing. When the wealth of the offender is considered in an unsystematic way, a high fine might be imposed on a poor offender who committed a severe offence and on a wealthy offender who committed a minor offence. Hence, the nominal amount of the fine does not express the severity of the crime. With day fines on the other hand, the number of days clearly reflects the severity of the crime, irrespective of the wealth of the offender. In fact, in some countries it is practised to report in the media the number of the imposed days rather than the total amount of the fine (for example Sweden). This not only improves transparency, but also contributes to the censure of punishment. The first element of the day fine – the number of days – explicitly communicates the blameworthiness of the offender who received the fine.

In light of its advantages, an increasing number of countries in Europe[2] are moving away from a fixed fine system and towards adopting the day fine system. By 2020, already half of the European countries are applying day fines. Yet little is known about the practice of those countries with this model of fines. Given the fact that currently not a single English-speaking country is implementing day fines, the international literature and the information on the different practices with this fine are scarce. This book is the first to offer a comprehensive interdisciplinary and comparative analysis of day fines, their advantages and disadvantages, the practices of the different countries and challenges with implementation.

1.2 DAY FINES AROUND THE WORLD

Wealth-dependent fines are not the invention of the twentieth century. In England already in the thirteenth century, fines were higher for richer offenders.[3] This was then theoretically discussed by Montesquieu[4] in the eighteenth century and by Jeremy Bentham in the nineteenth century.[5] However, the modern version of such fines – nowadays termed day fines – seems to have emerged only in the twentieth century. Scandinavian countries pioneered the discussion and the adoption of day fines in Europe with Finland being the first to implement the fine in 1921, shortly followed by Sweden (1931) and Denmark (1933). As the country chapters in this book demonstrate, those countries also served as an inspiration for other European jurisdictions to follow through and to adopt similar models of pecuniary sanctions.

[2] When referring to European countries in this book, we mean the EU Member States and the states of the Schengen Area.
[3] Note, 'Fines and Fining – An Evaluation', 1013, 24.
[4] Montesquieu, *The Spirit of Laws*, p. 108.
[5] Bentham, *Theory of Legislation*, p. 353.

Over the years, day fines were also introduced in countries outside Europe, such as in Peru (1924), Cuba (1936), Brazil (1969), Costa Rica (1972) and Bolivia (1972).[6] Furthermore, during the late 1980s, several American counties experimented with this model of fine. Day fines were believed to provide an opportunity for a wider use of pecuniary sanctions and consequently, to reduce the heavy burden on prisons. In particular, wealth-dependent fines were believed to have a sufficient deterrent effect on poor as well as on rich offenders and thus could reduce the reliance on imprisonment sentences.[7] In those pilot programmes, not only the minimum and maximum number of days were provided, but also tables with guidelines for different categories of offences were constructed which guided the courts about the ranges of days that should be imposed for each category. The daily unit constituted approximately two thirds of the offender's net daily income after deductions.[8] Evaluations of those programmes yielded positive results in terms of rates of payments, the average imposed fines and the court's perception of the ease of the process.[9] Despite the perceived success of the experiments, day fines were not retained in all counties where they were piloted and also did not become widespread in the USA.[10] Even though they can be found in some Codes of particular States in the USA[11] their use is very limited. One explanation for the failure to further implement day fines in the USA might be the 'wrong' timing. The period between the 1970s and the 1990s was characterised by a punitive turn. People lost faith in the idea of rehabilitation and incapacitation became more widespread. Therefore, the political environment at the time might not have been ripe for a reform that would increase the use of pecuniary sanctions and decrease custodial sentences.[12]

Australia, as well, recognising the inequality created by fixed fines, discussed several times over the years the possibility to introduce day fines in their sentencing system. Although courts seem to be guided to account for the offender's

---

[6]   Albrecht and Johnson, 'Fines and Justice Administration: The Experience of the Federal Republic of Germany', 3, 6.

[7]   Farrell, 'The Day-Fine Comes to America', 592.

[8]   McDonald *et al.*, *Day Fines in American Courts: The Staten Island and Milwaukee Experiments*, pp. 21–2.

[9]   McDonald *et al.*, *Day Fines in American Courts: The Staten Island and Milwaukee Experiments*, pp. 6–7; Winterfield & Hillsman, 'The Staten Island Day-Fine Project', p. 5; Vera Institute of Justice, 'Structured Fines: Day Fines As Fair And Collectable Punishment In American Courts', pp. 15–16.

[10] Zedlewski, *Alternatives to Custodial Supervision: The Day Fine*, p. 10.

[11] ALA. CODE para. 12-25-32(2)(b)(8); OKLA. STAT. tit. 22, para. 991a(A)(1)(y).

[12] Kantorowicz-Reznichenko, 'Day Fines: Reviving the Idea and Reversing the (Costly) Punitive Trend', 333–72.

financial capacity, it was unclear how this information should be incorporated in the setting of the fine. Nevertheless, this initiative was rejected time after time. The main arguments against day fines were the complexity of collecting the information and calculating the fine, which could result in delays. In addition, the potential infringement of privacy was stressed as the court would need to access different sources of information about the offender's financial capacity. Finally, remaining problems of inequality were mentioned such as offenders with low income but with assets and significant potential for high earnings in the future, or concealment of income by wealthy offenders.[13] Similarly, day fines were considered and rejected in New Zealand and in Canada.[14]

The day fine model has faced objections also in Europe. A potential reform was discussed in the Netherlands at the end of the 1960s.[15] The advantages that were emphasised with respect to a wealth-dependent fine were the equality between poor and rich offenders, the transparency of the fine due to its two separate components and the potential increased deterrent effect of tailored fines. Nevertheless, the arguments against day fines eventually outweighed its advantages. First, the possible outcome of disproportionate fines for especially wealthy offenders for minor offences was considered unacceptable. Second, it was unclear how a day fine system should operate alongside a fixed fine system, which was rendered still useful for minor violations. Third, the determination of what should be included in the daily unit and the collection and calculation of the fine were perceived as being too complex.[16] However, in light of its advantages, the increasing number of countries in Europe that introduced day fines and the possibilities that advancements in technology provide, it remains to be seen whether past objections will prevent more European countries from adopting this model.

1.3 SYNOPSIS AND STRUCTURE

This book first, in Chapter 2, offers a theoretical analysis of the day fine model to understand its potential to fit two of the main purposes of the criminal

---

[13] See *e.g.* Australian Law Reform Commission, Sentencing, ALRC 44 (1988), para. 114; Australian Law Reform Commission, Sentencing of Federal Offenders, Discussion Paper No. 70 (2005) at 109–10, paras. 7.10, 7.15. See also, Bartl, 'The Day Fine-Improving Equality before the Law in Australian Sentencing', 47–78.

[14] Warner, 'Equality Before the Law and Equal Impact of Sanctions: Doing Justice to Differences in Wealth and Employment Status', pp. 232–3.

[15] In 1969 an extensive governmental report was prepared on day fines which was then used to make the decisions for the reforms of the Criminal Code which eventually entered into force in 1983.

[16] Kantorowicz-Reznichenko and Luining, 'De Dagboete: Reden voor Nieuwe Overpeinzing?', 6–13.

sentencing system – retribution and deterrence. Even though deterrence seems to be one of the potential advantages of day fines, it is less self-evident that such structure will fit the proportionality principle of retributive justice. Following this analysis, we also discuss the different features of the model that would make it optimal. Such exercise provides a benchmark against which to assess the actual models practiced by the countries.

The theoretical analysis is followed by Chapters 3 to 18 that cover all the European countries[17] that currently (or previously) implemented the day fine system, in chronological order of their introduction.[18] Those chapters are especially important to demonstrate the experience of the countries with this type of fine, the different challenges they face(d) with its implementation and their practices. To allow for a comparative analysis, all the chapters are structured in a similar manner and cover the most important aspects of the model, that is (a) the historical development of day fines in the country and the rationale for introducing it; (b) the legal framework and the structure of the fine, including questions concerning access to financial information of the offender which are important for the optimal calculation of the fine; (c) the practical implementation in terms of how widely it is actually used and for which offences; (d) the public and professional perception of day fines; and finally (e) the special challenges each country faces with respect to this model of pecuniary sanctions. Among the country chapters we also include England and Wales, which is an interesting case study due to the failure of day fines in the country. 'Unit fines' (as they were termed in England and Wales) were introduced at the beginning of the 1990s and were abolished only seven months later. We believe this chapter can shed additional light on the complexity of day fines and reasons and circumstances that can lead to its rejection.

Learning from the experience of the countries can prompt research on the topic on the one hand and can assist policy-makers who consider introducing (or improving) the day fine system in their countries on the other hand. Therefore, in Chapter 19 we provide a comparative analysis, based on the country chapters. This analysis integrates the findings and reflects on the strengths and weaknesses of the implementation, with some thoughts on how to overcome the hurdles. In addition, we reflect on issues of legal transplants.

---

[17]   By this we mean the entire Schengen area, rather than just EU Member States. For that reason we also included a chapter on Switzerland. Liechtenstein is the only European country that is not included in the book. They have adopted day fines in 1988, but their model was entirely copied from the Austrian system.

[18]   The information in this book includes developments until December 2019. Any legal changes adopted afterwards, are not included. Furthermore, we focus on the system of adult criminal justice. Juvenile legal rules are mostly excluded.

REFERENCES

ALA. CODE § 12–25-32(2)(b)(8); OKLA. STAT. tit. 22, § 991a(A)(1)(y).

Albrecht, H. and Johnson, E. H. 1980. 'Fines and Justice Administration: The Experience of the Federal Republic of Germany', *International Journal of Comparative and Applied Criminal Justice* 4: 3–14.

Bartl, B. 2012. 'The Day Fine-Improving Equality before the Law in Australian Sentencing', *University of Western Sydney Law Review* 16: 47–78.

Bentham, J. 1891. *Theory of Legislation*. Kegan Paul, Trench, Trübner & Co.

Farrell, P. G. 1990. 'The Day-Fine Comes to America', *Buffalo Law Review* 38: 591–617.

Kantorowicz-Reznichenko, E. 2018. 'Day Fines: Reviving the Idea and Reversing the (Costly) Punitive Trend', *American Criminal Law Review* 55: 333–72.

Kantorowicz-Reznichenko, E. and Luining, E. 2016. 'De Dagboete: Reden voor Nieuwe Overpeinzing?', *Trema Straftoemetingsbulletin* 39(1): 6–13.

McDonald, D. C. *et al.* 1992. 'Day Fines in American Courts: The Staten Island and Milwaukee Experiments', *National Institute of Justice, U.S. Department of Justice* 136611, 21–22.

Montesquieu, 2001. *The Spirit of Laws*. Kitchener, Ont.: Batoche Books.

Note, F. 1953. 'Fines and Fining – An Evaluation', *University of Pennsylvania Law Review* 101: 1013–30.

Vera Institute of Justice. 1995. 'Structured Fines: Day Fines as Fair and Collectable Punishment in American Courts', *Vera Institute of Justice* 1522.

Warner, K. 2012. 'Equality Before the Law and Equal Impact of Sanctions: Doing Justice to Differences in Wealth and Employment Status' in Zedner, L. and Roberts, J. V. (eds.), *Principles and Values in Criminal Law and Criminal Justice: Essays in Honour of Andrew Ashworth*. Oxford: Oxford University Press, pp. 225–43.

Winterfield, L. L. and Hillsman, S. T. 1993. 'The Staten Island Day-Fine Project', *National Institute of Justice, U.S. Department of Justice* Ncj 138538: 1–7.

Zedlewski, E. W. 2010. 'Alternatives to Custodial Supervision: The Day Fine', *National Institute of Justice, U.S. Department of Justice* Ncj 230401: 1–12.

2

Theoretical Perspectives on Day Fines

Elena Kantorowicz-Reznichenko

2.1 INTRODUCTION

In order to understand the additional value of day fines to the classical pecuniary sanctions, it ought to be analysed in light of the theoretical justifications of the criminal sanctioning system. The justification of punishment is an old inquiry that goes back to the ancient times of the Greek philosophers. Even though in modern times the criminal justice system and the right of the state to punish individuals are taken for granted, there are different theories that provide the justification for that practice. This chapter reviews the two main (relevant) justifications discussed in the legal philosophy literature – deterrence (utilitarian) and retribution – and analyses day fines in light of these approaches. Since day fines are inherently different from fixed fines, in terms of the amount of the fine and its calculation, it is important to analyse whether this model is in line with the theoretical justifications of punishment. There are, of course, other purposes of punishment such as incapacitation,[1] rehabilitation,[2] and restitution.[3] However, since fines in general and day fines in particular are not expected to meet these objectives when imposed as a sole sanction, those justifications are not discussed here.[4]

---

[1] Blumstein, Cohen and Nagin, *Deterrence and Incapacitation: Estimating the Effect of Criminal Sanctions on Crime Rates.*

[2] Von Hirsch and Ashworth, *Principled Sentencing: Readings on Theory and Policy.*

[3] Johnstone, *Restorative Justice: Ideas, Values, Debates.*

[4] For a more comprehensive discussion of punishment justifications and their criticism see, for example, Honderich and Chester, *Punishment: The Supposed Justifications.* One may, of course, suggest that day fines incapacitate the offender by taking on a daily basis a significant portion of his or her income. Similarly, day fines can be relevant to rehabilitation in the sense that if it served as an alternative to imprisonment, it has a potential to avoid the criminogenic effect of imprisonment. In other words, it allows the person for example to maintain his or her employment, not to associate with other criminals, etc. and indirectly enables this person to start over. However, such interpretations are not traditional and go beyond the scope of this chapter.

In addition, this chapter discusses a theoretically optimal structure of a day fine model. This will constitute a benchmark to evaluate the day fine models that are implemented in practice in different European countries.

2.2 JUSTIFICATIONS OF PUNISHMENT AND DAY FINES

2.2.1 *Retribution and Just Desert*

The most notable proponent of the old 'retribution'[5] or 'retaliation' justification for punishment is Immanuel Kant.[6] According to Kant, no person can be treated as merely a means to an end. In other words, the punishment does not serve the purpose of threatening other potential offenders. A sanction may be inflicted upon an individual only for the reason that he or she has committed a crime. The rationale behind this approach is that any act that the criminal commits against another person should be seen as if he or she committed it against himself or herself.[7]

When discussing the question of how severe the punishment should be, the retribution justification stresses the concept of 'an eye for an eye' and the principle of equality. A person deserves a punishment that would be equal to his or her wrongdoing and expresses his or her internal wrongfulness. For instance, the only proper penalty for a murderer is the death penalty and no other means may be used to punish such a crime. Therefore, a punishment needs to fit exactly the crime.[8] In a broader sense, the Kantian retribution approach seeks to restore the equilibrium. It is believed that once a person commits a crime, he or she places him or herself in an advantageous position as compared to law abiding citizens. Thus, in order to restore the initial state, the offender must be punished.[9]

A similar modern approach to retribution is termed 'desert'. This is a past-looking theory that asserts that a person should be punished for his or her crimes because he or she *deserves* it.[10] The punishment conveys a criticism in order to

---

[5] Some parts of this section are based on my unpublished PhD dissertation (Reznichenko, 'Cost-Effective Criminal Enforcement: A Law and Economics Approach').

[6] There are different streams of retributive justice, focusing on different aspects of the justification of punishment. I do not profess that this chapter provides a comprehensive account of all the various approaches to retributive justice. In this account, I simply provide the fundamental notions of the general and the widespread approach to serve as the basis for the analysis of day fines.

[7] Kant, *The Philosophy of Law*, pp. 195–8.

[8] *Ibid.*

[9] Murphy, *Kant: The Philosophy of Right*, p. 121.

[10] Von Hirsch, *Doing Justice: The Choice of Punishments, Report of the Committee for the Study of Incarceration*, p. 46.

express society's discontent of the criminal's behaviour. Bearing this in mind, the gravity of punishment should be proportionate to the crime. Inasmuch as the criminal sanction carries blame, severer crime should be punished more harshly. This way the punishment itself can express the discontent towards the prohibited act. Thus, two offenders who committed the same crime should receive the same punishment.[11] This approach as well aims at restoring the initial balance of rights and responsibilities between the citizens. In other words, when a criminal violates the law he or she, on the one hand, still enjoys the benefits from living in a society where others follow the law, but at the same time, gains additional benefits from violating his or her own responsibilities to follow the law. Imposing a punishment corrects this imbalance and creates equal rights and obligations for all members of society.[12]

A central principle in retributive justice theory is proportionality. The severity of punishment must be proportional to the blameworthiness and the culpability of the offender.[13] Blameworthiness focuses on the offences committed and addresses the seriousness of the imposed or potential harm, and culpability normally refers to the level of intent of the offender to commit the crime.[14] In this respect we need to meet the test of the cardinal and the ordinal proportionality.[15] The former refers to the requirement of the punishment not to be too lenient or too harsh in absolute terms. For instance, minor theft should not be punishable by a life imprisonment and a murder should not be punished just by imposing a fine. The latter – ordinal proportionality – refers to the relative gravity of the sanction. People committing the same offence should receive the same punishment and people committing different offences should receive different sanctions, based on the degree of severity of the offence committed. Consequently, the cardinal proportionality principle sets the general limits to the punishment for each offence and the ordinal proportionality principle guides the distribution of sanctions across different offences.[16]

Fulfilment of the proportionality condition, prima facie, poses a problem with the implementation of day fines. With fixed fines, the nominal amount is

[11]   Von Hirsch, *Censure and Sanctions*, p. 9.
[12]   Haist, 'Deterrence in a Sea of Just Deserts: Are Utilitarian Goals Achievable in a World of Limiting Retributivism', 802.
[13]   Von Hirsch, *Censure and Sanctions*, p. 15. It should be noted though, that if retribution is only about compensating for the unfair advantage that was gained by the criminal through his or her criminal act, proportionality of punishment is not so self-evident. However, this is not the only justification according to retributive justice approach (see pp. 7–9).
[14]   Frase, 'Excessive Prison Sentences, Punishment Goals and the Eighth Amendment: Proportionality Relative to What', 590.
[15]   Von Hirsch, *Censure and Sanctions*, pp. 18–19.
[16]   Perry, 'The Role of Retributive Justice in the Common Law of Torts: A Descriptive Theory', 182.

set in proportion to the crime's severity. However, in the case of day fines, the total amount differs across offenders who committed the same crime, depending on their wealth. Whether the principle of proportionality is really a challenge for the day fine system heavily depends on the chosen meaning of *proportionality*. Should the objective size of the punishment fit the severity of the crime, or should the subjective 'pain' which is inflicted on the offender be proportionate to the crime committed?

The former understanding of the concept would lead to the conclusion that day fines violate the objective principle of proportionality. Imposing different amounts of fine on two offenders who committed the same crime, means that at least in one of these cases, the punishment is not proportionate to the crime. This effectively means a violation of the ordinal proportionality principle. Furthermore, day fines might result in high fines for minor offences (when the offender is wealthy) and low fines for severe offences (when the offender is poor). One such example can be found in the highly publicised case in Finland where a CEO of Nokia received a fine of more than 100,000 euros for speeding.[17] Consequently, also the principle of the cardinal proportionality would be violated.[18]

However, a narrow and strict view of the proportionality principle does not seem to be widespread. Accounting for solely the severity of the criminal *act*, while completely disregarding the *person* who committed it would require ignoring such aspects as the offender's criminal record.[19] Yet, to the best of my knowledge, most if not all criminal justice systems treat the criminal record as a relevant factor in determining the punishment. Moreover, it should be noticed that even criminal justice systems which favour the fixed fine models, do not render a person's ability to pay as an irrelevant factor for the pecuniary punishment.[20] One major distinction between such systems and jurisdictions which apply day fines, is that only in the latter the financial state of the

---

[17] Nokia Boss Gets Record Speeding Fine, BBC NEWS (14 January 2002, 2:29 PM), https://perma.cc/RQ7F-B4GF. [Hereinafter: 'the Nokia case'].

[18] Perry and Kantorowicz-Reznichenko, 'Income-Dependent Punitive Damages', p. 871.

[19] There are theorists who indeed support such view, see Roberts, 'The Role of Criminal Record in the Sentencing Process', pp. 316–19. However, such view does not seem to hold in practice given the disparity in sentencing between first-time offenders and recidivists who committed the same crime.

[20] For instance, in England and Wales, para. 164, Part 12, Chapter 1 to the Criminal Justice Act 2003 requires the courts to inquire about the offender's financial capacity and account for this information in the size of the fine. Similarly, Article 24 of the Dutch Penal Code prescribes to account for the offender's financial ability when setting the fine. Also in the USA such provisions can be found: in federal laws – 18 U.S.C. para. 3572(a) (2012); as well as state laws – e.g. N.Y. Penal Law para. 80.00(1) (McKinney 2016); ALA. R. Crim. P. 26.11(b).

offender is accounted in a systematic manner and is a mandatory factor to incorporate in the calculation of the fine. Therefore, it seems that even in fixed fine systems a strict and narrow meaning of the proportionality principle is not followed.

A broader definition of proportionality would suggest that the level of 'suffering' from the punishment should be proportionate to the crime and not only the punishment's objective size. This point can relate to the 'subjectivist' approach to criminal sanctions.[21] In its extreme, it is suggested that since people experience sanctions differently, depending on their level of sensitivity, their punishment should be calibrated to their level of suffering. For example, when considering an imprisonment sanction, the length of the prison sentence should not only depend on the severity of the crime, but also on the level of distress one experiences when being locked up.[22]

The day fine system does not suggest to completely individualise the fine. Many aspects of how a person experiences his or her punishment are unobservable. Therefore, the extreme view of the subjectivists is not feasible in practice even if it were desirable on moral grounds. However, wealth or income is an objective factor that is expected to affect the level of a punished person's suffering. Its observable characteristic and relevance can be derived also from the frequent obligation not to ignore wealth in jurisdictions that use fixed fines. Put in economic terms, the utility loss of a poor person from each additional unit of deprived wealth is expected to be higher than that of a rich person. The disposable income of a poor person is much lower, thus any additional deprivation of wealth results in a deprivation of more basic needs. In fact, a fixed fine can be viewed as a regressive fine. The poorer the offender, the larger portion of his or her wealth he or she needs to forgo to cover the same amount of fine as a rich offender. For example, a 500 euro fine constitutes 50 per cent of a person's monthly income if he or she earns 1,000 euros per month. On the other hand, the exact same fine constitutes only 5 per cent of the monthly income of a person whose monthly income is 10,000 euros. Consequently, imposing an equal absolute fine on offenders who committed the same crime, yet differ in their income, results in de facto harsher punishment for the poor offender. In order to place wealthy and poor offenders on relatively equal terms the portion of their deprived income should be equal rather than the total amount of the fine.

[21]   Bronsteen, Buccafusco and Masur, 'Happiness and Punishment', pp. 1037–82; Kolber, 'The Subjective Experience of Punishment', pp. 182–236; Kolber, 'The Comparative Nature of Punishment', pp. 1565–608.

[22]   Kolber, 'The Subjective Experience of Punishment', pp. 182–236.

One should note that even supporters of a more objective approach to punishment and those who explicitly object to the subjectivist approach, do not render wealth-dependent fines as objectionable. The claim goes that a model such as day fines can still be ex ante objective across persons.[23] Looking at the two components of the day fine, it is easy to see that the number of days is an objective component. This component meets even the strict criteria of the narrowly defined proportionality principle. The number of days, similarly to any other 'time' punishment such as prison or community service, depends heavily on the severity of the crime, even though other factors such as culpability and criminal record also play a role. It assures that the sanction is not arbitrary and is directly connected to the severity of the criminal act. Furthermore, the number of imposed days can independently convey the level of disapprobation of the criminal act (either as a way to communicate it to the offender himself[24] or to the society as a whole).[25] And finally, the component of the number of days can meet the requirements of cardinal proportionality as well as ordinal proportionality. Any system can set the absolute limits on the number of days that can be imposed for each particular offence (and many systems actually do).[26] Furthermore, this component of the day fine model enables the courts to impose a different number of days depending on the gravity of the offence, thus meeting the ordinal proportionality condition.

The second component – the daily unit, which depends on the person's wealth or income – is seemingly subjective. However, even in this case an objective element can be found. The jurisdictions that apply the day fine model usually set a uniform *portion* that should be taken from the offender's daily unit, irrespective of his or her wealth. This is in fact a moderate approach, since taking the subjective experience of punishment to its extreme would suggest accounting for each individual's utility loss from a fine. Consequently, not only the total amount would differ across offenders, but also the portion of their wealth which is taken from them. Therefore, the day fine model seems to meet the middle ground between an extreme objective approach (disregarding entirely the persons who committed the crime and focusing only on the criminal act) and the extreme subjective approach (tailoring the punishment entirely to the person).

[23] Markel and Flanders, 'Bentham on Stilts: The Bare Relevance of Subjectivity to Retributive Justice', pp. 956–7.
[24] *Ibid.*, pp. 931–2.
[25] Von Hirsch, *Censure and Sanctions*, pp. 15–16.
[26] See the country chapters for a review of the number of days that can be imposed for different offences.

2.2.2 *Deterrence*

The deterrence theory is a utilitarian concept[27] that rationalises an act by its consequence. Deterrence as the main justification for imposing punishment can be traced back to Protagoras (as reinstated in the writings of Plato):

> For no one punishes a wrong-doer in consideration of the simple fact that he has done wrong, unless one is exercising the mindless vindictiveness of a beast. Reasonable punishment is not vengeance for a past wrong – for one cannot undo what has been done – but is undertaken with a view to the future, to deter both the wrong-doer and whoever sees him being punished from repeating the crime.[28]

Therefore, as opposed to the retribution approach, according to the deterrence theory the state has the right to punish not for the *reason* that the offender committed a crime, but rather for the *purpose* of preventing future crimes. Already at this stage, the theory includes both individual and general deterrence. Whereas the former seeks to discourage the punished criminal from repeating his or her crimes, the latter intends to dissuade other potential offenders from committing similar misconducts.[29]

Many centuries later, philosophers revived the idea of punishing individuals in order to deter prospective crimes. In the eighteenth century, Cesare Beccaria asserted that the right of the sovereign to impose a sanction is restricted to the sole purpose of protecting the society. He repeated the idea that inasmuch as the punishment cannot undo past crimes, the drive for imposing a sanction is the deterrence of offenders from committing wrong-doings in the future. Consequently, according to Beccaria the severity of punishment should be balanced between the necessity to leave an impression on potential criminals and the need to refrain from imposing senseless suffering.[30]

Following Beccaria, Jeremy Bentham promoted punishment as the instrument that the state may use with the aim of preventing future crimes through imposition of fear.[31] According to his utility theory, if the enforcement

---

[27] Deterrence is not the only goal in the utilitarian approach. Incapacitation and rehabilitation are also relevant according to this approach for the justification of punishment. See generally Frase, 'Punishment Purposes', p. 70. However, deterrence seems to be the only, or at least the most relevant utilitarian justification for pecuniary sanctions. Therefore, I focus here on deterrence.

[28] Cooper and Hitchinson, 'Protagoras', p. 759.

[29] For a more comprehensive definition see Zimring and Hawkins, *Deterrence; The Legal Threat in Crime Control*, pp. 71–2.

[30] Beccaria, *An Essay on Crimes and Punishments*, pp. 36–7.

[31] Bentham, *Theory of Legislation: Principles of the Penal Code*, p. 41.

authorities would generate a threat of costs higher than the potential benefits from crimes, it would discourage people from committing those crimes. Hence, the first objective of punishment is to deter all crimes. Inasmuch as not all crimes can be deterred, Bentham justifies proportionality in punishment to preclude the most severe crimes. If sanctions vary, the potential criminal would choose to commit those crimes that have the threat of a lighter sanction.[32] This objective is referred to as 'marginal deterrence'.

In modern times, the deterrence theory was translated into an economic model of rational choice and is now well established in the Law and Economics literature. According to this model, criminals are rational individuals and utility maximisers, thus, they choose to commit crimes only when it provides them benefits which outweigh their expected costs. Enforcement authorities in turn are able to create a threat of punishment that would constitute expected costs for potential criminals and to ensure those costs outweigh crime benefits.[33] Deterring crime is justified to prevent purely involuntary transactions, which are generally inefficient due to misallocation of scarce resources.[34]

When turning to pecuniary sanctions, according to the utilitarian approach, the size of the fine needs to be set in a way that deters the criminal from committing the crime (imposing higher expected costs as compared to the benefits of the crime). There are different theoretical models investigating the optimal fine and the way of its calculation. These models discuss whether the size of the fine should be equal to the harm[35] or the gain[36] resulting from the crime and what should be the optimal probability of punishment. The problem with these models is that their effectiveness entirely depends on the probability of detection. Only when the likelihood to be detected is perfect, can fine-equals-harm or fine-equals-gain deter offenders from committing their crimes. In reality, the probability of detection almost never equals one and the necessary higher fine to compensate for it often increases the amount of the fine to such an extent that it cannot be afforded by low-income offenders.[37]

From a deterrence perspective, a (fixed) fine, which is not dependent on wealth, can never equally deter all types of offenders. Low fines are suitable to

[32] Bentham, *An Introduction to the Principles of Morals and Legislation*, pp. 178–9.
[33] Becker, 'Crime and Punishment: An Economic Approach', pp. 169–217.
[34] Posner, 'An Economic Theory of the Criminal Law', pp. 1193–231.
[35] Polinsky and Shavell, 'The Optimal Tradeoff between the Probability and Magnitude of Fines', pp. 880–91.
[36] Polinsky and Shavell, 'Should Liability Be Based on the Harm to the Victim or the Gain to the Injurer?', pp. 427–37.
[37] Kantorowicz-Reznichenko, 'Day-Fines: Should the Rich Pay More?', pp. 481–501.

deter low-income offenders.[38] However, they merely create a pricing system for wealthier offenders, who can decide the offence is worth paying for. On the other hand, too high fines, which are adjusted to deter wealthy offenders, result in inability to pay for the poor offenders. Consequently, poorer criminals will receive alternative sanctions (e.g. community service or imprisonment), which are harsher than a fine in terms of limitation on liberty. This, in turn, creates de facto two parallel criminal sentencing systems for the poor and the rich.

An additional issue is the proportionality of the sanction to the severity of the crime. Also in the utilitarian approach, as we have seen above, proportionality plays a role.[39] It provides marginal deterrence (if not all crimes can be prevented, imposing harsher sanctions for severer crimes should increase the deterrence level of committing such crimes as compared to less severe crimes). In theory, for this discussion it does not seem to matter whether we adopt the objective, narrow definition or the more subjective meaning of proportionality. In both cases, as the severity of the crime increases so will the punishment, thus, prima facie, achieving marginal deterrence. The reason for that is that marginal deterrence is relevant for the first component of the day fine – the number of days. It is the number of days that needs to increase as a function of the crime's severity. The daily unit is irrelevant at this stage. However, as demonstrated above, disregarding a person's wealth (as would be required under the strict and narrow meaning of proportionality) would harm the general and individual deterrence. If we are unable to achieve individual and general deterrence, marginal deterrence seems to lose its value.

Take an example of a wealthy offender who can easily afford the amount of fixed fines imposed by the courts for many of the offences. Incremental increases in such fines would not have a strong effect on his or her behaviour. For instance, the court imposes fine X for causing an accident due to negligent behaviour and 2X for hit-and-run. The idea of increasing the fine for a hit-and-run offence is to assure that the perpetrator stays and provides help to the victim. Therefore, the increase in punishment is meant to achieve marginal deterrence. However, if the fine is not adjusted to the wealth of the offender

---

[38]   Under the assumption, of course, that the fine is not too low even for a low-income offender.

[39]   Robinson and Darley, 'Utility of Desert', pp. 746–90. Besides marginal deterrence, the utilitarian approach supports the proportionality principle in the sense of matching the costs of the punishment to its benefits ('ends proportionality'). Furthermore, among the different alternative punishments, one should always choose the option that costs the least, while achieving the same goal ('means proportionality'). See Frase, 'Excessive Prison Sentences, Punishment Goals and the Eighth Amendment: Proportionality Relative to What', p. 592. Due to the limited scope of this chapter and the fact day fines are not being compared to other types of sanctions (e.g. imprisonment), this aspect is not addressed here.

and 2X constitutes a very small portion of the wealthy offender's income, he or she might choose to commit the harsher crime, in order to reduce the probability of his or her detection. The same can also apply to a poor offender. If a low-income offender does not have the means to cover fine X, he or she also does not have the means to cover fine 2X. Therefore, in both cases he or she might face an imprisonment sentence and prefer to commit the harsher crime to avoid detection all together. Consequently, the fine neither achieves individual deterrence, nor marginal deterrence.

Day fines mitigate those problems by constituting a kind of price discrimination system. Accordingly, this model of pecuniary sanctions creates similar incentives to commit the offence, irrespective of a person's wealth. The idea of wealth dependent-fines was already explicitly promoted by Jeremy Bentham:

> A pecuniary punishment, if the sum is fixed, is in the highest degree unequal ... Fines have been determined without regard to the profit of the offense, to its evil, or to the wealth of the offender ... Pecuniary punishments should always be regulated by the fortune of the offender. The relative amount of the fine should be fixed, not its absolute amount; for such a part of the offender's fortune.[40]

The modern model of day fines follows this logic. The number of days (with respect to each specific offence), as well as in many cases the portion of wealth or income, which is counted for in the daily unit, constitutes the fixed component of the fine. Consequently, despite the varying total amount, the relative amount of the fine is fixed. This structure of a pecuniary sanction has the potential to achieve all three types of deterrence promoted by the deterrence theory. As the fine is adjusted to the person's wealth, individual deterrence should be achieved to the same extent for any offender irrespective of his or her wealth. The fine is no longer a one-size-fits-all solution and thus should not lead to under- or over-deterrence of specific groups in the population, depending on their wealth. Similar logic applies to general deterrence. If a potential offender knows that the size of the fine will be adjusted to his or her wealth, as well as to the seriousness of the offence, the 'price' of such a fine might be too high to make it worth committing the crime. This system should result in equal distribution of fine defaulters and imposition of alternative (more severe) sanctions on offenders who fail to pay their fines. Finally, given the theoretical success of individual and general deterrence, marginal deterrence should be achieved through the increasing number of days imposed as a function of the seriousness of the crime.

---

[40] Bentham, *Theory of Legislation: Principles of the Penal Code*, pp. 132–3.

2.3 THEORETICALLY OPTIMAL DAY FINE MODEL

Until now I have discussed whether the day fine model may fit the two main (and most relevant) justifications of punishment – retributive justice and deterrence (utilitarian approach). From the analysis it seems, at least under certain conditions, that this model of pecuniary sanctions might be superior to the fixed fine system. However, there are several aspects of this model that can vary from system to system and that have an effect on its optimal structure. This section discusses the main theoretical features,[41] which can achieve optimal deterrence and/or a more proportionate fine in terms of its retributive value.[42]

2.3.1 *The Scope of Wealth*

The first question is the desirable scope of wealth that should be counted for in the daily unit. As will be shown in the country chapters, jurisdictions differ in the wealth they instruct to capture when calculating the daily unit. It can range from only employment income to the entire wealth of the offender. Should the court take into account only what the offender has obtained through employment, or should it also consider everything the offender owns and all other sources of income, such as profits from investments, assets, inheritance, etc.?

From the deterrence theory perspective, accounting for anything less than the entire wealth of the offender in the daily unit, can potentially lead to under-deterrence of some groups. If a person's main or sole income is not from employment, threatening him or her with a fine that is entirely based on employment income is expected to be ineffective.[43] Take for example a potential unemployed offender whose income is derived from inheritance. If the daily unit is entirely based on employment income that would mean that

---

[41] Other theoretical aspects are also relevant, such as the number of days, the enforcement instruments and the threatened sanctions in case of not paying. However, due to the limited scope of this chapter, only the features which concern the financial aspect of the day fine model are covered. Making the fine dependent on one's wealth is what makes this model unique and distinguishable from fixed fines and this is also the reason that this aspect is analysed in this chapter.

[42] The theoretical points discussed in this section were touched upon in Kantorowicz-Reznichenko (2015). However, this chapter provides a deeper theoretical analysis of those points and especially adds the implications of considering the retributive justice approach.

[43] In this type of argument I do not account for the effect of stigma and having a criminal record as such. Those factors can play a role in deterring a potential offender, especially first-time offenders, who bear the costs of losing their reputation. However, for the purpose of the current analysis, I only look at the deterrent effect of the pecuniary aspect of the punishment.

the daily amount he or she needs to pay is zero. Therefore, irrespective of the number of days he or she will receive for a committed offence the total fine would equal zero. This, in theory, significantly reduces any type of deterrence (individual, general and marginal). Less extreme cases are possible where the potential offender receives employment income, but has other sources of income as well. His or her fine would be a positive amount but will fail to reflect the adequate portion from his or her wealth in order to achieve optimal deterrence.

In terms of retributive justice, accounting for the entire wealth might also be the optimal strategy. If we adopt the middle-ground approach as discussed in this chapter, the goal is to equalise the impact the pecuniary punishment has on the offender, while using an observable measure of variation (wealth). In other words, the number of days needs to be proportionate to the severity of the crime. The *portion* of the deprived wealth should be fixed and reflected by the fine. In any other case, the fine is not proportionate based on the middle-ground approach. Take as an example two offenders who committed the same crime and have the same wealth. However, offender A's wealth is entirely from his or her employment salary and the main source of income of offender B is the interest he or she receives on the money he or she inherited. Assume both offenders receive ten days of fine for their crime and the fixed portion for the daily unit is 50 per cent of their daily income. Given the identical wealth and offence committed by the two offenders, a proportionate fine should be the same for both. However, if the daily unit is solely based on the employment income, offender A will have to pay a fine and offender B's fine will equal zero. This outcome clearly violates the equality before the law principle and the principle of proportionality.

2.3.2 *The Limit on the Daily Unit*

Another theoretically relevant question is whether there should be placed a limit on the daily amount that can be deprived from the offender? In many jurisdictions which are using fixed fines there is a limit on the fine that can be imposed for different offences. In addition, aside from the life imprisonment sentence, all 'time' sentences have an upper bound. In other words, there is a number of (conditional or unconditional) imprisonment months that can be imposed on a convicted offender, a number of community hours and a number of months or days of driver licence revocation. Therefore, a question arises, even if the portion of income for the daily unit is fixed, should there be a limit on the total amount that can daily be deprived from an offender?

From the deterrence theory perspective, there should not be an upper bound for the daily unit. Such limit would inherently decrease deterrence of the richest offenders. For instance, let us assume the daily unit of a fine cannot exceed 100 euros. If the fixed portion of wealth for the daily unit is 50 per cent, then such model can obtain an optimal deterrence only for offenders whose daily income (wealth) is less than 200 euros. For people whose income is above this amount, the maximum allowed daily unit no longer constitutes 50 per cent of their daily wealth. Therefore, a person who earns, for example, 1,000 euros per day, loses only 10 per cent of his or her daily income if the installed limit in the day fine model is 100 euro per day. Such legal limitation is in theory bound to create under-deterrence of certain groups of offenders.

From a retributive justice perspective, creating no upper bound for the daily unit raises concerns of disproportionate fines. As has been mentioned before, there were already cases where an extremely high fine was imposed for a minor offence such as speeding. Such examples give a sense of arbitrary criminal fines that punish rich people for being rich. However, if considering the middle-ground approach advocated in this chapter, one should remember the separate elements of the day fine model. It is the number of days, rather than the total amount of the fine, which should be assessed with respect to the blameworthiness of the offender. As long as this element is proportionate to the severity of the crime, the fine should be considered proportional. Even in the most cited example, the Nokia case, the driver received fourteen days of fine for his offence. This number does not seem to be disproportionate (given that the general maximum prescribed by the law in Finland is 120 days). It was the driver's especially high income that increased the total fine. Not following the day fine model structure creates a regressive fine that increases the portion of the deprived wealth of poorer offenders. There seems to be a conceptual difficulty to accept the notion that a regressive fine is disproportionate to the severity of the offence, while a 'flat' fine (same portion of wealth for the daily unit irrespective of wealth) is proportionate.

2.3.3 *Information on the Financial Status of the Offender*

A crucial challenge to an optimal day fine is the asymmetric information between the offenders and the authorities with respect to the offenders' income. Even if we decide that the scope of the fine is the entire wealth and there is no limit on the daily unit, the authorities must have full access to a person's financial capacities in order to achieve optimal deterrence. If the court is aware of only some sources of a person's income and bases its calculation on this information, the fine is expected to lead to under-deterrence.

Full access to financial information is also necessary to achieve proportionality in sentencing, at least for the middle-ground approach advocated in this chapter where the fine is tailored to the offenders' relevant observable features. A fine that is based on incomplete wealth of the offender will impose a lesser burden on him or her and will constitute a lesser portion of his or her deprived wealth than is intended. Consequently, the fine will not be proportionate to the blameworthiness (specifically, the portion of the wealth) and will also not be relatively equal across offenders who committed the same crime.

In theory, two conditions need to be met to fulfil this theoretical requirement for an optimal fine. First, courts need to have legal access to all sources of information about the person's financial state (for example tax reports, bank statements and property registration). Second, courts need to use the entire information in order to calculate the daily unit. Violation of either of these two conditions will hinder the application of an optimal fine. When one considers these conditions in practical terms, their fulfilment is not easy due to privacy issues as well as to the costs of obtaining the information. However, the practical side of the theoretical conditions is the objective of Chapter 19 in this book.

2.4 CONCLUSION

In this chapter, I have analysed the day fine model from the perspective of the two main approaches to the justification of criminal punishment: deterrence (utilitarian) and retribution. Day fines are relatively easy to advocate when considering the deterrence theory. However, the analysis is less straightforward with respect to retributive justice. Strict interpretation of this approach – focusing on its potential total amount rather than on its components – would render wealth-dependent fines as unacceptable. Nevertheless, I have tried to demonstrate that the day fine model actually offers a middle ground between the objective and the subjective interpretation of the principle of proportionality, which is crucial in the retributive justice approach. Looking at the separate components of the day fine model allows capturing many important aspects in criminal law – proportionality to the offence, equality before the law, fairness and deterrence.

The following chapters review and analyse the day fine models practised in all the European criminal justice systems (aside from Liechtenstein). In the last chapter of this book (Chapter 19), we take a comparative look at the practices of the different jurisdictions. In particular, we analyse how the actual applied models are structured as compared to the theoretically optimal model of day fines. We discuss the reasons of the gap between theory and practice and provide some policy recommendations.

REFERENCES

Beccaria, C. 1983. *An Essay on Crimes and Punishments*. Boston: International Pocket Library (first published in Italian in 1764).

Becker, G. 1968. 'Crime and Punishment: An Economic Approach', *Journal of Political Economy* 76(2),169–217.

Bentham, J. 1840. *Theory of Legislation: Principles of the Penal Code*. Boston: Weeks, Jordan & Company (translated from French by Etienne Dumont).

Bentham, J. 2007. *An Introduction to the Principles of Morals and Legislation*. New York: Dover Publications, INC. (first published in 1780).

Blumstein, A., Cohen, J. and Nagin, D. (eds.) 1978. *Deterrence and Incapacitation: Estimating the Effect of Criminal Sanctions on Crime Rates*. Washington DC: The National Academies Press.

Bronsteen, J., Buccafusco, C. and Masur, J. 2009. 'Happiness and Punishment', *University of Chicago Law Review* 76: 1037–82.

Frase, R. S. 2004. 'Excessive Prison Sentences, Punishment Goals, and the Eighth Amendment: Proportionality Relative to What', *Minnesota Law Review* 89: 571–651.

Frase, R. S. 2005. 'Punishment Purposes', *Stanford Law Review* 58: 67–84.

Haist, M. 2008. 'Deterrence in a Sea of Just Deserts: Are Utilitarian Goals Achievable in a World of Limiting Retributivism', *Journal of Criminal Law & Criminology* 99: 789–822.

Honderich, T. and Chester, W. 2005. *Punishment: The Supposed Justifications*. London: Pluto Press.

Johnstone, G. 2013. *Restorative Justice: Ideas, Values, Debates*. London: Routledge.

Kant, I. 1974. *The Philosophy of Law*. New Jersey: Augustus M. Kelly Publishers (first published in English in 1887).

Kantorowicz-Reznichenko, E. 2015. 'Day-Fines: Should the Rich Pay More?', *Review of Law & Economics* 11(3),481–501.

Kolber, A. J. 2009. 'The Subjective Experience of Punishment'. *Columbia Law Review* 109: 182–236.

Kolber, A. J. 2009. 'The Comparative Nature of Punishment', *Boston University Law Review* 89: 1565–608.

Markel, D. and Flanders, C. 2010. 'Bentham on Stilts: The Bare Relevance of Subjectivity to Retributive Justice', *California Law Review* 98: 907–87.

Murphy, J. G. 1994. *Kant: The Philosophy of Right*. Macon GA: Mercer University Press.

Perry, R. 2005. 'The Role of Retributive Justice in the Common Law of Torts: A Descriptive Theory', *Tennessee Law Review* 73: 177–236.

Perry, R. and Kantorowicz-Reznichenko, E. 2017. 'Income-Dependent Punitive Damages', *Washington University Law Review* 95: 835–85.

Plato. 1997. 'Protagoras'. In Cooper, J. M. and Hutchinson, D. S. (eds.), *Plato: Complete Works*. Cambridge, MA: Hackett Publishing Company, 746–90.

Polinsky, M. and Shavell, S. 1979. 'The Optimal Tradeoff between the Probability and Magnitude of Fines', *The American Economic Review* 69: 880–91.

Polinsky, M. and Shavell, S. 1994. 'Should Liability Be Based on the Harm to the Victim or the Gain to the Injurer?', *Journal of Law, Economics, & Organization* 10: 427–37.

Reznichenko, E. 2015. *Cost-Effective Criminal Enforcement: A Law and Economics Approach*. Unpublished PhD dissertation, available at http://hdl.handle.net/1765/78227.

Roberts, J. V. 1997. 'The Role of Criminal Record in the Sentencing Process', *Crime and Justice* 22: 316–19.

Robinson, P. H. and Darley, J. M. 1996. 'Utility of Desert', *Northwestern University Law Review* 91: 453–99.

Von Hirsch, A. 1976. *Doing Justice: The Choice of Punishments*, Report of the Committee for the Study of Incarceration. New York: Hill and Wang.

Von Hirsch, A. 1993. *Censure and Sanctions*. Oxford: Clarendon Press.

Von Hirsch, A. and Ashworth, A. (eds.) 1998. *Principled Sentencing: Readings on Theory and Policy*. Oxford: Hart Publishing.

Zimring, F. E. and Hawkins, G. J. 1976. *Deterrence: The Legal Threat in Crime Control*. Chicago: The University of Chicago Press.

3

Day Fines in Finland

Raimo Lahti

3.1 HISTORICAL DEVELOPMENT OF DAY FINES IN FINLAND AND THEIR LEGISLATIVE REASONS[1]

The day fine system was adopted in Finland in 1921. Thus, Finland was the first Nordic country to introduce this punishment into its system of criminal sanctions. The Finnish Penal Code (PC) had been enacted in 1889 in the spirit of the so-called classical school. Before the reform of 1921, (penal) fines had been fixed at a certain amount of marks. The main reason for adopting the new system, according to the official argumentation for the statute, was an attempt to introduce a system where fines would have an equal impact on people with varying means. For this reason, the fine was to be made more dependent than before on the offender's financial status. The system was also intended to render the size of the fine more independent of fluctuations in the value of money. The introduction of the day fine system was strongly supported by the leading scholar in criminal law of his days, Allan Serlachius, who represented ideologically the so-called sociological school.[2]

It is noteworthy that, according to the *travaux préparatoires* of the legislation in question, the idea was also, instead of setting the term of imprisonment following non-payment of a fine (that is, conversion into imprisonment) according to a predetermined scale, to leave the term to the discretion of the court in a new trial on the matter. However, no reform was carried out in this respect, as the day fine reform was regarded as a temporary measure and the legislator intended to limit change to what was absolutely

[1] See in more detail Lahti, 'Criminal Sanctions in Finland: A System in Transition', 121–57, 131, 142, 149, 153.

[2] Serlachius, 'Päiväsakkojärjestelmä', 201–10.

necessary.[3] Nevertheless, it turned out that the day fine reform was not a temporary measure, although in recent decades the system of pecuniary (financial) sanctions has diversified in many ways.

After 1921, reform of the legislation on fines was suggested several times, but not until the last few decades were any significant changes made. For example, the committee which was formed to consider measures to prevent criminality and formulate appropriate proposals and which submitted its report in 1930, criticised the practice whereby many fines led to conversion into imprisonment. During the 1920s, there was a great increase in the number of people who were imprisoned for the non-payment of fines. The committee's proposal, which was not adopted at the time, was that fines should be payable in instalments and that it should be possible to grant an extension of the period during which the fine was supposed to be paid. The committee also proposed that in some cases the non-payment of fines should not lead to conversion into imprisonment.[4]

In 1963 and 1969, following proposals which had been made on several occasions, the legislation on fines was finally reformed. First, in 1963 it was made possible to pay a fine in instalments and an extension of the period during which the fine had to be paid was allowed. Second, in the 1969 statute conversion into imprisonment was left to the discretion of the court in a new trial on the matter and the maximum fine was lowered from 300 to 120 day fines, the maximum conversion being reduced from 180 to 90 days. The main aim of these reforms was to lessen the number of people imprisoned for not paying fines.[5] This aim was reached in so far as the number of serving prison sentences as a result of conversion decreased to under a tenth of what it had been before the reforms (the number of those serving conversion sentences was 9,075 in 1962 and 539 in 1974).[6]

In 1976, the monetary value of the day fine was increased with the desire to improve the applicability of fines. To this end, the statute provided that the size of the day fine (the daily unit) had to be set according to gross income and more detailed rules for fixing the size of the day fine were given. The goal was

---

[3] See Government Bill No. 36/1920. In the legal literature there was also criticism against the introduction of the day fine system, inter alia by relying on a comparative survey according to which only Portugal had adopted it into its legislation in 1852. See Ignatius, 'Sakkorangaistuksesta', 1–44, 27. As to the history of Portuguese legislation, *cf.* Faraldo-Cabana, *Money and the Governance of Punishment, A Genealogy of the Penal Fine*, p. 90.

[4] See, in more detail, *Komiteanmietintö* [Committee report] No. 1931:2.

[5] Regarding the goals of these reforms, see Government Bill No. 15/1963 and Government Bill No. 174/1967.

[6] This decrease was also greatly influenced by the decriminalisation of drunkenness in 1968, since many of those in conversion imprisonment had originally been fined for this offence.

that the general-preventive effect of the higher fines should be equivalent to that of the shorter terms of imprisonment and thus constitute an alternative. At the same time, the lesser offences would continue to be met with mild fines. That would be made possible by lessening the number of day fines. With the noticeable increase in the monetary value of the day unit, it was regarded as especially important to make a more just evaluation of the offender's ability to pay fines and to avoid disparity in judicial practice.[7] The success of the 1976 reform is indicated by the fact that during recent decades about 90 per cent of all, in ordinary or summary proceedings, convicted offenders have been sentenced to pay a day fine (see Section 3.3).

In the same year, 1976, the general provisions on the meting out of punishment (fine or imprisonment) were reformed in Chapter 6 of the Penal Code and that reform also reflected the emphasis on the general-preventive effect of the punishment and the idea of the justness of sentences. In accordance with the proportionality principle, the punishment must correspond to the harmfulness and dangerousness of the offence and to the offender's culpability as manifested in the offence. In addition, the consistency in juridical practice is a consideration of major importance.[8]

In late 1976, the report of the Penal Law Committee for a total reform of Finnish criminal law was also finalized.[9] In regard to the fines it was proposed that the system should be differentiated along the following lines. Day fines, based on the ascertained financial position of the offender, would be a sanction having a noticeable effect on his or her standard of living, while, on the other hand, fee-type sanctions, fixed at a specific amount of money, would be applied specifically to mass petty criminality. The methods of enforcing fines should be made more effective and the possibility of conversion into imprisonment would prevail until a sufficiently effective enforcement system had been developed.

The Penal Law Committee recommended a simple and clear system of criminal sanctions arguing that such a system would be more effective as far as general prevention is concerned and, from the point of view of furthering consistency in judicial decisions, is more certain than a system based on a number of different types of sanctions. The use of prison sentences should be reduced, because those sentences do not rehabilitate and they are also very expensive in a cost-benefit assessment. Therefore, long prison terms should, when possible, be transferred into short prison terms and short prison terms

---

[7]　Government Bill No. 109/1975 (II).
[8]　Government Bill No. 125/1975 (II).
[9]　See generally *Komiteanmietintö* (Committee report) No. 1976:72.

into other punitive measures such as fines, warnings and supervisory non-institutional sentences.

An important objective of the total reform of Finnish criminal law (1980–2003) was to reduce the number of custodial sentences and, therefore, the increased use of financial sanctions had a preference.[10] Part of this endeavour was the adoption of the summary penal fee by a special Act in 1983. This penal fee, which is fixed at a specific small amount, is applicable only to minor traffic offences and other similar petty (criminalised) misdemeanours (infractions, violations), which are specifically listed by the legislation in question. The penal fee may not be converted into imprisonment. Because it is a question of criminalised misdemeanours, it can fall under fixed fine (instead of penal fee), as mentioned in Table 3.1 (Section 3.3).

The revised provisions on day fine, conversion sentence and summary penal fee were enacted in 1999. These provisions are still the basis for the regulation in the field, although several amendments have been made during the last few years, as reflections of fluctuations in criminal policy thinking.

3.2 CONTENTS OF THE PROVISIONS ON DAY FINES, CONVERSION SENTENCES AND THE ENFORCEMENT OF IMPOSED FINES[11]

The main principle is that a fine shall be passed as day fines, although since 2009 the fixed fines for traffic offences have de facto been more common than the imposed day fines (see in Section 3.3). The minimum number of day fines is 1 and the maximum number is 120. For a special reason, the specific minimum or maximum number may be provided by an Act, within the limits of 1–120.

The amount of a day fine (daily unit) is defined in detail in a separate provision of the Penal Code[12] (PC 2a:2; 808/2007 with later amendments):

(1) The amount of a day fine shall be set so that it is reasonable in view of the solvency of the person fined.

---

[10] As to this total reform in general, see *supra* note 1, 151; Lahti, 'Towards a More Efficient, Fair and Humane Criminal Justice System: Developments of Criminal Policy and Criminal Sanctions during the Last 50 Years'. From a comparative point of view, see the reviews of Lappi-Seppälä, 'Penal policies in the Nordic Countries 1960–2010', 85–111; *Supra* note 3Faraldo-Cabana, p. 167.

[11] Chapter 2a of the Penal Code, 550/1999 and the Act on the Enforcement of Fines, 672/2002, both with later amendments.

[12] An unofficial translation of the Penal Code is available from the website of the Ministry of Justice (the amendments up to 766/2015 included): www.finlex.fi/fi/laki/kaannokset/1889/e n18890039_20150766.pdf.

(2) One sixtieth of the average monthly income of the person fined, less the taxes and fees defined by a Decree of the State Council and a fixed deduction for basic consumption, is deemed to be a reasonable amount of a day fine. The maintenance liability of the person fined may decrease the day fine.

(3) The primary basis for the calculation of the monthly income is the income of the person fined as indicated in his or her taxation. If the income of the person fined cannot be reliably ascertained from the tax records or it has essentially changed since the most recent taxation, it may also be assessed on the basis of other information.

(4) In court, the day fine is set on the basis of the information available at the time of the court proceedings and in proceedings on the basis of the Fine and Summary Penal Fee Act (754/2010), the day fine is set on the basis of the information available at the time when the fine is set or when the request for a summary penal fee is made. However, the prosecutor shall set the day fine on the basis of the information available at the time the summary penal fee is issued, if it has become evident that the solvency of the person for whom the summary penal fee has been requested has in the meantime essentially changed.

(5) More detailed provisions on the taxation which is the basis for the calculation of the monthly income, calculation of the average monthly income, the rounding-off of the amount of the day fine, the amount of the fixed deduction for basic consumption, the manner in which the maintenance liability is to be taken into account and the minimum amount of a day fine shall be issued by a Decree of the State Council.

As can be noticed from paragraph (2) above, the amount of the daily unit equals roughly half of the offender's daily income after taxes (that is, net income). Until the reform of 1999, the basis for determining the amount of a day fine was the gross income. Although the exact amount results from a rather complicated calculation, the Decree clarifies details and the criminal justice officials in question have available a handbook for the assessment. The Decree regulates, inter alia, how the net income must be calculated, the amount of the fixed deduction for basic consumption (= 255 euros since 2001), the deduction of the maintenance liability per person (= three euros and concerns primarily minor children) as well as the minimum of the daily fine (= six euros since 2001). The criminal justice officials (primarily police) have access to the previous year's taxation files through protected SMS-data from the taxation authorities.

In 1999, Finland also criminalised giving false information of one's income to the police in order to illegally reduce the amount of fines. However, due to the easy electronic access to the relevant taxation information, very few cases of the offence called 'fine deception' (PC 16:6) appear in practice and have been brought to the court.

It is noteworthy that in 1999–2007 not only wages or income from capital, but also wealth, when its value was 85,000 euros or more, affected the amount of a day fine. The main reason to give up this criterion was the abolition of the tax on property in the general taxation reform in 2006.[13] There was a strong emphasis on the practicability in the access to the relevant documents on the solvency of the person fined.

The total amount of the fine is equal to the number of day fines times the amount of a day fine. No upper limit for the amount of the daily unit has been enacted. Special provisions determine the relationship between the total amount of a fine and the amount of a summary penal fee, as well as setting a joint punishment for offences punishable by a fine and a summary penal fee.

The decision-makers in imposing fines vary according to the type of procedure. In the normal criminal proceedings the court decides and then, in non-serious criminal cases (where the maximum punishment for the accused crime is four years' imprisonment or lower), the day fines are decided by one legally trained judge sitting alone in the court. Summary proceedings for imposing day fines and penal fees are regulated by a special Act from the year 2010 (754/2010), which came into force in late 2016.

There are the following common preconditions for the applicability of the summary proceedings according to the Act of 2010: it must be a simple and clear case and the suspect and the possible victim must agree to the summary proceedings without an oral handling before a court. Summary penal proceedings for imposing day fines are possible when the maximum punishment for the offence in question is a fine or a six month imprisonment or lower. The decision-maker is the prosecutor or, if at most twenty-day fines are imposed for specified minor offences, the police. The decision-maker for summary penal fees (fixed fines) is either the police (primarily) or the prosecutor. From 1 January 2021 a legal amendment (602/2019) will come into force, according to which when within a year six times or more a fine has been imposed in a summary proceedings and the similarity of the offences as a whole shows heedless of the prohibitions and commands of the law, sentencing in the summary proceedings is not possible. The main goal of this amendment is related to the presumed improvement of the general-preventive effect,

[13] Government Bill No. 25/2007.

because the unpaid day fine imposed by the court in the ordinary proceedings could later lead to a conversion sentence.[14]

There are detailed provisions on the conversion sentence. A person who has been sentenced to a fine and from whom the collection of the fine has failed, shall be sent to imprisonment to replace the unpaid fine.

Duration of the conversion sentence for day fines (PC 2a:5; 983/2005):

(1) A conversion sentence for a fine is imposed so that three unpaid day fines correspond to imprisonment for one day. If the number of day fines to be converted is not divisible by three, the remainder is not converted. If only a part of a day fine has been paid, the day fine is deemed unpaid.

(2) A conversion sentence shall be passed for at least four days and at most sixty days. A conversion sentence may not be passed without a special reason if the unpaid day fines are less than twelve daily units.

(3) If two or more fines are to be converted at the same time, only one conversion sentence shall be passed.

(4) On grounds provided in section 6 and section 7, a court may pass a conversion sentence that is shorter than what has been provided in this section, but nevertheless at least four days.

The legislation on the conversion sentence has been reformed in 2019 (603/2019) so that the amendments will come into force on 1 January 2021. The amendments will make the system more lenient: first, from 2021 the conversion sentence shall be imposed so that four unpaid day fines correspond to imprisonment for one day and the maximum of a conversion sentence will be forty days. Second, a fine shall not be converted into imprisonment, if (1) the fine has been imposed in the procedure provided in the Fine and Summary Penal Fee Act; (2) fewer than twenty day fines are unpaid; or (3) the offence resulting in a fine had been committed below the age of eighteen years (PC 2a:4.2).

In addition (PC 2a:6), a court may discretionarily waive a conversion sentence if it is to be deemed unreasonable or unnecessary, taking into consideration (1) the personal circumstances or state of health of the person fined, (2) the participation of the person fined in social and healthcare measures, (3) a sentence of imprisonment or community service order imposed on the person fined on the basis of another offence. Until the effective date of the legislative amendment of 1 January 2021, there is also the following discretionary waiving ground to be decided by the court: the offence

---

14   Government Bill No. 178/2018. It was argued that the amendment would further the credibility of the criminal justice system, in particular in the minor cases of shoplifting.

for which the fine was imposed, taking into consideration its detrimental nature, is to be deemed petty when assessed as a whole. The deletion of this ground is based on an aim of increased emphasis on general prevention by enlarging the scope of the conversion sentence.

A special public authority, the Legal Register Centre, is responsible for the enforcement of fines, certain compensations paid to the State, forfeitures, several administrative financial penalties and certain other sanctions subject to separate provisions.[15] The first opportunity to pay a fine is to use the fine or bank transfer form, which has been given by the police, an authority or a court. Authorities and courts send the information on the fines and other sanctions to the Legal Register Centre's enforcement system. The Legal Register Centre may grant a term of payment. If the fine is not paid by the date stated in the Legal Register Centre's demand for payment, the case will be sent for enforced collection. This will be done about one month after the demand for payment has been sent. The bailiff will then deal with all matters related to the payment.[16]

The biggest part of fines are paid voluntarily – regarding the fixed fines even circa 80 per cent. As for the day fines which have been imposed in summary proceedings, the portion of voluntarily paid fines is circa 65 per cent; but for the day fines which have been imposed in an ordinary procedure, the corresponding portion is only one third. This low portion is explained by the (one average) lower social position and lower income (solvency) of offenders and the divergent composition of the offences in question: summary proceedings deal primarily with minor traffic offences, while ordinary procedures cover traditional offences such as theft and assault.[17]

In all, the majority of the fines can be collected either by the voluntary payments or by execution. A conversion sentence is needed only in a minority of the cases. In 2010, in about 11,000 cases, a procedure for a conversion sentence was initiated. The amount of the court decisions delivered to the Legal Register Centre for the enforcement of conversion sentences was lower, circa 8,000, because a part of those sentenced pay their fines during the proceedings. The majority of those who serve their conversion sentence are users of intoxicants, have health problems or are otherwise socially vulnerable.[18]

---

[15] See, in more detail, Act on the Enforcement of Fines; 672/2002 with later amendments.

[16] See, in more detail, Enforcement Code; 705/2007. An unofficial translation of this Act is available from the website of the Ministry of Justice: www.finlex.fi/fi/laki/kaannokset/2007/e n20070705_20070987.pdf.

[17] *Supra* note 13, Chapter 2.1.

[18] *Ibid.*

TABLE 3.1 *The distribution of penalties in 2017*

	N	%
Court decisions 2017	50,045	100
Prison	4,812	10
Community service	1,522	3
Supervision order	192	0
Conditional imprisonment	12,205	24
Juvenile penalty	8	0
Day fines by the court	30,519	61
Waiver of the sentence	341	1
Other decisions (summary proceedings) 2017		
Fine orders by the prosecutor	41,573	
Fine orders by the police	87,772	
Fixed fines by the police (mostly traffic offences)	330,988	

Source: *Tilastokeskus (Statistics Finland)*

Finland is a country which has a well-developed social security legislation. For instance, different types of social assistance are secured as the last resort for covering the necessary daily living expenses of the person and his or her family in question. However, fines are not listed as such expenses.[19]

3.3 PRACTICAL IMPLEMENTATION OF THE DAY FINE SYSTEM

The distribution of penalties in Finland in 2017 shows – in Table 3.1 – how a large part of the penalties consists of fines and how a small part of the fines is decided by the court instead of the prosecutor or the police.[20] During the last years the competence and role of the police have been enlarged for the expedience reason '*minima non curat praetor*'.

The number and amount of day fines as well as the total amounts of fines in 2008–17 are presented in Tables 3.2 and 3.3. In addition, the distribution of the total amounts of day fines in 2017 is presented in Table 3.4.

---

[19] Social Assistance Act; 1412/1997. An unofficial translation of this Act is available from the website of the Ministry of Justice: www.finlex.fi/fi/laki/kaannokset/1997/en19971412_20101390 .pdf.

[20] In this section, Tables 3.1–3.4 are derived from H. Niemi (ed.), *Seuraamusjärjestelmä* [The System of Criminal Sanctions] 2017 (Report No. 32, University of Helsinki, The Institute for Criminology and Legal Policy, Helsinki 2018), Chapter A.6, Tables 3.1, 18–20.

TABLE 3.2 *Number and amount of the day fines and the portion of the minimum day fines in 2008–17*

	Number of day fines average amount			Amount of a day fines (daily unit) in euros, average			Minimum day fines*, portion of all %		
	C	S	All	C	S	All	C	S	All
2008	38	14	17	12	15	14	58.7	44.9	46.7
2009	38	14	18	13	15	15	60.2	46.6	48.6
2010	38	14	18	13	15	15	60.9	47.5	49.5
2011	38	14	18	12	16	15	61.2	46.6	48.8
2012	38	14	18	13	16	16	60.3	45.8	48.1
2013	39	14	18	13	17	16	59.9	44.9	47.3
2014	39	14	19	14	17	17	58.4	43.9	46.3
2015	39	14	18	13	18	17	59.7	43.4	45.9
2016	39	14	18	13	18	17	60.1	42.9	45.7
2017	39	13	20	13	19	17	61.5	44.6	46.8

Source: *Tilastokeskus (Statistics Finland)*
C = imposed by the court (judge) in ordinary proceedings
S = imposed in summary proceedings (prosecutor or – from 2017 – police)
All = imposed by the court or in summary proceedings
* Minimum amount of a day fine is six euros, as in 2001 legally determined.

Some conclusions from Tables 3.2–3.4 can be drawn: the average amount of daily units (Table 3.2) as well as of the total amounts of day fines (Table 3.4) are relatively low and the high amounts of day fines are mostly imposed for traffic offences. These observations are explained primarily by the fact that fines are extensively used as a penalty for low-income offenders of traditional crime (such as theft and assault); high-income fined offenders are mostly among those violating traffic rules.

There is no provision in the Finnish legislation according to which the day fine would be excluded due to the offender's lack of means. A fine is regarded as the mildest penalty (after waiving of the sentence) and – according to the general principle of sentencing – the choice of a more severe penalty is to be determined step by step taking into account the seriousness of the offence, the offender's culpability and his or her possible recidivism.[21] Among scholars, criticism has been expressed against the minimum daily unit of six euros with reference to the general provision of PC 2a:2.1, which prescribes that the amount of a day fine shall be set so that it is reasonable in view of the solvency

---

[21] See Government Bill No. 44/2002, Chapter. E., para. 1 (p. 185). See also above, Chapter 1.

Day Fines in Finland

TABLE 3.3 *Total amount of day fines in 2008–17*

| | Average | | | | | | |
| | C | | S | | All | | Penal fees |
	TrO	Others	TrO	Others	TrO	Others	TrO
2008	510	359	237	114	268	177	80
2009	516	351	239	115	275	183	80
2010	533	361	241	121	277	185	78
2011	545	356	248	124	284	189	77
2012	572	374	256	127	295	202	78
2013	618	395	273	130	314	211	78
2014	644	393	282	134	328	216	79
2015	640	384	287	134	328	205	101
2016	638	385	296	132	324	212	155
2017	631	379	310	127	317	213	155

Total amount of (day) fines in euro

| | C | | S | | All | | Fixed Fines (max.) |
	TrO	Others	TrO	Others	TrO	Others	TO
2008	115,960	62,730	59,44	8,622	115,960	29,550	115
2009	50,600	29,550	24,170	11,370	50,600	46,760	115
2010	81,540	46,760	32,256	7,400	81,540	16,700	115
2011	18,780	16,700	50,100	66,530	50,100	66,530	115
2012	33,735	9,090	36,320	3,930	36,320	60,350	115
2013	32,664	60,350	95,000	18,600	95,000	151,480	115
2014	82,665	65,050	21,528	7,072	82,665	65,050	115
2015	54,795	42,900	36,450	12,384	54,795	42,900	200
2016	114,768	32,160	40,120	5,256	114,768	32,160	240
2017	77,808	52,140	33,936	10,310	77,808	52,140	240

Source: Tilastokeskus (Statistics Finland)
C = imposed by the court (judge) in ordinary proceedings
S = imposed in summary proceedings (prosecutor or – from 2017 – police)
All = imposed by the court or in summary proceedings
TrO = traffic offences

of the person fined.[22] On the other hand, the regulation of a conversion sentence (PC 2:2a:4–6) includes limitations in its use, inter alia, by enabling the waiving of the conversion sentence when the personal circumstances or state of health of the person fined support this.

---

[22] Matikkala, *Rikosoikeudellinen seuraamusjärjestelmä*, p. 73.

TABLE 3.4 *The distribution of the total amounts of imposed day fines in 2017*

Euros	Traffic fines %	Others %
1–40	1.2	8.0
41–60	3.8	17.0
61–80	2.3	7.6
81–100	3.7	12.0
101–150	6.9	18.6
151–200	25.7	7.8
201–300	19.5	11.7
301–400	12.3	5.3
401–500	7.6	4.0
501–1,000	12.6	5.2
1,001–2,000	3.7	2.1
2,001–3,000	0.6	0.4
3,001-	0.3	0.2
In total	100	100
Amount (N)	107,128	57,493

Source: *Tilastokeskus (Statistics Finland)*

Tapio Lappi-Seppälä has analysed the use of fines in Finland and other European countries.[23] The Tables 3.5–3.6 (taken from his article) are based on the European Sourcebook Statistics. Table 3.5 includes all types of offences and Table 3.6 illustrates the use of fines and other sanctions in assault and theft offences; both tables concern the year 2006.

Table 3.5 shows that Finland has the highest overall conviction rate (4,158), but three out of four convictions were for traffic offences.

Tables 3.5 and 3.6 indicate that fines are imposed to a very great extent in Finland and other Nordic countries. As explained in Sections 3.1 and 3.2 above, there has been a systematic trend in criminal policy-thinking to reduce the use of prison sentences and to further the use of its alternatives, among which the fine is a typical penalty. The monetary value has been increased, thus making fines more credible alternatives to short-term prison sentences.

As to the effectiveness of fines, there is a well-known observation that offenders who have been punished with a fine have lower recidivism rates than those whose punishment has been more severe. For example, in Finland about 25 per cent of those receiving fines became reconvicted for some form of

[23] Lappi-Seppälä, 'Fines in Europe', 1637–48.

TABLE 3.5 *The use of fines in Europe 2006*

	General application of fines				Application by offenses			
	A	B	C	D	E. Theft (all) F.		G. Assault (all) H.	
	All convictions/ pop	Imposed fines/ pop	Fines % of all convictions	Non-traffic convictions / pop	Sanctions / pop	Fines %	Sanctions / pop	Fines %
Finland	4,158	3,659	88	1,413	582	91	207	54
England & Wales	2,455	1,768	72	2,445	184	13	60	7
Belgium	1,805	1,661	92	380	80	53	47	68
Hungary	1,419	412	29	1,120	311	21	67	24
Sweden	1,319	712	54	1,023	267	47	97	19
Scotland	1,318	659	50	1,164	291	30	296	46
Switzerland	1,308	497	38	703	37	1	12	9
Poland	1,214	231	19	804	175	6	103	6
Netherlands	1,025	318	31	722	174	18	107	23
Germany	945	756	80	709	147	71	67	61
France	940	357	38	522	115	12	86	19
Croatia	730	66	9	679	127	4	50	3
Slovakia	700	28	4	650	124	2	38	6
Czech Rep.	675	27	4	675	141	2	26	4
Portugal	623	473	76	306	34	37	51	77

Country	A	B	C	D	E	F	G	H
Austria	489	191	39	489	98	30	64	59
Latvia	435	30	7	435	138	1	19	9
Slovenia	404	28	7	381	97	5	38	4
Romania	234	44	19	196	64	1	62	44
Albania	222	84	38	214	32	4	14	44
Cyprus	204	80	39	204	51	25	9	56

Source: Lappi-Seppälä 2014, based on *European Sourcebook of Crime and Criminal Justice Statistics 2010* (Aebi et al., 2010), columns E and F based solely on the sourcebook. 'Pop' means per 100,000 in population.

A = Convictions either by the court or prosecutor. All offences and infractions
B = Imposed fines (both courts and prosecutor) / 100,000 population
C = The share of fines (%) of all convictions (A)
D = The number of non-traffic convictions / 100,000 population
E = The number of fines imposed for theft offences / 100,000 population
F = The share of fines (%) of all sanctions imposed for theft
G = The number of fines imposed for assault offences / 100,000 population
H = The share of fines (%) of all sanctions imposed for assault
Country order by column A.

TABLE 3.6 *The use of fines and other sanctions in assault and theft offences in Europe 2006*

		Theft (all)			Assault (all)		
		Fine/ pop	Other/ pop	All	Fine/ pop	Other/ pop	All
Nordic							
	Finland	530	52	582	112	95	207
	Sweden	125	142	267	18	79	97
Western 1							
	Switzerland	0	37	37	1	11	12
	Germany	104	43	147	41	26	67
	Austria	29	69	98	38	26	64
Western 2							
	Netherlands	31	143	174	25	82	107
	France	14	101	115	16	70	86
	Belgium	42	38	80	32	15	47
UK							
	England &Wales	24	160	184	4*	56*	60*
	Scotland	87	204	291	136	160	296
South							
	Portugal	13	21	34	39	12	51
	Slovenia	5	92	97	2	36	38
East							
	Poland	11	165	175	6	97	103
	Slovakia	2	122	124	2	36	38
	Czech Rep.	3	138	141	1	25	26
	Hungary	65	246	311	16	51	67
	Latvia	1	137	138	2	17	19
ALL (21)	**Mean**	**34**	**119**	**153**	**22**	**50**	**72**

Source: Lappi-Seppälä 2014, based on *European Sourcebook of Crime and Criminal Justice Statistics 2010* (Aebi et al., 2010), columns E and F based solely on the sourcebook. 'Pop' means per 100,000 in population.
* The low number of assaults in England & Wales compared to earlier editions of statistics suggest that the definition has been changed in a manner that prevents reliable comparisons.

penalty during the following five years whereas the figure of those sentenced to prison was 75 per cent. However, these figures as such cannot be used as a basis, because the initial recidivism risk in these two groups is different. Nevertheless, there is fairly little systematic research with control groups about the effects of fines on recidivism.[24]

---

[24] Lappi-Seppälä, 'Fines in Europe', chapter on Effectiveness, with references.

3.4 PUBLIC PERCEPTION OF DAY FINES

In the legislative reform of 1999, the day fines based on gross income were replaced by net income. According to the *travaux préparatoires* of the reform, the aim was 'to introduce a more just fining system, whereby the size of the fine is perceived as fair among different income-groups'. There is a general pre-condition that the legitimacy of a penal system and its general-preventive effect that the system as a whole can be regarded as fair. In Scandinavian criminal policy-thinking it is emphasised that the use of punishment should demonstrate a socio-ethical reproach and, in this way it influences the sense of morals and justice (so-called positive general prevention). From the point of view of legitimacy, the actual realisation in criminal justice of such principles of justice as equality and proportionality as well as the fairness of the proceed-ings is of central importance.

A separate follow-up research was carried out by Tapio Lappi-Seppälä in order to measure the degree of perceived fairness of the fining system.[25] A total of 2,966 persons were interviewed at four different stages before and after the reform during the years 1999–2001. The results of this research are interesting also since in the late 1990s and early 2000s the Finnish fining system received worldwide attention due to extraordinarily large day fines (over tens of thousands of euros) imposed on offenders with an extraordinar-ily high income.

Three out of four interviewed persons considered that the system with day fines was in generally fair. Just below 60 per cent considered traffic fines generally to be fair, about one fifth considered them too low and about one sixth too severe. The respondents' critical attitudes towards the day fine system grew along with income-level. However, the degree of their satisfaction with the fining system did not differ according to the fact whether the fines were calculated on the basis of gross or net income – contrary to what the govern-ment assumed.

3.5 ACTUAL CHALLENGES OF THE FINING SYSTEM

During the last few years the day fines and the fining system in general have received quite much attention in the Finnish public debate and criminal policy-thinking. In particular, following issues have raised differing opinions and led to disputed legislative solutions or proposals:

---

[25] Lappi-Seppälä, 'Public Perceptions and the Fairness of the Dayfine System. An Evaluation of the 1999 Dayfine Reform', 386–97.

(1) What should be the monetary values of a day fine and of the fixed fine?
     How should the summary proceedings be organized – for example, what
     should be the roles of the police and the prosecutor and how should the
     legal safeguards, the appeal and other remedies be regulated?

(2) To what extent should the conversion sentences be used and how
     should the discretion of the court in its decision-making be regulated?

(3) To what extent should penal administrative fees (administrative fines)
     be introduced? How much would this trend lead to the decriminalisa-
     tion of minor offences and how much would there in future exist
     parallel punitive sanction systems and problems with double jeopardy?

As to the first issue, in 2016 the Finnish government proposed that the
monetary amount of day fines, fixed fines and corporate fine (corporate
criminal liability was introduced by the Act of 743/1995)[26] would be essentially raised and the public finances were presented as the main argument for
the reform. This Government Bill was turned down in the Parliament,
because that financial argument was not accepted as a primary important
one when taking into account the constitutional limits of criminalisation
and punishment.[27]

The current legislation on the conversion sentences has been described
above (Section 3.2). As explained there, the latest amendments of the legislation in question have had divergent aims. In the public debate the amendment
which limits the discretion of the court in the conversion process to reduce or
waive the conversion sentence has been strongly criticised. It has been referred
to the probable unfair effect where those who will be targets of the tightened
practice belong to the socially disadvantaged groups.

As to the trend of the increased introduction of penal administrative
fees instead of relying on the punishability of minor offences, a great legislative challenge is that no general, systematic legislation (like for
Ordnungswidrigkeiten in German) has been created in Finland, although
there are numerous special legal Acts regulating penal administrative sanctions in the various fields of public administration. For example, the new
Road Traffic Offences Act (729/2018; into force on 1 June 2020) introduces
a new punitive fee for minor violations of that Act. Not even a recent report
(2018) of a working party set up by the Ministry of Justice proposes such

---

[26] See, in more detail, Lahti, 'Finnish Report on Individual Liability for Business Involvement in
      International Crimes', 257–66, Chapter 3.

[27] See Government Bill No. 1/2016 and the Statement of the Constitutional Committee of the
      Parliament on it, No. 9/2016.

a unified legislation, which would make the system of punitive sanctions more consistent and coherent.[28]

One of the recent pecuniary punitive sanctions whose exact position or nature is unclear is victim surcharge. It was introduced by special Act 669/2015. If an offender is sentenced for such an offence for which imprisonment may be imposed, he or she will also be ordered to pay a victim surcharge. The adoption of the victim surcharge was justified with the objective of strengthening public funding for the measures of support to the victims of crime.

A person over eighteen years of age who has committed an offence is liable to pay the victim surcharge. The amount of the surcharge is determined based on the penal provision irrespective of whether the offence has a victim or not. Legal persons, such as companies and corporations, that have been sentenced to a corporate fine are also liable to pay the victim surcharge. The amount of the victim surcharge to be imposed on an individual offender is forty or eighty euros. The victim surcharge is imposed in criminal proceedings and there is no discretion entrusted to the authority or court who imposes this pecuniary sanction.

In all, there is an urgent need for coordinating various punitive sanctions (whether they are criminal in nature or administrative). In an acceptable regulation model, it must be balanced with various pros and cons whether it is necessary to rely on criminalisation and the strong safeguards of the criminal justice process or whether there are more compelling reasons for administrative fines instead of penal fines (criminal punishment).

3.6 CONCLUSION

The day fine system has been in force in Finland for nearly one hundred years. There has been general satisfaction with the fining system, in which the role of day fines has been remarkable. Several factors have contributed to the success of this pecuniary sanction. First, the public perception and official criminal policy ideology have regarded it as furthering fairness of the fining system and, more generally, the fairness of the whole criminal justice system. Second, the official criminal policy has aimed at reducing the use of imprisonment as a criminal sanction but has sparingly developed new alternatives to imprisonment. Third, the efficiency of the day fine system has been furthered by the detailed provisions on the assessment of the person's income[29] (and the easy access to his or her taxation data) and the effective enforcement of fines.

---

[28] See, in more detail, Lahti and Rainiala, 'Alternative Investigation and Sanctioning Systems for Corporate and Corporate-Related Crime in Finland', 131–63.

[29] *Cf.*, for instance, the situation in the Czech Republic and its critical assessment by Drápal, 'Day fines: A European comparison and Czech malpractice', 461–80, 477.

Nevertheless, there are several challenges in further developing the fining system (see above Section 3.5). A big issue, also on the level of the European Union, is how to coordinate the different types of penal and administrative fines and make the comprehensive system of pecuniary sanctions more coherent. Finally, I refer to the concluding prospect expressed by Patricia Faraldo-Cabana: to build such a nexus between money and personal liberty in the sense of consumerism that would make pecuniary sanctions for serious offences more palatable.[30]

REFERENCES

Aebi, M. F., Aubusson de Cavarlay, B., Barclay, G., Gruszczyñska, B., Harrendorf, B., Heiskanen, M., Hysi, V., Jaquier, V., Jehle, J.-M., Killias, M., Shostko, O., Smit, P. and Porisdottir, R. (2010). *European Sourcebook of Crime and Criminal Justice Statistics* – 2010. 4th edition. The Hague: Boom Juridische Uitgevers. [Onderzock en beleid series, no. 285, Ministry of Justice, Research and Documentation Center (WODC)] (382 p., ISBN 978-90-8974-299-5).

Act on the Enforcement of Fines; 672/2002 with later amendments.

Drápal, J. 2018. 'Day Fines: A European Comparison and Czech Malpractice', *European Journal of Criminology* 15: 461–80.

Enforcement Code; 705/2007. An unofficial translation of this Act is available from the website of the Ministry of Justice: www.finlex.fi/fi/laki/kaannokset/2007/e n20070705-20070987.pdf.

Faraldo-Cabana, P. 2017. *Money and the Governance of Punishment, A Genealogy of the Penal Fine.* London: Routledge.

Government Bill No. 36/1920.

Government Bill No. 15/1963.

Government Bill No. 174/1967.

Government Bill No. 109/1975 (II).

Government Bill No. 125/1975 (II).

Government Bill No. 44/2002, Chapter E, 1 §, p. 185.

Government Bill No. 25/2007.

Government Bill No. 1/2016.

Government Bill No. 178/2018.

Ignatius, K. 1922. 'Sakkorangaistuksesta', *Lakimies* 20: 1–44.

Komiteanmietintö, No. 1931:2 (Helsinki, 1931).

Komiteanmietintö, No. 1976:72 (Helsinki, 1977).

Lahti, R. 1977. 'Criminal Sanctions in Finland: A System in 'Transition', *Scandinavian Studies in Law* 21: 121–57.

Lahti, R. and Rainiala, M. 2019. 'Alternative Investigation and Sanctioning Systems for Corporate and Corporate-Related Crime in Finland', *Revue Internationale de Droit Pénal* 90: 131–63.

---

[30] *Supra* note 3 Faraldo-Cabana, pp. 221–2.

Lahti, R. 2017. 'Finnish Report on Individual Liability for Business Involvement in International Crimes', *Revue Internationale de Droit Pénal* 88: 257–66.

Lahti, R. 2017. 'Towards a More Efficient, Fair and Humane Criminal Justice System: Developments of Criminal Policy and Criminal Sanctions during the Last 50 Years', *Cogent Social Sciences* 3: 1303910.

Lappi-Seppälä, T. 2004. 'Public Perceptions and the Fairness of the Dayfine System. An Evaluation of the 1999 Dayfine Reform', *Tidskrift, utgiven av Juridiska Föreningen I Finland* 140: 386–97.

Lappi-Seppälä, T. 2012. 'Penal Policies in the Nordic Countries 1960–2010', *Journal of Scandinavian Studies in Criminology and Crime Prevention* 13: 85–111.

Lappi-Seppälä, T. 2014. 'Fines in Europe', in Bruinsma, G. and Weisburd, D. (eds.), *Encyclopedia of Criminology and Criminal Justice*. New York: Springer, pp. 1637–48.

Matikkala, J. 2010. *Rikosoikeudellinen seuraamusjärjestelmä*. Helsinki: Edita.

Niemi, H. (eds.) 2017. *Seuraamusjärjestelmä* (Report No. 32, University of Helsinki, The Institute for Criminology and Legal Policy, Helsinki 2018), Chapter A.6, Tables 1, 18–20.

Serlachius, A. 1921. 'Päiväsakkojärjestelmä', *Lakimies* 19: 201–10.

Social Assistance Act; 1412/1997. An unofficial translation of this Act is available from the website of the Ministry of Justice: www.finlex.fi/fi/laki/kaannokset/1997/e n19971412_20101390.pdf.

4

Day Fines in Sweden

Jacob Öberg

4.1 INTRODUCTION

As in other areas of social engineering, Sweden is considered and perhaps considers itself as world-leading in creating systems that address social inequality. One of the cases in point is the Swedish day fine system. The idea that the amount of a fine ought to be settled in accordance with the daily income of the accused was devised as early as the beginning of the twentieth century by Professor Johan Thyrén.[1] The perceived inequality between wealthy and poor offenders created by fixed fines were strong motivations when Sweden introduced its day fine system in 1931. The Swedish day fine system has been considered as pioneering by systematically considering both the wealth of the offender and the seriousness of the offence when imposing the penalty.[2]

This chapter considers in depth the Swedish day fine system. The case study of Sweden is illustrative for two reasons. First, as there was extensive debate in Sweden prior to introducing the system and discussions on extending the use of day fines in the beginning of the 2000s, this chapter can give us a certain understanding of the pros and cons for introducing such a system.[3] Sweden is thereto a pertinent example for day fine studies as it has very detailed prosecutorial guidelines for calculating the fine.[4]

The first part of the chapter considers the history and rationale for introducing the day fine system. It discusses the arguments for and against introducing the system. Thereafter the main provisions on day fines and the legal structure

---

[1] Thornstedt, 'The day fine System in Sweden', 307; Thyrén, *Principerna för en strafflagsreform I.*
[2] See Eriksson and Goodin, 'The Measuring Rod of Time: The Example of Swedish Day-fines', 125; Kantorowicz-Reznichenko, 'Day Fines: Reviving the Idea and Reversing the Costly Punitive Trend', 333, 342–3; Hillsman, 'Fines and Day Fines', 49.
[3] See Section 4.2, Section 4.5 and Section 4.6.
[4] See Section 4.3.2.

of the system are discussed comprehensively in conjunction with an examination of the prosecutorial guidelines. Subsequently, the relevant case law and practice is analysed, particularly in relation to the adjustment of day fines. Finally, public reception and academic debates in switching to a system that imposes day fine penalties are accounted for. The chapter concludes with a summary of the main findings and some reflections on the main challenges with an extensive use of fines (and day fines) as a criminal penalty.

4.2 HISTORICAL DEVELOPMENT OF DAY FINES IN THE SWEDISH LEGAL SYSTEM

The fine as a criminal penalty has traditionally had a central role in the Swedish criminal justice system. Already in the criminal justice system of the ancient county laws, fines were prescribed as a penalty. Historically, the scope for using the fine as a penalty has varied. Initially, the thinking behind the penalty was the perception that through his behaviour the criminal is in debt to society and shall pay this debt. Furthermore, by paying the fine, offenders should financially compensate victims for their violations. As the state incrementally claimed a stake in the enforcement of the fines it obtained the character of a proper punishment entailing a very heavy burden for individuals. If the fines were not paid, they could be converted to death penalty or other draconian physical penalties. This development must be seen in the context of the fact that the King and the Church under the medieval times increasingly gained stronger powers. The consequence of this was that the criminal punishment system became harsher and more retributory in its nature. When fines were ordered by the court, they were to a large extent converted to corporal punishment, for example flogging or whipping. One of the rationales for reducing the use of fines was that the offender could not often or did not wish to pay the penalty. The scope, choice and intensity of the fine was also an arbitrary exercise depending on who imposed the penalty. The somehow cruel and harsh view of penalties survived throughout the enlightenment period as the King and the Church still had a strong influence over the state's imposition of penalties. At some point, the flogging and whipping punishments were, however, removed from the penalty sanctioning system entailing that fines and the short imprisonment sentence became a more common sanction to address petty offences. Many fine sentences were, however, still converted to imprisonment sentences, leading to very high prison populations.[5]

---

[5] See Bäcklund, 'Böter som alternativ och komplement till andra påföljder – praktiska frågor', 264, 266; Aspelin, 'Straffets grunder – historisk bakgrund', 108, 107–12, 121.

In response to the overpopulation of prisons and the gradually increasing calls for social justice, in the beginning of the twentieth century politicians and lawyers commenced to seriously discuss a reform of the fine system. Johan Thyrén was the primary proponent of revising the previous fine system with a day fine system. He developed his thinking in a review article of 1927[6] proposing what later on was going to constitute the basis for the key provisions in the Swedish Criminal Code on the determination of the day fine.[7]

The system was justified primarily on the basis of social justice – the previous fine system was unfair – and punishment should instead be imposed equally to all members of the society. Thyrén's model suggested that the punishment needed to consider two components: (1) that the punishment was proportionate to the gravity of the offence; and (2) that the financial burden of the fine would be justified given the offender's general financial circumstances. This fine would thus allow imposing an equal 'relative'[8] burden of punishment on all offenders regardless of their wealth thus systematically considering the socio-economic status of the offender. The day fine system partly recasted the underlying principle in the previous fine system which was designed primarily to impose punishments that were commensurate with the seriousness of the offence (proportionality).[9] In his work for the Law Commission,[10] Thyrén made a comprehensive review of other criminal justice systems and argued that several other systems had introduced similar ways of considering the wealth of the offender when determining the fine. There was a simple rule (applied then in Germany, Italy, Norway and Switzerland) which entailed that the court had to assess both the seriousness of the offence and the offender's financial circumstances when setting the fine.[11] In those systems the poor offender was treated more leniently when he had committed an equally serious offence as the rich offender. The simple rule, however, prescribed no clear guidelines in how the different components should be measured.

Those who advocated the 'simple rule' claimed that the 'day fine' system in practice might turn out just to be the 'simple rule'. The division of the assessment in two parts would be fictive as both components had to be assessed when determining the final amount. They also contended that it would be too

---

6   Thyrén, 'Om Bötesstraffets Reformering', 353.
7   Chapter 25 (2) (2) Swedish Criminal Code, ('Brottsbalk', 1962:700).
8   See *Supra* note 2, Kantorowicz-Reznichenko, 335, 338 for this expression.
9   *Supra* note 6, 354–8.
10 The Law Commission was the body responsible for preparing the new legislation on day fines: See *Kungliga Maj:ts Proposition till riksdagen med förslag till lag om ändring av vissa delar av strafflagen m.m*, Prop 1931:188.
11 See *ibid.*, 14–18.

complicated to specify both a specific punishment in terms of time and set a specific sum to be paid each day. These problems would lead to unjustified penalties, entail heavier burdens for the prosecutor and the judges as well as higher procedural costs. In addition, the system would be unreasonably intrusive for offenders with good financial circumstances whilst its deterrent effect for offenders with lower incomes would be questionable. The application of the day fine system would have unacceptable ramifications for 'wealthy' offenders in the lower scale of the penalty range which previously had been punished with a fixed fine and after the introduction of the day fine system would be subject to a very intrusive penalty. These arguments, however, did not persuade the proponents of the day fine system. To the main criticism – which was that the day fine system would be too complicated – they responded that the use the of the 'simple rule' is to employ the 'day fine' system in camouflage. They observed that the offender's financial circumstances, regardless of which system was chosen, had to be considered when the fine would be converted into a prison sentence. Furthermore, if the offender's motive for the offence was personal profit, the fines could potentially be set at a level which factored in the profit and risk for apprehension that the offender would be exposed to.[12]

Further, the day fine system had the advantage that it invited the court to express explicitly its judgment about the seriousness of the crime and to thus communicate censure (or 'stigma').[13] Under the 'simple rule' system, a high fine was ambiguous: it might signal a serious crime committed by someone with low income or it might signal a petty crime committed by someone with high income. Under the 'simple rule', the text of the law would specify a fine scale ranging from a low minimum to a very high maximum and judges would be given discretion to set a fine anywhere on that scale. By specifying in the statute that the punishment for a given offence is a certain number of days, the day fine system facilitates controlling the exercise of judges' discretion. Most importantly, the day fine system would visibly demonstrate that rich and poor are treated alike by the legal system and were indeed equal before the law, something considered indispensable given the political climate of the early twentieth century in Sweden. It was thus emphasised that the signals the law sent to ordinary people were of the utmost importance – the punishment for an offence should not be such as to constitute a major burden for a poor person

---

[12] See *ibid.*, 23. The latter reasoning is coherent with the traditional 'deterrence' model devised by Bentham and refined by economists and modern criminology: Bentham, *The Rationale of Punishment*, 1–23; Becker, 'Crime and Punishment: An Economic Approach', 169, 207–8; Paternoster, 'How Much Do We Really Know about Criminal Deterrence?', 765.

[13] *Supra* note 10, 15.

but hardly to be felt at all by a rich person.[14] Ultimately, it was also conceived that the introduction of day fines to a large extent would replace shorter prison sentences which were deemed unacceptable since they were claimed to have no positive feature attached to them.[15]

The result of the law commission's report was a proposal for implementing day fines as an additional sanction. The ideas expressed in the report also constituted the basis for the design of the key provisions on day fines in the Swedish Penal Code as it stands today.

4.3 THE LEGAL FRAMEWORK OF DAY FINES

4.3.1 *The Central Provision on Day Fines*

The basic provision on day fines can be found in Chapter 25, Section 2 of the Swedish Penal Code. It is appropriate to restate it *in extenso*:

> Day fines shall be determined in number to at least thirty and at most one hundred and fifty. Each day fine shall be imposed as a fixed amount from thirty up to and including one thousand Swedish crowns, having regard to what is judged to be reasonable with account taken of the income, wealth, obligations to dependants and other economic circumstances of the accused. If special reasons exist, the amount of the day fine may be adjusted. The lowest amount for a day fine is four hundred and fifty Swedish crowns.[16]

In the day fine system, the 'number' of day fines represents the gravity of the offence and the 'unit' of each day fine is estimated in accordance with the financial situation of the accused. In Sweden, the 'number' of day fines is not prescribed specifically for the offence in question, but there is a general scale for all offences ranging from 30 to 150 intended to fit both petty offences and more serious offences.[17] Day fines shall be used for the offence in question if a particular form of fine is not prescribed for the crime,[18] unless the offence is punishable with less than thirty day fines in which case summary fines shall be used.[19]

---

[14] *Supra* note 10, 15, 44, 86; *supra* note 2, Eriksson and Goodin, 130.
[15] *Supra* note 6, 358–9.
[16] This extract comes from a translation of the Swedish Criminal Code provided by the Ministry of Justice – see Ds 1999:36.
[17] Berggren *et al., Brottsbalken- en kommentar, kap.* 25–38 (Norstedts Juridik, 2012), BrB 25:1, 1–4.
[18] Chapter 4 (6) of the Swedish Penal Code illustrates the formula (emphasis added) which indicates the use of day fine as a sanction: 'A person, who, without authorisation, intrudes or remains in an office, factory, other building or vessel or at a storage area or other similar place, shall be *sentenced* for unlawful intrusion to *a fine*'.
[19] Chapter 25 (1) Swedish Penal Code.

If a person is sentenced at the same time for several offences, he or she must be sentenced to a joint punishment, which cannot exceed 200 day fines.[20] The daily 'unit' of a day fine in Sweden is 30 to 1,000 crowns (approximately between 3–94 euros or 3–104 dollars). Accordingly, the highest sum of day fines which can be imposed in one sentence is 150,000 crowns for one offence (150 X 1,000) or 200,000 crowns for more than one offence (200 X 1,000). Even if the provision allows for adjustment,[21] a day fine with a lower amount than 450 crowns (approximately 42 euros or 46 dollars) cannot be imposed.[22]

The setting of the day fine thus involves two steps. The first step consists in determining a fitting punishment in terms of the number of days for which fines could be extracted in such a way as to reflect the gravity of the offence. The second step consists in assigning an amount of money to be paid for each of those days considering the offender's financial circumstances. To ensure the transparency of the system, the judges do communicate the number of day fines separately from the daily unit.[23] This practice is also accepted in media where reports of judgments seems to include the number of day fines and regularly the total fine amount (including the daily unit).[24]

The thinking behind the day fine system is that the amount of the daily unit, taking into consideration his or her financial circumstances, would correspond to what the offender at the time of the sentence is able to dispense on a daily basis without being deprived of the necessities in life. The day fine system is thus employed to deprive people of pleasures, calibrated in temporal terms, that is, of a certain number of days' pleasures.[25]

4.3.2 *Guidance from the Prosecutor-General in Determining Day Fines*

As the determination of the day fine is a key issue for courts and prosecutors in daily legal practice, the Prosecutor-General has – to ensure uniformity in the

---

[20]   Chapter 25 (6) Swedish Penal Code.

[21]   Adjustment entails that the fine sentence can be reduced if certain exceptional circumstances pertaining to the offender are at hand. Adjustment of fines is discussed in more detail in Section 4.4.

[22]   Chapter 25 (2) and (6) Swedish Penal Code. For convenience, the respective exchange rates: 100 crowns = €9,43 / $10,39 / £8,05 (25 November 2019).

[23]   See NJA 1991, p. 692; NJA 1996, p. 195; NJA 1999, p. 286; NJA 2012, p. 16.

[24]   See e.g.: www.dagensmedia.se/nyheter/journalist-far-dagsboter-for-kokaininnehav-6228727; www.dagensmedia.se/nyheter/medievarldens-arkiv/dn-medarbetare-far-dagsboter-for-brott-vid-ubatsjakt/; www.blt.se/karlskrona/dryga-dagsboter-for-24-aring-som-hotade-polis-pa-hasslofestiva len/; www.gp.se/nyheter/sverige/%C3%A4ventyrade-rikets-s%C3%A4kerhet-fick-70-dagsb%C3 %B6ter-1.4473685.

[25]   *Supra* note 10, 188, 87; *supra* note 2, Eriksson and Goodin, 127–9; *supra* note 5, Bäcklund, 264–6.

practice of the prosecutors – provided guidelines for this purpose.[26] The courts are formally not bound by the guidelines but should make an independent interpretation of the provisions in the criminal code. A brief review of the Supreme Court's case law in this respect, however, suggests that the guidelines and their method for calculating the fine have had a significant influence on the courts' case law.[27]

The most recent and updated version of the Prosecutor-General's guidelines in setting the daily unit of the day fine is from 2007.[28] It proceeds from the following formula. The amount of the day fine in ordinary cases is based on the offender's expected gross annual income with deductions for costs incurred for acquiring the income at the date when the court's sentence is delivered. Income is defined broadly and includes continuous sources of income or contributions to the accused including unemployment benefits, financial contributions, study assistance benefits, scholarships, housing allowance and maintenance benefits.[29] The annual income also encompasses 'assets' and other streams of 'unearned' income, for example pension, interest and annuities.[30]

The offender's own statement about his annual income shall be accepted if they are considered credible in light of the investigation.[31] In cases where the offender's statement does not appear credible, the annual income should be estimated to a reasonable amount based on the latest taxable income and other available information. However, in order to compensate for Sweden's progressive tax system, the estimated annual income is deducted with 20 per cent of that portion of the taxable earned income that exceeds the lower tax threshold (2019: 490,700 crowns) and with 5 per cent of that portion of the income that exceeds the higher tax threshold (2019: 689,300 crowns).[32] There is also a deduction for every dependent child amounting to half of the price basic amount.[33] The daily unit of the fine is fixed to 1/1,000 of the calculated wealth pursuant to the preceding steps. On the basis of indirect taxes, this amount is then reduced by 50 crowns. If the suspect would have net assets[34] which

[26] *Supra* note 1, 309.
[27] See NJA 1991, p. 692 for support of this proposition.
[28] See Riksåklagarens Riktlinjer, 'Beräkningen av dagsbotsbeloppet vid strafföreläggande', RåR 2007:2.
[29] *Ibid.*
[30] See *supra* note 1, 309–10.
[31] Section 4 of the Decree on Preliminary Investigation ('Förundersökningskungörelse', 1947: 948).
[32] Chapter 65 (5) Swedish Income Tax Act ('Inkomstskattelag', 1999:1229).
[33] Chapter 1 (6) National Insurance Act ('Lagen om allmän försäkring', 1962:381).
[34] It refers to monetary assets deposited in bank and not fixed assets pertaining to industry, trade or real estate: *supra* note 1, 309–10.

exceeds 1,500,000 crowns the day fine is increased by 50 crowns and by a further 50 crowns for every 500,000 crowns.[35]

4.3.3 *Welfare Benefits Relevant for Assessing the Daily Unit of the Day Fine*

Welfare benefits in Sweden are wide-ranging and have for the largest part of post-war history been considered 'generous' in terms of payment levels. The Swedish social security system is to a certain extent earnings-based whilst some benefits are 'universal' and linked to residence or citizenship. The system is primarily financed through compulsory payments on the wage to a nationally administered social security system managed by the Swedish Social Insurance Agency ('Försäkringskassan').[36] Two important principles of the Swedish social insurance system are those of universality (encompassing the entire population) and of compensation for loss of income ('principen om inkomstbortfall').[37] In the modern Swedish welfare system, there are three basic components: (1) citizenship/residence benefits including old age pension systems and certain family benefits (for example child assistance benefits); (2) earnings-related social insurance benefits (for example unemployment allowance); (3) income-tested benefits such as housing benefits for families with children and the elderly.[38] Several benefits are regulated by the Social Insurance Code which provides detailed provisions on the conditions for obtaining the benefits.[39] In the following the most generous benefits are accounted for.[40]

The central family benefits are parental benefits (job-protected leave from employment to care for a child following its birth),[41] child assistance benefits (which parents obtain for every child)[42] and maintenance allowance (payments that a non-custodial parent makes as a contribution to the costs of

---

[35] 'RåR 2007:2', 1.1–1.4.

[36] Chapter 2 (3) and (4) Social Insurance Code ('Socialförsäkringsbalk', 2010:110).

[37] See for discussion of the Swedish welfare system: Edebalk, 'Emergence of a Welfare State – Social Insurance in Sweden in the 1910s', 537; Bergh, *The Rise, Fall and Revival of the Swedish Welfare State: What are the Policy Lessons from Sweden?*; Palme, Fritzell and Bergmark, 'End of Equality? The Welfare State Model Beyond the Crisis', 5–8.

[38] *Ibid.*, Palme, Fritzell and Bergmark, 5–6.

[39] See Hessmark *et al.*, *Socialförsäkringsbalk : en kommentar Avd. A-C och Avd. D-H* for an extensive commentary to the code.

[40] See European Commission, *Your social security rights in Sweden* (2019), for a more extensive overview in English of welfare benefits in Sweden.

[41] Chapters 11 and 12 of the Social Insurance Code.

[42] *Ibid.*, Chapters 15 and 16.

raising her or his child).[43] Parental benefits can add up to comparatively high amounts. If a person is employed and is entitled to the maximum amount of parental benefits by means of SGI (sick leave-based income) a person may obtain as much as 372,000 crowns per year. Compared to parental benefits, compensation from sickness insurance is less extensive.[44] The highest reimbursement from the sickness insurance is 791 crowns per day when the applicant applies for sick leave. This amounts to approximately 23,330 crowns per month. Should the applicant be permanently incapable to work due to sickness, the applicant obtains sick leave compensation which maximally amounts to 225,641 crowns a year.[45]

The two most extensive benefits outside the Social Insurance Code are study assistance benefits and unemployment benefits. Study assistance benefits is regulated in the Study Assistance Act ('Studiestödslag', 1999:1395). Those benefits are divided in the form of a grant and a loan and it is possible to only apply for the grant. Currently, students are entitled to 10,676 crowns (in total) a month or 5.74 of the price base amount[46] at full time studies.[47] Unemployment benefits are governed by the Act on Unemployment Insurance ('Lag om arbetslöshetsförsäkring', 1997:238). To qualify for the benefits, the applicant needs to have been a paying member for the unemployment fund for at least a year and fulfil the requirement of having worked at least 80 hours per month for at least six months. The maximum amount that can be obtained per day is limited to 910 crowns (the first 100 days, after that 760 crowns). This amounts to approximately 20,020 crowns per month which corresponds to the payment levels of the sick leave compensation.[48]

All this suggests that the amounts of the different welfare benefits vary considerably.[49] A substantial day fine may thus entail hardship for individuals having only sick leave compensation, study assistance benefits or unemployment benefits. Considering, however, that the financial circumstances of the offender is factored in when setting the daily unit of the fine, it appears that individuals obtaining less generous benefits nonetheless may have the means to pay a higher day fine.

---

43 *Ibid.*, Chapters 17 and 19.
44 See Ryberg-Welander, *Socialförsäkringsrätt : om ersättning vid sjukdom* for more extensive discussion of this benefit.
45 Försäkringskassan, *Aktuella belopp*.
46 The price base amount of 2019 is 46,500 crowns.
47 Sections 11 and 12 of the Study Assistance Act.
48 Sections 24–48 of the Act on Unemployment Insurance.
49 See Försäkringskassan, *Aktuella belopp* for detailed information on the different amounts which can be obtained through the discussed welfare benefits.

4.3.4 *The Procedure for Imposing Day Fines and Summary Fines*

A day fine is pursuant to the main rule in criminal proceedings imposed *ex officio*[50] by the court in its sentencing decision.[51] The court is thereto mandated to make a proper investigation into the offender's personal and financial circumstances to have sufficient material for its fining decision.[52] The prosecutor will not advance a specific claim for a day fine but will argue for a specific penalty in the final pleadings.[53] An important exception to the main rule is that the prosecutor is competent to advance a claim for a specific day fine and impose such a fine by means of summary penalty orders.[54] An order for summary penalty means that the suspect is, subject to his or her approval, ordered to pay a fine according to what the prosecutor considers that the offence deserves.[55] When an order has been submitted for approval within a specified period, the issue of criminal liability for the offence may not be taken up again before the expiration of the period. Orders approved shall have the same effect as a judgment that has entered into force.[56] Orders for summary penalties shall be signed by the prosecutor and identify: (1) the suspect, (2) the individual circumstances of the offence required for its identification, (3) the applicable statutory provisions and (4) the punishment submitted to the suspect for approval. The suspect's approval of an order of summary penalty is made by his signing a declaration that he admits the commission of the act and accepts the sanction included in the order and by delivering the declaration to the proper authority.[57]

4.3.5 *Standardised Fines and Summary Fines*

In addition to day fines, there are fines of the traditional kind in the Swedish legal system which are imposed by the court or the prosecutor directly at a certain sum of money. Such fines are today only used for petty offences. Summary fines shall be levied to an amount of at least 100 crowns and at most 2,000 crowns. However, if a lower maximum amount is specially provided for,

---

[50] However, there are precedents suggesting that the court should not go beyond what the prosecutor has argued for: NJA 1996, p. 541; NJA 2001, p. 614.
[51] See Chapter 30 (5) Swedish Procedural Code (Rättegångsbalk, 1942: 740).
[52] See Chapter 46 (4) and (9) Swedish Procedural Code.
[53] See Chapter 46 (10) Swedish Procedural Code; Ekelöf, Edelstam and Pauli, *Rättegång* V, pp. 203–5.
[54] See Chapter 48 (1) Swedish Procedural Code.
[55] A summary penalty may even concern a conditional sentence, or such a sanction coupled with a fine: Chapter 48 (2) Swedish Procedural Code.
[56] See Chapter 48 (4) Swedish Procedural Code.
[57] Chapter 48 (6) and (9) Swedish Procedural Code.

it shall be applicable. Standardised fines are fines that, pursuant to what is provided for the crime, shall be determined according to a special basis of computation.[58] The lowest amount for a standardised fine is 100 crowns.[59] Standardised fines are employed for a very rare number of offences and seem therefore overall of minor significance in the Swedish sanctioning system.[60]

Summary fines can also be employed if the crime is punishable with less than thirty day fines.[61] The amount can vary between 100 and 2,000 crowns. However, if a lower maximum amount is specially provided for, it shall be applicable.[62] The thinking behind the system is that day fines are a more serious penalty than summary fines.[63] Herein, a value rule is applied to determine which type of fine should be imposed. If the property stolen or the amount of the fraudulent conduct or the value of goods which has been subject to trespassing exceeds sixty crowns, a day fine should be imposed – otherwise summary fines should be employed.[64] For certain offences, summary fines are levied as a rule of thumb, including unlawful intrusion,[65] all offences in the Act on Public Order ('Ordningslag', 1993:1617), offences in the Act on Unlawful Possession of Certain Radar and Laser Instruments ('Lag om förbud mot vissa radar- och laservarnare', 1988:15), minor smuggling offences and customs offences in the Act on Smuggling Offences ('Lag om straff för smuggling', 2000:1225), illegal driving, breach of drivers licence regulation and certain offences in the Weapons' Regulation ('Vapenförordning', 1996:70). In sum, it appears that summary fines are levied either for ordinary minor property offences or traffic offences of minor nature or for violations of administrative regulations (administrative offences). The latter could be conceptualised as an example of the expanding scope of regulatory criminal law where the summary fine is imposed to ensure respect for certain regulatory commands.[66]

---

[58] The expression 'standardised fines' is not used in the relevant criminal provisions which use this type of sanction. The expression 'standardised fines' refers only to the fact that fines are calculated according a special basis for computation. Section 41 of the Swedish Fishing Act (Fiskelag, 1993:787) for example prescribes that the fines must be calculated on the basis of the numbers of kilowatt of the engine of the fishing boat.

[59] Chapter 25 (3) and (4) Swedish Penal Code.

[60] See Jareborg and Zila, *Straffrättens påföljdslära*, p. 31. See Section 41 of the Fishing Act for an example of use of this type of sanction.

[61] Chapter 25 (1) Swedish Penal Code.

[62] Chapter 25 (3) Swedish Penal Code.

[63] NJA 2010, p.155.

[64] Åklagarmyndigheten, 'Strafföreläggande i bötesmål – en sammanställning av tillämpade påföljder', 7; Borgeke, Månsson and Sterzel, *Studier rörande påföljdspraxis med mera*, pp. 499–505.

[65] Chapter 4 (6)(2) Swedish Penal Code.

[66] See Ashworth, 'Is the Criminal Law a Lost Cause', 226–7, 255–6 for this observation.

4.3.6 *Enforcement and Collection of Fines*

The provisions of the Enforcement of Fines Act ('Bötesverkställighetslag', 1979:189) governs the collection and enforcement of fines. If the fines have not been paid by the offender, they will be collected by the Swedish Enforcement Authority. If it is impractical to collect the fine from the offender the judge may, upon the request of the prosecutor, convert the fine to an imprisonment sentence if it is apparent that the offender intentionally has failed to pay the fines or if conversion due to other special reasons is justified from a general perspective. The conversion penalty may be set to an imprisonment sentence of at least fourteen days and at the maximum of three months.[67] In the absence of clarifications in case law and preparatory works there is substantial uncertainty on what criteria is used for determining the conversion penalty (that is, what quantity of day fine deserves one month imprisonment and two month imprisonment and so forth). However, the lower instances which have issued conversion penalties in published case law have intriguingly settled for the same conversion penalty of one month imprisonment.[68]

The conversion penalty is envisaged to be employed with caution and only where strong reasons for conversion exist. Such reasons may exist where offenders who are capable of paying their fines through diverse disloyal acts have made it impossible to collect the fines or by mere defiance fail to pay the fines. The conversion penalty can also be used in other instances against offenders which repetitively have been involved in petty offences but do not have the will or financial capacity to pay the fines and where disloyalty or defiance has not been established. In the latter scenario, the circumstances must be flagrant, meaning that a failed punitive reaction would seriously provoke the general sense of justice.[69]

In practice, conversion is so rare that statistics are no longer published. Only in a couple of instances a year the imprisonment sentence is actually served.[70] Sentences to fines lapse after five years have expired from the date when the judgment acquired final legal force, regardless of the reason for why the fine was not paid. This does not apply if, at the expiry of the stated period, the

---

[67] See Sections 15 and 22 of the Enforcement of Fines Act; Chapter 25 (8) Swedish Penal Code. To clarify there are no other alternative sanctions (e.g. community services) available for conversion of fines than imprisonment.

[68] The Court of Appeal in NJA 2012, p. 22 and the District Court in RH 2004:28 imposed such a conversion penalty.

[69] See NJA 2012, p. 22; 'Proposition om ändring i brottsbalken m. m.', 1982/83:93, 15, 16, 34, 43.

[70] It has been observed that the Swedish system on conversion is met with genuine consternation in other European countries where 'day fine' prisoners are a serious concern. See *supra* note 60, pp. 33–4.

sentenced person has been notified of an application for conversion of the fine and this application has not been finally determined. If the application does not lead to conversion of the fine, it shall lapse when the court's final decision in the case acquires final legal force.[71] A conversion penalty lapses if the conversion decision has not been enforced, three years from the date when the judgment acquired final legal force.[72]

4.4 PRACTICAL IMPLEMENTATION OF THE DAY FINE SYSTEM

4.4.1 *Relevant Case Law of the Courts*

This section discusses the key judgments in this area followed by an account of some recent statistics on day fines.

The Supreme Court's Approach to Determining the Day Fine

A central judgment on day fines is NJA 1991, p. 692. In this judgment the court held that the Prosecutor-General's guidelines, whilst not binding on the court, should be taken as a point of departure when setting the fine. The basis for the court's calculation was that the day fine should amount to 1/1,000 of the annual income. Given, however, that the offender was married and had to contribute to his wife's sustenance, this fact had to be considered when determining the fine to ensure that the offender did not incur a heavier financial burden than a single person. Given the relationship between the incomes of the married couple, a reasonable outcome would be achieved if the husband's annual income, 300,000 crowns, was reduced by 1/6 (50,000 crowns). The remaining income would then be 250,000 crowns and 1/1,000 of this 250 crowns. From this amount the prosecutor had deducted thirty crowns from indirect taxes that would incur to the offender and thereafter twenty-six crowns corresponding to 1/1,000 of 20 per cent of the part of the annual income which exceeded the cut-off point in the income taxation scale. The court thus accepted the Prosecutor-General's claim that the offence would carry a day fine of 190 crowns.[73]

---

[71] See Chapter 35 (7), Swedish Penal Code.
[72] See Section 21 of the Enforcement of Fines Act.
[73] This way of calculating the fine is consistent with the Prosecutor General's guidelines 'RåR 2007:2' as discussed in Section 4.3.

Case Law on Adjustment of the Amount of the Day Fine

On a number of occasions, the Supreme Court has explored whether the amount of the day fine could be adjusted due to the existence of special reasons.[74] The court displays restraint in its approach and has held that this provision should be interpreted narrowly. In NJA 1996, p. 195, the court suggested that there are certain instances where the application of the day fine provisions results in a penalty which entails excessive hardship for the offender.[75] This is the case where a high number of day fines is imposed and the offender's solvency is seriously compromised because of long-term illness or a serious disability. In this instance, the amount of the day fine should be adjusted to ensure that the penalty is not beyond the offender's financial capacity. Within groups with insignificant incomes – for example certain juveniles, dependents with children and the retired – the circumstances may be such that the minimum amount of a day fine needs to be adjusted to ensure that the penalty does not entail unreasonable hardship. The possibility to adjust the day fine should, however, be applied restrictively and only where there are special reasons for adjustment. General exceptions for primary school students or other pupils cannot therefore be accepted but there must be an individual assessment on the basis of the circumstances in the specific case. One example where adjustment of the minimum amount can be accepted is where the number of day fines due to the penal value of the crime[76] is deemed very high and the penalty for this reason would entail serious hardship. Another instance of adjustment would be where someone lives under strained social circumstances and the penalty therefore becomes a heavy financial burden to incur. In the case at hand the offender was sixteen years old and she was enrolled in a normal elementary school education. Whilst she had no income or assets, she lived under similar financial circumstances as elementary school pupils in general. Given this, there were no special reasons for adjustment.

In NJA 1999, p. 286 the court held that that there could be special reasons for adjustment where the crime's penal value lies in the lower range of the penalty scale for day fines and the offender has such good financial circumstances that the

---

[74] It may be clarified that the 'number of day fines' can never be adjusted – it is only the 'daily unit' of the fine, the amount which can be adjusted: see Chapter 25(2) Penal Code.

[75] See 'Prop 1990/91:68', 117.

[76] As mentioned above in Section 4.3, the 'number of day fines' is assessed according to the concrete penal value of the offence pursuant to the general principles in Chapter 29 of the Swedish Penal Code. The leading provision here is Chapter 29 (1) of the Swedish Penal Code which prescribes that 'punishment shall . . . . be determined within the scale of punishments according to the penal value of the crime or crimes taken. In assessing the penal value, special consideration shall be given to the *damage, wrong or danger occasioned by the criminal act, to what the accused realised or should have realised about this and to the intentions or motives* he may have had' (emphasis added to underline the different elements of the penal value).

threshold effect – pertaining to the fact that a day fine rather than a summary fine is imposed for the crime – is objectionable. The court suggested that such special reasons for adjustment of the day fine amount may present itself in minor assault instances. Where the offence consists of correcting minors, legal practice shows that the circumstances may vary considerably. In the case at hand the evidence suggested that the offender's actions had been caused by the fact that the victim and his friends at nightfall had entered into the offender's garden, made high noises and climbed into a chestnut tree. The offender lost his temper when he got hold of the victim and asked what he was doing and the victim subsequently responded that 'this was not his business'. Whilst the offender's action to give the victim a blow was not excusable and he thereby committed minor assault, it was considered disproportionate to impose a fine of 13,000 crowns which would be the result if the ordinary principles for calculating day fines would be applied. The fine was therefore adjusted to 3,750 crowns.

The age of the offender may – in line with general principles of sanctioning – also be a reason for adjusting the day fine.[77] The Supreme Court held in NJA 2012, p. 16 that there was space for adjusting the day fine if the juvenile offender had turned eighteen years to ensure consistency in the criminal justice system. The court held that the penal value of the petty theft offence at issue was 110 day fines which entailed that this value should be adjusted to 80 day fines to duly consider the age of the offender.

In a judgment from the Court of Appeal in 2010 the court considered whether a day fine could be adjusted for an asylum seeker. It restated that the provision on adjustment should be applied restrictively and only where special circumstances were at hand. It admitted that the amount of the penalty, 6,500 crowns, was substantial given the offender's financial and social situation. The Court of Appeal, however, found that there were no specific circumstances in the case showing that the offender's situation diverged from other asylum seekers. Furthermore, if the number of day fines would be decisive for the assessment it would lead to a practice of standardised judgments in a way that would not be consistent with the Supreme Court's proposition that assessments must be individual. It could also be envisaged that such a practice would entail boundary problems and threshold effects. Given all this, the Court of Appeal decided to not accept the adjustment of the day fine.[78]

---

[77] Chapter 29 (7) Swedish Penal Code.
[78] RH 2010: 63.

The Basis for Determining the Day Fine

In a judgment of 2001 the Court of Appeal examined which financial information was pertinent for determining the daily unit of the day fine. It initially observed that the idea behind the system was that the day fine should be determined to an amount that the suspect could dispense with, without suffering hardship or fail to fulfil his maintenance duties.[79] The suspect had stated in hearings that he was a businessman, healthy and working with an annual income of 400,000 crowns, assets of 100,000 crowns and maintenance duties to three children. He also had voluntarily the same day deposited an amount of 27,300 crowns. Thereafter he issued a power of attorney for another person to admit the offence and accept the penalty summary order on the condition that the order contained no higher penalty than what followed from that order. In the proceedings in the District Court the suspect subsequently submitted a certificate wherein he pledged pursuant to the German Procedural Code that he did not have any assets or any income.[80] The Court of Appeal considered that the initial evidence in the preliminary investigation regarding the offender's circumstances was credible. The certificate that the offender subsequently submitted indicated that he, sixteen months after the committal of the offence, had no assets or income. Given that the offender, however, voluntarily deposited a sum of 27,300 crowns at the time of the offence suggested that he was capable at that stage of paying the mentioned amount without suffering hardship or fail to satisfy his maintenance duties. The court concluded that the day fine should be determined on the basis of the financial information that was provided at the time of the offence.[81]

4.4.2 *Statistics on Fines*

To the best of the author's knowledge no empirical study has been pursued which measures the relative effectiveness of day fines in deterring crime (for example as compared to fixed fines or other alternative sanctions). There are, however, some reliable official statistics on the frequency of the use of day fines and fines as sanctions in judgments and summary penal orders.

---

[79] This is in line with the thinking in the preparatory works to the provision: *supra* note 10, 35, 87.

[80] To clarify, the German Procedural Code had no specific relevance in the case. It was simply a certificate from the offender which had been issued pursuant to the German Procedural Code. The evidentiary value of the certificate had no specific evidentiary value in the case and was considered of secondary importance to the fact that the offender had deposited an amount of 27,300 crowns which according to the court evinced the offender's capacity to pay the fine at the time of the commission of the offence.

[81] See RH 2001:57.

Fines issued either by judgments or accepted summary penal order are seemingly the most common form of sanction. In 2018, 58 per cent of the total number of conviction decisions carried fines as the principal sanction. Among the remaining 42 per cent, imprisonment sentences counted for approximately 10 per cent, waiver of prosecution for 19 per cent, suspended sentences[82] for 10 per cent whilst the remaining sanctions totalled 10 per cent of all conviction decisions. The statistics of 2018 also suggest that the fine sanctions are distributed evenly among the sexes; 60 per cent of the main sanctions against women and 58 per cent of the main sanctions among men consisted of fines by summary penalty orders or judgment. Fines were also the most common sanction in all age groups over seventeen. In 2018, 55–72 per cent of the principal sanctions for that age group consisted of fines. Only for the youngest age group, fifteen to seventeen, the ratio of fine sanctions of all convictions was lower (34 per cent), which can be explained by the fact that young offenders regularly are convicted to special sanctions such as youth care orders.[83] Compared to 2009, the sanctioning structure has also slightly changed. The largest change is that the overall share of fine sanctions (fines in judgments and summary penal orders) has increased by 6 per cent. In addition to the changes in sanctioning structures, there has been a rediversion of the different types of fine penalties. The share of fines which are issued by courts has increased whilst the share of fines through summary penal orders has been reduced since 2009. In 2018 it was equally common that fines were issued by courts as by summary penal orders – each counted for 50 per cent of the total amount of fine penalties. This could be compared to 2009 when fines issued by courts consisted of 43 per cent of the total amount of fine penalties. Among the different fine penalties, the day fine penalty was the most commonly imposed fine in 2018. Among the total number of 65,760 fine penalties, 55,650 constituted day fine sanctions (84 per cent), whilst summary fines were imposed in 10,105 (15 per cent) of conviction decisions and standardised fines only in five conviction decisions.[84] In terms of offences, fines are most commonly used in relation to offences in the Road Traffic Offences Act (7,761), in relation to offences in the Crimes Against the Drugs (Penal) Act (9,351), for offences in the Road Traffic Ordinance (3,072), as well as for theft and other robbery offences (3,595).

---

[82]   Among them there were 3,273 suspended sentences combined with 'community service' (see Chapter 28 (2)(a) Swedish Penal Code).

[83]   See Chapter 32 of the Swedish Penal Code.

[84]   See Brottsförebyggande Rådet (Swedish Crime Prevention Authority), 'Kriminalstatistik 2018 – Personer Lagförda för Brott, Slutlig statistik', 20-1, 24. See also the webpage of the Swedish Crime Prevention Authority: www.bra.se/bra-in-english/home/crime-and-statistics/crime-statistics/persons-found-guilty-of-offences.html.

On the basis of these statistics it may also be inferred that the higher range of the scale for day fines is rarely used.[85] In 2018, 6,536 out of 55,650 day fines were imposed in the highest range of the penalty scale (100–200 number of day fines) which equals 11.7 per cent.[86] The latter finding is coherent with perceptions among scholars which is that courts exceptionally impose higher penalties than 100–120 day fines.[87]

4.5 PUBLIC PERCEPTION AND CRITICISM OF THE DAY FINE SYSTEM

Historically, it appears that day fines have been perceived in a positive light among practitioners and academics.[88] Commentators have suggested that the fine penalty entails an inconvenience by means of the intrusion in the offender's financial circumstances. If high fine penalties are imposed against offenders with scarce resources, this may act as a disincentive for other less wealthy offenders to commit a similar offence. The day fine system indeed allows for the imposition of penalties which in the specific case may entail serious financial repercussions for the individual concerned. Another advantage pertaining to the fine penalty is that the application of the criminal law proportionality principle – that the penalty should reflect the seriousness of the offence – becomes more transparent through the day fine system. Since the number of day fines is aligned with the seriousness of the offence, it becomes possible to ascertain the penal value that is attached to the offence.[89]

The main criticism against day fines is its limited capacity to act as a deterrent sanction. When the day fine system was implemented, Thyrén suggested that day fines did not communicate anything in particular. He argued that the central issue for the general public would instead be what behaviour had caused the imposition of day fines.[90] This view is, however, in hindsight contestable. In contrast to the proposition advanced by Thyrén, it appears that traditional views of imprisonment as the only deterrent sanction

---

[85] As mentioned above Chapter 25 (2) and (6) of the Swedish Penal Code allow the court to impose up to 150 number of day fines for a single offence and 200 number of day fines in the case of a consolidated punishment.

[86] See Swedish Official Statistics, 'Tabell 500, Bötespåföljder, efter huvudbrott, samt böternas art och storlek', 2018. Available at: www.bra.se/statistik/kriminalstatistik.html.

[87] See Borgeke and Heidenborg, *Att bestämma påföljd för brott*, pp. 66–7; *supra* note 1, 308.

[88] See *supra* note 1, 311–12; Strahl, 'Något om böter', 203.

[89] See *supra* note 5, Bäcklund, 265–7.

[90] *Supra* note 6, 354–5; Ulväng holds similar views at least in terms of shorter imprisonment sentences: Ulväng, 'Böter i stället för fängelse? Några anteckningar i anslutning till Nils Jareborgs uppsats', 243, 247–8.

are strongly held among politicians and practitioners in the criminal justice system.[91] This view finds support in a body of scholarship which argues that fines do not communicate sufficient social censure to be a serious alternative to imprisonment.[92] The general public approach in Sweden to day fines seems to be that this kind of penalty is attached to minor or petty offences, imposing a feeble moral stigma on the offender.[93] Another deterrence concern pertains to the execution stage where the imposition of fines do not per se have a clear linkage to the offender. A fine can be paid by another individual than the offender. In terms of a juvenile offender, it is regularly the case that the parent of the offender actually pays the fine. In terms of juvenile offenders and individuals with serious mental disturbance it may also be questioned whether fines are a rational penalty. These offenders normally have a limited capacity to pay and the treatment aspect is central when choosing the sanction towards them.[94]

Although the social justice aim of the day fine system to punish offenders according to their wealth is appreciated by several observers, legitimate critique has been advanced to the threshold effects that are caused by imposing high day fines on affluent offenders. In a review article of 2003, Bäcklund has compellingly illustrated the justice concerns arising from considering the wealth of the offender as the central feature in fine sentencing. Within the range of monthly incomes of 15,000–40,000 crowns, the divergence in the final day fine sentence is significant. A single parent with a monthly income of 15,000 crowns would pay 18,000 crowns in day fines for minor theft of a value of 700–800 crowns.[95] A corresponding amount at a monthly income of 20,000 crowns would be 25,200 crowns in day fines and at a monthly income of 40,000 crowns the day fine sentence would amount to 48,000 crowns. It is contestable whether differences in living standard, with respect to the progressive tax system and the social welfare system, justifies those strongly diverging fine

[91] See *ibid.*, Ulväng, 246–7 for this observation.
[92] For a selection of literature sharing this view: Kahan, 'What Do Alternative Sanctions Mean?', 593; Coffee Jr, 'No Soul To Damn – No Body To Kick – An Unscandalized Inquiry into the Problem of Corporate Punishment', 386, 433, 447; Öberg, 'Is It "Essential" to Imprison Insider Dealers to Enforce Insider Dealing Laws?', 111, 130–3; Öberg, 'Criminal Sanctions in the Field of EU Environmental Law', 402.
[93] There is certain support from press articles in Sweden that fines do not carry sufficient moral censure to constitute a credible sanction for certain offences, including drug offences and minor assault: www.svd.se/narkotikapolis-boter-ar-verkningslost; www.expressen.se/kvallspos ten/sport/fotboll/superettan/par-hansson-boter-ar-inte-avskrackande-nog/.
[94] See *supra* note 2, Eriksson and Goodin, 130, 131, 134; *supra* note 5, Bäcklund, 264–6.
[95] Bäcklund's estimation of the fine penalties is based on the sentencing standards of 2003 in relation to minor theft. The amount of the day fine in her example would probably be higher today to be aligned with a general increase in living standard and incomes.

penalties.[96] Heidenborg and Borgeke have voiced similar criticisms. The fact that the amount of the daily unit for the fine varies between 50 and 1,000 crowns whilst the number of day fines varies between 30 and 150 (or 200 in the case of joint offences) entails that the daily unit clearly is more significant than the number of day fines for the final sentence. Even if it is exceptional that the daily unit is set at 1,000 crowns, it appears that the law imposes five times more weight to the offender's financial circumstances (the amount of the daily unit) than the seriousness of the offence (the number of day fines). It could be questioned if this is a reasonable system from the perspective of justice and equality.[97]

Having enunciated these criticisms, the overall impression from the debate is, however, that the day fine system is well-entrenched among the actors in the criminal justice system and perceived as a well-functioning way of sentencing offenders for less serious crimes.

4.6 SPECIAL CHALLENGES: SWITCHING TO DAY FINES FROM SHORT IMPRISONMENT SENTENCES

There have been proposals for extending the application of day fines to more serious offences. Jareborg has in particular argued for replacing short imprisonment sentences for certain offences such as assault or drunk driving with day fine penalties and conditional sentences on the basis that imprisonment intrinsically is an 'inhumane' and 'ineffective' penalty.[98] Jareborg's preference for fines over imprisonment is shared by other Swedish scholars who contend that the hardship of imprisonment should not be imposed for other crimes than serious offences.[99] The ideas and principles underlying Jareborg's proposal were critically discussed by Magnus Ulväng in a response article in *Svensk Juristtidning* ('Swedish Law Journal') of 2003. Several issues were outlined as problematic. First, the concern with imposing day fines for criminal offences which in the past had been punished with shorter imprisonment sentences, pertained to the principles of the Swedish sanctioning system. Pursuant to a key principle in this system the court shall, when choosing the sanction, particularly consider any circumstance that argues for the imposition of a less severe punishment than imprisonment. As a reason for imprisonment, the court

---

[96] See *supra* note 5, Bäcklund, 266.
[97] See *supra* note 86, pp. 67–8; *supra* note 1, 308.
[98] See Jareborg, 'Böter i stället för fängelse?', 231, 232–6.
[99] *Supra* note 60, pp. 94–7, 139; *supra* note 1, 312; *supra* note 89, Ulväng, 243–4, 262–4; Aspelin, 'Böter i stället för frihetsstraff', 53.

may consider besides the penal value and nature of the crime or crimes, the fact that the accused has previously been guilty of committing a crime.[100] The conventional interpretation of this provision and the preparatory works attached to it is that offences must have a penal value of twelve months in order for an imprisonment sentence to be imposed.[101] However, as an exception to this principle, the case law suggests that there is a presumption that certain offences by nature ('*artbrott*')[102] must be sanctioned with an imprisonment sentence, for example drunk driving and unprovoked assault, even if the offence does not have a higher penal value than six months' imprisonment. Previous criminality is also a strong reason for imprisonment which may speak in favour of such a sentence even if the penal value of the present offence is less than one year.[103] To switch to day fines for such offences would entail that the courts would need to substantially revise settled case law. It would perhaps even require an amendment of the established sanctioning principles in Chapter 30, Section 4.[104] This may be politically very difficult to achieve in the present Swedish political climate where politicians endeavour to win against their opponents with proposals for harsher sentencing policies.[105]

Another contested issue in this debate is whether the current way of calculating the day fine can be maintained if shorter imprisonment sentences are replaced with day fine sentences. The premise here is that even a shorter prison sentence is more deterrent than a fine of 1,000 euros. The argument is thus that the smallest day fine penalty imposed by the current system must be raised significantly if they are to replace shorter imprisonment sentences. Otherwise the legitimacy of the system would be jeopardised. Imposing high day fine penalties for recidivists instead of short imprisonment sentences may thereto be difficult to defend on the basis of the principles of the sanctioning system. The credibility of the system would be undermined if abundant previous criminality was not considered as a reason for imposing an

---

[100] See Chapter 30 (4) Swedish Penal Code.
[101] 'Regeringens proposition om ändring i brottsbalken m. m. (straffmätning och påföljdsval m. m.)', 1987/88:120, 100; *supra* note 60, pp. 143–4.
[102] The concept of nature of crime suggests that these offences are so frequently occurring that imprisonment is needed to ensure sufficient deterrence: *supra* note 60, pp. 140–3; 'Prop 1987/88:120', 100, 116–17.
[103] *Supra* note 60, pp. 127–9, 143–4; NJA 1998, p. 713; NJA 1992, p. 590.
[104] See *supra* note 89, Ulväng, 246–7.
[105] See the debate article in the daily newspaper *Dagens Nyheter*: www.dn.se/debatt/svagt-stod -i-forskningen-for-att-hardare-straff-minskar-brotten/ where several professors in criminology at Stockholm University condemned the political debate on harsher sentencing prior to the Swedish elections in September 2018.

imprisonment sanction.[106] The current system is based on a moral principle that previous criminality should be considered when determining the magnitude of the penalty and when choosing the type of sanction.[107] Ulväng did, in contrast to Jareborg's proposition, advance a proposal where shorter imprisonment sentences employed in cases of recidivism and for '*artbrott*' offences would be replaced by day fine penalties in conjunction with another alternative sanction. The latter would be feasible within the current sanctioning system and clearly communicate the censure of the offence. He proposes concretely that day fine sentences should be imposed, either on a self-standing basis or as an additional sanction to an alternative sanction such as conditional sentences,[108] for offences of a lesser penal value than six months' imprisonment. This suggests that more serious alternative sanctions such as conditional sentences with community service[109] and probation sentences with special provisions[110] should be employed for offences carrying a penal value exceeding six months' imprisonment.[111]

4.7 CONCLUSIONS: DAY FINES AS AN ALTERNATIVE CRIMINAL SANCTION

One of the main points of this chapter is that the Swedish day fine system overall must be considered as a largely successful project which holds general acceptance by courts and practitioners. The common view is that it is a merit of the system that it forces the courts to consider the economic circumstances of the accused and to articulate openly for the way in which such consideration has been done.[112] As discussed in the previous section there have also been ideas to extend the application of day fines as an alternative to short imprisonment sentences,[113] in particular for offences such as theft and other property crimes of normal gravity.[114]

It is easy to understand why fines and day fines are the most commonly advocated sanction to be used as an alternative to imprisonment. In a cost-benefit analysis of the choice between fines and imprisonment, the cost side of

---

[106] See *supra* note 89, Ulväng, 247–8, 250–1, 253–4.
[107] See Chapter 29 (4) and Chapter 30 (4) Swedish Penal Code.
[108] See Chapter 30 (8) Swedish Penal Code.
[109] See *ibid.*, Section 7.
[110] See *ibid.*, Section 9.
[111] See *supra* note 89, Ulväng, 256–7, 260–3.
[112] *Supra* note 87.
[113] Svensson, 'Gammalt straffsystem', 608, 611–14; *supra* note 97.
[114] Statens Offentliga Utredningar, 'Ett reformerat straffsystem', SOU 1995:91; *supra* note 5, Bäcklund, 271, 277 discussing this reform.

the analysis may favour fining because the cost of collecting a fine from someone who can pay is lower than the cost of imprisonment. By imposing fines rather than imprisonment it is also possible to ensure that the criminal is still a working member of the society whilst the society obtains a certain financial contribution by the penalty. Since the day fine system is supported by an effective implementation system it also carries a certain deterrent function. Furthermore, in terms of white-collar crimes where crimes are driven by financial gain, fines may be an effective sanction. If 'optimal fines' are imposed (where the amount of the fine factors in the probability of detection and prosecution as well as the potential profits of the offence) they may impose a genuine disincentive for a potential offender.[115]

The central argument against fines (and day fines) in the scholarly debate is that such sanctions are not considered sufficiently deterrent in the sense that a fine is not capable of providing a relevant threat for potential offenders to refrain from wrongdoings.[116] Whilst to date there has not been undertaken an empirical study of the deterrent nature of the Swedish day fine system, the evidence of the public opinion discussed above suggests that fines are not considered a sanction capable of communicating moral censure.[117] When used as an alternative to imprisonment, fines seem to convey the normative message that society is willing to accept the offender's behaviour. By viewing fines as mere prices for committing an offence, the seriousness of the offence is depreciated. As discussed above, there is also a deterrence problem relating to the execution stage where the imposition of the fine does not entail a personal duty for the offender to pay the fine.[118] The fine can thus be paid by another individual than the offender. This is particularly commonplace with regard to juvenile offenders.[119] Another concern is that potential offenders for most offences do not at all consider the threat of monetary sanctions, due to the offenders' lack of wealth or because white-collar offenders can regularly transfer or hide their wealth.[120] As observed in this chapter, there are also statutory limits restraining the amount and number of day fines that can be

---

[115] See Posner, 'Optimal Sentences for White-Collar Criminals', 409; *supra* note 5, Bäcklund, 264–7; Ivancevich, Konopaske and Gilbert, 'Formally Shaming White-Collar Criminals', 401, 406; *supra* note 12, Becker, 207–9.

[116] See *supra* note 91 for references to this scholarship.

[117] See above Section 4.5.

[118] See Kraakman, 'Corporate Liability Strategies and the Costs of Legal Controls', 857 for a detailed law and economics analysis of the downfalls of the shifting of personal liability from a deterrence perspective.

[119] See above Section 4.5.

[120] See Mann, Wheeler and Sarat, 'Sentencing the White-Collar Offender', 479, 496–9; Spagnolo, 'Saving the Banks, But Not Reckless Bankers', at www.voxeu.org/article/criminal-sanctions-how

imposed by courts.[121] In conjunction with the facts that courts rarely seem to impose fines in the higher range of the penalty scale,[122] it seems to be difficult to ensure that 'optimal penalties' for the offender are imposed. There is thus some support for the view that it is appropriate, as a matter of policy and philosophy, to employ prison sentences indiscriminately for more serious offences.[123]

On an endnote, this all suggests that the day fine system, although well-perceived among practitioners and academics as a way of achieving social justice through sanctioning and as a way of avoiding the use of the hardship of imprisonment sentences, carries a limited deterrent function. There are furthermore clear prospects of redesigning the system to ensure that the wealth component of the assessment is not given too much significance to the detriment of the idea of proportionate sentencing (aligning the penalty with the seriousness of the offence). This should not be conceived of as a criticism of the system as such but merely as a way of articulating openly what the system is able to achieve in terms of policy outcomes and the intrinsic limits of this way of sanctioning (in ensuring just desert and deterrence).

REFERENCES

Åklagarmyndigheten, 'Strafföreläggande i bötesmål – en sammanställning av tillämpade påföljder', *RättsPM* 2012: 7.

Ashworth, A. 2000. 'Is the Criminal Law a Lost Cause', *Law Quarterly Review* 116: 225–56.

Aspelin, E. 1973. 'Böter i stället för frihetsstraff', *Nordisk Tidsskrift for Kriminalvidenskab* 66: 53–72.

Aspelin, E. 1999. 'Straffets grunder – historisk bakgrund', *Svensk Juristtidning* 84:, 108–31.

Bäcklund, A. 2003. 'Böter som alternativ och komplement till andra påföljder – praktiska frågor', *Svensk Juristtidning*, 264–78.

Becker, G. 1968. 'Crime and Punishment: An Economic Approach', *Journal of Political Economy* 76: 169–217.

Bentham, J. 1830. *The Rationale of Punishment*. London: Robert Heward.

-save-banks-without-rewarding-bankers; McDermott, 'Occupational Disqualification of Corporate Executives: An Innovative Condition of Probation', 604, 614–15.

[121] See Chapter 25 (II), Swedish Penal Code.

[122] See above Section 4.4.2.

[123] See Coffee Jr, 'Corporate Crime and Punishment: A Non-Chicago View of the Economics of Criminal Sanctions, 419; *supra* note 91, Kahan, 620–2, 650; Hristova, 'The Case for Insider-Trading Criminalization and Sentencing Reform', 267, 301–2; Stone, 'The Place of Enterprise Liability in the Control of Corporate Conduct', 1, 29–30.

Bergh, A. 2011. *The Rise, Fall and Revival of the Swedish Welfare State: What are the Policy Lessons from Sweden?*, IFN Working Paper No. 87.

Borgeke, M. and Heidenborg, M. 2016. *Att bestämma påföljd för brott*. Stockholm: Jure.

Borgeke, M., Månsson, C. and Sterzel, G. 2013. *Studier rörande påföljdspraxis med mera*. Stockholm: Jure.

Brottsförebyggande Rådet. 2019. 'Kriminalstatistik 2018 – Personer Lagförda för Brott, Slutlig statistik' (Brottsförebyggande rådet).

Coffee Jr, J. C. 1980. 'Corporate Crime and Punishment: A Non-Chicago View of the Economics of Criminal Sanctions', *American Criminal Law Review* 17: 419–76.

Coffee Jr, J. C. 1981. 'No Soul To Damn – No Body To Kick – An Unscandalized Inquiry into the Problem of Corporate Punishment', *Michigan Law Review* 79: 386–459.

Edebalk, P. G. 2000. 'Emergence of a Welfare State – Social Insurance in Sweden in the 1910s', *Journal of Social Policy* 29: 537–51.

Ekelöf, P. O., Edelstam, H. and Pauli, M. 2011. *Rättegång V*. Stockholm: Norstedts Juridik.

Eriksson, L. and Goodin, R. E. 2007. 'The Measuring Rod of Time: The Example of Swedish Day-fines', *Journal of Applied Philosophy* 24–2: 125–36.

European Commission. 2019. *Your social security rights in Sweden.*

Försäkringskassan. 2019. *Aktuella belopp.*

Hessmark, L. G. *et al.* 2015. *Socialförsäkringsbalk: en kommentar Avd. A-C och Avd. D-H.* Stockholm: Norsteds Juridik.

Hillsman, S. T. 1990. 'Fines and Day Fines', *Crime and Justice* 12: 49–98.

Hristova, M. V. 2012. 'The Case for Insider-Trading Criminalization and Sentencing Reform', *Tennessee Journal of Business Law* 13: 267–308.

Ivancevich, J. M., Konopaske, R. and Gilbert, J. A. 2008. 'Formally Shaming White-Collar Criminals', *Business Horizons* 51: 401–10.

Jareborg, N. 2003. 'Böter i stället för fängelse?', *Svensk Juristtidning* 231–42.

Jareborg, N. and Zila, J. 2014. *Straffrättens påföljdslära*. Stockholm: Norstedts Juridik.

Kahan, D. M. 1996. 'What Do Alternative Sanctions Mean?', *University of Chicago Law Review* 63: 591–653.

Kantorowicz-Reznichenko, E. 2018. 'Day Fines: Reviving the Idea and Reversing the Costly Punitive Trend', *American Criminal Law Review* 55: 333–72.

Kraakman, R. H. 1983–4. 'Corporate Liability Strategies and the Costs of Legal Controls', *Yale Law Journal* 93: 857–900.

Kungliga Maj;ts Proposition till riksdagen med förslag till lag om ändring av vissa delar av strafflagen m.m, Prop 1931:188.

Mann, K., Wheeler, S. and Sarat, A. 1980. 'Sentencing the White-Collar Offender', *American Criminal Law Review* 17: 479–500.

McDermott, M. F. 1982. 'Occupational Disqualification of Corporate Executives: An Innovative Condition of Probation', *Journal of Criminal Law and Criminology* 73: 604–41.

Öberg, J. 2011. 'Criminal Sanctions in the Field of EU Environmental Law', *New Journal of European Criminal Law* 2: 402–25.

Öberg, J. 2014. 'Is it "Essential" to Imprison Insider Dealers to Enforce Insider Dealing Laws?', *Journal of Corporate Law Studies* 14: 111–38.

Palme, J., Fritzell, J. and Bergmark, Å. 2008. 'End of Equality? The Welfare State Model Beyond the Crisis', in *Framtider*, Institute for Future Studies, International edition, 4–12.

Paternoster, R. 2010. 'How Much Do We Really Know about Criminal Deterrence?', *Journal of Criminal Law and Criminology* 100: 765–824.

Posner, R. 1980. 'Optimal Sentences for White-Collar Criminals', *American Criminal Law Review* 17: 409–18.

Ryberg-Welander, L. 2018. *Socialförsäkringsrätt: om ersättning vid sjukdom*. Stockholm: Norstedts Juridik.

Spagnolo, G. 2012. 'Saving the Banks, But Not Reckless Bankers', *Vox*.

Stone, C. D. 1980. 'The Place of Enterprise Liability in the Control of Corporate Conduct', *Yale Law Journal* 90: 1–77.

Strahl, I. 1951. 'Något om böter', *Nordisk Tidsskrift for Kriminalvidenskab* 39, 203–24.

Svensson, B. 1981. 'Gammalt straffsystem', *Svensk Juristtidning*, 608–14.

The Swedish Penal Code.

The Swedish Procedural Code.

Thornstedt, H. 1975. 'The Day Fine System in Sweden', *Criminal Law Review* June: 307–12.

Thyrén, J. C. N. 1912. *Principerna för en strafflagsreform I*. Lund: Gleerup.

Thyrén, J. C. N. 1927. 'Om Bötesstraffets Reformering', *Svensk Juristtidning*, 353–63.

Ulväng, M. 2003. 'Böter i stället för fängelse? Några anteckningar i anslutning till Nils Jareborgs uppsats', *Svensk Juristtidning* 243–63.

5

Day Fines in Denmark

Thomas Elholm[*]

5.1 HISTORICAL DEVELOPMENT OF DAY FINES IN THE COUNTRY

The first comprehensive Criminal Code in Denmark dates back from 1866. It contained a provision on lump sum fines (Section 30a), but nothing about day fines. However, according to Section 59 of the Criminal Code from 1866, special consideration was to be given to the offender's 'wealth' and his ability to pay the fine, when a lump sum fine was to be calculated. Thus, the same key criteria as used today within the day fine system were inherent in the system of calculating lump sum fines.

The Criminal Code was the subject of a comprehensive reform at the beginning of the twentieth century and a number of committees and experts voiced their opinions. When the first Criminal Code Commission made its report in 1912, it did not propose any substantial changes regarding fines. The rule in Section 59 concerning particular consideration of wealth and the ability to pay was upheld, albeit with the additional remark that the fine has to be measured within the limits set by the seriousness of the offence. According to the Commission, a petty offence should not lead to a high fine simply because the offender is rich, nor should a person, who has been found guilty of a serious offence, get away with quite a small fine simply because he is poor. Thus, the main contradiction between the supporters of the two different views – whether the seriousness of the offence or the ability to pay should be given main priority – was visible already at this point in the legal development.

[*] Part of this contribution is based on: Lars Bo Langsted, Peter Garde, Vagn Greve and Thomas Elholm, 'Denmark', in Frank Verbruggen abd Vanessa Franssen (eds.), *International Encyclopaedia of Laws: Criminal Law*, 5th ed., Alphen aan den Rijn: Kluwer Law International, 2019.

In 1917, the very influential professor Carl Torp came up with a report in which he argued that, for two reasons, the ability to pay the fine should be decisive: (1) because a fine ought to strike rich and poor equally hard and (2) because it would reduce the number of fines that cannot be paid and therefore, in fact, becomes a custodial sentence. Torp found the previous rules on fines to be inadequate in order to obtain these objectives. He proposed a fine measuring system in which all matters influencing the offender's ability to pay should be considered. However, Torp did not propose a day fine system.[1]

Torp's idea was inspired by the International Criminalist Association's annual meeting in 1891, where Von Liszt recommended that fines be settled according to the criminal's ability to pay. In addition, Torp was influenced by the negotiations at the criminal congress in Stockholm in 1911, also stressing the importance of wealth and ability to pay a fine.

The Second Criminal Law Commission drafted a report in 1923 based on Torp's ideas.[2] The basic idea was to reorganise the system of fines to make fines an alternative to short-term custodial sentences, and in particular it should be designed to take account of the criminal's ability to pay. The Commission proposed a day fine system, according to which account must be taken of the criminal's 'assets, income, financial obligations and other matters'. However, it was left to the courts with a large margin of appreciation to determine the size of the individual day fine (the daily unit).

A minority of two of the Commission members opposed the setting up of a day fine system. Instead, they suggested the lump sum fine system to continue with a slightly changed wording. They believed that penalties should be calculated primarily to be preventive and that day fines for crimes involving financial gain (achieved or intended) could not adequately meet that purpose.

The final proposal for a new Criminal Code (1930)[3] followed the ideas of the majority of the Committee, supporting the idea of a day fine system. However, certain offences were excepted from the day fine system, because it was considered unnecessary and impractical (minor offences). The tax area was also excepted due to special 'fiscal views'. Finally, it was proposed that day fines should be applied only to violations of the criminal code and solely by the imposition or adoption of fines in court (not administrative fines). The day fine system was introduced with the new Criminal Code (on which the present is based) in 1930.

---

[1] Carl Torp, *Betænkning angaaende de af den under 11. August 1905 nedsatte Straffelovskommission udarbejdede Forslag indeholdende Udkast til Love vedrørende den borgerlige Straffelovgivning med Motiver*, København 1917, p. 76.
[2] *Betænkning afgiven af Straffelovskommissionen af 9. November 1917*, København 1912.
[3] *Straffelov Nr. 126 af 15. April 1930*. The Criminal Code came into force in 1933.

The heavy debate during the first decades of the twentieth century about the foundation of the Danish system of fines continued into the mid-twentieth century. Criticism voiced by law professor Krabbe, led to the insertion of a new Section in the Criminal Code (the revision of the Criminal Code from 1938–9), offering the court a possibility to avoid using day fines for economic crimes and instead imposing lump sum fines. According to this new section, the lump sum fine should be calculated, not according to the perpetrator's ability to pay or the need for equal treatment of rich and poor, but according to the financial gain (actual achieved or intended). 'It would be unreasonable to impose a fine on illegal fishing for the captain's wages if the fishery was to secure a very large profit to the master or his employer', the Minister of Justice said.[4]

Thus, to a certain extent, Krabbe's resistance won the audience, also among the advocates of the day fine and it has become evident that all the exceptions from the day fine system mentioned above, combined with a certain reluctance among judges to use day fines, have resulted in a system where day fines are relatively rare compared to the total numbers of fines for violations of Danish criminal law provisions.[5]

Since the mid-twentieth century there has not been much debate about the day fine system and there has been no comprehensive research on the consequences or perception of the system.

5.2 THE LEGAL FRAMEWORK AND THE STRUCTURE OF DAY FINES

5.2.1 *Legal Basis for Day Fines*

The Danish system of fines is regulated in Section 51 of the Danish Criminal Code, containing rules on both day fines and lump sum fines. According to this provision, day fines are the general rule. However, there are four exceptions to the rule, which makes the actual use of day fines rather secondary.

First of all, only fines imposed for violations of the Criminal Code may be day fines, compare Criminal Code Section 51 (1). Thus, fines for traffic offences according to the Road Traffic Act,[6] fines for drug related crimes according to the Drugs Act and fines for violation of safety and health regulations (outside the Criminal Code) can be only lump sum fines. These fines

---

[4] Rigsdagstidende 1938–39, Tillæg A, sp. 3766.

[5] See further on the historical background and the present use of day fines in Thomas Elholm, *8:11 om bøder og proportionalitet i specialstrafferetten*, Jurist- og Økonomforbundets Forlag, København 2010.

[6] Law No. 1324 of 21 November 2018.

outnumber by far the fines for violation of the Criminal Code. However, if – under the same criminal case – offences of both the Criminal Code and, for example, Road Traffic Act occur, the judge will impose a day fine covering both offences.

Secondly, day fines can be issued only in court. Day fines are either imposed by the judge or accepted by the defendant in court (the latter according to Section 899 of the Administration of Justice Act;[7] if the court finds no reason to doubt that the defendant is guilty, the judge may propose a fine, which has to be accepted by the prosecutor as well). Thus, neither the police, nor the prosecutor nor any other public authority can impose/issue a day fine. Administrative fines issued by the police or any other public authority with competence of issuing fines (so-called compound fines) will always be lump sum fines, even though they are issued for violations of the Criminal Code, for example for petty theft or shoplifting etc. according to Section 276 of the Criminal Code.

Thirdly, even though a fine is imposed by or accepted in court for violation of the Criminal Code, the judge has a certain margin of appreciation according to Section 51 (2) of the Criminal Code: where a fine is to be imposed with respect to an offence by which the person concerned obtained or intended to obtain a considerable financial gain for himself or another person, and where the application of day fines would result in the penalty being fixed at a lower amount than is considered reasonable, having regard to the amount of the profit that has been or might have been obtained by the offence, the court may impose a fine other than in the form of day fines.

Finally, fines which are imposed as supplementary punishment to another legal consequence may only be lump sum fines, compare Criminal Code Section 51 (1). Thus, if the judge chooses to combine a fine with, for example, imprisonment, the fine must be a lump sum fine. The same applies in cases, where a fine is supplementary to conditional sentences (suspended imprisonment), compare Criminal Code Section 58 (1) and if a fine is supplementary to community service, compare Criminal Code Section 64. In addition, waiver of prosecution can be subject to payment of a fine, compare Administration of Justice Act, Section 723(1)1 and this fine is also a lump sum fine.

5.2.2 *Legal Basis for Calculating Day Fines*

According to Section 51 (1) of the Criminal Code, the number of day fines shall be fixed at not less than one, nor more than sixty, having regard to the

---

7 Law No. 1284 of 14 November 2018.

nature (seriousness) of the offence and the circumstances referred to in Section 80 of the Criminal Code.

The amount of the single day fine (the daily unit) shall be fixed at a sum corresponding to the average daily earnings of the person concerned; in fixing the amount, account ought to be taken of the convicted person's living conditions, including his capital resources, family responsibilities and any other circumstances affecting his capacity to pay, compare Section 51 (1) of the Criminal Code. The daily unit may in no case be fixed at an amount lower than two Danish kroner,[8] but Section 51 (1) of the Criminal Code gives no upper limit to the amount of the daily unit.

Thus, there are two significant provisions of the Criminal Code regulating the calculation of day fines: the general sentencing provision in Section 80 and the special provision regarding fines in Section 51.

Section 80 stipulates the three main criteria for measuring criminal penalties in the Danish penal system: (1) the principle of uniformity in sentencing, (2) the seriousness of the offence and (3) various information about the offender. In practice, the seriousness of the offence is the most important factor, making proportionality between the offence committed and the actual sentencing the main sentencing factor. In assessing the seriousness of the offence consideration shall be given to the harm, danger and violation involved, as reflected in, for example, the value of the stolen goods, the profit of tax evasion or the amount of narcotics possessed. Generally, *mens rea* is also of relevance for the assessment of the seriousness of the offence and hence for the calculation of the fine. However, the importance of *mens rea* varies from area to area and case to case. In some cases, it is hardly of any importance. This is often the case, if, for example, the penalty scale covers both intentional and negligent behaviour.

According to Section 80 information about the offender is also a relevant factor for sentencing. In assessing the information about the offender consideration shall be given to the offender's general personal and social circumstances, the offender's circumstances before and after the offence and the offender's motives for committing the offence. It is of general importance in the Danish legal system, whether the offender has committed a first or a repeated offence. In many areas, the fine is calculated higher (often doubled) in cases of second time and also in cases of third time offending etc. (although not doubled again).

Rules on aggravating and mitigating circumstances in Sections 81–83 of the Criminal Code serve as guidelines for sentencing too. Sections 81 and 82 are

---

[8] For convenience, the respective exchange rates: 100 DKK = €13.40 / $14.50 / £12.30 (6 August 2019).

the most relevant ones regarding the calculation of fines, although most of them are only rarely mentioned explicitly in the court's reasoning for the calculation of the fine. According to Sections 81 and 82 the court 'shall' use the circumstances mentioned in measuring a criminal penalty. However, the margin of appreciation for the judge is generally wide concerning the 'weight' of such circumstances. Furthermore, the lists of mitigating and aggravating circumstances are not exhaustive.

According to Section 83 of the Criminal Code, the penalty may be reduced within the prescribed statutory range (the penalty scale) when information about the offence, the offender or other circumstances conclusively support it. In particularly mitigating circumstances, the penalty may be remitted. By referring to Sections 83 in combination with Section 82, the minimum sentence can (in theory) always be reduced to just one day fine or even be totally remitted, despite the minimum sentence of the specific provision.

5.2.3 *Institutions Involved in Providing Information and Collection of Fines*

According to Section 51 (4) of the Criminal Code, the police may, together with other public agencies, make enquiries necessary for fixing the fine. Furthermore, the police may request the information regarding the conditions of the person concerned, which is found to be important for fixing the fine, from registers kept by public authorities, including the court. Notification shall be in writing or by direct data transfer.

According to Section 90 (2)1 of the Corrections Act,[9] fines must be paid to the police unless otherwise determined. The fine-collecting authority is, as a rule, the police and the police can allow the deferment of or withholding payment of the fine on the debtors' request. If the debtor does not pay the fine charged before a specified deadline, the police will transfer the case to a special recovery/dept authority (a special branch within the Tax Authority, hereafter the Debt Authority). The Debt Authority may on the basis of assessment of the ability to pay, etc. allow a longer time limit or suggest an instalment plan (rates of payment). If it is not possible to recover a fine in whole or in part, but the debtor is deemed to have the ability to pay, the Dept Authority sends the case to the police, who then has to decide whether the fine has to be converted into imprisonment ('replacement penalty' of imprisonment).

---

[9] Law No. 1491 of 13 December 2017.

5.2.4 *Conversion of Day Fines to Imprisonment*

At the same time as the court imposes a fine and calculates the amount of the fine, the court must also decide on the length of any possible replacement penalty. Day fines can be converted into imprisonment only. Thus, conversion into community service or other kinds of penalty is not possible.

According to Section 54 (1) of the Criminal Code, the replacement penalty is calculated so that one day fine equals one day of imprisonment. However, the replacement penalty may in no case be less than two days and normally not more than sixty days. In special cases, however, the replacement penalty may be increased to a maximum of nine months.

In situations, where it is not possible to recover the fine, but the debtor is deemed capable of paying, replacement is normally mandatory, compare Section 53 of the Criminal Code, but it is waived where special circumstances speaks heavily against, for example if the debtor is less than eighteen years of age. In practice, the Danish system has changed the administrative tradition in the last one to two decades, so that the authorities are trying as far as possible to avoid conversion into imprisonment, and instead collecting the fine by the means available. Conversion is applied only a few times each year (some years it is even not used at all).

Some provisions within special Acts allow for the imposition of fines, without the usual liability conditions being fulfilled, for example without *mens rea*. In these cases, the fine cannot be converted into imprisonment.

Remission is possible but rarely used. If the case has been sent from the Dept Authority to the police, because the debtor has not paid, and the police has to decide, if the fine should be converted, an alternative to replacement is remission. Remission is regarded as a pardon, following the rules of competence etc. of a pardon. The chief of police has the competence to pardon fines, if the amount is less than DKK 100,000.[10]

5.3 THE PRACTICAL IMPLEMENTATION OF DAY FINES

5.3.1 *The Application of Day Fines*

As mentioned above in subsection 5.2.1, there are numerous exceptions from the rule of day fines. In fact, the use of day fines is somewhat limited in practice. Day fines are only used in court and only for violation of the Criminal Code.

---

[10]   Remission etc. is regulated by Order No. 624 of 25 June 2009 and Order No. 409 of 6 April 2015.

Furthermore, although a fine is sometimes imposed for violations of the Criminal Code, the Code is generally reserved for provisions regarding serious crimes, in which case the penalty will often be imprisonment (suspended or unsuspended), thus limiting the applicable area for day fines.

In 2017, the percentage of cases in which fines were imposed (out of all imposed sentences) for violation of the Criminal Code was 44 per cent (12,541 judgments in 2017). The percentage of cases in which imprisonment sentences were imposed (out of all sentences) for violation of the Criminal Code was 46 per cent (12,939 judgments, hereof 6,417 unsuspended).

There are no statistics on the distribution of day fines *vs.* lump sum fines for violation of the Criminal Code. However, the exception from the day fine system in Section 51 (2) of the Criminal Code (where a fine is to be imposed with respect to an offence by which the person concerned obtained or intended to obtain a considerable financial gain for himself or another person) is rarely used. Thus, most of the 12,541 fines mentioned above had to be day fines.

Relatively few Danish court decisions are published.[11] However, it can be derived from the source of published cases that day fines are used for a broad range of violations of the Criminal Code, including violence of or threat against public servant (Section 119), chicane of public servant (Section 119 (a)), unlawful access to places and devices, including social media (Section 263–264), obscene behaviour (Section 232), possession of child pornography (Section 235), negligent manslaughter (Section 241), assault (Section 244), negligent infliction of serious harm (Section 249), theft (Section 276) and damage of things etc. (Section 291), just to mention some of the offences.

Out-of-court settlement of criminal cases, where the penalty is most likely to be a fine, is very common in Denmark. The compound fine (a lump sum fine) plays a very important role. Several hundreds of thousands of cases[12] are settled by means of the compound fine, more than half of all criminal cases. A compound fine is used in all cases, where the prosecution does not claim a higher penalty than a fine. Instead of referring the case to the court, the prosecutor will send a letter to the accused setting out the alleged offence

---

[11] Some High Court judgments and all Supreme Court cases are published by a private company, see www.karnov.dk. Cases from the city courts can be obtained by writing to the specific court indicating the case of interest and paying twenty-four euro per each case.

[12] NB: Unfortunately, the official Danish statistics on fines for violations of the Road Traffic Act do not (with a few exceptions) entail fines lower than 2,500 DKK. Thus, the number of criminal penalties in 2017 (184,924) are only penalties of 2,500 DKK. or more (or 1,000 DKK. or more regarding violations of some of the other special Acts). The majority of fines are normally below 2,500 DKK.

exactly as in a normal indictment and adding that the case may be settled by payment of a fine stipulated in the letter.[13] If the accused pays the fine indicated, the case is closed, otherwise the case is referred to court.

In 2017, the number of criminal penalties was 184,924, approximately 15 per cent hereof for violations of the Criminal Code.[14] The number of cases in which fines were imposed was 164,135 (106,378 hereof were compound fines). As mentioned above, day fines can be imposed only for violations of the Criminal Code. Thus, from an overall perspective the day fine system plays a minor role looking at the Danish system of penal sanctions.

In 2017, the percentage of cases in which fines were imposed (out of all sentences) for violation of other Acts than the Criminal Code was 97 per cent. Some of the relevant Acts were the Road Traffic Act, Acts on Drugs, Acts on Weapons, Acts regarding transport, health and environmental Acts. Fines for violation of these Acts will automatically be lump sum fines, unless the fine is imposed for violations of the Criminal Code and specific Acts combined.

As mentioned above, day fines were introduced in 1939 as an alternative to short-term custodial sentences. It has not been possible to find statistical evidence about the consequences of the introduction of the day fine (for example, if the percentage of imprisonment decreased following the adoption of day fines), but it is quite clear from the statistics mentioned above that the majority of penalties in the Danish penal system are fines; even violations of the Criminal Code are often sanctioned by fines (44 per cent).

The potential of day fines to replace more repressive sanctions is hard to estimate. However, since the day fine system was introduced many years ago and the courts have applied the system in a stable way for a long time, adhering to the principle of uniformity in sentencing (the main sentencing criteria according to Section 80 of the Criminal Code), it is unlikely to believe that the day fine system would have great potential replacing more repressive sanctions – at least with the present, rather repressive, political climate in Denmark.

The rather limited potential is underlined by the fact that the possibility provided in Section 82/83 of the Criminal Code, whereby a penalty can be reduced even below the penalty scale, is rarely used. Thus, the courts will rarely use a fine instead of an imprisonment, if the penalty scale prescribes imprisonment as a minimum. This said of course does not exclude the possibility of using day fines at a larger extent than is presently the case.

[13] The legal basis for compound fines is Section 832 of the Administration of Justice Act.
[14] NB: see *supra* note 11.

There are neither general official and publicly accessible statistics on the number of day fines imposed on a yearly basis nor statistics on the daily unit applied. A search among the judgments published[15] reveals that most frequently the number of day fines are between four and twenty, only rarely above twenty and below four.

One relatively recent example of a very high number of day fines is the case U 2014.1540 H, where High Court changed the judgment of the city court increasing the number of day fines from forty to fifty (see further on the case Section 5.3.2).

When the number of day fines are calculated above twenty, the court will usually apply a scale, making it unlikely (but not impossible) to find judgments with the number of day fines other than: twenty-five, thirty, forty, fifty or sixty.

There are no empirical or other studies conducted in the Danish legal context regarding the effectiveness of the fines in deterring criminals. In 2016, the percentage of recidivism two years after a fine was 28 per cent, while the percentage two years after release from imprisonment was 65 per cent. This is of course not an indication of the effect of fines on recidivism, due to the selection bias (offenders who are sent to prison are usually characterised by higher recidivism risk). It has not been possible to find statistics on the rate of payment, the trend of fine defaulters, etc.[16]

5.3.2 *Calculation of Day Fines in Practice*

Denmark is a welfare state. Medical and hospital treatment is free. Schools, high schools and universities are free. Everybody who turns sixty-seven years is entitled to an annual pension from the state; there is social security aid for the unemployed etc. Students are entitled to a monthly allowance from the State of around 6,000 DKK. The average yearly pre-tax income for all persons aged fifteen years and above was around 320,000 DKK (EUR 43,000) in 2017. Of all households, 57 per cent owned their own dwelling (house or flat). The average housing size for a household with two adults was around 135 m2 (one of the highest in the EU). The gross national product for 2016 was DKK 2,100 billion (EUR 280 billion). This is equivalent to about EUR 48,400 per inhabitant, from infant to pensioner, only surpassed in the EU by

---

[15] Published in either TfK (Tidsskrift for Kriminalret) or UfR (Ugeskrift for Retsvæsen), both journals available online via the same search formular at www.karnov.dk.

[16] *Kriminalitet 2017*, Danmarks Statistik, Årgang 76, Marts 2019, p. 133. Available at: www.dst.dk /da/Statistik/Publikationer/VisPub?cid=28072.

Luxembourg and Ireland. The unemployment rate is low (3–4 per cent of the work force). The total burden of taxation is one of the highest in the world (45 per cent in 2018).

As a clear point of departure, the prosecutor (the police) has – before the court hearing starts – obtained information on the person's income situation (see subsection 5.2.3 above). In cases where the prosecutor has not obtained the information, the defendant is asked – in court – to account for his income at the time of the offence, and the fine is calculated on the defendant's own information.

Concerning the issue of determining the number of day fines, the nature of the offence must be taken to account and concerning the amount of the daily unit information about the offender is decisive, see the statutory requirements described in subsection 5.2.2 above.

In practice, however, the courts adhere far from always to the statutory requirements for calculating the day fines. While the system of day fines has been successful in Finland and Sweden, Danish courts have to a certain extent refused the idea of day fines. Much suggests that the courts are counting backwards. First, they decide on how much a fine should be, based exclusively or mainly on the seriousness of the offence (not the income of the offender). Thereafter, they convert the amount to day fines based on fairly free considerations,[17] thus leaving the income etc. of the defendant almost without consideration. This procedure is probably due to the fact that the vast majority of fines (imposed in court) are the result of the defendant not having accepted a compound fine. In cases like this, the judge will, if he finds the defendant guilty, normally be inclined to impose a fine of the same amount as the compound fine.

However, case law suggests that the judges at least in some cases do respect the idea of the day fine system. In the case U 2017.3516 V, the city court imposed a fine for chicane of public servant (Section 119(a) of the Criminal Code). The fine was calculated to four day fines of a daily unit of 500 DKK. The High Court referred to the fact that the legislator in the work préparatoires had indicated a minimum fine of 7,500 DKK.[18] However, the High Court adjusted the fine with reference to the low

---

[17] See Vagn Greve, *Straffene*, 2002, pp. 147 *et seq.*, Knud Waaben, *Strafferettens almindelige del. Sanktionslæren*, 2001, p. 75 and Gorm Toftegaard Nielsen, *Strafferet 2. Sanktionerne*, 4. ed. 2014, pp. 69 *et seq.*

[18] The minimum fine was indicated in the work préparatoires, not in the provision of the Criminal Code itself. It is a special feature of the Danish criminal system that the legislator often gives (sometimes rather detailed) directions to the courts in the work préparatoires and the courts are very careful to follow the directions.

income of the defendant and imposed six day fines of a daily unit of 625 DKK, equivalent to 50 per cent of the normal minimum fine indicated by the legislator.

In the case U 2014.1540 H, two legal persons (a television and a broadcast company) were both sentenced to fifty day fines of 100,000 DKK for violation of Section 114(e) of the Criminal Code (promoting terrorist activity). The judgment is a very rare example, because (1) a legal person is sentenced to day fines, (2) the number of day fines is exceptionally high and (3) the daily unit is very high, calculated on the basis of the annual turnover of the company in a four to five years period (approximately 250 million DKK for the entire period).

The prosecutor, the police and other authorities with the competence of issuing compound fines (for example the Tax Authority), have detailed lists of 'normal fines', that is lump sum fines for standard offences. These so-called 'fines catalogue' are prepared or agreed by the Attorney General. The amounts of the normal fine indicated in the lists are generally followed by the courts. The main principles of the catalogue have been subject to test cases in court, sometimes even by the Supreme Court, so it could be said that the police and prosecution follow the courts rather than the other way round. As the lists are public (www.anklagemyndigheden.dk or www.skat.dk), the majority of the accused do not attempt to contest the case in court.[19]

Section 55 of the Criminal Code sets a scheme for converting minor lump sum fines into imprisonment. According to the provision, a compound fine of DKK 10,000 or less, is converted by the following scale: Fines between 0–499 DKK (two days), 500–999 DKK (four days), 1,000–3,999 DKK (six days), 4,000–5,999 DKK (eight days), 6,000–10,000 DKK (ten days).

Based on published judgments and my own experience with judges, there are reasons to believe that in practice the conversion table is used by the judges as a guideline for calculating the number of day fines. Thus, the judge will take his point of departure in the amount of the compound fine (which has been calculated according to the 'fines catalogue') and convert this amount into day fines by using the scale in Section 55. Thus, the income of the defendant does not play the role originally intended with the day fine system.

---

[19] Lars Bo Langsted, Peter Garde, Vagn Greve and Thomas Elholm, 'Denmark', in Frank Verbruggen and Vaness Franssen (eds.), *International Encyclopaedia of Laws: Criminal Law*. Alphen aan den Rijn: Kluwer Law International, 2019, p. 201.

5.4 PUBLIC PERCEPTION OF DAY FINES

There is no research on the level of acceptance of day fines among the general population in Denmark. There seems to be no significant debate about day fines either. This *might* be an indication that the day fine system is generally perceived as legitimate.

The last ten to twenty years have been characterised by a repressive criminal policy in Denmark.[20] At first glance, this development seems to be supported by the majority of the population. However, comprehensive research on the public sense of justice reveals that (1) the population is not well informed about the actual sentencing practice of the courts, (2) they sometimes believe that sentencing is more lenient than it actually is, (3) if they are informed and asked to give their own opinion about a reasonable penalty in specific cases, they prefer from time to time a more lenient practice than court practice. Sometimes they prefer a fine instead of imprisonment.[21] Unfortunately, the research mentioned focusses on custodial sentences and fines are not systematically investigated in this research.

Likewise, the level of acceptance of day fines in professional circles has not been investigated. There are several statements regarding the perception of a relatively reluctant attitude among judges and other legal professionals.[22]

The debate on and criticism of the day fine system has been declining and is rather absent today, but it was present in, for example, 1975 during the meetings of the Nordic Committee of Criminal Law, where the conclusion says that the Danish delegates rejected the idea of the day fine system, believing that the defendant's ability to pay could be taken to account by other means. Furthermore, according to the Nordic Committee, the Danish experience of the day fine system shows that there is a risk of the system not being applied in accordance with its purpose, because the judges calculate the fine by determining first the overall amount of the fine and therefrom deduct the number of day fines and the daily unit. Therefore, it was to be expected that the Standing Committee of Criminal Law in Denmark would propose an abolition of the day fine system.[23] However, the day fine system was not

---

20 Thomas Elholm, 'The Symbolic Purpose of Criminal Law', in Reindl-Krauskopf, Zerbes, Brandstetter, Lewisch and Tipold (eds.), *Festschrift für Helmut Fuchs*. Verlag der Österreichischen Akademie der Wissenschaften, Wien 2014, pp. 137–52.

21 Flemming Balvig, *Danskernes retsfølelse og retsfornuft – et forspil*, Det Juridiske Fakultet, Københavns Universitet, 2010, p. 19. Available at: justitsministeriet.dk/sites/default/files/medi a/Arbejdsomraader/Forskning/Forskningspuljen/2011/2010/Retsbevidsthedsundersoegelse n_2010.pdf.

22 Straffelovrådets Betænkning om Straffastsættelse og strafferammer, Nr. 1424/2002, pp. 416 *et seq.*

23 Nordisk Strafferetskomité, *Betenkning om bøtestraffen*, NU 1975:5, p. 12.

abolished (and not proposed to be abolished either). Although the criticism was repeated in 2002, when the Standing Committee of Criminal Law in Denmark made a comprehensive investigation on sentencing and penalty scales, the members of the Standing Committee of Criminal Law did not agree to propose an abolition of the system.[24]

5.5 SPECIAL CHALLENGES

The idea of the day fine system was to make it possible to reflect the seriousness of the offence through the number of daily units and at the same time taking into account the perpetrator's financial capacity through the amount of each daily unit. Thus, the punishment should be equally hard in terms of blame by imposing the same number of day fines for rich and poor, but also equally hard financially by adjusting each of the daily fines in accordance with the financial capacity of the offender.

However, as mentioned above quite often the judges do not fully implement the idea of the day fine system – for different reasons. While the system of day fines has been more successful in Finland and Sweden, Danish courts have to a certain extent opposed the idea of day fines.[25]

The reason for this reluctance – if it is true – is hard to assess, but it might have to do with the fact that the judges are often dealing with cases, where a compound fine (lump sum) has been proposed by the prosecutor, but declined by the defendant. In these cases, the judge will often try to calculate a day fine somewhat equivalent to the amount of the compound fine.

Furthermore, guidelines of sentencing levels – for example prepared by the Attorney General or indicated in the work préparatoires – will normally operate with fixed amounts (lump sums), hereby they indicate the right calculation for compound fines, which are the most important fine in practice seen from a quantitive perspective. Thus, there are few guidelines (except from what can be derived from previous case law) on, for example, how to calculate the number of day fines.

A few features would probably increase the functionality of the day fine system: (1) if the judges had online access to the relevant financial information about the offender, (2) if it was made clear exactly which financial information is relevant, (3) if there was a special calculating mechanism (calculating the daily unit by giving the relevant information into the system) and (4) if the

---

[24] Straffelovrådet, *Betænkning om Straffastsættelse og strafferammer*, Nr. 1424/2002, pp. 416 *et seq.*

[25] See *ibid.* and Thomas Elholm, 8:11 *om bøder og proportionalitet i specialstrafferetten*, Jurist- og Økonomforbundets Forlag, København 2010, pp. 97 *et seq.*

legislator in work préparatoires or special guidelines would indicate the reasonable number of day fines for a certain offence, instead of indicating (as it is often done) the lump sum fine applicable. Interestingly, all of these features seem to be provided in the Finnish day fine system,[26] where the day fine system seem to function better and to be a more integrated part of the penalty system than it is the case in Denmark.

REFERENCES

Balvig, F. 2010. *Danskernes retsfølelse og retsfornuft – et forspil*, Det Juridiske Fakultet, Københavns Universitet, p. 19. Available at: www.justitsministeriet.dk/sites/default/ files/media/Arbejdsomraader/Forskning/Forskningspuljen/2011/2010/Retsbevidsthed sundersoegelsen_2010.pdf.

Betænkning afgiven af Straffelovskommissionen af 9 November 1917, København 1912.

Elholm, T. 2010. *8:11 om bøder og proportionalitet i specialstrafferetten*. København: Jurist- og Økonomforbundets Forlag.

Elholm, T. 2014. 'The Symbolic Purpose of Criminal Law', in Reindl-Krauskopf, S., Zerbes, I., Brandstetter, W., Lewisch, P. and Tipold, A. (eds.), *Festschrift für Helmut Fuchs*.Wien: Verlag der Österreichischen Akademie der Wissenschaften.

Greve, V., *Straffene*, 2002, pp. 147 *et seq.*

Kriminalitet 2017, Danmarks Statistik, Årgang 76, Marts 2019, p. 133. Available at: www .dst.dk/da/Statistik/Publikationer/VisPub?cid=28072.

Langsted, L. B., Garde, P., Greve, V. and Elholm, T. 2019. 'Denmark', in Verbruggen, F. and Franssen, V. (eds.), *International Encyclopaedia of Laws: Criminal Law*. Alphen aan den Rijn, NL: Kluwer Law International.

Law No. 1491 of 13 December 2017.

Law No. 1284 of 14 November 2018.

Law No. 1324 of 21 November 2018.

Nielsen, G. T. 2014. *Strafferet 2. Sanktionerne*. København: Djøf Forlag, pp. 69 *et seq.*

Nordisk Strafferetskomité, *Betenkning om bøtestraffen*, NU 1975:5, p. 12.

Order No. 624 of 25 June 2009.

Order No. 409 of 6 April 2015.

Rigsdagstidende 1938–9, Tillæg A, sp. 3766.

Straffelov nr. 126 af 15 april 1930.

Straffelovrådet, *Betænkning om Straffastsættelse og strafferammer* 1424/2002, pp. 416 *et seq.*

Torp, C. 1917. *Betænkning angaaende de af den under 11 August 1905 nedsatte Straffelovskommission udarbejdede Forslag indeholdende Udkast til Love vedrørende den borgerlige Straffelovgivning med Motiver*. København, p. 76.

Waaben, K. 2001. *Strafferettens almindelige del. Sanktionslæren*. Copenhagen: Thomson GadJura.

---

[26] Elholm *ibid.*, pp. 277 *et seq.*

6

Day Fines in Germany

Hans-Joerg Albrecht

6.1 HISTORICAL DEVELOPMENT OF DAY FINES IN GERMANY

A day fine system was adopted in Germany in 1975. The move towards replacing conventional summary fines with day fines was the result of a Comprehensive Criminal Law Reform 1969/1975. This reform was implemented in two steps: it brought in 1969 a complete revision of the system of criminal penalties as well as sentencing rules, in 1975 the day fine system and, besides that, large-scale decriminalisation by downgrading many misdemeanour offences to administrative offences (which carry a summary administrative fine only).

In 1969, the first step of the Comprehensive Criminal Law Reform led to the introduction of a priority rule in favour of fines (then still imposed as summary fines) and a close to prohibition rule on prison sentences below six months. The second step, completed in 1975, transformed the summary fine into a day fine system. While the blueprint of the German day fine system originated from Scandinavia,[1] the decision to give fines priority over (short) prison sentences is rooted in a criminal policy programme devised at the end of the nineteenth century by Franz von Liszt (1883, called the 'Marburg Programme') and expressing deep distrust in prisons' and imprisonment's rehabilitative capacity. According to Franz von Liszt, in particular short prison sentences (prison sentences up to three months accounted for approximately 80 per cent of all prison sentences at that time)[2] must not only be considered to be completely ineffective but, moreover, to have adverse effects on rehabilitation and reintegration of offenders. He concluded that instead of incarcerating offenders it would be better to do nothing and let offenders go free,[3]

---

[1] Grebing, 'Die Geldstrafe im deutschen Recht nach Einführung des Tagessatzsystems', p. 79.
[2] *Ibid.*, see p. 30.
[3] Von Liszt, 'Der Zweckgedanke im Strafrecht'; Von Liszt, 'Die Kriminalität der Jugendlichen', p. 338.

anticipating thus conclusions drawn from labelling and radical non-intervention theory almost a hundred years later.[4] The Marburg Programme offered an effective medicine against adverse consequences of prison sentences in the form of fines and other alternatives to imprisonment, alternatives coming with less stigma and less encouragement to reoffend. In contrast, the Marburg Programme advised to restrict the scope of imprisonment and focus – through long prison sentences and rehabilitative efforts (and incapacitative sentencing) – on a small group of serious recidivists and habitual offenders.

The narrative drawn from the programme of Franz von Liszt in Germany still today denounces prisons as 'schools of crime' and praises alternatives to imprisonment. This narrative encouraged already a first legislative move towards fines at the beginning of the 1920s[5] and was then in the 1960s very successful in furthering a criminal policy which gave priority to fines and cut back significantly short prison sentences. In fact, the incarceration rate fell sharply after the adoption of the priority rule in 1969. Prisoner rates decreased immediately from 96/100,000 (1968) to 76/100,000 (1970). The share of fines at all criminal penalties imposed after 1969 climbed to approximately 80 per cent (see Figure 6.2) and remained then rather stable for the last fifty years.[6] From a comparative (and European) view, the adoption of a priority rule for fines resulted in Germany in a rather unique distribution of criminal penalties.[7] No other country in Europe displays a comparable share of fines at criminal sentences at large. Austria followed in the 1970s the policy script Germany had adopted but displayed always more appetite for short and longer prison sentences and resorted then, at the beginning of the new millennium, to diversionary practices and herewith reduced conviction rates (and fines) significantly.[8] Switzerland implemented in 2007 a criminal law reform which sought and managed to replace short prison sentences by fines (and community service). However, the reform drew heavy criticism[9] and a revision of Swiss criminal law re-allows from 1 January 2018 short prison sentences.[10]

---

[4] Becker, *Outsiders: Studies in the Sociology of Deviance*; Schur *Radical Non-Intervention – Rethinking the Delinquency Problem.*

[5] Peters, *Die Entwicklung von Sanktionspraxis und Strafrechtsreform 1871 bis 1933*, p. 68.

[6] Albrecht, 'Sentencing in Germany: Explaining Long-Term Stability in the Structure of Criminal Sanctions and Sentencing'.

[7] Albrecht, 'Die Geldstrafe in Ländern der Europäischen Union – Normative Strukturen und praktische Anwendung'.

[8] Fink, Jehle and Pilgram, 'Strafrechtliche Sanktionen im internationalen Vergleich Deutschland – Österreich – Schweiz', 86; *supra* note 7.

[9] Killias, 'Korrektur einer verunglückten Gesetzgebung: Zur erneuten Revision des AT-StGB'; Besozzi and Kunz, 'Kurze Freiheitsstrafen und ihr Ersatz. Eine Revision der Revision?'.

[10] www.ejpd.admin.ch/ejpd/de/home/aktuell/news/2016/2016-03-29.html.

The introduction of a day fine system in 1975 then should compensate for an apparent problem of summary fines: unequal treatment of rich and poor offenders. Criminal fines internationally have been subject to criticism based on the allegation that rich offenders can buy their way out of the criminal justice system while the poor are exposed to the risk of fine default and default imprisonment thus suffering disproportionally.[11] Day fines came with the promise to respond effectively to this problem. While the number of day fines addresses the criminal wrong and is determined on the basis of crime seriousness, the size of a day fine unit is calculated on the basis of the net income of a defendant. By separating these steps, day fines reflect both the criminal wrong and the financial situation of an offender. And a Law and Economics analysis suggests that day fines are not only better suited to achieve justice but are also a more cost-efficient method of controlling crime.[12]

A review of penal reform debates before introducing the day fine system reveals that there have been other suggestions regarding the development and application of criminal fines. For example, in the 1960s, a group of German law professors drafted a model penal code.[13] They introduced a concept which was called 'instalment fine', a model which combines day fines with a system of mandatory instalments. The intent of this type of fine was to deprive the offender, for a fixed period of time, of all the income which the offender could spare, thereby relegating the offender's income to a subsistence level. Whereas possession of money is perceived to guarantee freedom, it was hoped that an instalment fine would amount to something like 'partial imprisonment' or 'restricted liberty', since offenders would be deprived of resources necessary for mobility. This model was ultimately rejected in Germany and never received support in other European countries.[14]

Despite the remarkably successful implementation of the day fine system and the important role fines (and financial penalties at large) play in Germany, implementation and evaluation of the day fine system (and financial penalties in general) does not form a distinct field of systematic empirical (criminological) research as do imprisonment and prisons. Only few studies scattered over the last fifty years address fines, day fines, fine enforcement and the impact of fines on recidivism in Germany.[15]

---

[11] *Supra* note 1, p. 43.
[12] Kantorowicz-Reznichenko, 'Day-Fines: Should the Rich Pay More?'.
[13] Baumann, *Alternativentwurf eines Strafgesetzbuches. Allgemeiner Teil.*
[14] *Supra* note 1, pp. 82–4.
[15] Albrecht, *Strafzumessung und Vollstreckung bei Geldstrafen*; Albrecht, *Legalbewährung bei zu Geldstrafe und Freiheitsstrafe Verurteilten*; *supra* note 7; Janssen, *Die Praxis der*

6.2 THE COMPREHENSIVE CRIMINAL LAW REFORM, DAY FINES AND THE SYSTEM OF CRIMINAL PENALTIES

Prioritisation of fines in 1969 and the introduction of day fines in 1975 were part of a reform package which – beyond the narrative of Franz von Liszt and also driven by a social-democratic/liberal coalition government's agenda (the coalition had come to power in 1969) – sought decriminalisation, rehabilitation, cleansing the criminal code book from moral penal law, reduction of penal stigma, in general inclusionary criminal justice practices and – in face of increasing caseloads – a cost-effective system of criminal sanctions.

The criminal law reform of 1969 downgraded contraventions/misdemeanours (punishable by short prison sentences or fines) from criminal offences to administrative offences (administrative disobedience, 'Ordnungswidrigkeiten'). Administrative offences carry an administrative fine ('Geldbuße') only and are investigated and prosecuted in a simplified procedure (spelled out in the Law on Administrative Offences, 'Ordnungswidrigkeitengesetz'). However, basic standards of criminal law and criminal procedure apply also in cases of administrative offences. The introduction of administrative offences was a response to the dynamic development of motor vehicle traffic where regulation through contraventions (and short prison sentences) had been extensively used in the 1950s and 1960s and therefore relief was sought for prosecution services and criminal courts.[16] Moreover, the introduction of the concept of administrative offences was based on the consideration that criminal wrongs should be restricted to those acts which result in serious harm for victims and society. In fact, a controversial debate on whether a clear line can be drawn between criminal wrongs on the one hand and wrongs that should be dealt with outside the criminal law and on the basis of administrative or police law can be traced back to the nineteenth century with Goldschmidt at the turn of the nineteenth and twentieth century presenting for the first time a systematic analysis of separating criminal from administrative wrongs.[17] Administrative fines, however, are imposed as lump sum fines, and according to tariffs, which do not seek individualisation of punishment and do not consider individual income (except when it comes to a decision on whether to grant payment accommodation

---

Geldstrafenvollstreckung; Bögelein, Ernst and Neubacher, *Vermeidung von Ersatzfreiheitsstrafen. Evaluierung justizieller Haftvermeidungsprojekte in Nordrhein-Westfalen*; Bögelein, 'Money Rules: Exploring Offenders' Perceptions of the Fine as Punishment'.

[16] Kaiser, *Verkehrsdelinquenz und Generalprävention*.

[17] Goldschmidt, *Das Verwaltungsstrafrecht*.

through instalments). Administrative fines, moreover, cannot be converted into default imprisonment when collection efforts are not successful.

The reform package implemented in 1969 and thereafter increased the power of prosecutors to significantly divert and finalise criminal cases.[18] The 1960s and 1970s saw a sharp increase in police recorded crime (and corresponding levels of criminal suspects) which in turn resulted in amendments of the criminal procedural code softening up the strict legality principle through introducing discretionary powers of the public prosecutor to dismiss criminal cases.[19] In 1963, paragraph 153 of the Code of Criminal Procedure (hereafter CPC) was introduced which empowers the public prosecutor to dismiss cases on the ground of minor guilt (petty offences); in 1975, this power was expanded in order to cover more serious criminal offences. Paragraph 153(a) CPC allows dismissal of a case if the defendant agrees with fulfilling certain conditions proposed by the public prosecutor (conditions may include payment of a lump sum either to the treasury or a charity, community service, reparation, victim-offender reconciliation). With respect to the condition to pay a 'fine' statutory minimums and maximums are not defined through paragraph 153(a) CPC, but are subject to (and limited by) the proportionality principle. If conditions are not complied with, then criminal proceedings will continue with a full trial. Furthermore, the public prosecutor may decline public prosecution of selected offences (among them insult, criminal damage, simple assault, trespassing) and refer a victim to the possibility of private prosecution of the offence (paragraph 374 CPC).

Seen from a comparative perspective and from the aim of identifying the role day fines play in a system of criminal penalties, it is important to take into account – when looking at absolute and relative numbers of criminal convictions (and related sentences) – the definition of criminal offences (and the role administrative offences play) as well as dismissal (diversionary) powers and practices of prosecution services. The finding of significant variation of conviction rates in Europe (with a minimum of circa 120 and a maximum of circa 3,800 criminal convictions per 100,000)[20] reflects simply – besides some variation in crime – variation in the scope of criminal offence definitions and in dismissal practices. This in turn will impact the rates and distribution of criminal sanctions imposed.[21]

---

[18] Albrecht, *Simplification of Criminal Procedure: Settlements out of Court – A Comparative Study of European Criminal Justice Systems.*

[19] *Ibid.*

[20] See Aebi *et al.*, *European Sourcebook of Crime and Criminal Justice Statistics 2014*, p. 156.

[21] *Supra* note 7.

Day fines may be considered the backbone of the system of penal sanctions in Germany. However, they apply in adult criminal law only. Juvenile criminal law (Youth Court Law) does not allow sentencing a youthful (or young adult) offender to a fine as penalties should be exclusively geared towards education and rehabilitation of youthful offenders. Neither does German criminal law know criminal corporate liability as the concept of criminal blame (guilt) is understood as being carried by human agency and the capacity to decide freely between right and wrong. But, administrative corporate liability may be established for criminal and/or administrative offences committed by executive officers of a corporation and violating obligations of the corporation. In such cases an administrative fine may be imposed on the corporation (maximum ten million euros (which corresponds to the maximum of a day fine).[22]

The German system of criminal sanctions is simple and essentially provides for two penal sanctions only, day fines and prison sentences. Day fines may not be suspended. However, in exceptional cases, paragraph 59 Criminal Code (hereafter CC) allows for cautioning an offender and imposing a conditional (suspended) day fine (up to 180 day fine units). This option is only rarely used by criminal courts (in 2017 circa 1 per cent of all convicted offenders have been cautioned). This is tentatively explained by the fact that most cases that were suitable for cautioning were already dismissed by public prosecutors for reasons of expediency (see Figure 6.1). Prison sentences in general may range from one month up to fifteen years (or amount to life imprisonment). Prison sentences of up to two years may be suspended (paragraph 56 CC) and (punitive and rehabilitative) conditions may be attached to a suspended prison sentence. Such conditions may include payment of an amount of money determined by the court and either to be paid to a charity or to the treasury, reparation/compensation, victim-offender reconciliation or community service, placement under probation supervision (paragraph 56(b) CC). Statutory minimum and maximum do not exist with respect to a condition of payment of an amount of money and the principles of day fines do not apply. However, proportionality standards must be complied with. The 'fine' imposed as a condition of suspension of a prison sentence must be both just and reasonable (seen from the financial capability of the offender). Research shows that in approximately 60 per cent of the suspended prison sentences an additional 'fine' is imposed.[23] Non-payment may have the consequence of revocation of suspension and execution of the prison sentence (paragraph 56(f) CC).

---

[22] Para. 30 Law on Administrative Offences.
[23] Trapp, *Rechtswirklichkeit von Auflagen und Weisungen bei Strafaussetzung zur Bewährung*, p. 197.

A day fine in principle may be imposed besides a prison sentence in cases where an offender has sought financial advantages (paragraph 41 CC). This option is only rarely used by criminal courts as it should be applied in exceptional cases only[24] and may neither be imposed in the pursuit of forfeiting proceeds of crime (here, only forfeiture rules (paragraphs 73 *et seq.* CC) are applicable) nor with the motive to downsize a prison sentence in order to allow for suspension of the prison sentence.[25] In 2017, in 0.08 per cent of all criminal convictions, a day fine was imposed besides a prison sentence.

While the introduction of community service as an intermediate criminal penalty has been called for at various occasions[26] the German legislator has been reluctant to widen the scope of criminal penalties beyond day fines and suspended and unsuspended prison sentences. A comprehensive report on the German system of criminal sanctions concluded in 2000 that there was no need to add further standalone penalties to day fines and prison sentences[27] but suggested minor revisions only (expansion of cautioning (paragraph 59 CC) and strengthening of community service as well as compensation of crime victims as substitutes of default imprisonment). In the following years, reforms of the system of sanctions have been discussed in the Federal Parliament. But, obviously, there was neither political interest nor political will to implement necessary legislative steps. The basic structure of the system of criminal penalties remained unchanged.[28]

The choice between a day fine and a short prison sentence (below six months) is strictly (and effectively) regulated through paragraph 47 CC which gives day fines priority over prison sentences below six months. Paragraph 47 CC says that a short prison sentence may be imposed only in exceptional situations. These exceptional situations are defined through:

(1) specific facts found in the offence or the offender;
(2) which necessitate a prison sentence;
(3) either due to a particular need to exert (rehabilitative) influence on an offender (through imprisonment or conditions attached to suspended prison sentences);
(4) or to a particular need to maintain public confidence in the legal order.

---

[24] Fischer, *Strafgesetzbuch. Kommentar*, p. 355.
[25] See, for example, Federal Court of Justice, Judgment as of 13 March 2019, 1 StR 367/18.
[26] Böhm, 'Gemeinnützige Arbeit als Strafe: Zu einer Gesetzgebungsinitiative des Bundesrates'.
[27] Kommission zur Reform des strafrechtlichen Sanktionensystems 2000.
[28] Arendt, *Quo vadis, Geldstrafe? Möglichkeiten und Grenzen einer ambulanten Sanktion*, pp. 60–2.

An analysis of German jurisprudence with respect to exceptional circumstances reveals that it is mostly persistent (petty) offenders who still attract short prison sentences.[29] Persistent petty offenders have turned out as a particular problem group as they exhibit a disposition of neither being amenable to fines nor to prison sentences. It is with respect to this group that courts evidently favour short prison sentences on the ground that reinforcement of public confidence in the legal order requires such punishment. If a prison sentence below six months is imposed after a trial, however, the CPC (paragraph 267 (III)) requests explicit reasoning as to why the priority rule was not applied. The financial situation of an offender (and an assessment of whether he/she will be able to pay the fine) may not be considered when deciding on whether to impose a day fine or a prison sentence below six months. The financial situation is to be taken into account only when deciding on the size of a day fine unit and payment accommodations.

Most criminal offence statutes in the German Criminal Code do not prescribe a minimum sentence, but only define the maximum penalty and explicitly allow for both, either day fines or prison sentences. For criminal offences (felonies) considered the most serious minimum penalties are statutorily defined, the most common minimum penalty is one year imprisonment. However, for selected serious crimes (in particular aggravated robbery, rape, serious forms of drug trafficking, homicide) the minimum is raised to two, three, five years, in exceptional cases to ten years). But, such increased minimums from one year imprisonment and more regularly come with a provision which reopens the minimum and provides for a lesser minimum in case of crimes of less seriousness ('minder schwere Fälle'). In almost all of these cases reduced minimums then result in the possibility to suspend a prison sentence, in some in the possibility to impose fines. Paragraph 47 II CC allows fining an offender although an offence statute does not carry a day fine if mitigating circumstances result in lowering the minimum below six months.

The use of day fines is then backed up by a procedural option. The prosecutor may decide to initiate simplified penal proceedings. With simplified proceedings a full criminal trial can be circumvented (and resources saved) with resorting to the imposition of a penal order ('Strafbefehl') if a case remains within a certain range of seriousness and does not pose problems of evidence (parasgraphs 407–412 CPC). A penal order does not require a trial at the consequence of restricting the sentence imposed in the penal order to a day fine or a suspended sentence of imprisonment of

---

[29] Streng, 'Para. 47. Kurze Freiheitsstrafe nur in Ausnahmefällen', p. 2051.

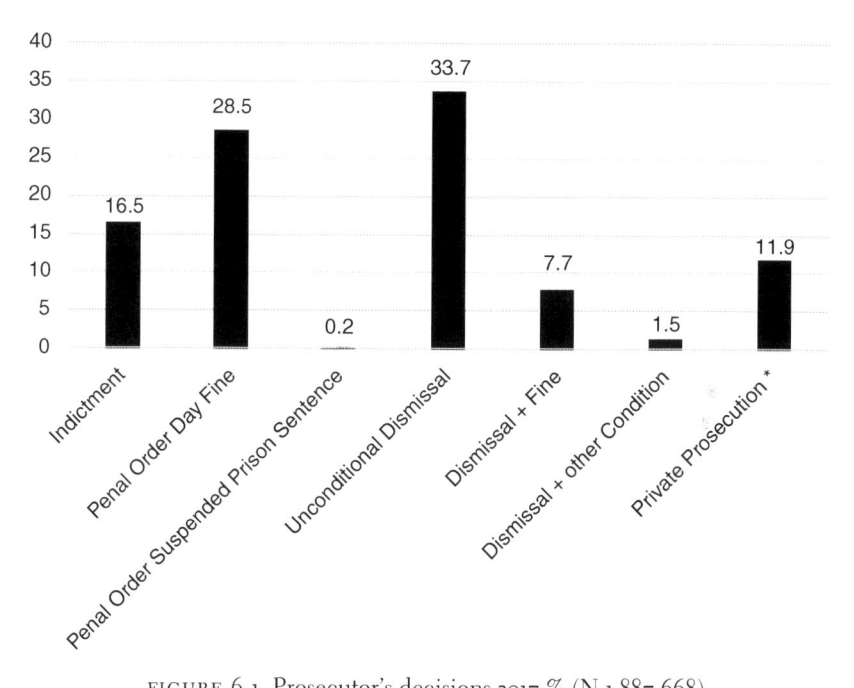

FIGURE 6.1 Prosecutor's decisions 2017 % (N 1,887,668)
*The public prosecutor may decline prosecution for selected criminal offences listed in para. 374 CPC and refer a complainant to private prosecution.
Source: Statistisches Bundesamt, Rechtspflege. Staatsanwaltschaften, p. 48.

a maximum of one year (the latter, introduced in 1993, however, is possible only if the defendant is represented by a defence counsel).[30] The option of a penal order results in an important incentive for prosecutors and judges (1) to resort to lower penalty ranges and (2) to impose a fine as it allows for quick and convenient finalisation of proceedings. Also, defendants and defence counsels prefer penal orders as they do not expose offenders to a public trial and offer a discrete way to conclude a criminal case.

Data in Figure 6.1 show that public prosecutors make extensive use of paragraphs 153 and 153(a) CPC. In 2017, more than 40 per cent of suspects (who in principle could have been brought to court) had their cases dismissed either unconditionally or with a condition. In another 12 per cent of cases, public prosecutors found that public interest did not warrant public prosecution and referred complainants to the option of private prosecution (provided by paragraphs 374–394 CPC).

[30] *Supra* note 18.

Almost 30 per cent of the cases are finalised by prosecutors through applying for a penal order (virtually exclusively aiming at a day fine) and, finally, 16.5 per cent go – after indictment – to a criminal court (where again most sentences concern day fines).

Prosecutors, in a first step, sort out petty offences by way of implementing non-prosecution policies at a large scale or referring victims to private prosecution (paras. 153 and 374 CPC). In a second step, conditional dismissals (most of them imposing a lump sum fine, see Figure 6.1) address more serious forms of criminal offences. Then, in a third step, the initiation of simplified proceedings results in the imposition of a day fine in a penal order. Overall, financial penalties (including day fines) dominate criminal law-based responses within the range of criminal offences qualifying for conditional dismissal and sentences of less than six months. Also, with respect to sentences between six months and two years, financial penalties prevail, as suspended prison sentences normally come with the condition to pay a (lump sum) fine.[31] Hence, day fines in Germany have adopted the role of an intermediate penal sanction and a response to more serious forms of crime distinct from the role summary fines usually play in criminal justice systems.[32]

6.3 THE STRUCTURE OF DAY FINES AND FINING

6.3.1 *Minimums and Maximums*

Day fines come with a minimum of 5 day fines and a maximum of 360 day fines (paragraph 40 (I) CC, in case of sentencing multiple offences up to 720 day fines may be imposed). Determination of the number of day fines is subject to general rules on sentencing (paragraph 46 CC). However, other than prison sentences, day fines may not be suspended (except in case of cautioning, paragraph 59 CC, which always comes with a suspended day fine of up to 180 day fine units).

The amount of a day fine unit (reflecting the net income of the defendant) may range from 1 to 30,000 euros (paragraph 40 (II) CC). The upper limit of the amount of a day fine was raised from 5,000 to 30,000 euros in 2009 and is far above what other day fine systems in Europe determine as a maximum.[33] The move towards raising the upper limit of a day fine was rather made for symbolic reasons. A significant catalyst of this move is found in an economic

---

[31] *Supra* note 23.
[32] Tonry and Lynch, 'Intermediate Sanctions'.
[33] *Supra* note 7.

criminal trial dealing with a merger between Mannesmann and Vodafone which resulted in allegations of 'breach of trust' against the board members of the Mannesmann company, the most prominent member of which was the then CEO of Deutsche Bank.[34] This case came amidst public debates on grossly inflated salaries of board members of big stock market listed corporations and ultimately led to a discussion on whether the German day fine system was equipped to effectively respond to the top earners in big corporations. In a remarkably short period of time and in an almost unanimous decision (it was only the faction of Die Linke which abstained from voting) on 29 June 2009, the Federal Parliament adopted a law which raised the maximum of a day fine unit from 5,000 to 30,000 euros.[35] There was a discussion on whether to completely abolish a maximum and follow the Finnish example, which was considered to comply with constitutional standards of predictability as everybody should know his/her net income and thus be able to calculate the size of criminal fines.[36] However, the Parliament ultimately opted for a fixed maximum, as it was also under the influence of an earlier judgment of the Federal Constitutional Court which declared unconstitutional a financial penalty ('Vermögensstrafe') which did not set a maximum but would have allowed a criminal court to forfeit the total of the assets of a criminal offender.[37] The total amount of a day fine may now range between a minimum of 5 euros (five day fine units at 1 euro each) and a maximum of 10,800,000 euros (360 day fine units at 30,000 euros each; in case of multiple offences 21,600,000 euros).

6.3.2 *The Net Income Principle*

The starting point of determining the size of a day fine unit is the net income of an offender (or the net income an offender could have) at the time of the trial (or when issuing the penal order). However, the net income had been debated controversially when drafting the Comprehensive Criminal Law Reform. It was suggested not to use the net income but to deduct from the net income the minimum income needed to exist and to forfeit with a day fine unit only the income above that level.[38] The legislator did not follow the

[34] Kolla, 'The Mannesmann Trial and the Role of the Courts'.
[35] Zweiundvierzigstes Gesetz zur Änderung des Strafgesetzbuches – Anhebung der Höchstgrenze des Tagessatzes bei Geldstrafen, as of 29 June 2009.
[36] Deutscher Bundestag 2009, p. 7.
[37] Federal Constitutional Court, Judgment as of 20 March 2002, 2 BvR 794/95.
[38] Wilde, 'Die Geldstrafe – ein unsoziales Rechtsinstitut?'; Wilde, 'Wenn Armut zur Strafe wird. Die freie, gemeinnützige Arbeit in der aktuellen Sanktionspraxis'.

proposal to spare income below the subsistence level from being accessible for day fines and adopted ultimately the net income principle. But the net income principle has been softened down. When calculating the final amount, the law says (paragraph 40 (II) CC) the court has – beyond the net income – to consider personal and financial circumstances. This gives the judge some discretion (as part of sentencing discretion) when fixing the size of a day fine unit and allows for deviating from the net income.

The net income is defined through all sorts of income, including benefits in kind. It is still disputed whether and how assets in the form of real estate, stocks etc. which do not result in constant or immediate income should be treated when calculating the size of a day fine unit. In general, however, it is concluded that assets should only very restrictively be included in the determination of a day fine unit as day fines may not pursue the goal of confiscation.[39]

Fiscal law may serve as guidance in interpreting net income, but, net income remains a concept which is autonomously defined in penal law.[40] Whereas most offenders do not own considerable assets the problem of exactly what should be taken into consideration (in terms of personal and economic circumstances), in order to lower or decrease the day fine level, is much more important. One of the most important factors concerns liability for maintenance and actual maintenance payments, that is, financial support for children or other family members. Calculation of the size of maintenance must respect standard maintenance rates which are fixed annually in the civil court system responsible for civil maintenance lawsuits.[41]

Opinions vary as to whether debts in general or permanent financial obligations, other than maintenance payments, should be considered when determining the income. In general, a rather restrictive approach is favoured.[42] It is suggested that only those obligations which correspond to reasonable and plausible economic behaviour should be deducted. This would include, for example, debts resulting from the purchase of an apartment or a house and would not include payments for a luxury automobile. Other, more general debts, are excluded from consideration. More recently, the discussion centres around compensation and reparation resulting from the crime and the position of the needs of the victim vis-à-vis a day fine. As a part of the general movement toward better treatment of victims in the criminal

---

[39] Kinzig, 'Para. 40. Verhängung in Tagessätzen', p. 755.
[40] Brandis, *Geldstrafe und Nettoeinkommen*.
[41] *Supra* note 39, p. 756.
[42] *Supra* note 24, p. 352.

justice system, the idea that day fine levels should be adjusted in order to allow for effective victim compensation and reparation is receiving growing support.[43] But, the legislator chose to take into account reparation of crime victims not at the stage of fixing the size of a day fine but when deciding on payment accommodations (paragraph 42 CC). The court should allow for payment accommodations if without that compensation the victim would be 'seriously at risk' (paragraph 42 (3) CC).

In order to compensate for progressive effects of high numbers of day fine units, namely for the disproportionate increase of the financial burden in the case a higher number of days also combined with a high daily unit, it is also accepted that with an increasing number of day fines the size of a day fine unit may be lowered.[44]

The decision of the legislator to also include net income which an offender could have has drawn heavy criticism. But, an understanding of that clause prevails which restricts net income an offender could have to situations where somebody forwent potential income with the intent to reduce the amount of a day fine unit.[45] The 'could have' clause may not be invoked to force somebody into adopting more lucrative work opportunities.[46]

6.3.3 *Transfer Dependent (Incomeless) Offenders and Marginal Groups*

Marginal groups present serious problems for any system relying on fines, whether they are day fines or fixed sum fines. Beyond these groups, among them prisoners, homeless persons or drug dependent individuals, it is also students, asylum seekers, the unemployed and partners/wives/husbands who do not hold a job but manage the household (and child-rearing) who do not fit into the model of the day fine (which is based on constant income from a regular job). Technically, it does not appear that there would be much of a problem to simply base day fine units on the income offenders receive as social security payments, pensions, stipends or maintenance payments. Moreover, the rather modest lower limits of day fine units should allow for adjustment to such low levels of income. Therefore, the German day fine system operates under the premise that everybody has (or could have) income (also unemployed prisoners or asylum seekers, who are not allowed to hold a job, will receive what is called 'pocket money').

---

[43] Albrecht, 'Para. 40. Verhängung in Tagessätzen', p. 1869.
[44] *Supra* note 24, p. 354.
[45] BayObLG, judgment as of 2 February 1998, 1 St RR 1/98.
[46] *Supra* note 24, p. 349; *supra* note 39, p. 754.

With respect to partners/wives/husbands who do themselves not have income but are maintained under the umbrella of a family (or household), it is argued that the basis for calculating the size of a day fine unit should be what he/she actually receives in terms of maintenance.[47] For students, net income is based on stipends (or constant financial support from others). However, it should be recognised that in all those cases where the offender is dependent on some type of social security, the state provides resources thought to represent a minimum level of maintenance. Prisoners, asylum seeking persons, individuals living on social security (or unemployment benefits), homeless people either do not have regular income (prisoners may be able to earn some 200 to 300 euros a month through prison labour, but part of that income is to be saved to support after prison release while another part is devoted to allow purchasing certain everyday supplies while in prison) or income (including payments in kind) which places them close to the subsistence level. Payments in kind in fact should not be considered as income at all as such payments cannot be turned into cash and used to pay a day fine. However, some High Courts ('Oberlandesgerichte') have decided that payments in kind (for example, accommodation and food stamps provided for asylum seekers) may be considered when determining a day size unit.[48] But, in case of a prisoner, involuntary accommodation in prison as well as other services provided may not be counted as income.[49]

Part of the resources provided by social security (or corresponding support schemes), then, are taken away by another agency of the state under the day fine system. A potential inconsistency (in a welfare state) is presented in attempting to keep people slightly above a subsistence level on the one hand and, on the other hand, pushing them below that minimum level with a day fine. Essentially, this problem may be resolved by always resorting to the minimum level for a day fine (which in principle is possible as discretion of trial courts in this respect is rather wide)[50] or, still better, by providing non-custodial alternatives to the day fine for these groups of offenders.

6.3.4 *Estimating the Net Income*

Paragraph 40 (III) CC authorises the court to estimate the income, assets and other circumstances relevant for determining the size of a day fine unit. The

---

[47] *Ibid.*

[48] High Court (Oberlandesgericht) Oldenburg, Ss 205/07 (I 61), Judgment as of 30 July 2007.

[49] Oberlandesgericht Hamm, Judgment as of 6 January 2015, 3 RVs 102/14.

[50] See Oberlandesgericht Köln, Judgment as of 17 June 2015, III-1 RVs 101/15.

possibility to replace exact determination of the income by an estimate is grounded first of all on the proportionality principle. As a suspect or an accused has the right to refuse giving evidence on his/her income (as an obligation would amount to self-incrimination) and tax secrecy law prevents prosecutors and courts to have access to tax information, full investigation of the financial situation of an offender by way of witness testimony or other investigations is considered to be disproportional especially in the case of small fines and lengthy proceedings resulting from efforts to find the 'true' income.[51] However, the power to estimate may not be used to force somebody to disclose financial information. An estimate must have a sound basis from which then an estimate is made. Estimations (or rather guesses) which do not have a factual foundation – according to a recent judgment of the Federal Constitutional Court – would amount to arbitrariness.[52] Although it is unanimously accepted that valid income information is of paramount importance for the effective implementation of the day fine system, police (responsible for the investigation of criminal offences) in general does not assign much relevance to personal (and financial) information on suspects.[53]

The lack of systematic (and valid) information collected during the investigative stage of criminal proceedings is of particular relevance as most day fines are imposed in the penal order procedure (see Figure 6.1). In practice, information on the professional status of the offender, as well as the offender's standard of living, is regarded as sufficient and, in fact, actually provide quite accurate estimates in most cases. Some cases, however, do pose problems, even considering the power to make estimates.[54] These difficult cases involve, for example, professions where variation in income is rather large. However, the cases where this occurs (for example, tax, economic and environmental offences) are rather rare.

Assessment of net income and determination of the size of a day fine by the trial court may be appealed separately and is considered by defence lawyers to play a significant role in defence strategies.[55] As day fine sentences originate mostly from trial courts at the lowest level of the court hierarchy ('Amtsgerichte'), most jurisprudence on specific day fine issues is generated by the High Courts ('Oberlandesgerichte'). Only on rare occasions day fine cases are dealt with by the Federal Court of Justice ('Bundesgerichtshof').

---

[51] Bundesgerichtshof (Federal Court of Justice) Judgment as of 25 April 2017, 1 StR 147/17).
[52] Federal Constitutional Court, Judgment as of 1 June 2015, 2 BvR 67/15).
[53] Albrecht, *Strafzumessung und Vollstreckung bei Geldstrafen.*
[54] *Ibid.*
[55] Rademacher and Gerhardt, 'Reduzierung der Tagessatzhöhe als Verteidigungsziel'.

6.3.5 *Payment Accommodations*

The court may grant payment accommodations when sentencing an offender to a day fine (paragraph 42 CC). However, payment in instalments or a payment extension must be granted only if it would be unreasonable in the light of the financial situation of the offender to expect prompt payment of the total amount. Collection of day fines has to comply with the principle of speedy enforcement (paragraph 2 Law on Enforcement of Criminal Sentences). Research on fine enforcement has shown that court practices are rather generous in this respect but may then result in lengthy enforcement proceedings.[56] Payment accommodations or modifications therefrom may also be issued during the fine collection process.

6.3.6 *Enforcement of Day Fines*

After a judgment has become final, an enforcement procedure will be initiated by the prosecutor's office (the prosecutor is responsible for the collection and enforcement of fines) if the convicted person did not pay the fine within the delays fixed by law (two weeks). The Law on Enforcement of Criminal Sentences ('Strafvollstreckungsordnung') and the Law on Recovery of Public Claims ('Justizbeitreibungsgesetz') apply.

The fine collection procedure involves as a first step a formal reminder, which – if not successful – is followed by a conventional civil enforcement process. Civil enforcement may be implemented in the form of seizure of personal property or in the form of attachment of claims. The initiation of civil collection proceedings may be waived if information available shows that such steps would not be successful. If a fine cannot be collected in civil proceedings or if collection has been waived then – according to paragraph 43 CC – the fine is replaced by default imprisonment with one day fine corresponding to one day in prison. The correspondence ratio of one day fine unit and one day imprisonment has drawn criticism. Critical voices point to Austrian criminal law which has adopted a ratio of two day fine units equalling one day imprisonment[57] and argue that loss of liberty should outweigh the loss of income and should therefore come with a ratio reflecting such difference.[58]

If it has been stated by the public prosecutor that the fine cannot be collected, the prosecutor will issue an order to enforce default imprisonment. Default imprisonment may not be suspended. It is criticised that a separate

---

[56] *Supra* note 53, p. 233.
[57] *Supra* note 43, p. 1885.
[58] *Supra* note 28, p. 141; *supra* note 39, p. 767.

detention order by a judge is not considered to be necessary as imprisonment and the length of imprisonment is already spelled out in the original judgment imposing a day fine.[59] However, the defendant may apply with the court for waiving the fine because of particular hardship brought by fine enforcement (paragraph 459(f) CPC). Moreover, the court may order not to enforce the fine (or parts of it) if in the same or separate criminal proceedings a prison sentence has been imposed and fine collection could impede rehabilitation and reintegration of the offender (paragraph 459(d) CPC). As default imprisonment corresponds to a regular (unsuspended) prison sentence, rules on early release (parole) apply (paragraph 57 CC). A fine default prisoner may be released after serving two third of the prison sentence. However, in practice not many fine defaulters will profit from early release as a minimum of two months has to be served and a significant share of day fines falls below sixty day fine units (see Table 6.3).

6.3.7 *Community Service*

While the (Federal) Criminal Code is silent about other ways of enforcing day fines than either through payment or through default imprisonment, the Introductory Law to the Criminal Code gives the states ('Bundesländer') power to introduce legislation which allows replacement of default imprisonment by community service.[60] In the 1980s, all Laender made use of this power; after reunification in 1990, the new Laender in the East of Germany followed.

A look at ordinances of the Laender which regulate community service reveals that similar conversion rates apply (with three to six hours of community service replacing one day of default imprisonment). Similarities prevail also in the rules regarding initiation and revocation proceedings.[61]

6.4 IMPLEMENTING THE DAY FINE SYSTEM

6.4.1 *The Structure of Criminal Sanctions*

As was outlined above, the introduction of the priority rule in 1969 (paragraph 47 CC) immediately resulted in a large-scale change in the structure

---

[59] Köhne, 'Abschaffung der Ersatzfreiheitsstrafe?'; Seebode, 'Problematische Ersatzfreiheitsstrafe'; Wissenschaftliche Dienste, *Ersatzfreiheitsstrafe gemäß para. 43 StGB. Rechtsvergleich, Verfassungskonformität und Alternativen*, p. 4.

[60] Article 293, Einführungsgesetz zum Strafgesetzbuch.

[61] Ministerium der Justiz Nordrhein-Westfalen 2019.

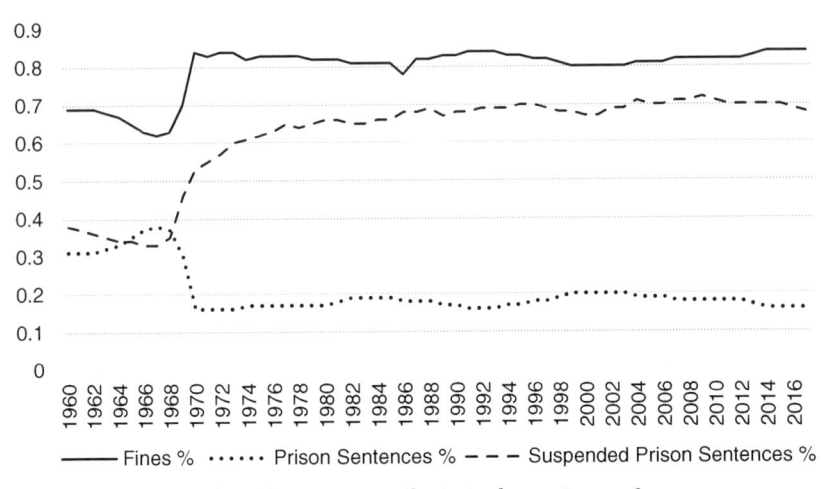

FIGURE 6.2 The structure of criminal sanctions 1960–2017
Source: Statistisches Bundesamt, Strafverfolgung.

of criminal sanctions. The proportion of fines at criminal penalties meted out increased to more than 80 per cent and remained at that level since then. The introduction of the day fine system in 1975 did not bring further increases in the use of fines. However, as the move towards introducing a day fine system was known already in 1969 when implementing the first part of the reform package, the changes in the structure of penalties may be attributed to the legislator's intent to replace short prison sentences through a credible fine system and full compliance of prosecutors and judges with that goal (which was certainly furthered by incentives to resort to simplified penal order proceedings). Besides the increase in the use of fines and the corresponding decrease in the use of prison sentences, the rate of suspended prison sentences starts to increase after 1969, too. The rate of suspended prison sentences reaches a plateau in the mid-1980s with some 70 per cent of suspended prison sentences (and conditions attached, see above). What seems remarkable then is the stability of the structure of criminal sentences in Germany. During the last fifty years, the proportion of fines at all criminal sentences did not change.

The reunification (and extension of West German criminal law to the East of Germany) in 1990 did not interrupt the flat lines either. Not only the criminal code books of the Federal Republic of Germany (FRG) were almost completely and immediately after concluding the reunification treaty transplanted to the East of Germany. In addition, after the reunification East German judges and prosecutors have been replaced by lawyers from West Germany; sentencing laws and sentencing practices thus have been transplanted successfully.

When looking at the structure of penal sanctions in detail and for 2017, Table 6.1 reveals that the goals of the Comprehensive Criminal Law Reform have been achieved with respect to replacing short term imprisonment by fines. In the penalty range up to one month exclusively, fines are meted out as by law the minimum of prison sentences is established at one month. Within the range of one up to six months, day fines prevail with representing some 48 per cent of total sentences and almost 90 per cent of sentences in that category. Most sentences between six months and two years are suspended prison sentences; day fines account for approximately 10 per cent of all sentences imposed within this range. Penalties above two years (which cannot be suspended) total circa 1.5 per cent of all criminal sentences. Thus, the structure of criminal sentences displays a reversed J-curve reflecting sentencing practices (and sentencing doctrine[62]) which keep criminal sentences effectively and constantly within the lower third of the range of sentences carried by criminal offence statutes and close to the minimum allowed by criminal offence statutes thus placing criminal cases under the rule of paragraph 47 CC which requests a day fine instead of prison sentences. In fact, the reversed J-curve distribution of sentencing

TABLE 6.1 *Structure of criminal sanctions 2017, % column and total, () row %*

Penalty range	Day fine (%)	Suspended prison sentence (%)	Imprisonment (%)	N (%)
< 1 month	36.2 (100)			237,403 (100)
1–6 months	47.5 (88.4)	4.6 (8.6)	1.6 (3.0)	352,208 (100)
7–12 months	0.5 (8.4)	4.0 (71.6)	1.1 (19.9)	36,660 (100)
1–2 years	0.04 (1.2)	2.2 (70.0)	0.9 (28.7)	20,653 (100)
2–3 years			0.7 (100)	4,497 (100)
3–5 years			0.5 (100)	3,299 (100)
5–10 years			0.2 (100)	1,447 (100)
10–15 years			0.02 (100)	116 (100)
Life			0.01 (100)	91 (100)
Total	(84.1)	(10.8)	(5.1)	656,376 (100)

Source: *Statistisches Bundesamt, Strafverfolgung 2017, pp. 160–1, 198–9.*

[62] See *supra* note 6.

outcomes can be traced back to the beginning of the twentieth century. Already for the first decades of the twentieth century, Franz Exner[63] pointed out that criminal sentences were not normally distributed over the penalty range prescribed in a criminal offence statute but – in those cases for which data back then were accessible – come in the form of a reversed J-distribution curve, placing the bulk of penalties close to the minimum prescribed by a criminal offence statute.

Rates of day fines for selected offence categories are to be found in Table 6.2. The offence categories included in Table 6.2 concern theft, forgery, fraud and assault which carry sentencing ranges between a minimum of five day fines and a maximum of five years' imprisonment. Aggravated assault (paragraph 224 CC) and burglary (paragraph 244 CC) carry sentencing ranges between six months and ten years imprisonment and do not explicitly mention day fines. However, for less serious offences the minimum is lowered for both, aggravated assault and burglary, to three months to five years which authorises the court according to paragraph 47 II CC to resort to day fines. For robbery offences a penalty range between one and fifteen years is available (paragraph 249 CC) but for less serious offences of robbery (and additional mitigating circumstances) day fines are again applicable if the minimum is moved below six months. In contrast, drug offences, sexual offences, immigration offences and motor traffic offences cover a wide range of criminal offence statutes displaying various degrees of seriousness and varying minimums and maximums.

The data demonstrate that day fines prevail when the range of sentences available according to an offence statute does not establish a minimum (and thus allows for the absolute minimum of five day fine units) and sets the maximum at five years' imprisonment. Theft, fraud, forgery, motor traffic offences and assault fall into this category. In general, at least four out of five offenders convicted and sentenced for these crimes receive a day fine. Also, immigration offences (including illegal immigration and illegal overstaying as well as smuggling offences) come with the same pattern of sentencing. Sexual and drug offences also show a significant share of day fines, too. With respect to sexual offences, it is in particular possession of child pornography, sexual harassment and sexual abuse of children (with no physical contact) which lead to the imposition of day fines. Drug offences include possession, purchase or smuggling of small amounts of (soft and hard) drugs where in case of repeat offending day fines are imposed. Then, more serious criminal offences such as burglary and aggravated assault come with rates of day fines of circa 20 and 30 per cent. Finally,

---

[63] Exner, Studien über die Strafzumessungspraxis der deutschen Gerichte, pp. 75–85.

TABLE 6.2 *Selected offence categories and the share of day fines 2002–17*

	2002	2003	2004	2005	2006	2007	2008	2009	2010	2011	2012	2013	2014	2915	2016	2017
Theft	81.4	81.3	81.7	81.2	80.6	81.42	80.9	81.23	81.5	82.1	82.8	84.3	85.3	86.5	86.4	85.6
Burglary	17.8	18	18.4	19.1	18.5	21.2	21.5	22	21.1	22.5	21.7	23.9	23.9	23.8	22.9	20.8
Fraud	82.9	79.8	81.7	83.2	82.5	84.3	83.7	83.8	84	84.2	83.6	84.3	85.4	85.6	85.6	85.6
Assault	79.1	78.4	78.9	79.8	79.1	79.4	78.9	78.6	79.1	79.7	80	80.2	81.4	81.9	82.1	81.9
Aggravated Assault	27.4	25.4	25.4	26.3	26.1	24.6	24.2	24.2	23.9	25.4	26	26.6	27	27.6	27.8	28.4
Robbery	3.7	2.6	2.0	3.0	3.5	3.3	2.2	2.2	2.9	1.6	2.3	3.1	3.1	3.3	2.8	2.2
Forgery	73.6	73.7	76.6	77.7	78.2	79.3	79.1	79.9	80.2	81.5	81.7	83.7	84.1	84.1	84.4	85.4
Sexual Offences	33.4	34.6	37.3	36.7	36.6	37.7	40.3	38.8	34.7	34.8	36.7	38.4	40.8	40.7	39.4	41.4
Drug Offences	53.8	54.4	56.2	58.5	59.3	62.1	65.9	65.2	65.2	67	67.9	69.4	71	71.5	72.4	73.1
Immigration Offences	85.3	85.7	85.8	85.3	87.4	88.8	87.1	87.9	88.4	89.3	90	91.5	88.7	81	78.7	89.3
Motor Traffic Offences	91.6	91.9	91.4	91.7	92	92.3	92.2	92.4	92.7	93	93.2	93.5	94	94.1	94.3	94.6

Source: Statistisches Bundesamt, Strafverfolgungsstatistik 2002–17.

TABLE 6.3 *Day fine units by day fine size % (in () row percentages)*

Day fine units	Day fine size (€)					Total
	<5 € (%)	5–10 € (%)	10–25 € (%)	25–50 € (%)	>50 € (%)	
5–15	8.3 (1.6)	9.6 (29.2)	9.2 (38.6)	8.0 (28.4)	5.9 (2.2)	48,594
16–30	27.1 (1.4)	31.6 (24.7)	34.3 (36.9)	36.9 (33.9)	33.1 (3.2)	188,809
31–90	50.7 (1.8)	49.4 (27.0)	48.3 (36.4)	48.8 (31.3)	52.1 (3.5)	269,733
91–180	13.3 (3.1)	9.0 (32.1)	7.7 (37.5)	5.8 (24.3)	6.9 (3.0)	41,455
181–360	0.6 (1.9)	0.4 (21.0)	0.5 (35.7)	0.5 (29.7)	2.0 (11.6)	3,110
Total	9,611 (1.7)	147,568 (26.7)	203,174 (36.8)	173,276 (31.4)	18,072 (3.3)	551,701

Source: Statistisches Bundesamt, Strafverfolgung 2017, pp. 198–201.

robbery still leads to a rate of 2–3 per cent day fines (due to mitigation rules and applicability of paragraph 47 (II) CC explained above).

A look at the number and the size of day fine units observed in 2017, Table 6.3 shows that the majority of day fines does not exceed 25 euros (which equals a net income of some 750 euros per month). Two third of the offenders sentenced to day fines fall into this income bracket. The rather low net income calculated by judges (compared to the average net income of employees in Germany amounting to 1,890 euros per month in 2017)[64] may be explained by (1) a high number of offenders convicted and sentenced coming from marginal and economically deprived groups and (2) by judges tending to lower levels when estimating the net income.

In fact, almost 30 per cent of day fine units do not exceed 10 euros (equalling a monthly net income of 300 euros at most) which corresponds to the amount of social welfare payments. On the other hand, it is rather rare that a high number of day fine units (>180) comes with a size of day fines of more than 50 euros. Most of these cases involve tax offences and economic crimes.

6.4.2 *Collection of Fines and Default Imprisonment*

The fine collection procedure starts after the sentence has become final. Enforcement of fines is the task of public prosecution services. The legal framework is found in the CC, CPC, the Law on Enforcement of Criminal

---

[64] de.statista.com/themen/293/durchschnittseinkommen/.

Sentences ('Strafvollstreckungsordnung') and the Law on Recovery of Public Claims ('Justizbeitreibungsgesetz') as outlined above.

Research on the fine collection process in Germany is restricted to two studies.[65] One of these studies was carried out shortly after the introduction of the day fine system and also includes a comparison of enforcement of fines before and after the introduction of the day fine system.[66] Another study was launched in North Rhine-Westphalia and laid the emphasis on the fine collection process.[67] Both studies arrive at comparable results with respect to fine collection. Circa 50 per cent of fines are paid immediately after the conviction became final. Payment accommodation (mostly instalments) were granted in approximately one third of the cases and in some 15 per cent execution of default imprisonment was ordered. After an order of execution was issued, two third of the defaulters settled the debt.[68] The introduction of the day fine system in 1975 did not have any impact on the fine collection process and its outcomes.[69]

After a finding that the fine cannot be collected, the public prosecutor will order execution of default imprisonment. Official statistics on the fine collection process and default imprisonment for the whole of Germany do not exist. However, pieces of information on day fine enforcement may be drawn from Statistics on Public Prosecution (which account for the number of fine collections initiated by public prosecution services and the number of cases where community service replaced default imprisonment). Some states ('Bundesländer') operate prison statistics which allow for identifying fine defaulters among prison admissions while federal prison statistics offer head counts (of fine defaulters) at certain dates. The latter do not provide for a complete picture of default imprisonment but underestimate the number of default prisoners as default prison sentences are short prison sentences. As data on the average time default prisoners serve are not available for Germany, estimates must be based on selected studies and on data published occasionally by state ('Bundesländer') justice systems (which allow for calculating the average time served on the basis of flow and stock data on default prisoners).

Upon notification that default imprisonment will be enforced a significant share of fines will be paid.[70] The enforcement pattern corresponds to what

[65] *Supra* note 53; *supra* note 15, Janssen.

[66] *Supra* note 53.

[67] *Supra* note 15, Janssen.

[68] *Supra* note 53, p. 233.

[69] *Ibid.*, p. 313.

[70] Jehle, Feuerhelm and Block, *Gemeinnützige Arbeit statt Ersatzfreiheitsstrafe*, p. 12 report payment of fines in 77 per cent of cases after a formal declaration of fine default and notification that default imprisonment will be enforced, serving of default imprisonment in 14 per cent and community service in 8 per cent.

Albrecht[71] found with respect to collection of fines and default imprisonment in the 1970s.

In North Rhine-Westphalia, 8 per cent of day fines result in default imprisonment.[72] A rate of approximately 8 per cent in 2017 can be calculated on the basis of prison admission data also for Bavaria.[73] In Mecklenburg-Vorpommern the rate of default imprisonment was circa 7 per cent in 2017.[74] The rate of default imprisonment reported for Hessen is slightly higher,[75] but its calculation is based on prison admission data which come with some overestimating of 'true' prison admissions (due to double counting of prisoners changing prison facilities).

Data in Figure 6.3, covering the whole of Germany, result from federal statistics on public prosecution which account for the numbers of day fine collection proceedings initiated and default imprisonment replaced by community service and on estimates of rates of default imprisonment based on head counts and an estimate of an average of thirty days default imprisonment.[76] When assuming an average of thirty days, the rate of fine defaulters serving default imprisonment is rising and in 2017 stands at approximately 10 per cent of all day fines for which collection has been initiated by public prosecution services. In conclusion, and taking into account the estimates drawn from statistics provided by individual states ('Bundesländer') mentioned above, the rate of default imprisonment today may be assessed to be close to 10 per cent for Germany at large. On the basis of this evidence it can be concluded that: (1) the rate of default imprisonment has doubled during the last forty years (from circa 5 per cent in the mid-1970s to some 10 per cent in 2017); (2) a significant proportion of day fines cannot be collected and instead short prison sentences are executed and (3) community service replaces day fines at a rate of some 5 per cent during the last fifteen years, but the rate is on the

---

[71] *Supra* note 53, p. 253.

[72] Bögelein, Ernst and Neubacher, 'Wie kann die Vermeidung von Ersatzfreiheitsstrafen gelingen? Zur Lebenssituation der Verurteilten und zur Zusammenarbeit staatlicher und nichtstaatlicher Organisationen', 285.

[73] Bayerischer Landtag, *Schriftliche Anfrage. Ersatzfreiheitsstrafe in bayerischen Justizvollzugsanstalten*, p. 4.

[74] Landtag Mecklenburg-Vorpommern, 'Kleine Anfrage. Ersatzfreiheitsstrafen', p. 2.

[75] Hessisches Statistisches Landesamt, *Der Strafvollzug in Hessen im Jahr 2017. Teil 2: Bestand und Bewegung in den Justizvollzugsanstalten.*

[76] Villmow, *Geldstrafen – Gemeinnützige Arbeit – Ersatzfreiheitsstrafen. Aktuelle Probleme und Reformbedarf*, p. 4, prisoner entry and head count data for Bavaria in fact result in an estimate of approximately thirty days served on average for fine default, see *supra* note 73, p. 4 and Statistisches Bundesamt, *Strafverfolgungsstatistik 2017*, p. 6.

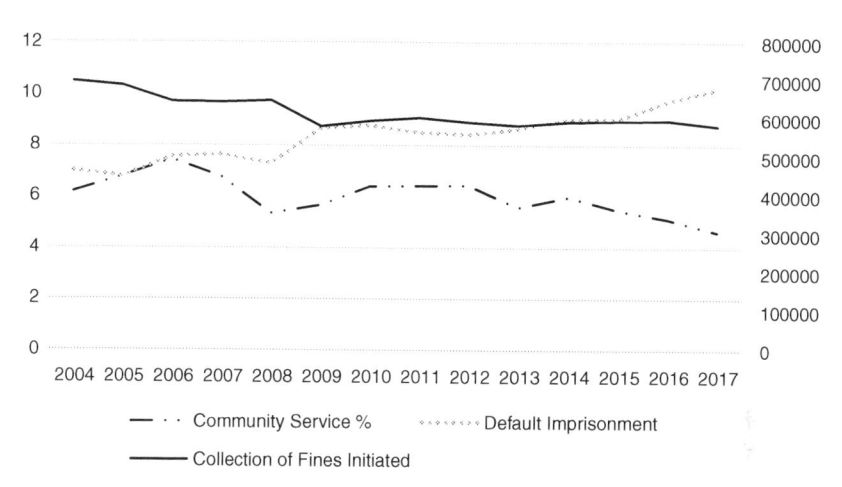

FIGURE 6.3 Fine collection initiated (right Y-axis), community service %, default imprisonment % (both left Y-axis)
Sources: Statistisches Bundesamt, Staatsanwaltschaftsstatistik 2004–2017; Statistisches Bundesamt, Strafvollzug 2004–2017; Villmow, Geldstrafen – Gemeinnützige Arbeit – Ersatzfreiheitsstrafen. Aktuelle Probleme und Reformbedarf.

decline and there is no evidence to assume that it replaces effectively default imprisonment.

Although community service has been hailed as a promising medicine against default imprisonment (and short prison sentences), the core of fine defaulters seems to resist not only conventional fine enforcement but also to miss the escape ramp provided by the offer of community service. The evident increase in fine collection problems (including default imprisonment) tentatively can be explained by a significant increase in precarious labour conditions (including low wage jobs and temporary employment). This coincides with immigration and increasing numbers of immigrants confined to disadvantaged financial and social conditions not least due to restricted access to labour markets or precarious employment.[77]

Research on fine defaulters (serving default imprisonment) shows consistently high rates of unemployment, persistent (petty) offending, mental health problems, drug addiction and homelessness, in general the profile of socially

---

[77] Brinkmann, Dörre and Röbenack, *Prekäre Arbeit. Ursachen, Ausmaß, soziale Folgen und subjektive Verarbeitungsformen unsicherer Beschäftigungsverhältnisse*, p. 42.

marginalised and psychologically impaired individuals.[78] Furthermore, criminal offences for which day fines cannot be collected and result in default imprisonment reflect in general petty, though persistent offending, low numbers of day fine units and rather small day fine sizes.[79] Fare dodging, simple theft, trespassing, vandalism and assault account for significant proportions of criminal offences committed by fine defaulters.[80] As many of these cases are finalised through penal orders or in criminal proceedings which do not emphasise personal circumstances of offenders, criminal files do not contain information which could effectively guide the decision-making of fine enforcement authorities.[81] The conclusion drawn from data on fine defaulters serving default imprisonment first of all concerns strengthening and widening proactive approaches in order to reach out to those who ultimately are at risk of default imprisonment.[82] However, it is in fact questionable whether community service replaces default imprisonment. As community service is offered to all those for whom default imprisonment is ordered, it might present an alternative also for those who – without the option of community service – would have paid the fine in a last-minute move.

The significant rate of fine default certainly is the price of implementing effectively the rule (paragraph 47 CC) which gives fines priority over prison sentences and the unique distribution of criminal penalties in Germany. Sentencing rules (paragraph 47 CC) evidently are strictly followed by criminal courts and generate a small group of fined offenders exhibiting a profile (social status, age, prior record, prison experiences) very close to those offenders with suspended and unsuspended prison sentences.[83]

Treig and Pruin[84] complain about a particularly high number of default prisoners in Germany and, in fact, when ranking European countries on the basis of shares of default prisoners counted at the total of sentenced prisoners in 2014,[85] Germany is placed on top. However, when calculating the share of default prisoners at the number of fines imposed, then a different picture

---

[78] *Supra* note 53; Dolde, 'Zum Vollzug von Ersatzfreiheitsstrafen. Eindrücke aus einer empirischen Erhebung', p. 585; *supra* note 72, p. 284.

[79] *Supra* note 15, Janssen, p. 217.

[80] *Ibid.*, p. 214; Caritas, *Vermeidung von Ersatzfreiheitsstrafen bei Bagatelldelikten (Schwarzfahren u.a.)*, p. 2; Mosbacher, 'Sitzen fürs Schwarzfahren. Gerechte Strafe für strafwürdiges Unrecht oder kontraproduktiver Freiheitsentzug für Bagatellen?', 1069.

[81] *Supra* note 72, p. 286.

[82] *Supra* note 15.

[83] *Supra* note 53, pp. 268–70.

[84] *Ibid.*, p. 324.

[85] Aebi, Tiago and Burkhardt, *Council of Europe Annual Penal Statistics: SPACE I – Prison Populations: Survey 2015*, p. 73.

emerges. The Netherlands, for example, display a ratio of 1.2 per cent default prisoners while Germany with 0.8 per cent is well below.

6.4.3 *Day Fines and Recidivism*

Despite its massive use, day fines did not attract much research in Germany with respect to recidivism and comparative effectiveness. Also, internationally, evaluation research including day fines does not exist. A meta-analysis of research studying the effects of custodial versus non-custodial sanctions on reoffending covering the period between 1961 and 2013 found but one study including fines[86] and, therefore, does not provide for a basis of assessing the comparative effectiveness of fines versus prison sentences.

Data in Figure 6.4 show recidivism rates in Germany for adult offenders convicted and sentenced to day fines, suspended and unsuspended terms of imprisonment in 1994, 2004 and 2007. Data have been retrieved from the Federal Register of Criminal Convictions ('Bundeszentralregister').

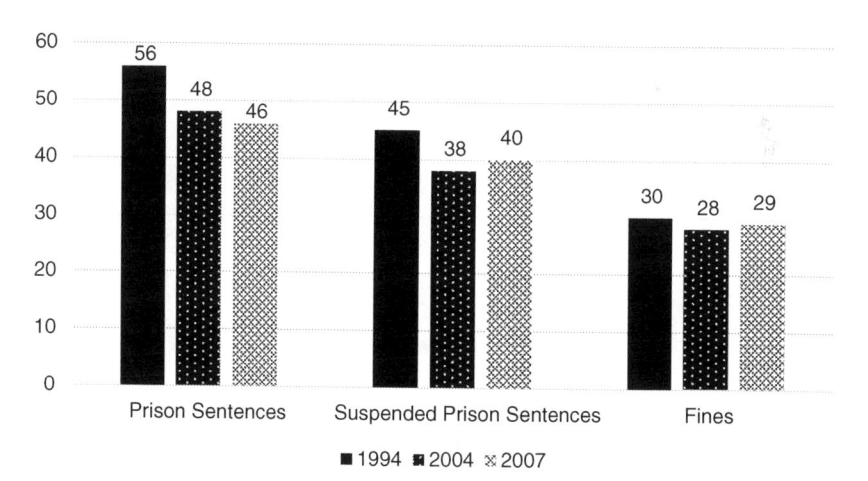

FIGURE 6.4 Reconviction rates after fines, suspended prison sentences and imprisonment
Sources: *Jehle, Heinz and Sutterer (2003)*, Legalbewährung nach strafrechtlichen Sanktionen; *Jehle, Albrecht, Hohmann-Fricke and Tetal (2010)*, Legalbewährung nach strafrechtlichen Sanktionen; *Jehle, Albrecht, Hohmann-Fricke and Tetal (2016)*, Legalbewährung nach strafrechtlichen Sanktionen.

---

[86] Villettaz, Gillieron and Killias, *The Effects on Re-offending of Custodial vs. Non-custodial Sanctions: An Updated Systematic Review of the State of Knowledge.*

Differences in recidivism rates after day fines and prison sentences are significant, but reflect of course a selection carried out by courts on the basis of sentencing rules which consider besides seriousness of the criminal offence prior records and various other circumstances impacting on recidivism.

In Germany, research has shown that recidivism rates of offenders sentenced to fines and short imprisonment before and after the reform of 1969 (giving priority to fines) did not change.[87] Another study on recidivism after fines, suspended prison sentences and imprisonment found that controlling for prior record, gender, age, family status, offence (and other variables likely to be correlated with reoffending) differences in recidivism rates were reduced significantly. The results were interpreted as demonstrating that fines, suspended prison sentences and imprisonment (within variations allowed by law and jurisprudence of the Federal Court of Justice) are interchangeable with respect to prevention of recidivism.[88] However, it was also shown that most of the serious reoffending after fines was concentrated within a (small) group of offenders who ultimately served substitute imprisonment. Approximately 80 per cent of fined offenders who were sentenced to immediate imprisonment in case of recidivism (within a period of five years) were fine defaulters.[89] German sentencing practices evidently result in imposing day fines also in cases where reoffending risks are high but offence seriousness does not call for prison sentences.

Summarising research on recidivism after day fines (and significant changes in sentencing practices), it may be concluded that the German (day fine) experiment did not affect patterns of reoffending and, furthermore, did not impact on crime rates. The latter is also evident when looking at the course of crime rates during the last decades which show for Germany (from the late 1990s on and comparable to the crime decline in many industrial countries) a significant decrease in police recorded property and violent crime.[90]

6.5 PUBLIC OPINION AND DAY FINES

In the drafting period of the Comprehensive Law Reform of 1969/1975 there was only little opposition voiced by politicians, criminal justice professionals

---

[87] Kiwull, *Kurzfristige Freiheitsstrafen und Geldstrafen vor und nach der Strafrechtsreform*, pp. 80–1.

[88] *Supra* note 15, Albrecht, p. 227; see also Hohmann-Fricke, *Strafwirkungen und Rückfall. Lässt sich mit Hilfe prozesserzeugter Daten der Strafrechtspflege der spezialpräventive Anspruch des Strafrechts prüfen?*, p. 157 finding that variation in criminal sentences for theft (fines versus prison sentences) does not add to explanation of variance in reoffending after controlling for prior record, age and gender).

[89] *Supra* note 15, Albrecht, p. 238.

[90] Albrecht, 'Der Rückgang der Jugendkriminalität setzt sich fort'.

TABLE 6.4 *The German public's penalty preferences for burglary 1989/2005 and sentences for burglary 2005*

	1989 %	2005 %	Sentences imposed for burglary Germany 2005 %
Fine	8.8	11.3	19.3
Imprisonment	13.0	19.8	32.4
Suspended prison Sentence	12.3	13.3	48.3
Community service	60.0	50.5	not available
Other sentence	1.8	3.1	not available
Don't know	4.0	2.0	
Total	5,274	2,025	9,004 (convictions and sentences for burglary)

Survey Question: 'People have different ideas about the sentences which should be given to offenders. Take for instance the case of a 21 years old man who is found guilty of burglary for the second time. This time he's taken a TV. Which of the following sentences do you ... '.
The 1989 and 2005 surveys had different sample sizes; the 1989 survey was restricted to West Germany.
Sources: SPSS Files International (European) Crime Survey 1989, 2005; Statistisches Bundesamt. Strafverfolgung 2005, p. 144.

and lawyers with respect to widening the scope of fines and reducing short prison sentences. The move towards the fine and away from the prison was also supported by criminal law doctrine embracing rehabilitation and special prevention while sidelining repression and general deterrence.[91] Public opinion surveys in these years did not specifically target attitudes towards fines or day fines. However, a survey carried out in 1966 shows that reform of criminal law was among issues the German public was least interested in.[92]

Germany participated in the 1989 and 2005 waves of the International Crime Survey.[93] The ICS 1989 and 2005 included items on sentencing preferences in a burglary case. The data in Table 6.4 reveal (although the waves of 1989 and 2005 cannot be strictly compared because they are different in terms of sample sizes and the region covered and a recidivist male burglar stealing a television set may not represent the average burglary case brought to a criminal court) that

[91] Roxin, 'Franz v. Lisztvon Liszt und die kriminalpolitische Konzeption des Alternativentwurfs'.
[92] Noelle and Neumann, *Jahrbuch der Öffentlichen Meinung 1965–1967*, p. 153.
[93] *Criminal Victimisation in International Perspective. Key findings from the 2004-2005 ICVS and EU ICS.*

(1) the German public would impose a prison sentence at a much lower rate as do in fact German courts (33.1 versus 80.7 per cent);

(2) preference for a fine is voiced by circa 11 per cent of the respondents while fines are imposed in 19 per cent of burglary cases by courts;

(3) both waves show clear preference of the public for a community service sentence.

The most recent German crime survey[94] studied also sentencing preferences for different criminal cases (presented to interviewees with various sentencing options). Of course, cases presented to interviewees cannot be strictly compared to offence categories in the Criminal Court Statistics. However, some conclusions can be drawn from contrasting responses of interviewees and statistics on conviction and sentencing. The offence categories in the German Crime Survey 2017 concern fraud, theft, burglary, assault, malicious damage and robbery. The penalty options were: fine, suspended or immediate imprisonment and compliance with a condition (community service, reparation, victim-offender mediation).

With one exception fines do play lesser roles in public attitudes towards penalties compared to (real) sentences imposed in 2017. With respect to burglary, however, the public would impose a fine at a rate which comes close to the rate of day fines imposed for burglary by German courts in 2017. But, the public would sentence a burglar – and that underlines the ICVS data – at a significantly lower rate to imprisonment (50 versus 75 per cent) compared to actual sentencing outcomes in German criminal courts.

Differences are then especially marked when comparing sentences and sentence preferences for robbery. While 24 per cent of the public see a fine as appropriate punishment, in 2017 only in 2 per cent of robbery cases a day fine was meted out by criminal courts. Less than half of the respondents opt for a prison sentence while court statistics say that a prison sentence is the rule for robbery. In fraud, theft and malicious damage cases rates of prison sentences are comparable when contrasting survey data and 2017 court statistics. However, the public evidently is divided when it comes to the choice of a fine or conditions (community service, reparation etc. which are not available as sentencing options for courts). Finally, only assault cases trigger a more punitive answer (measured by the rate of prison sentences) among the public compared to actual sentencing outcomes.

---

[94] Birkel, Church, Hummelsheim-Doss, Leitgöb-Guzy and Oberwittler, *Der Deutsche Viktimisierungssurvey 2017. Opfererfahrungen, kriminalitätsbezogene Einstellungen sowie die Wahrnehmung von Unsicherheit und Kriminalität in Deutschland.*

TABLE 6.5 *Penalty preferences and sentences imposed for selected offence categories 2017*

	Survey penalty preferences 2017			Sentences imposed Germany 2017	
	Fine (%)	Compliance with conditions * (%)	Prison sentence (%)	Fine (%)	Prison sentence (%)
Fraud	45	37	11	91	9
Theft	42	42	14	86	14
Assault	22	34	42	82	18
Malicious Damage	46	47	5	94	6
Robbery	24	29	46	2	98
Burglary	23	25	50	26	74

* Community Service, Reparation, Victim-Offender-Mediation
Sources: Birkel, Church, Hummelsheim-Doss, Leitgöb-Guzy and Oberwittler, Der Deutsche Viktimisierungssurvey 2017, p. 97; Statistisches Bundesamt, Strafverfolgungsstatistik 2017.

On the basis of these surveys it may be concluded that the public not only is in line with a criminal policy which sought to reduce imprisonment, but, for selected offence categories endorses the widening of non-custodial sanctions. However, it is also evident that the public, while voicing support for non-custodial sanctions, is rather in favour of responses which request a restoration from offenders (in the form of community service or reparation) instead of simply transferring money to the state.

6.6 CHALLENGES

A particular challenge the German day fine system is facing is certainly default imprisonment. Default imprisonment has plagued the German criminal justice system (and policy-makers) not least because default imprisonment is short imprisonment which thus might rise again through the backdoor.[95] Default imprisonment therefore is used (a) as an indicator of success and failure of anti-short-term imprisonment policy (and the legacy of Franz von Liszt) and (b) as an indicator of how just the day fine system ultimately is.

Moreover, the question of cost-effectiveness is raised as the cost of default imprisonment outweighs by far the amount of day fines and places a heavy burden on the criminal justice administration.[96] The question of how to

[95] *Supra* note 59, Wissenschaftliche Dienste.
[96] *Supra* note 80, Caritas; *supra* note 80, Mosbacher.

reduce default imprisonment and whether to abolish default imprisonment completely has been discussed since the Comprehensive Criminal Law Reform 1969/1975 was designed and implemented.[97]

From the 1980s on, the focus was on offering community service as an alternative to default imprisonment and following a strongly proactive approach in order to compensate for social deficits of fine defaulters. More recently, the perspective of abolishing default imprisonment was presented in a draft law in Federal Parliament by the faction of 'Die Linke'.[98] Default imprisonment should be replaced completely by community service with three hours community service corresponding to one day fine unit. In case a fine cannot be collected, community service would automatically replace a day fine under the condition that the offender agrees with community service.[99] The drafters substantiated the call for abolishing default imprisonment by arguing that fine defaulters suffered from discrimination as the cause of default was in most cases poverty, unemployment, drug dependence and other disadvantages exposing them unfairly to the risk of imprisonment. Moreover, conclusions were drawn from comparative legal analysis which in fact shows that default imprisonment in some European countries is placed under more restrictions than in Germany.[100] However, the draft did not consider the rather restrictive use of day fines in these countries nor did the draft offer solutions if fine defaulters do not agree with community service or do not or not completely serve community service hours replacing the day fine. Ultimately, the draft law would have resulted in abolishing not only default imprisonment but also fine collection altogether in the group of fine defaulters and would have restricted community service to those who chose that option voluntarily. The draft law, however, did not find support in a hearing held by the Judicial Committee of the Federal Parliament.[101] Opinions voiced by various experts came to the (evident and simple) conclusion that abolishing default imprisonment would result in exempting those who chose not to do community service from criminal punishment.

Relief is then sought through strategies of decriminalisation and depenalisation.[102] Fine default and default imprisonment have triggered (again) a debate on decriminalising petty offences, in particular fare dodging

---

[97] *Supra* note 1.
[98] Gesetzentwurf der Fraktion Die Linke, *Entwurf eines Gesetzes zur Änderung des Strafgesetzbuchs und weiterer Gesetze – Aufhebung der Ersatzfreiheitsstrafe.*
[99] *Ibid.*, p. 3.
[100] *Supra* note 59, Wissenschaftliche Dienste.
[101] www.bundestag.de/presse/hib/633506-633506.
[102] Lorenz and Sebastian, 'Drei Überlegungen zur Entkriminalisierung des Schwarzfahrens'.

(paragraph 265(a) CC), which account for a significant share of default imprisonment.[103] While there is evidently also political support for downgrading fare dodging to an administrative offence or treating non-payment of fare completely as a civil law issue,[104] other petty offences (possession of small amounts of drugs, simple theft, trespassing) would then still attract criminal penalties (including day fines) and generate default imprisonment.

Another avenue is taken with calling for another method to calculate the size of a day fine unit (outlined above). Of course, deducting what is necessary to retain a subsistence level would result for marginalised offenders in the lowest day fine possible (one euro). In combination with proactive strategies of implementing payment accommodations and community service, this approach could in fact lead to better adjustment of day fines to financial capacities of offenders and subsequently to reductions in rates of default imprisonment.

Finally, a certain potential of reducing duration and impact of default imprisonment has been created by prison laws (of states, 'Bundesländer') through providing for the opportunity to work off the day fine in the prison or by admitting default prisoners immediately to open forms of imprisonment.[105]

REFERENCES

Aebi, M. F., Tiago, M. M. and Burkhardt, C. 2016. *Council of Europe Annual Penal Statistics: SPACE I – Prison Populations: Survey 2015*. Strasbourg: Council of Europe.

Aebi, M. F. *et al.* 2017. *European Sourcebook of Crime and Criminal Justice Statistics 2014*. Helsinki: HEUNI.

Albrecht, H.-J. 1980. *Strafzumessung und Vollstreckung bei Geldstrafen*. Berlin: Duncker & Humblot.

Albrecht, H.-J. 1982. *Legalbewährung bei zu Geldstrafe und Freiheitsstrafe Verurteilten*. Freiburg: Max-Planck-Institut für Ausländisches und Internationales Strafrecht.

Albrecht, H.-J. 2001. *Simplification of Criminal Procedure: Settlements out of Court – A Comparative Study of European Criminal Justice Systems*. Pretoria: South African Law Commission.

Albrecht, H.-J. 2012. 'Die Geldstrafe in Ländern der Europäischen Union – Normative Strukturen und praktische Anwendung', in Hilgendorf, E. and Rengier, R. (eds.), *Festschrift für Wolfgang Heinz zum 70. Geburtstag*. Baden-Baden: Nomos, pp. 565–79.

---

[103] *Supra* note 15, Janssen, p. 214.
[104] *Supra* note 80, Mosbacher.
[105] Treig and Pruin, 'Kurze Freiheitsstrafen und Ersatzfreiheitsstrafen als Herausforderung an den Strafvollzug – Möglichkeiten und Grenzen', pp. 336–7.

Albrecht, H.-J. 2013. 'Sentencing in Germany: Explaining Long-Term Stability in the Structure of Criminal Sanctions and Sentencing', *Law and Contemporary Problems* 76: 211–36.

Albrecht, H.-J. 2016. 'Der Rückgang der Jugendkriminalität setzt sich fort', *Recht der Jugend und des Bildungswesens* 64: 395–413.

Albrecht, H.-J. 2017. 'Para. 40. Verhängung in Tagessätzen', in Kindhäuser, U., Neumann, U. and Paeffgen, H.-U. (eds.), *Strafgesetzbuch*. Baden-Baden: Nomos, pp. 854–876.

Arendt, M. 2012. *Quo vadis, Geldstrafe? Möglichkeiten und Grenzen einer ambulanten Sanktion*. Frankfurt: Peter Lang Verlag.

Baumann, J. 1969. *Alternativentwurf eines Strafgesetzbuches. Allgemeiner Teil*. Tübingen: Mohr.

Bayerischer Landtag 2018. *Schriftliche Anfrage. Ersatzfreiheitsstrafe in bayerischen Justizvollzugsanstalten*. 10.09.2018, Drucksache 17/22054.

Becker, H. S. 1973. *Outsiders: Studies in the Sociology of Deviance*. New York: The Free Press.

Besozzi, C. and Kunz, K.-L. 2012. 'Kurze Freiheitsstrafen und ihr Ersatz. Eine Revision der Revision?', in Hilgendorf, E. and Rengier, R. (eds.), *Festschrift für Wolfgang Heinz zum 70. Geburtstag*. Baden-Baden: Nomos, pp. 580–93.

Birkel, C., Church, D., Hummelsheim-Doss, D., Leitgöb-Guzy, N. and Oberwittler, D. 2019. *Der Deutsche Viktimisierungssurvey 2017. Opfererfahrungen, kriminalitätsbezogene Einstellungen sowie die Wahrnehmung von Unsicherheit und Kriminalität in Deutschland*. Wiesbaden: Bundeskriminalamt.

Bögelein, N. 2018. 'Money Rules: Exploring Offenders' Perceptions of the Fine as Punishment', *The British Journal of Criminology* 58: 805–23.

Bögelein, N., Ernst, A. and Neubacher, F. 2014a. *Vermeidung von Ersatzfreiheitsstrafen. Evaluierung justizieller Haftvermeidungsprojekte in Nordrhein-Westfalen*. Baden-Baden: Nomos.

Bögelein, N., Ernst, A. and Neubacher, F. 2014b. 'Wie kann die Vermeidung von Ersatzfreiheitsstrafen gelingen? Zur Lebenssituation der Verurteilten und zur Zusammenarbeit staatlicher und nichtstaatlicher Organisationen', *Bewährungshilfe* 61: 282–94.

Böhm, A. 1998. 'Gemeinnützige Arbeit als Strafe: Zu einer Gesetzgebungsinitiative des Bundesrates', *Zeitschrift für Rechtspolitik* 31: 360–5.

Brandis, P. 1987. *Geldstrafe und Nettoeinkommen*. Köln: O. Schmidt.

Brinkmann, U., Dörre, K. and Röbenack, S. 2006. *Prekäre Arbeit. Ursachen, Ausmaß, soziale Folgen und subjektive Verarbeitungsformen unsicherer Beschäftigungsverhältnisse*. Bonn: Friedrich-Ebert-Stiftung.

Caritas 2018. *Vermeidung von Ersatzfreiheitsstrafen bei Bagatelldelikten (Schwarzfahren u.a.)*. Freiburg: Caritas.

Deutscher Bundestag 2009. *Gesetzentwurf der Bundesregierung. Entwurf eines …* Gesetzes zur Änderung des Strafgesetzbuches – Anhebung der Höchstgrenze des Tagessatzes bei Geldstrafen. Drucksache 16/11606, 16. Wahlperiode 15.01.2009.

Dolde, G. 1999. 'Zum Vollzug von Ersatzfreiheitsstrafen. Eindrücke aus einer empirischen Erhebung', in Feuerhelm, W., Schwind, H.-D. and Bock, M. (eds.), *Festschrift für Alexander Böhm zum 70. Geburtstag*. Berlin, New York: De Gruyter, pp. 581–96.

Exner, F. 1931. *Studien über die Strafzumessungspraxis der deutschen Gerichte*. Leipzig: Wiegandt.

Fink, D., Jehle, J. and Pilgram, A. 2015. 'Strafrechtliche Sanktionen im internationalen Vergleich Deutschland – Österreich – Schweiz',*Journal für Strafrecht* 2: 81–94.

Fischer, T. 2016. *Strafgesetzbuch. Kommentar*. München: Beck.

Gesetzentwurf der Fraktion Die Linke 2018. *Entwurf eines Gesetzes zur Änderung des Strafgesetzbuchs und weiterer Gesetze – Aufhebung der Ersatzfreiheitsstrafe*. Deutscher Bundestag Drucksache 19/1689, 19. Wahlperiode, 18.04.2018.

Goldschmidt, J. 1902. *Das Verwaltungsstrafrecht*. Berlin: Heymanns.

Grebing, G. 1978. 'Die Geldstrafe im deutschen Recht nach Einführung des Tagessatzsystems', in Jescheck, H.-H. and Grebing, G. (eds.), *Die Geldstrafe im deutschen und ausländischen Recht*. Baden-Baden: Nomos, pp.13–164.

Hessisches Statistisches Landesamt 2018. *Der Strafvollzug in Hessen im Jahr 2017. Teil 2: Bestand und Bewegung in den Justizvollzugsanstalten*. Wiesbaden: Statistisches Landesamt.

Hohmann-Fricke, S. 2014. *Strafwirkungen und Rückfall. Lässt sich mit Hilfe prozesserzeugter Daten der Strafrechtspflege der spezialpräventive Anspruch des Strafrechts prüfen?* Universität Göttingen.

International (European) Crime Survey 1989, 2005, SPSS Files 1989, 2005, p. 144.

Janssen, H. 1994. *Die Praxis der Geldstrafenvollstreckung*. Frankfurt: Peter Lang Verlag.

Jehle, J.-M., Albrecht, H.-J., Hohmann-Fricke, S. and Tetal, C. 2010. *Legalbewährung nach strafrechtlichen Sanktionen. Eine bundesweite Rückfalluntersuchung 2004 bis 2007*. Mönchengladbach: Forum Verlag.

Jehle, J.-M., Albrecht, H.-J., Hohmann-Fricke, S. and Tetal, C. 2016. *Legalbewährung nach strafrechtlichen Sanktionen. Eine bundesweite Rückfalluntersuchung 2010 bis 2013 und 2004 bis 2013*. Mönchengladbach: Forum Verlag.

Jehle, J.-M., Feuerhelm, W. and Block, P. 1990. *Gemeinnützige Arbeit statt Ersatzfreiheitsstrafe*. Wiesbaden: Kriminologische Zentralstelle.

Jehle, J.-M., Heinz, W. and Sutterer, P. 2003. *Legalbewährung nach strafrechtlichen Sanktionen. Eine kommentierte Rückfallstatistik*. Berlin: Bundesministerium der Justiz.

Kaiser, G. 1970. *Verkehrsdelinquenz und Generalprävention*. Tübingen: Mohr.

Kantorowicz-Reznichenko, E. 2015. 'Day-Fines: Should the Rich Pay More?', *Review of Law & Economics* 11: 481–501.

Killias, M. 2011. 'Korrektur einer verunglückten Gesetzgebung: Zur erneuten Revision des AT-StGB', *Zeitschrift für Schweizerisches Recht* 130: 627–40.

Kinzig, J. 2019. 'Para. 40. Verhängung in Tagessätzen', in Schönke, A. and Schröder, H. (eds.), *Strafgesetzbuch. Kommentar*. München: Beck, pp. 749–60.

Kiwull, H. 1979. *Kurzfristige Freiheitsstrafen und Geldstrafen vor und nach der Strafrechtsreform*. Universität Freiburg.

Köhne, M. 2004. 'Abschaffung der Ersatzfreiheitsstrafe?', *Juristische Rundschau* 79: 453–6.

Kolla, P. 2004. 'The Mannesmann Trial and the Role of the Courts', *German Law Journal* 5: 829–47.

Kommission zur Reform des strafrechtlichen Sanktionensystems 2000. *Abschlussbericht*. Berlin: Bundesministerium der Justiz.

Landtag Mecklenburg-Vorpommern 2018. '*Kleine Anfrage. Ersatzfreiheitsstrafen*' *in Mecklenburg-Vorpommern 2017*. 25.10.2018, Drucksache 7/2696.

Lorenz H. and Sebastian, S. 2017. 'Drei Überlegungen zur Entkriminalisierung des Schwarzfahrens', *Kriminalpolitische Zeitschrift* 2: 352–7.

Ministerium der Justiz Nordrhein-Westfalen 2019. *Maßnahmen zur Vermeidung von Ersatzfreiheitsstrafen*. Düsseldorf: Landtag.

Mosbacher, A. 2018. 'Sitzen fürs Schwarzfahren. Gerechte Strafe für strafwürdiges Unrecht oder kontraproduktiver Freiheitsentzug für Bagatellen?', *Neue Juristische Wochenschrift* 71: 1069–72.

Noelle, E. and Neumann, E. P. 1967. *Jahrbuch der Öffentlichen Meinung 1965 – 1967*. Allensbach, Bonn: Verlag für Demoskopie.

Peters, J. 2000. *Die Entwicklung von Sanktionspraxis und Strafrechtsreform 1871 bis 1933*. Aachen: Shaker Verlag.

Rademacher, M. and Gerhardt, F. 2006. 'Reduzierung der Tagessatzhöhe als Verteidigungsziel', *Zeitschrift für die Anwaltspraxis* 18: 427–32.

Roxin, C. 1969. 'Franz von Liszt und die kriminalpolitische Konzeption des Alternativentwurfs', *Zeitschrift für die Gesamte Strafrechtswissenschaft* 81: 613–49.

Schur, E. 1973. *Radical Non-Intervention – Rethinking the Delinquency Problem*. Englewood Cliffs: Prentice-Hall.

Seebode, M. 1999. 'Problematische Ersatzfreiheitsstrafe', in Feuerhelm, W., Schwind, H.-D. and Bock, M. (eds.), *Festschrift für Alexander Böhm zum 70. Geburtstag*. Berlin, New York: De Gruyter, pp. 519–52.

Statistisches Bundesamt 1961–2018. *Strafverfolgung*. Wiesbaden: Statistisches Bundesamt.

Statistisches Bundesamt 2003–18. *Strafverfolgungsstatistik 2002–2017*. Wiesbaden: Statistisches Bundesamt.

Statistisches Bundesamt 2005–18. *Staatsanwaltschaftsstatistik 2004–2017*. Wiesbaden: Statistisches Bundesamt.

Statistisches Bundesamt 2005–18. *Strafvollzug 2004–2017*. Wiesbaden: Statistisches Bundesamt.

Statistisches Bundesamt 2006. *Strafverfolgung 2005*. Wiesbaden: Statistisches Bundesamt.

Statistisches Bundesamt 2018. *Bestand der Gefangenen und Verwahrten in den deutschen Justizvollzugsanstalten 2017*. Wiesbaden: Statistisches Bundesamt.

Statistisches Bundesamt 2018. *Rechtspflege. Staatsanwaltschaften*. Wiesbaden: Statistisches Bundesamt.

Statistisches Bundesamt 2018. *Strafverfolgung 2017*. Wiesbaden: Statistisches Bundesamt.

Statistisches Bundesamt 2018. *Strafverfolgungsstatistik 2017*. Wiesbaden: Statistisches Bundesamt.

Streng, F. 2018. 'Para. 47. Kurze Freiheitsstrafe nur in Ausnahmefällen', in Kindhäuser, U., Neumann, U. and Paeffgen, H.-U. (eds.), *Strafgesetzbuch. Band 1*, Baden-Baden: Nomos, pp. 2048–55.

Tonry, M. and Lynch, M. 1996. 'Intermediate Sanctions', *Crime and Justice* 99: 99–144.

Trapp, E. 2003. *Rechtswirklichkeit von Auflagen und Weisungen bei Strafaussetzung zur Bewährung*. Tübingen: Institut für Kriminologie.

Treig, J. and Pruin, I. 2018. 'Kurze Freiheitsstrafen und Ersatzfreiheitsstrafen als Herausforderung an den Strafvollzug – Möglichkeiten und Grenzen', in Maelicke, B. and Suhling, S. (eds.), *Das Gefängnis auf dem Prüfstand. Zustand und Zukunft des Strafvollzugs.* Wiesbaden: Springer, pp.313–49.

Van Dijk, J., van Kesteren, J. and Smit, P. 2007. *Criminal Victimisation in International Perspective. Key findings from the 2004–2005 ICVS and EU ICS.* Meppel: Boom Juridische uitgevers.

Villettaz, P., Gillieron, G. and Killias, M. 2015. *The Effects on Re-offending of Custodial vs. Non-custodial Sanctions: An Updated Systematic Review of the State of Knowledge.* Oslo: The Campbell Cooperation.

Villmow, B. 2016. *Geldstrafen – Gemeinnützige Arbeit – Ersatzfreiheitsstrafen. Aktuelle Probleme und Reformbedarf.* www.sbh-berlin.de/wp-content/uploads/2017/10/201710 16Villmow_Vortrag_Folien.pdf.

Von Liszt, F. 1883. 'Der Zweckgedanke im Strafrecht', *Zeitschrift für die Gesamte Strafrechtswissenschaft* 3: 1–47.

Von Liszt, F. 1905. 'Die Kriminalität der Jugendlichen', in Von Liszt, F. (ed.), *Strafrechtliche Aufsätze und Vorträge.* Berlin: Guttentag, pp. 331–55.

Wilde, F. 2015. 'Die Geldstrafe – ein unsoziales Rechtsinstitut?', *Monatsschrift für Kriminologie und Strafrechtsreform* 98: 348–64.

Wilde, F. 2017. 'Wenn Armut zur Strafe wird. Die freie, gemeinnützige Arbeit in der aktuellen Sanktionspraxis', *Neue Kriminalpolitik* 29: 205–19.

Wissenschaftliche Dienste 2018. *Ersatzfreiheitsstrafe gemäß para. 43 StGB. Rechtsvergleich, Verfassungskonformität und Alternativen.* Berlin: Bundestag.

7

Day Fines in Austria

Christopher Kahl and Verena Weinberger

7.1 HISTORICAL DEVELOPMENT OF DAY FINES IN AUSTRIA

The system of day fines (*Tagessatzsystem*) was introduced into Austrian criminal law in 1975 with the creation of the new Criminal Code (*Strafgesetzbuch* – StGB). Before that, the Austrian system of criminal law (*Strafgesetz 1852* – *StG*) only provided for a system of fixed fines (e.g. trading with gunpowder was fined up to 25,000 *Schilling* – paragraph 445 StG). The court imposed a fine within the range laid down in the specific provision of the offence. The actual amount of the fine imposed was based on the severity of the offence and the guilt of the offender as well as his economic background (paragraph 241 StG). Since the economic background was only one of several factors determining the fine, it was not transparent why similar offences led to different sanctions. This resulted in a public perception of unequal treatment.[1] To counteract this kind of perception, courts imposed fines mainly based on the severity of the offence. Subsequently, poor offenders were disadvantaged compared to the wealthier ones.[2]

Combating this social inequality was one of the main reasons for the introduction of a day fine system in the Austrian Criminal Code.[3] One major aim of the reform of criminal law was the reduction of short-term imprisonment sentences because of their stigmatising effects without the preventive benefits of medium- to long-term imprisonment. Due to the possibility to adjust the fine to the individual economic background, the day fine system was regarded as an appropriate instrument to achieve this goal by imposing adequate fines.[4] Furthermore, the scope of fines was significantly

---

[1] Platzgummer, § 19 StGB, para. 5.
[2] Salimi, § 19 StGB, para. 7.
[3] ErläutRV (explanatory notes on the governmental draft) 30 BlgNR 13. GP, p. 93.
[4] *Ibid.*, p. 94.

broadened. Offences that were traditionally only punishable by imprisonment like petty cases of theft or fraud were opened up for monetary fining. Last but not least, the legislative materials highlighted further advantages of the introduction of the day fine system, like transparency of judgments, increased effectiveness of deterring crimes and easier access to legal remedies.[5] When introducing the day fine system, the Austrian legislator followed the Scandinavian system of day fines which provides a separate determination of the number of daily units and the amount of the daily unit.

7.2 THE STRUCTURE OF THE FINE

A fine under the system of the Austrian Criminal Code consists of two factors: the number of daily units and the amount of the daily unit. While the number of daily units is determined by the severity of the offence and the guilt of the offender, the amount of the daily unit depends on the personal circumstances and the financial capacity of the person. The total amount of the fine is calculated by multiplying these two factors. Since these fines are criminal penalties, their imposition is the task of only the criminal courts. The verdict must explicitly state the number of daily units and the amount of the daily unit imposed. It is not sufficient to simply refer to the result of the multiplication of these two factors, as this would not transparently illustrate the severity of the offence and the guilt of the offender.[6] The competent authority to collect a fine in Austria is an administrative officer under the direction of the President of the Higher Regional Court of Appeal of Vienna.

7.2.1 *The Number of Daily Units*

As a first step the court has to decide on the number of daily units. The minimum number is two daily units (paragraph 19(1) StGB), the court cannot go below this absolute threshold.[7] The maximum number of daily units depends on the offence committed and is provided for each offence separately. In most cases the maximum is 360 daily units (e.g. gross negligent assault, criminal defamation, theft and fraud), while more serious offences allow the imposition of 720 daily units (e.g. assault, counterfeiting legal documents and coercion). Only few alterations exist for minor offences, where the fine must not exceed 60 (e.g. appropriation) or 180 daily units (e.g. negligent assault,

[5] *Ibid.*
[6] *Supra* note 2, para. 10.
[7] *Ibid.*, para. 23.

certain offences against property committed within a family). In certain cases – like reoffending (paragraph 39(1) StGB) or offences committed by abusing an official position (paragraph 313 StGB) – these thresholds may be exceeded by up to 50 per cent.

There are no offences in the Criminal Code that are only punishable by fines. Whenever the Criminal Code stipulates fines, it also provides for the alternative possibility of imprisonment instead. With the amendment of the Criminal Code in 2016, the legislator established a correlation between the maximum length of imprisonment and the maximum number of daily units, as every day of threat of imprisonment corresponds to two daily units of fine.[8] Therefore, if an offence is punishable by up to six months of imprisonment, the Criminal Code alternatively provides the option of a fine up to 360 daily units. Accordingly, the threat of up to 720 daily units is alternatively combined with the threat of up to one year imprisonment. If the threat of imprisonment exceeds one year, no fines are alternatively foreseen. This correlation between imprisonment and fines only exits in the Criminal Code but not in criminal provisions in other legal acts. In these legal provisions outside of the Criminal Code, there are also criminal offences that are only punishable by fines (e.g. paragraph 57 (3) Wine Act).

The process of determining the actual number of daily units is equivalent to deciding on the length of imprisonment. The relevant factors are the severity of the criminal offence and the guilt of the offender.[9] Personal circumstances and the financial capacity of the delinquent are irrelevant. It is in the court's own discretion to decide on the number of daily units, as long as the sentence is equivalent to the culpability of the offender (paragraph 32 StGB – *Strafzumessungsschuld*). When sentencing the offender, the court has to take into account the aggravating and mitigating factors provided in paragraphs 33 *et seq* StGB. Those factors are only of a general nature. An exact conversion ratio for increasing or decreasing a sentence is not foreseen. It remains disputed whether considerations regarding the deterrence of the offender or other people from committing further criminal offences can influence the actual penalty imposed on the offender.[10]

Neither the Criminal Code itself nor other legal acts or documents contain official sentencing guidelines.[11] In practice the courts tend to start at the level of one third of the penalty foreseen by law and adjust this by taking aggravating

---

[8]   ErläutRV 689 BlgNR 25. GP 11.
[9]   *Supra* note 3, pp. 93 *et seq.*
[10] Medigovic, Reindl-Krauskopf and Luef-Kölbl, *Strafrecht Allgemeiner Teil II*, p. 67; Ebner, § 32 StGB, paras. 23 *et seq.*
[11] Austrian Supreme Court of Justice 19.06.2018, 11 Os 34/18m.

and mitigating factors into account.[12] However, this is an informal practice merely for imprisonment sentence and not a legal guideline in any way.

7.2.2 *The Amount of the Daily Unit*

In determining the amount of the daily unit, consideration must be given to the personal circumstances and the financial capacity of the offender at the time of the first instance conviction. The severity of the offence and the guilt of the offender must not be taken into account for the calculation of the amount of the daily unit, as they are already used for determining the number of daily units. The amount of the daily unit is to be set at a minimum of 4 euros and a maximum of 5,000 euros.

The idea behind the Austrian day fine system is to reduce the income of the offender to a level barely above the subsistence minimum for a period that is equivalent to the number of daily units. This is supposed to significantly lower the offender's standard of living for the number of daily units.[13] The scope of wealth, which can be taken into account for determining the amount of the daily unit, only includes the personal income. Since the Austrian day fine is not confiscatory in nature, personal assets must not be seized.[14]

7.2.2.1 The Notion of Income in Austrian Criminal Law

The starting point for calculating the amount of the daily unit is the net income of the offender, regardless of its legal or fiscal nature.[15] It may be the income from employment or self-employment, alimony payments, tips, non-cash benefits (e.g. company car), unemployment payment and other welfare benefits (e.g. social aid)[16] and pensions.[17] If assets generate profits, those are seen as income as well.[18] Hence, income from immovable property (e.g. rent), dividends and interest are considered income as well.

In case of a lack of income, the court has to determine a potential income for the offender. It has to be assessed how much the offender could potentially

---

[12] Grafl and Schmoller, *Entsprechen die gesetzlichen Strafdrohungen und die von den Gerichten verhängten Strafen den aktuellen gesellschaftlichen Wertungen? Gutachten zum 19. Österreichischen Juristentag*, p. 159; dissenting Austrian Supreme Court of Justice 19.06.2018, 11 Os 34/18m.

[13] Lässig, § 19 StGB, para. 8; Austrian Supreme Court of Justice 13 Os 65/75, SSt 46/32.

[14] *Supra* note 10, Medigovic, Reindl-Krauskopf and Luef-Kölbl, p. 41.

[15] *Supra* note 3, p. 96.

[16] In 2019 the level of social aid was 885 euros for single persons without children.

[17] *Supra* note 10, Medigovic, Reindl-Krauskopf and Luef-Kölbl, p. 40; *supra* note 2, para. 32.

[18] *Supra* note 2, paras. 33, 40 *et seq.*

earn using his skills, knowledge and resources to the maximum extent, without risking his health or breaking the law (*Anspannungsgrundsatz*).[19] Realising this potential income must actually be possible considering the situation on the job market. Furthermore, it must be reasonable to achieve. This principle also applies, if the offender could reasonably increase his income, for example by working more or generating profits by the use of assets.[20] This is why the possibility to rent out a vacant flat or work full-time instead of part-time may increase the income of the offender. In contrast, it may not be reasonable for a single parent to seek employment, if that risks the well-being of the child.[21] In cases where even by applying the *Anspannungsgrundsatz* no potential income can be assessed, the court sets the amount of the daily unit at the minimum of four euros.[22] Even if the offender has no means to pay the fine it is not possible to impose a daily unit of less than four euros.

7.2.2.2 The Calculation of the Amount of the Daily Unit

In a next step, the actual amount of the daily unit is calculated by reducing the total amount of income (actual or potential) by the subsistence minimum. The relevant amount to calculate is the annual income. Therefore, all income of the year is summed. This sum is divided by twelve to generate the actual monthly income.

Every year, the Ministry of Justice publishes a regulation for the amount of unseizable income, which represents the subsistence minimum. The level of subsistence is related to the actual net income, a higher income thus results in a higher level of subsistence minimum. In 2019, the minimum subsistence level is set at 1,088 euros per month, while the maximum is set at 1,877.60 euros.[23]

This result (net income minus subsistence minimum) can further be reduced by alimony payments. These are only deductible if the offender has a legal obligation that he actually meets. The deductible amount of alimony payments is capped as stated in the regulation of the Ministry of Justice. Voluntary contributions without a legal obligation are not to be taken into account.[24]

Further expenses like costs of living (e.g. rent, transportation, leasing rates) do not reduce the amount of the daily unit, as they already influence the level of the subsistence minimum. Exemptions may be made if the offender needs

---

[19] Austrian Supreme Court of Justice 13 Os 65/75, SSt 46/32.
[20] *Supra* note 2, paras. 34 *et seq.*
[21] Austrian Supreme Court of Justice 9 Os 154/75, SSt 47/6.
[22] *Supra* note 10, Medigovic, Reindl-Krauskopf and Luef-Kölbl, pp. 40 *et seq.*
[23] www.justiz.gv.at; given that there is no obligation to pay child support.
[24] *Supra* note 2, para. 73.

those payments to secure his livelihood, for example if the offender needs a car to carry out his job.[25]

7.2.2.3 Example

X earns a monthly income of 1,500 euros, 14 times a year and has to provide child support for his daughter. He has additional monthly expenses for renting his apartment (500 euros) and repaying the loan he took for his sports car (200 euros). Due to committing property damage, he is convicted to pay a fine of 40 daily units.

As a first step, the actual monthly income has to be calculated by multiplying the monthly income by 14 and then dividing this result by 12 ($1,500 \times 14/12 = 1,750$ euros). According to the regulation issued by the Ministry of Justice, his subsistence minimum – considering his income and obligation to pay child support – is 1,460.40 euros. This amount needs to be subtracted from his monthly income, as it cannot be seized for punitive purposes. Neither the expenses for the sports car nor the rent for the apartment can be deducted. As a result, 289.60 euros is the relevant monthly amount to determine the amount of the daily unit. This amount has to be divided by thirty to calculate the actual amount of the daily unit. Hence, one daily unit has to be set at 9.65 euros ($289.60/30$). In total, X has to pay a fine of 386 euros (9.65×40).[26]

7.2.2.4 Recalculation of the Amount of the Daily Unit

If the personal or economic circumstances of a person sentenced to a fine deteriorate in more than a merely minor manner, there is a possibility to reassess the amount of the daily unit of the remaining fine within the parameters stated above (paragraph 31a(2) StGB). However, if the offender intentionally caused the deterioration of circumstances, including by failing to take up reasonable employment, the amount of the daily unit cannot be recalculated. Even when recalculating the fine, the minimum amount for the daily unit of four euros still applies.

7.2.3 *Imprisonment in Default of Payment*

For the case that a fine cannot be recovered, the court has – at the time of the conviction – to prescribe imprisonment in default of payment (*Ersatzfreiheitsstrafe*). It is provided that two daily units correspond to

---

[25] *Supra* note 10, Medigovic, Reindl-Krauskopf and Luef-Kölbl, p. 42.
[26] Compare *supra* note 10, Medigovic, Reindl-Krauskopf and Luef-Kölbl, p. 42.

one day of imprisonment (paragraph 19 (3) StGB), in case of an odd number of daily units, it is rounded down to the next whole number. Hence, in the example above, the court has to prescribe imprisonment in default of payment for the duration of twenty days.

The offender cannot choose whether to pay the fine or serve imprisonment in default of payment, as the latter is only applicable if the fine is uncollectable by the means of execution.[27] Amounts already paid by the offender reduce the time of imprisonment in default of payment.[28]

Instead of serving imprisonment in default of payment, the offender has the possibility to apply to perform community service (paragraph 3(a) *Strafvollzugsgesetz* – StVG). Four hours of community service correspond to one day of imprisonment, hence two hours of community service equal one daily unit. In the example above, if the fine is uncollectable, X would have to perform eighty hours of community service, in order to prevent imprisonment in default of payment.

7.2.4 *Access to Financial Information*

Although the offender's financial status is a crucial element for calculating the amount of the daily unit, there are no legal provisions or guidelines on how to get this financial information. In practice, emphasis is laid on the information provided by the offender himself. However, the court may not rely on this information without further examination, if it has doubts concerning its plausibility.[29] Possible approaches for assessing the offender's financial status include requesting further documents, examining the collective agreement applicable and enquiring at the social security agencies or the offender's employer. If the process and efforts required to obtain the information is disproportionate, the court may also estimate the relevant income, taking into account for example the economic situation of the offender's company, the income situation in the relevant industry and the offender's lifestyle.[30] According to paragraph 76 Austrian Code of Criminal Procedure (*Strafprozessordnung* – StPO), mutual assistance may be requested by the court in order to receive information from other public authorities, particularly from the competent tax authority. Thus, it is possible to access the offender's income tax assessment against his will. In contrast, the court cannot access bank data without the offender's consent.

---

[27] *Supra* note 10, Medigovic, Reindl-Krauskopf and Luef-Kölbl, paras. 93 *et seq.*
[28] *Supra* note 2, para. 101.
[29] *Ibid.*, para. 88; Steininger, 'Drei Jahre Strafgesetzbuch', p. 135.
[30] *Supra* note 3, p. 97; *supra* note 13, Lässig, para. 28.

7.2.5 *Conditional Suspension of the Sentence*

If it can be presumed that the mere prospect of the enforcement of the fine will suffice to prevent the offender from committing other offences and that the enforcement of the fine is not needed to deter others from committing offences, the court has to conditionally suspend a part of that fine (paragraph 43(a)(1) StGB). Since 2010 a full conditional suspension of the fine has no longer been possible, at least one quarter actually needs to be enforced.[31]

Under certain circumstances,[32] it is possible that the court imposes a fine instead of one part of the imprisonment sentence. In this case the fine must not exceed 720 daily units and the remaining part of the imprisonment is to be conditionally suspended.

7.2.6 *Act on the Responsibility of Legal Entities for Criminal Offences*

Since 2006, according to the Act on the Responsibility of Legal Entities (*Verbandsverantwortlichkeitsgesetz* – VbVG) it is possible to convict legal entities because of a criminal conduct of their decision-makers or staff. The court imposes a corporate fine (*Verbandsgeldbuße*). Different systems of sanctioning were discussed in the legislative process, but in the end the Austrian legislator chose to adjust the traditional day fine system for the means of criminal liability of legal entities.[33] While the number of daily units is determined by the severity of the offence and the organisational default, the amount of the daily unit depends on the economic situation of the legal entity. Due to the similarity in the systems, this chapter only covers the differences in between.

The corporate fine is the primary penalty under the VbVG (paragraph 4 VbVG). The minimum number of daily units that must be imposed on the legal entity is one daily unit. The maximum number of daily units that can be imposed is linked to the maximum threat of imprisonment for individual persons, who committed the offence within the legal entity. The legal entity faces a maximum of

- 180 daily units, if the offence is punishable by lifelong imprisonment or imprisonment up to 20 years (e.g. murder);

---

[31] According to the legislative materials the full conditional suspension of fines would not be sufficiently 'effective' (ErläutRV 981 BlgNR 24. GP, p. 88).

[32] See para. 43(a)(2) StGB: The offender would be sentenced to imprisonment for more than six months but no more than two years and the requirements for a conditional suspension of the whole penalty (the mere prospect of the enforcement of the sentence is sufficient with regard to special and general deterrence) are not met.

[33] ErläutRV 994 BlgNR 22. GP, p. 25.

- 155 daily units, if the offence is punishable by imprisonment up to 15 years (e.g. aggravated robbery with the use of a weapon);
- 130 daily units, if the offence is punishable by imprisonment up to 10 years (e.g. aggravated fraud with a damage of more than 300,000 euros);
- 100 daily units, if the offence is punishable by imprisonment up to 5 years (e.g. extortion);
- 85 daily units, if the offence is punishable by imprisonment up to 3 years (e.g. money laundering);
- 70 daily units, if the offence is punishable by imprisonment up to 2 years (e.g. aggravated property damage with a damage between 5,000 and 300,000 euros);
- 55 daily units, if the offence is punishable by imprisonment up to 1 year (e.g. negligent killing, petty cases of theft);
- 40 daily units in all other cases (offences that are only punishable by fine).

The amount of the daily unit depends on the economic capacity of the legal entity. As a general rule, the relevant amount of the daily unit shall be equal to one 360th of the yearly proceeds of the legal entity. Alternatively the court may exceed or fall short of this amount by not more than one third (paragraph 4 (4) VbVG). According to the legislative materials the relevant yearly proceeds for calculating the amount of the fine is the surplus after taxes of the legal entity that may be distributed to shareholders, taking into account the necessary investments and the expenditures for outside capital.[34] In doctrine, it has been suggested that this may be the wrong approach and other figures like the revenue, the return on sales or the cash flow would be more adequate for sentencing purposes.[35]

The main goal of this penalty system is to seize any surplus for the duration of the sentence without risking the integrity of the legal entity.[36] However, there is a minimum of 50 euros and a maximum of 10,000 euros.[37] As a consequence, the range for the corporate fine in total is from 50 euros to 1.8 million euros.[38]

7.2.7 *Withdrawal from Prosecution (Diversion)*

For cases of minor or medium criminal offences, the StPO provides for the withdrawal from prosecution (*Diversion*) in paragraphs 198 *et seq.* StPO, where

---

[34] *Ibid.*
[35] Zirm and Limberg, 'Zur Tagessatz-Bemessung im VbVG', pp. 708–16.
[36] *Supra* note 33.
[37] If the association serves charitable, humanitarian or church purposes or is not profit-oriented, the daily unit is fixed at a minimum of 2 euros and a maximum of 500 euros.
[38] For the criticism on the maximum amount of the fine, see Section 7.4.

the cases are settled with non-stigmatising sanctions only and without a formal conviction. In practice, the withdrawal from prosecution is highly relevant, the number of withdrawals from prosecutions even exceeds the number of convictions.[39] Requirements for the withdrawal are (1) the threat of punishment for the offence is not more than five years of imprisonment, (2) the guilt of the accused is not to be regarded as grave, (3) the offence did not result in the death of a person, (4) the punishment does not appear to be necessary in the light of specific and general deterrence and (5) a basis of sufficiently clear facts exists. Both the public prosecutor and the court can apply these provisions and impose one of the four measures of diversion: the payment of an amount of money, the performance of community service, the imposition of a probation period with or without certain duties (e.g. probation service) and the settlement of the conflict with the victim (victim-offender-mediation). In relation to legal entities, the Austrian law provides for a corresponding provision of diversion in paragraph 19 VbVG. This chapter only focuses on the first measure of diversion, the payment of an amount of money to the benefit of the federal state according to paragraph 200 StPO.

Although the fine according to the StGB and the payment of an amount of money as a measure of diversion are different in their criminal nature (the fine is a penalty, whereas the payment of an amount of money is explicitly not a penalty but an alternative measure), the system of the calculation of the amount due in principle is the same. This means, it also has to be differentiated between the number of daily units and the amount of the daily unit. In contrast to the StGB, it is sufficient for the public prosecutor or the court to propose the payment of a sum of money without making transparent the specific number of daily units and the amount of the daily unit.[40]

The amount of money must not exceed the sum that corresponds to a fine of 180 daily units, plus the costs of the criminal proceedings that the accused would have to reimburse in the event of a conviction. The extent of the amount of money is determined by the severity of the offence and the personal circumstances and the financial capacity of the accused. Additionally, the withdrawal from prosecution after payment of an amount of money has to be made dependent upon the accused compensating the damage caused by the offence, unless exceptional circumstances apply. Another major difference to the fine according to the StGB is that this

---

[39] Federal Ministry for Constitutional Affairs, Reforms, Deregulation and Justice, Sicherheitsbericht 2017, p. 30, with 52,175 cases of diversion versus 31,415 convictions.

[40] Schroll, '§ 200 StPO', para. 2/2.

amount of money actually has to be paid and cannot be conditionally suspended.[41] Upon payment of the amount of money and, if applicable, compensation of the damage, the public prosecutor or the court must withdraw from any prosecution.

7.2.8 *Act on Fiscal Offences*

The Act on Fiscal Offences (*Finanzstrafgesetz* – FinStrG) deals with various fiscal offences at the expense of the Austrian state. Depending on the amount of the evaded taxes, the competence for leading the procedure and sanctioning is divided between administrative authorities and criminal courts (paragraph 53 FinStrG). There is a separate administrative authority, namely the fiscal offence prosecution authority, which in minor cases – where the evaded tax is less than 100,000 euros[42] – investigates, prosecutes and adjudicates on its own. If the damage of the tax evasion exceeds 100,000 euros, the criminal courts are competent to adjudicate.

7.2.8.1 Fines in the FinStrG

The FinStrG contains a system of penalties which is completely different compared to the rest of the criminal law. Whereas the Criminal Code provides for both imprisonment and fines as primary penalties, in fiscal penal law for most of the offences fines are the only primary penalty, imprisonment may only be imposed additionally.

Furthermore, fines are calculated in a different way compared to the Criminal Code. In fiscal penal law, most of the fines are imposed as a sum (*Geldsummenstrafe*) and depend on the amount of the taxes or the duties which have been evaded. This is the assessment basis of the fine (*strafbestimmender Wertbetrag*). Depending on the fiscal offence committed, the maximum amount of the fine is a multiple of the assessment basis. It is calculated by taking half (e.g. certain fiscal misdemeanours), the single (e.g. gross negligent tax evasion), the twofold (e.g. intentional tax evasion) or the threefold (e.g. tax evasion by a gang) of the relevant assessment basis. For example, if the intentionally evaded amount of taxes is 500,000 euros, this amount is multiplied by the factor 2, thus the maximum fine for the offence of tax evasion is 1 million euros. According to the jurisprudence of the Supreme Court, the assessment basis is no element of the offence and

---

[41] *Ibid.*, para. 2/3.
[42] Or 50,000 euros when it comes to the evasion of custom duties.

therefore has not to be covered by the intent of the offender.[43] It is sufficient that the offender acts with the intent to cause any damage, but it is not required that he has an intent with regard to a specific amount.[44] In contrast to fines of the StGB, this kind of fine has no absolute limit.[45] It is only capped by the result of multiplying the amount of evaded taxes with the relevant factor. Concerning the minimum of this fine, the FinStrG lays down both an absolute and relative minimum. The fine has to be at least twenty euros (paragraph 16 FinStrG) or 10 per cent of the maximum fine (paragraph 23 (4) FinStrG). Hence, in the example above, the court has to impose a fine of at least 100,000 euros. In case of negligent conduct only this kind of fine can be imposed. If the offender acts intentionally, the court may also impose a sentence of imprisonment in addition to the fine.

Only few offences are punishable by a fixed fine, meaning that the fine is capped at an absolute amount (e.g. up to 1.5 million euros). These offences basically form two categories. On the one hand, there are severe offences that are primarily punishable by imprisonment (e.g. tax fraud). In these cases, the court may also impose a fine in addition to imprisonment. On the other hand, there are minor or medium serious fiscal offences that are only punishable by fixed fines with an absolute amount. This can be explained by the fact that these administrative offences only sanction breaches of obligations (e.g. breach of obligation to disclose certain information to the tax authority) and lack a specific assessment base like the amount of evaded taxes. The minimum of twenty euros also applies. Analysing the various fixed fines, no system, how the legislator determined the maximum amount of these fines, is evident.

The aim of the imposition of a fine under the FinStrG is in principle the same as in the Criminal Code, since the severity of the offence, the guilt of the offender as well as his personal circumstances and financial capacity have to be taken into account. However, the process of sentencing is not a two-step (number of daily units and amount of daily unit) but a one-step process and there are no rules how this should happen. In contrast to the daily unit system, the maximum fine is not linked to the economic capacity of the offender but the amount of the evaded taxes or the fixed amount of the fine. In consequence, it is difficult, in some cases impossible, to achieve the goal of an adequate fine. On the one hand there is no mechanism to take into account the economic situation of the offender, on the other hand the maximum amount is not dependent on the income of the

[43] Austrian Supreme Court of Justice 04.10.1988, 15 Os 88/88; 18.09.2001, 14 Os 84/01; 15.03.2006, 14 Os 145/05p.

[44] Kert, 'Legal Framework and Practice of the Fight against VAT Fraud in Austria', pp. 87 *et seq.*

[45] The only exception is para. 49(a)(3) FinStrG, which limits the fine to 20,000 euros.

offender, since the amount of evaded taxes is not necessarily a limit connected to his financial capacity. The non-transparency of this system also makes it difficult to demonstrate the guilt of the offender.[46]

There are no legally binding sentencing guidelines, paragraph 23 (2) FinStrG only highlights the importance of aggravating and mitigating factors as laid down in the StGB.

7.2.8.2 Imprisonment in Default of Payment

For the case that a fine cannot be recovered, the fiscal offence prosecution authority or the court has – at the time of the conviction – to prescribe imprisonment in default of payment. It is in the discretion of the fiscal offence prosecution authority or the court to decide on the length of imprisonment in default of payment.[47] This discretion is limited by paragraph 20 FinStrG, depending on the competent authority and the severity of the offence. While the court can impose up to one year of imprisonment in default of payment (in exceptional cases up to two years), the fiscal offence prosecution authority can only impose up to six weeks or three months, if decided in a chamber consisting of three members.

7.2.8.3 Current Criticism on the System

Parts of the doctrine criticise the sanctioning system of the FinStrG. Since the system for determining the fines of the StGB highly differs from the one of the FinStrG, some criticise that it is hard to comprehend whether offences with a similar degree of wrongdoing face a similar threat of punishment. It is not transparent whether for fiscal offences a punishment that is comparable to equally severe offences under the StGB or other criminal provisions is foreseen.[48] Although it has been argued that this contradicts the principle of equal treatment, the Austrian Constitutional Court has recently approved the sanctioning system of the FinStrG.[49]

Another concern is that the personal circumstances and the economic capacity of the offender are not sufficiently taken into account for determining the fine since the maximum amount of the fine is highly dependable on the evaded tax. For example if an accountant intentionally assists a multinational

---

[46] See Section 7.2.8.3.
[47] Leitner, Brandl and Kert, *Handbuch Finanzstrafrecht*, para. 1089.
[48] *Supra* note 12, Grafl and Schmoller, p. 135.
[49] Austrian Constitutional Court 10.10.2018, G 49–50/2017.

corporation in the evasion of taxes without gaining personal benefits and causes a loss in the amount of forty million euros, the maximum fine would be eighty million euros (because the offence of intentional tax evasion is punishable by up to the twofold of the amount of the evaded taxes). Given the mandatory minimum of 10 per cent, he would at least have to pay a fine of eight million euros. It is evident that this employee normally will not have the capacity to come up with that amount of money. As a consequence, in case of default of payment imprisonment often seems inevitable. It is doubtful whether such results are reasonable and appropriate.[50] Therefore, several representatives of the doctrine demand the adoption of the day fine system also for fiscal offences.[51]

7.2.9 *Act on Administrative Offences*

In addition to the criminal law, in Austria a system of administrative penal law for minor offences exists. According to the prevailing opinion, it is not criminal by law, but penal in nature. These offences are investigated, prosecuted and adjudicated not by courts but by administrative authorities. While these administrative offences are laid down in various acts, the Act on Administrative Offences (*Verwaltungsstrafgesetz* – VStG) specifies common rules for this administrative penal liability. Administrative offences are constituted by various misconducts, like exceeding a speed limit, driving a vehicle under the influence or violating health and safety regulations at work, as long as no damage to a person or property occurs.

In contrast to the Austrian Criminal Code, in administrative penal law a system of fixed fines applies.[52] The maximum amount of the fixed fine is stated in the relevant acts. The VStG only provides for a maximum amount of 218 euros, in case the relevant acts lack a maximum amount. For instance, according to paragraph 99 (1) of the Road Traffic Act, driving under the influence of more than 1.6 per cent blood alcohol level is punishable by a fixed fine up to 5,900 euros. Recent developments show a significant increase of the maximum amount of administrative fines in certain areas of law, as for example banking law (e.g. five million euros or three times the amount of the profits gained or losses avoided for the infringement of the prohibition of insider dealing, paragraph 154 Austrian Stock Exchange Act [*Börsegesetz*]). The minimum amount of the fixed fine also depends on the specific

---

[50] Brandl, 'Strafen und Strafbemessung', para. 1132; *supra* note 48, p. 136.
[51] Scheil, 'Das Sanktionensystem nach der FinStrG-Novelle 2010', p. 206.
[52] Schulev-Steindl, *Verwaltungsverfahrensrecht*, para. 523.

provisions in the administrative acts (e.g. for driving under the influence, a minimum of 1,600 euros is foreseen), however, an absolute minimum of 7 euros exists.

There was a debate in the 1970s and 1980s on whether to introduce the day fine system of the StGB in administrative penal law in order to adjust the administrative fine more appropriately to the individual offender. Due to the minor nature of administrative offences and the fact that these are cases of mass delinquency, the legislator decided to keep the system of fixed fines, since the administrative authorities do not have the capacity to determine the personal circumstances and financial capacity of the offender. By now, this debate is virtually non-existent.[53]

At the time of the imposition of the fine, the administrative authority has to prescribe imprisonment in default of payment for the case that a fine cannot be executed. Due to a lack of a day fine system, there is no fixed relation between the fine imposed and the length of imprisonment in default of payment. It is thus in the discretion of the administrative authority to decide on the length of imprisonment in default of payment. Unless stated otherwise, the duration of this imprisonment in default of payment must not exceed two weeks and an absolute maximum of six weeks exists (paragraph 16 VStG).

7.3 THE PRACTICAL IMPLEMENTATION OF DAY FINES

This section focuses on the practical implementation of the Austrian model of day fines. The Ministry of Justice annually publishes a report on the activity of the criminal law enforcement authorities, which is the main source of information for this section. Additionally, Statistics Austria publishes judicial criminal statistics that list all criminal convictions and categorises them in-depth (e.g. age, sex or nationality of offender, imposed sentences).

As a starting point, it has to be highlighted that a comparison between the fixed fine system used in the old StG and todays daily unit system implemented in 1975 is not possible, due to significant changes in the criminal provisions, the population, the crime rate and the lack of data.

7.3.1 *Ratio of Fines*

In a first step, in Figure 7.1 the significance of fines in relation to other sanctions is analysed. In 2017, 30,746 persons in total were convicted. In

---

[53] Wiederin, *Die Zukunft des Verwaltungsstrafrechts, Gutachten zum 16. Österreichischen Juristentag*, pp. 72, 74.

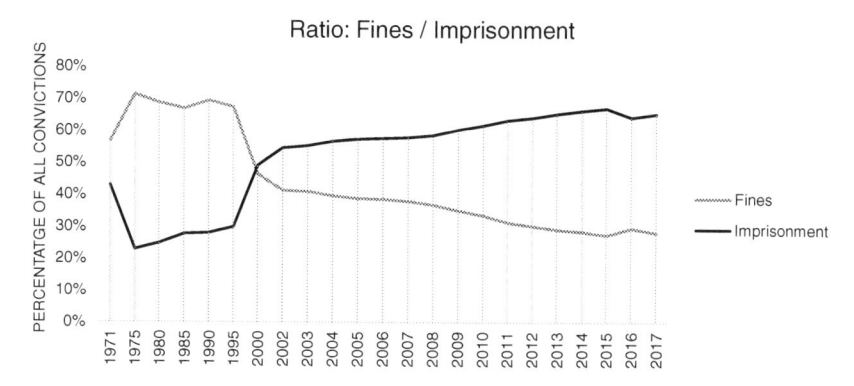

FIGURE 7.1 Ratio fines/Imprisonment.
Source: own figure based on data from *Statistik Austria*, Verurteilungsstatistik 2017, chapter 3

8,693 cases fines were imposed, compared to 20,100 sentences of imprisonment. This corresponds to a ratio of 28.3 per cent to 65.4 per cent.[54]

Data show that the amendment of the StGB along with the introduction of the day fine system in the year 1975 led to a significant increase of the importance of fines compared to the time before.[55] Since the day fine system was regarded as very effective, it was an appropriate instrument to replace short-term imprisonment and its stigmatising effects.[56] This explains the high level of fines from 1975 until 2000. The sudden decline in 2000 was caused by the introduction of the instrument of the Diversion.[57] In many cases that used to be sanctioned by a fine before the introduction of Diversion, now diversional measures have been applied. Since then, the ratio of fines to sentences of imprisonment has steadily declined.

7.3.2 *Categories of Offences*

Next, it is analysed for which categories of offences the system of day fines is used. The following list contains the most relevant offences or categories of offences for which fines are foreseen. The figures in parenthesis show the number of convictions with fines compared to the total number of

---

[54] The remaining amount to 100 per cent consists of conditional partial suspension of sentence of imprisonment combined with a fine and other sanctions.

[55] Between 1971 and 1974 the relative amount of fines increased from 57 per cent to 63 per cent, this means 6 per cent in three years. With the introduction of the day fine system the relative amount increased from 63 per cent to 72 per cent (in 1975) within only one year.

[56] Criminal report 1980, III-114 BlgNR 15. GP, pp. 106 *et seq.*

[57] See Section 7.2.7; Grafl, 'Entwicklung der Sanktionen in Österreich seit 1922', pp. 389 *et seq.*

convictions. It has to be highlighted that these offences and groups of categories also include more severe forms of conduct for which no fine is applicable
(e.g. theft with a weapon).

Negligent assault (792/1,008)
Negligent killing (84/148)
Assault (1,592/3,024)
Coercion (183/938)
Dangerous threat (209/1,304)
Offences of threat against property (2,951/10,770)
Property damage (576/1,026)
Theft (1,500/5,754)
Fraud (471/2,044)
Counterfeiting legal documents (152/336)
Suppression of legal documents (155/383)
Offences against non-cash means of payment (26/162).

These figures only show a rough overview of the practical implementation,
given the data available it is not possible to assess whether there is a gap
between the extent the day fine system can be utilised and the actual implementation. One of the few conclusions that can be drawn from the data
available is that there are no categories of offence where the judicial practice
does not use the possibility of day fines that is given de jure.

7.3.3 *Number of Daily Units Imposed*

Since every sentence strongly depends on the facts of the individual case, statistics
can only give a rough overview on the number of daily units imposed. As a general
tendency, the number of daily units imposed has increased over the last few
years.[58] While in the year 1988 only 8 per cent of all imposed fines had more than
120 daily units, this ratio increased to 25 per cent in the year 2013. Regarding
individual categories of offences, data show that the ratio of fines imposed for
assault exceeding 120 daily units has increased from 2 per cent to 13 per cent within
25 years in the court district of the Higher Regional Court of Appeal of Vienna
(*Oberlandesgericht* – OLG). The ratio of fines imposed for theft shows a similar
development (2 per cent to 10 per cent). This increase of fines exceeding 120 daily
units was significantly stronger in the court district of the OLG Innsbruck (assault:
6 per cent to 49 per cent; theft: 9 per cent to 48 per cent).[59]

---

[58] *Supra* note 12, Grafl and Schmoller, p. 68.
[59] *Ibid.*, p. 69.

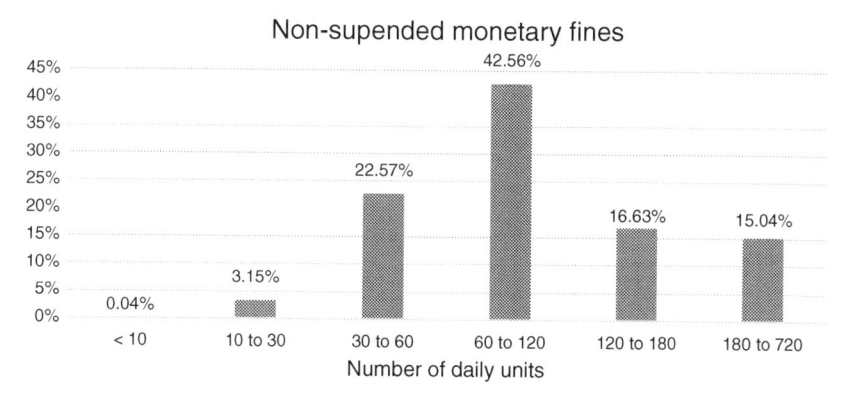

FIGURE 7.2 Number of daily units imposed – non-suspended monetary fines
Source: own figure based on data from *Statistik Austria*, StatCube (www.statistik.at
/web_de/services/statcube/index.html)

In 2017, in cases of non-suspended fines most of the fines imposed were in the range of 60 to 120 daily units. The majority of partially suspended fines was in the range of 60 to 180 daily units. Although – depending on the offence committed – it is often possible to impose up to 360 or 720 daily units, fines exceeding 180 daily units are only imposed in 15 per cent (non-suspended fines) or 25 per cent (suspended fines) of all cases. The following Figures 7.2 and 7.3 show the statistical distribution of the number of daily units in the year 2017.[60]

7.3.4 *Regional Differences*

The decision whether a fine or a sentence of imprisonment is imposed does not primarily depend on the category of the offences committed, but on the court which makes the decision. Data show a significant difference in sentencing between the four different areas of Higher Regional Courts of Appeal and their District and Regional Courts, as shown in Figure 7.4. Several studies show significant differences in sentencing between the different parts of Austria (so-called 'west-east-gap'). The ratio of fines varies between 17.7 per cent and 66.1 per cent in the different court districts of the Higher Regional Courts of Appeal. While in the court district of the OLG Vienna in 17.7 per cent of all cases a fine was imposed, the ratio of fines in the district of the OLG Linz was 26.2 per cent and in the district of the OLG Graz it was 29.5 per cent. By far the highest ratio of fines is imposed by the courts in the district of the OLG Innsbruck with 66.1 per cent.

[60] Statistics Austria, statcube.at/statistik.at/ext/statcube/jsf/tableView/tableView.xhtml#.

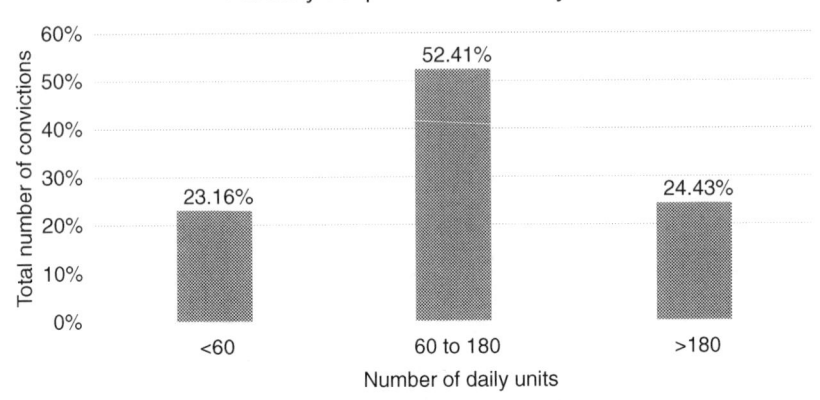

FIGURE 7.3 Number of daily units imposed – partially suspended monetary fines
Source: own figure based on data from *Statistik Austria*, StatCube (www.statistik.at
/web_de/services/statcube/index.html)

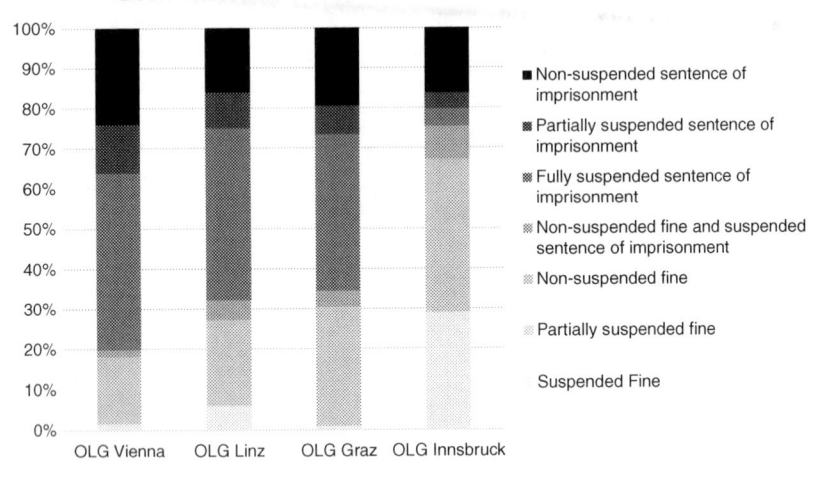

FIGURE 7.4 Overview of convictions in different court districts
Source: own figure based on data from *Statistik Austria*, StatCube (www.statistik.at
/web_de/services/statcube/index.html)

While in the court district of the OLG Innsbruck nearly half of all fines
are conditionally suspended, this instrument is rarely used in the other
court districts. In contrast, the instrument of the conditional suspension of
sentences of imprisonment is rarely applied in the court district of the OLG

Innsbruck. While in other court districts the conditional suspension of sentences of imprisonment is frequently used, the courts of the district of the OLG Innsbruck impose fines for minor and medium offences and use imprisonment sentences without conditional suspension for severe offences. As a consequence, offenders who would face a conditional suspension of a sentence of imprisonment in the court district of the OLG Vienna may very well face a fine in the court district of the OLG Innsbruck. Data also show that the number of daily units imposed on an offender is significantly higher in the court district of the OLG Innsbruck compared to the rest of Austria.[61] This higher number of daily units imposed is not surprising, since courts in the court district of the OLG Innsbruck tend to impose fines in cases where other courts would impose sentences of imprisonment.

The graph shows a quite different attitude towards fines in the different court districts. Whereas some courts (especially in the Western parts of Austria) regard fines as effective instruments to sanction criminal behaviour even in more serious cases, other courts regard them as less effective than imprisonment sentences. The latter ones often argue that a fine does not make any sense if the offender has no sufficient financial means and cannot pay the fine. However, the financial situation of the offender must not be an argument against the imposition of a fine.

7.3.5 *Level of Recidivism*

The criminal data available do not allow a comparison of the level of recidivism between the systems of fixed fines and the day fine system. However, there are data on recidivism rates of offenders sanctioned to different types of sentences. The data show that the level of recidivism increases with the severity of the initial sanction. Compared to non-suspended sentences of imprisonment, the system of fines is followed by less reoffending. It should be noted, nonetheless, that the most severe penalties are imposed in cases of recidivism and severe offences which may be one reason why the recidivism in cases of non-suspended imprisonment is comparatively high. Therefore, due to the selection bias and lack of a randomised study, it is not possible to draw any conclusion with respect to the relative deterrent effect of day fines.

The following Figure 7.5 shows the percentage of recidivists in 2017, based on the initial sanction imposed on the offender in 2013.

---

[61] *Supra* note 12, Grafl and Schmoller, pp. 69 *et seq.*

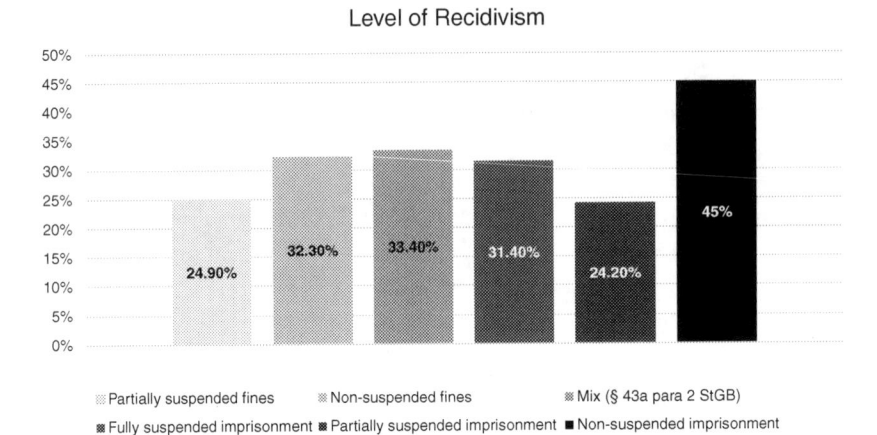

FIGURE 7.5 Level of recidivism.
Source: own figure based on data from *Statistik Austria*, Verurteilungsstatistik 2017, chapter 4

7.4 PUBLIC PERCEPTION OF DAY FINES

Recently, a certain disproportion between the criminal sanctions for offences against property and offences against life and limb and sexual integrity has been discussed on a political level. This led to an amendment of the Austrian Criminal Code in 2016, which increased the sanctions for offences against life and limb and sexual integrity.[62] This discussion is still ongoing, but its main focus lies on an increase of the duration of imprisonment for certain offences.[63] As a reflex, it could be possible that for some offences that are currently alternatively punishable by imprisonment or fine, the latter option of sanctioning is no longer possible. Furthermore, since the number of daily units that can be imposed for an offence is currently directly linked to the threated duration of a sentence of imprisonment (one day threat of imprisonment equals the threat of two daily units), it could be possible that aforementioned discussion also leads to higher fines, for example the increase from 360 to 720 daily units.

Public perception of criminal sanctions is mainly influenced by media coverage.[64] Since only minor offences are punishable by fines, these cases are barely reported in the news. Even if the cases make it to the headlines, the media only state the amount of the fine imposed in total, without specifying

---

[62] Strafrechtsänderungsgesetz 2015, BGBl I 2015/112.
[63] Report of the Criminal Task Force (2019).
[64] *Supra* note 12, Grafl and Schmoller, p. 7.

the calculation of the fine. In media reports usually it is not transparent how many daily units were imposed on the offender and how his personal circumstances and financial capacity influenced the total amount of the fine. As a result, the public does not recognise what the effects of the day fine system are.

On a professional level, the existence of the day fine system is widely accepted. Since this system has been in force for the last forty-five years, barely any criticism exists concerning the system as such. In recent years, only details were subject to discussion, particularly the minimum and maximum amount of the daily unit.

The minimum amount of the daily unit (four euros) has been criticised as too high. There are a number of cases where even a daily unit of four euros is disproportionate, since the offender has no or only little income and/or gets social assistance. As a consequence, this offender cannot afford to pay the fine and risks going to prison. This contradicts the aim to avoid short-term imprisonment. In order to ensure that the amount of the daily unit is actually congruent to the personal circumstances of the offender and his financial capacities, it has been suggested to lower the minimum amount of the daily unit to 1 euro or to remove it altogether.[65]

Furthermore, it has been criticised that the maximum amount of the daily unit (5,000 euros) is too low to sanction very rich people, especially in comparison to the German Criminal Code. Although an amendment of the StGB in the year 2009 increased the maximum amount of the daily unit from 500 to 5,000 euros, it is proposed by some to further increase this maximum to a level that is internationally comparable.[66] However, these concerns are only relevant for very few cases, since a daily unit of 5,000 euros only applies to people with a monthly average income of approximately 150,000 euros.

A similar discussion concerns the maximum amount of the daily unit of corporate fines according to the Act on the Responsibility of Legal Entities. Particularly in comparison to the high sanctions of European Competition Law, the maximum amount of the daily unit (10,000 euros) and the maximum fine of 1.8 million euros in total for the most severe offences seem to be very low. Hence, the corporate fine risks not to be sufficiently deterrent for financially strong corporations. It also shows that the current legal situation is no longer in accordance with the initial concept of the legislator determining the maximum amount of the corporate fine. At the time of the adoption of the VbVG, the maximum corporate fine was ten times as high as the maximum

---

[65] Birklbauer, 'Das StrÄG 2001 und die strafrechtliche Enquete-Kommission', 165.
[66] *Supra* note 2, para. 27; Triffterer, *Strafrecht Allgemeiner Teil*, pp. 474 *et seq.*

fine for individual persons (180,000 euros). But while this maximum amount increased to 3.6 million euros due to the increase of the maximum number of daily units to 720 and the maximum amount of the daily unit to 5,000 euros, the corporate fine stayed the same. To correct this disproportionality, some suggest increasing the maximum amount of the daily unit for the corporate fine to at least 100,000 euros.[67] It is worth mentioning that in spite of these relatively low corporate fines, the introduction of a criminal liability of legal entities has had deterrent effects, as corporations are afraid of other consequences of a criminal proceeding, as, for example, negative reports in media. Therefore, the majority of corporations have implemented compliance systems to avoid criminal liability. However, the fines provided for are too low to sanction corporations which are not willing to comply with legal obligations.

7.5 CONCLUSION

The day fine system has been in force in Austrian Criminal Law for the last forty-five years. Its introduction has been regarded as an important achievement for fair, equal and transparent sanctioning of criminal offenders. The long period of application has led to sufficient experience in the Austrian court system. Especially the potentially complex task of determining the personal circumstances and the financial capacity of the offender to calculate the amount of the daily unit does not seem to excessively burden the courts. The advantages of the day fine system seem to be so evident that in areas, where other systems of fines exist, the adoption of the day fine system is discussed.

REFERENCES

Birklbauer, A. 2001. 'Das StrÄG 2001 und die strafrechtliche Enquete-Kommission', *Juridikum* 1: 164–7.

Brandl, R., 2017. 'Strafen und Strafbemessung', in R. Leitner, R. Brandl and R. Kert (eds.), *Handbuch Finanzstrafrecht*. Vienna: Linde Verlag, pp.366–400.

Criminal report 1980, III-114 BlgNR 15. GP.

Ebner, J., 2018. '§ 32 StGB', in F. Höpfel and E. Ratz (eds.), *Wiener Kommentar zum Strafgesetzbuch*. Vienna: Manz'sche Verlags- und Universitätsbuchhandlung.

ErläutRV 30 BlgNR 13. GP.

ErläutRV 994 BlgNR 22. GP.

ErläutRV 981 BlgNR 24. GP.

Federal Ministry for Constitutional Affairs, Reforms, Deregulation and Justice, Sicherheitsbericht 2017 (Vienna: Federal Ministry for Constitutional Affairs, Reforms, Deregulation and Justice, 2019).

---

[67] *Supra* note 12, Grafl and Schmoller, p. 141.

Grafl, C., 2018. 'Entwicklung der Sanktionen in Österreich seit 1922', *Journal für Strafrecht* 5: 387–90.

Grafl, C. and Schmoller, K., 2015. *Entsprechen die gesetzlichen Strafdrohungen und die von den Gerichten verhängten Strafen den aktuellen gesellschaftlichen Wertungen? Gutachten zum 19. Österreichischen Juristentag.* Vienna: Manz'sche Verlags- und Universitätsbuchhandlung.

Kert, R., 2019. 'Legal Framework and Practice of the Fight against VAT Fraud in Austria', in A. Farkas (ed.), *Criminal Law Aspects of the Protection of the Financial Interests of the EU.* Budapest: Frakas/Dannecker/Jacsó.

Lässig, R., 2010. '§ 19 StGB', in F. Höpfel and E. Ratz (eds.), *Wiener Kommentar zum Strafgesetzbuch.* Vienna: Manz'sche Verlags- und Universitätsbuchhandlung.

Medigovic, U., Reindl-Krauskopf, S. and Luef-Kölbl, H., 2016. *Strafrecht Allgemeiner Teil II.* Vienna, Graz: Neuer Wissenschaftlicher Verlag.

Platzgummer, W., 1980. '§ 19 StGB', in E. Foregger and F. Nowakowski (eds.), *Wiener Kommentar zum Strafgesetzbuch.* Vienna: Manz'sche Verlags- und Universitätsbuchhandlung.

Report of the Criminal Task Force (2019).

Salimi, F., 2016. '§ 19 StGB', in O. Triffterer, C. Rosbaud and H. Hinterhofer (eds.), *Salzburger Kommentar zum Strafgesetzbuch.* Vienna: LexisNexis Verlag.

Scheil, A., 2013. 'Das Sanktionensystem nach der FinStrG-Novelle 2010', in R. Leitner (ed.), *Finanzstrafrecht 2012.* Vienna: Linde Verlag, pp. 189–223.

Schroll, H. V., 2016. '§ 200 StPO', in H. Fuchs and E. Ratz (eds.), *Wiener Kommentar zur Strafprozessordnung.* Vienna: Manz'sche Verlags- und Universitätsbuchhandlung.

Schulev-Steindl, E., 2018. *Verwaltungsverfahrensrecht.* Vienna: Verlag Österreich.

Steininger, H., 1978. 'Drei Jahre Strafgesetzbuch', in Bundesministerium für Justiz (ed.), *Strafrechtliche Probleme der Gegenwart.* Vienna: Federal Ministry of Justice.

Triffterer, O., 1994. *Strafrecht Allgemeiner Teil.* Vienna: Springer Verlag.

Wiederin, E., 2006. *Die Zukunft des Verwaltungsstrafrechts, Gutachten zum 16. Österreichischen Juristentag.* Vienna: Manz'sche Verlags- und Universitätsbuchhandlung.

Zirm, M. and Limberg, C., 2009. 'Zur Tagessatz-Bemessung im VbVG', *Österreichische Juristen-Zeitung* 16: 708–16.

8

Day Fines in Hungary[1]

Csaba Győry

8.1 HISTORICAL DEVELOPMENT OF DAY FINES IN HUNGARY

Day fines were introduced into Hungarian Criminal Law by the new Criminal Code in 1978. The institution of fine, however, was introduced much earlier. The first Hungarian Criminal Code in 1795, which remained a draft, introduced the possibility of the defendant opting to pay a fine instead of going to prison. In effect, it enabled those sentenced to a term of imprisonment to pay for their freedom instead.[2]

The second draft Criminal Code from 1843, which equally never entered into force, already turned the institution upside down: now its non-payment led to imprisonment and not the other way around. The draft Code of 1843 also extended the range of crimes where it was applicable.[3]

This trend continued with the first Criminal Code which entered into force (named Csemegi-kódex in Hungarian after its drafter, Károly Csemegi) in 1878.[4] In the sanction system of the new Code, fines were considered to be an auxiliary sanction ('mellékbüntetés').[5] As such, however, it was applicable to seventy crimes, a significant portion of the crimes in the Code. More importantly, the Code allowed the judge to deviate downwards from the sentencing range and the available sanction if he or she deemed the otherwise applicable sentence too harsh. In such circumstances, the judges could impose auxiliary sanctions as the main sanction. This proved very popular in judicial practice

[1] The chapter was prepared as part of the project 'The Impact of Punitive Criminal Policy in Sentencing and its Fiscal Effects', funded by the Hungarian National Research, Development and Innovation Office (K_125442).
[2] Pápai-Tarr and Sipos, 'A pénzbüntetés fejlődésének hazai mérföldkövei', p. 316.
[3] *Ibid.*, p. 317.
[4] Act No. 5 of 1878 on the Criminal Code.
[5] This is the Hungarian equivalent of the German institution of 'Nebenstrafe'.

and by 1910 the number of fines imposed as the main sanction rivalled those of imprisonment.[6]

This judicial practice was then adopted by the first comprehensive reform of the Hungarian criminal law in 1928.[7] This reclassified the fine as a main sanction and made it applicable to all misdemeanours and minor crimes.

The pendulum then swung back. Partly due to ideological reasons (fine instead of imprisonment had a whiff of capitalism about it) and partly due to the general return to a more oppressive criminal law during the communist dictatorship, the next criminal law reform which took place in 1950, demoted the fine to an auxiliary sanction. The number of fines imposed dropped sharply accordingly.[8] As the brutal crackdown following the revolution of 1956 turned into a slow consolidation and thaw, criminal law was reformed again in 1960. This, though it failed to reclassify fines as a main sanction, reintroduced judicial discretion in going below the sentencing range and the applicable sanction if the latter would be too harsh. Through this back door, the fine was again applicable as the main sanction and its number rose quickly, reaching the 30 per cent of all sanctions by the end of the 1960s.[9]

This was the state of affairs when the institution of day fines was introduced into Hungarian criminal law with the new Criminal Code of 1978. The introduction of alternatives to imprisonment and various other legal institutions aimed at the individualisation of sentences was part of general overhaul and modernisation of the Hungarian criminal law. The institution was based on the day fines provisions of the German Criminal Code (StGB – *Strafgesetzbuch*) – it was almost a literal translation of the corresponding paragraphs of the StGB. There is no historical research on the considerations of the codifiers why to adopt the German model, but the general influence of the criminal law scholarship of the then West Germany on the Hungarian criminal law certainly played a role.

While the new Code contained only a few crimes where day fine was the only applicable sanction, it retained the general rule of judicial discretion allowing the judge to substitute imprisonment with day fines if this better befits the purpose of punishment. Because of this, it remained the leading alternative to imprisonment in the Hungarian judicial practice.

---

[6] *Supra* note 2, p. 319.
[7] Act No. 10 of 1928.
[8] *Supra* note 2, p. 323.
[9] *Ibid.*, p. 327.

8.2 THE LEGAL FRAMEWORK FOR DAY FINES[10]

8.2.1 *Day Fines in the System of Criminal Sanctions*

There are altogether nine forms of criminal sanctions in the Hungarian Criminal Code. These are imprisonment,[11] custodial arrest,[12] community service, day fine, prohibition of exercise of professional activity,[13] driving ban,[14] prohibition from residing in a particular area,[15] ban from visiting sports events[16] and expulsion.[17] Thus, there are no fixed fines in the criminal sanctions system.

There is no crime in the Hungarian Criminal Code which is solely punishable by a day fine: a day fine is always an alternative or substitute sanction and its selection underlies the discretion of the judge. The sole exception to this discretionary choice is the case where the crime has been committed for pecuniary gain and fixed-term imprisonment is meted out. In such cases, imposing a day fine is compulsory as an additional sanction.

Thus, the day fine as a criminal sanction might be applicable in five distinct cases in Hungarian law. First, day fines might be applied *as an alternative to imprisonment* for crimes that are punishable with a maximum of three years of imprisonment (Criminal Code Section 33 (4)). In such cases, day fines can be

---

[10] The following chapter is based on the law as it stands /stood on on 1 March 2020. Later amendments, changes and judicial decisions are not reflected in the text.

[11] Imprisonment might be a fixed-term imprisonment or life term. Fixed-term imprisonment has the minimum duration of three months and a maximum of twenty years (with the exception of crimes committed as part of a criminal organisation, as a repeat offender or a habitual recidivist, in which cases it is twenty-five years (Criminal Code Section 3)). Life term can be with or without the possibility of parole. In case of life with parole, the sentencing judge determines the earliest time of release, which can be a minimum of fifteen years and a maximum of forty years (Criminal Code Section 41).

[12] Custodial arrest is a short-term imprisonment with a minimum duration of five and maximum duration of ninety days (Criminal Code Section 46).

[13] A prohibition to exercise professional activity (such as being a teacher or a medical doctor) may be imposed on a person who has either committed a criminal act through the violation of the rules of his or her profession requiring professional qualifications or through using his or her profession (Criminal Code Section 52).

[14] A driving ban can be applied to perpetrators who either committed a criminal offence through traffic violation or used a motor vehicle for a criminal activity (Criminal Code Section 55).

[15] If the presence of a perpetrator is deemed contrary to the public interest, he or she can be banned from one or more municipalities or a designated part of a municipality or county (Criminal Code Section 57).

[16] Any person who committed a criminal offence during a sports event, during the travel to and from the sports event, or in the connection of a sports event can be banned from visiting particular types of sports events (Criminal Code Section 58).

[17] Perpetrators who do not hold Hungarian citizenship may be expelled if their presence in the country is not desirable (Criminal Code Section 59).

combined with other sanctions enumerated in the Section, that is, custodial arrest, community service, prohibition of exercise of professional activity, driving ban, prohibition from residing in a particular area and visiting sports events.[18]

Second, as per general rule, *if the minimum sentence is deemed too harsh by the judge based on the general principles of sentencing*, a less severe sanction might be imposed (Criminal Code Section 82 (1)). In such cases imprisonment of less than a year might also be imposed for crimes that are otherwise punishable with a minimum of one year of imprisonment (Criminal Code Section 82 (1)(d)). However, instead of the imprisonment term of less than a year, custodial arrest, community service, day fine or a combination thereof might be also imposed in such cases. Given the fact that in the logic of the Hungarian Criminal Code crimes punishable by up to three years of imprisonment (the default where day fines can be applied as alternatives) are less serious offences than those where the law defines a minimum of one year (with the upper limit in latter cases reaching higher than three years), this general discretionary rule opens up the applicability of day fines for more serious offences.

Third, *in case of attempt or aiding or abetting, should the sentence imposed under Section 82 (1) remain excessive*, a double lowering of the applicable sanction is possible (this equally underlies the discretion of the sentencing judge) (Criminal Code Section 82 (4)). This means imprisonment of less than a year, or alternatively community service, day fine or custodial arrest (or their combination) might be applied to crimes punishable by a minimum of two, maximum of five years of imprisonment.

Fourth, day fines might be applied *as an alternative or as a supplementary sanction to custodial arrest* (Criminal Code Section 33 (5)). In such cases day fines can again be combined with other sanctions enumerated in the section. These are again community service, prohibition of exercise of professional activity, driving ban, prohibition from residing in a particular area and visiting sports events.[19]

Fifth, *perpetrators sentenced to fixed-term imprisonment for a criminal offence committed with the purpose of financial gain ('haszonszerzés céljával'),*

---

[18] Section 33 (4) also lists expulsion, but under Section 33 (6) expulsion shall be combined with day fines and community service. This is a matter of simple practical consideration: enforcement would be difficult and likely costly against foreign citizens expelled from the country. Thus it can only be combined with custodial arrest, prohibition of exercise of professional activity, driving ban, prohibition from residing in a particular area and visiting sports events.

[19] Section 33 (5) also lists expulsion, but under Section 33 (6) expulsion shall be combined with day fines and community service. Thus it can only be combined with custodial arrest, prohibition of exercise of professional activity, driving ban, prohibition from residing in a particular area and visiting sports events.

provided they have sufficient assets or income, shall be also imposed a day fine (Criminal Code Section 50 (2)). For this section to apply, three criteria have to be met. First, the sanction applied must be a fixed-term imprisonment (but this can be suspended). This means – as opposed to the other options where day fines can be applied – there is no upper limit of imprisonment in such cases (though the custodial sentence cannot be life imprisonment as it is not a fixed-term in Hungarian law). Second, the perpetrator must have sufficient assets or income to pay the fine. And third, the crime must have been committed for pecuniary gain ('haszonszerzés céljából'). This is a form of special intent in Hungarian criminal law and an element of altogether twenty crimes in the Criminal Code, including the most widespread property offences such as theft and fraud.[20] In such cases there is no upper limit to the applicable imprisonment.

The determination whether the perpetrator has sufficient assets or income is a difficult issue that, though seemingly technical, touches upon fundamental issues concerning the *nullum crimen* principle.[21] When deciding whether the perpetrator has sufficient income, as well as when setting the daily unit of the fine, the court has to consider existing maintenance obligations such as child and parental support, as well as the average expenses of the perpetrator and others he or she might be providing for: there must be a sufficient income left beyond these expenses for covering the fines (even if only by payment in instalments).[22] The income of other members of the household with maintenance obligations[23] for other household members shall be considered, their contribution counted towards household expenses and the contribution of the

[20] These are: (1) illegal use of the human body (Criminal Code Section 175), (2) pandering (Criminal Code Section 200), (3) exploitation of child prostitution (Criminal Code Section 203), (4) misuse of personal data (Criminal Code Section 219), (5) misuse of public information (Criminal Code Section 220 Subsection 2), (6) harbouring a criminal (Criminal Code Section 282 Subsection 2), (7) legal malpractice (Criminal Code Section 285 Subsection 2), (8) criminal offence with authentic instruments (Criminal Code Section 346 Subsection 2), (9) odometer fraud (Criminal Code Section 348), (10) illegal immigrant smuggling (Criminal Code Section 353 Subsection 2), (11) Facilitation of unauthorised residence (Criminal Code Section 354), (12) Abuse of Family Ties (Criminal Code Section 355), (13) Extortion (Criminal Code Section 367), (14) fraud (Criminal Code Section 373), (15) Economic fraud (Criminal Code Section 374), (16) Information System Fraud (Criminal Code Section 375), (17) Compromising the integrity of technical protection (Criminal Code Section 386), (18), Falsifying data related to copyright management (Criminal Code Section 387).

[21] Probably this is the reason why it is the subject of an advisory opinion of the Criminal Law Collegium of the Supreme Court ('Büntető Kollégiumi Vélemény, BKV'). These are legally not binding under Hungarian law, but by all practical purposes they are.

[22] 25. Büntető Kollégiumi Vélemény. para. 4.

[23] Maintenance obligation is a duty under family law to provide for family members. Under Hungarian law, one has a duty to provide for his or her spouse or registered partner, should

perpetrator reduced.[24] However, only those under legal maintenance obligation can be considered and only within the limits of their legally mandated share of household expenses.[25] Only existing maintenance obligations of family members can be considered: whether there are others who could theoretically 'step in' instead of the perpetrator is irrelevant. This follows from the *nullum crimen* principle, as otherwise the criminal sanction would be borne by household members or descendants not legally responsible for the crime.

As it is clear from the above, having assets or income and thus the ability to pay is not a general prerequisite for applying day fines in Hungarian law: it is explicitly mentioned as such only in the distinct case of a sanction for crimes committed for pecuniary gain and thus it only applies to a fraction of cases where day fines can be meted out. In the interpretation of the Supreme Court, this means that the requirement that when setting the daily amount of the fine the court 'shall consider the assets and the income of the perpetrator, as well as his or her personal circumstances and everyday needs' does not amount to a general rule that day fines are not applicable to perpetrators who are unable to pay.[26] The sole exception from this general rule are juvenile defendants: in cases involving juveniles day fines can only be applied if they have sufficient income or assets to pay (Criminal Code Section 113 (1)).

8.2.2 *The Number of Days and the Daily Unit*

The minimum number of days in Hungarian law is 30, the maximum is 540 days. The minimum amount for a daily unit is 1,000 HUF (approximately 3 euros), the maximum is 500,000 HUF (approximately 1,500 euros). From this follows that the minimum day fine applicable is 30,000 (30x1,000) HUF,

these not be able to provide for themselves. Furthermore, one also has a duty to provide for descendants and/or ascendants if they cannot provide for themselves (Civil Code Book 4. Section 195–7). If there is more than one person with the obligation to provide, the burden shall be distributed according to their salary, income, assets and ability to provide (Civil Code Book 4. Section 201). Always the most immediate descendants or ascendants have this duty. Should they not be able to do so, the duty moves to the next one or ones in line (Civil Code Book 4. Section 196), but one level always has to be exhausted before moving on to the next (Civil Code Book 4. Section 201). Hungarian law establishes priority ranking of sorts in terms of claims to maintenance obligations: underage children come before full age children, children before spouses and registered partners, spouses and registered partners (including ex-spouses and partners) before parents and parents before other ascendants or descendants (Civil Code Book 4. Section 202). The duty to provide can also be established as a contractual duty, for example in a care agreement.

[24] *Supra* note 21, para. 7.
[25] *Ibid.*
[26] See the decisions Kúria *Bfv.II.1523/2014/10* and *Kúria Bfv. II. 538/2014/19.*

which is approximately 100 euros and the maximum is 270,000,000 (540x500,000) HUF, which is approximately 840,000 euros.

These numbers are lower for juvenile defendants. For them, the minimum number of days is 15, the maximum is 250, the minimum daily amount 500 HUF (approximately 1.50 euros), the maximum 50,000 HUF (approximately 150 euros). Thus, the minimum day fine applicable to juveniles is 7,500 HUF (approximately 25 euros) and the maximum is 12,500,000 HUF (approximately 38,000 euros).

8.2.2.1 The Number of Days

The number of days shall be determined on the basis of the seriousness ('tárgyi súly', literally 'substantial weight') of the offence (Criminal Code Section 50 (1)). There is no exact benchmark for determining the seriousness of the offence. Both legal scholarship and judicial practice distinguishes between the seriousness *in abstracto* and *in concreto*. Seriousness *in abstracto* means the severity of the crime in general. This can be derived from its position within the Criminal Code (which generally proceeds from the most serious crimes such as genocide towards lesser ones, reflecting the importance and significance of the legal interest the crime protects),[27] as well as from the applicable sanctions: more serious crimes have more severe sanctions. In the context of crimes where day fines are applicable, this means that a crime punishable by up to three years of imprisonment is more serious than one punishable by up to two years, one year or custodial arrest.

The seriousness *in concreto* refers to the seriousness of the concrete offence adjudicated. For example, the Criminal Code makes a distinction between battery which results in injury which heals in eight days ('könnyű testi sértés', simple battery) and battery that causes injuries taking more than eight days to heal ('súlyos testi sértés', aggravated battery). An injury that heals in fourteen days, even if it qualifies as aggravated battery, is less serious than one where healing takes six months.

Circumstances that are not elements of crime could also be considered to determine the seriousness of the offence. The impact on the victim, for example, or the victim's family can be an important factor in determining the *in concreto* seriousness.[28]

The harm caused by the crime is also a factor to consider. In the logic of the Hungarian criminal law, this is often reflected in the precise classification of

---

[27]   Protected Legal Interest ('védett jogtárgy') is the Hungarian equivalent of the German Rechtsgut.
[28]   Mészáros, A *pénzbüntetés*.

the crime and entails different applicable penalties[29] and thus factors into the *in abstracto* seriousness of the crime. Likewise, whether the pecuniary loss caused by the crime falls into the lower or the upper limits of a particular damage or loss category should influence the determination of the *in concreto* seriousness of the crime.

With that said, the Hungarian criminal law does not make a direct connection between the pecuniary harm caused by the crime and the requirement of applying a day fine. As stated above, the crime committed for pecuniary gain (where day fines are compulsory) only constitute a fraction of crimes where pecuniary losses are caused. Though in such cases day fines are imposed irrespective of the length of the applicable imprisonment (thus could be imposed in cases where very substantial losses were caused), statistical analysis does not show a significant correlation between losses and day fines (see Table 8.3).

8.2.2.2 The Daily Unit

When setting the daily unit, the judge shall consider both the assets and the income of the perpetrator, as well as personal circumstances and everyday needs (Criminal Code Section 50 (1)). Accordingly, the judge needs to reflect on the financial situation of the perpetrator in the broadest possible terms, not only on his or her income.

Section 50 (4) allows the judge to order the day fine to be paid in instalments. This decision shall also be made on the evaluation of the income and assets of the perpetrator. This means that the judge can order a higher daily unit, resulting in a higher final amount being paid in instalments, thus lessening the immediate financial burden on the defendant.

In terms of income, the court shall consider both the salary (if any) of the perpetrator as well as any other income, such as income from investment, rental income, even maintenance payment provided by spouses, ex-spouses or other family members if the beneficiary is the perpetrator (thus, child allowance paid to ex-spouses raising underage children, for example, cannot be

---

[29] The categories for value, damage or loss in the definition of a particular crime are: minor (50,001–500,000 HUF, approximately 170–1,700 euros), considerable (500,001 HUF–5,000,000 HUF, approximately 1,700–17,000 euros), substantial (5,000,001 HUF–50,000,000 HUF, approximately 17,000–170,000 euros), particularly considerable (50,000,001 HUF–500,000,000 HUF, approximately 170,000–1,700,000 euros) and particularly substantial (from 500,000,001 HUF, approximately 1,700,000 euros) (Criminal Code Section 459 (6)). Generally, crimes resulting in a substantial pecuniary loss or more are punishable by longer imprisonment than the range where day fines can be applied as an alternative sanction (up to three years of imprisonment).

considered).[30] From the income, legal maintenance obligations shall be deducted. There is no general rule in Hungarian criminal law (as opposed to other national criminal codes) that income should be considered after tax. Welfare payments (unemployment benefits, family allowance, etc.) can generally be considered as income, though how much they are considered as such by the judge is – lacking empirical research on the subject – not known.

Assets can be marketable movable or immovable properties, financial assets such as securities, as well as marketable legal claims (for example, creditorships).

When looking at personal circumstances and everyday needs, the court shall consider such factors as the existence and number of dependents (legal or otherwise),[31] extra financial burdens such as disabled dependents and other already existing payment obligations such as taxes.

As stated above, however, in the interpretation of the Supreme Court, the description of what judges shall consider when setting the amount of the daily unit is merely an advisory rule and does not amount a compulsory rule that without assets or income no day fines shall be imposed.[32] This is a questionable interpretation of the law, as a day fine that the perpetrator obviously cannot pay would defy the very purpose of a fine and would amount to an additional sanction of imprisonment.

A 2003 study, based on interviews with judges, found that although the law requires the judge to consider only the income of the defendant, in practice the overall income of the household is also considered.[33] According to this study, this is done as a part of the reflection of the everyday circumstances of the defendant. For example, if someone has a low-paying job, but lives in a household at a generally higher living standard than his or her own income would enable (provided for by a high-income spouse), then the overall household income is considered and divided by the number of the members of the household. This study dates from 2003. To the extent that this practice would still exist, it is problematic, since it implies that the fine is indirectly imposed on innocent parties as well.

8.2.3 *The Imposition of Day Fines*

There are two ways to impose a day fine in Hungarian criminal law. One is the novel institution of 'agreement on admitting guilt' ('egyezmény a bűnösség beismeréséről'). This is a version of a plea deal within the frame of the

---

[30] *Supra* note 27.
[31] *Ibid.*
[32] *Supra* note 25.
[33] Tóth, 'A pénzbüntetés kiszabásának gyakorlata'.

(inquisitorial) Hungarian criminal law. Most day fines, however, are imposed in a criminal sentence by a judge following a criminal trial establishing criminal liability.

8.2.3.1 Plea Deal

The new Code of Criminal Procedure, which came into force on 1 July 2018 introduced a new institution into Hungarian law: the so-called 'agreement on admitting guilt' (Code of Criminal Procedure Sections 407–11). This replaced the former institution of 'foregoing trial'. Both are forms of plea deals. The most crucial difference is that while foregoing trial (provided the evidence was clear, the defendant admitted the crime and his or her guilt and there were no grounds present excluding criminal liability) was only available in cases concerning 'simple' crimes where evidence was generally clear and uncomplicated, the agreement is a full-blown alternative avenue of justice not limited to certain crimes.

Provided the defendant admits the crime and accepts criminal liability and there are no grounds present to exclude liability, the prosecution and the defendant (represented by an attorney) can conclude an agreement, which contains (1) the narrative description of the facts of the case; (2) the legal classification of the offence; (3) the declaration of the defendant admitting the crime and accepting liability; and (4) the sanction to be applied (Code of Criminal Procedure Section 410 (2)). In return, a lower sentence shall be imposed. There is, however, no sentencing discount table for a defendant opting for an agreement. Instead, the Code of Criminal Procedure refers to the Section of the Criminal Code which allows judges to impose a lower sentence if the one applicable by law would be too harsh based on the general principles of sentencing (Criminal Code Section 83 (1)).[34] This section, as stated above, opens up the applicability of day fines to a whole range of more serious crimes, only punishable by imprisonment by default.

The agreement has to be accepted by a judge in a pre-trial hearing and be included in a summary judgment (Code of Criminal Procedure Section 732). The judge, however, cannot alter the agreement: he or she either accepts it or, if he or she does not, the case proceeds to trial (Code of Criminal Procedure Section 734).

An internal analysis of the Prosecution Service concluded, however, that the sanction agreed is predominantly suspended custodial sentence, in connection with reparations for the victim. Of the ninety-eight agreements analysed, not

---

[34]   See Section 8.2.1, point 2.

a single one contains day fines.[35] The institution of agreement on admitting guilt is, however, very new, thus we cannot yet speak of any established practice. It might very well be that day fines will be agreed on in the future.

8.2.3.2 Sentencing

Day fines, for all practical purposes (at least for now) are only imposed by judges in a judgment following a trial. There are no further specific rules beyond the requirement to consider the assets, income, the life situation and everyday needs of a defendant.

A crucial issue here is how the judges determine the adequate amount of the daily unit once all legitimate expenses have been deducted. The same 2003 study found that judges deem that about 50 to 80 per cent of the remaining daily income is the adequate range for the fine to have a real 'bite' and achieve the aim of the criminal sanction.[36]

8.2.3.3 Access to Financial Information

There are no dedicated rules in Hungarian law about the access to financial information about the defendant. Generally speaking, information about assets and income is derived from obtained evidence during the investigation or the trial phase.[37]

In practice, this can come from two sources. Most of the time, the information is collected in the course of the investigation by the police and the prosecution for the purpose of securing a warrant of attachment.[38] In Hungarian Criminal Procedure, assets could be seized for three distinct reasons: (1) to secure evidence; (2) to secure assets that can be subject to forfeiture (both 'lefoglalás', Law on Criminal Procedure Sections 308–23 and 'Zár alá vétel', Law on Criminal Procedure, Sections 324–32); and (3) to secure assets that can cover civil tort claims of the victim(s) (in Hungarian law under certain circumstances these can be adjudicated by the sentencing judge in the criminal trial).

---

[35] Egyezség a bűnösség beismeréséről. Legfőbb Ügyészség, Budapest, 2018.

[36] *Supra* note 32.

[37] There is no academic research on the topic in Hungary. The following description is based on personal communications with judges and prosecutors.

[38] This has two forms in Hungarian Criminal Procedure. First, it can serve the securing of evidence, as well as of assets that can be forfeited should the defendant be found guilty ('lefoglalás', Law on Criminal Procedure Sections 308–23). Second, it can serve the securing of assets that can cover civil tort claims of the victim (in Hungarian law under certain circumstances these can be adjudicated by the sentencing judge in the criminal trial) and potentially forfeitable assets ('Zár alá vétel', Law on Criminal Procedure, Section 324–32).

Theoretically, the judge can also order that evidence is presented at trial about the assets and income of the defendant. This can happen when no assets were seized during the investigation and thus the financial situation of the defendant was not investigated. Thus, at least theoretically, the whole toolbox judges can use to determine the existence, location and value of forfeitable assets in the inquisitorial model is available to investigate the financial situation of the defendant: he or she can order financial information such as bank, brokerage or other investment accounts to be disclosed, tangible property assessed and evaluated, etc. Practically, however, all this generally amounts to a couple of questions about income and assets, as well as the costs of the household. This is because judges are not eager to be bogged down in difficult questions of income and asset evaluation, so they usually tend to play it safe and set an amount that they believe the defendant is able to pay.[39]

8.2.4 *The Execution of Day Fines*

8.2.4.1 Administration

The execution of day fines is administered by the budget office ('gazdasági hivatal') of the court that imposed the sentence. Once the sentence is processed, the budget office notifies the defendant about the modalities of payment. From the day the defendant receives the notification, he or she has fifteen days to pay the full amount. In case the court ordered the day fine to be paid in instalments, the amount and the respective payment deadlines are also included in the notification. The payment has to be transferred to an account of the court or paid on a slip in the post office.[40]

The law does not require that the defendant pays the fine him- or herself and does not control the person making the payment. This means that by all practical purposes the fine can be paid by anybody, such as a family member. Once the payment is booked, it is considered paid and the budget office issues a certificate to that effect.[41]

8.2.4.2 Application for Payment Instalments

If the defendant can provide reasonable proof that the immediate payment of the whole amount of the fine would pose such a severe financial burden to the

---

[39] This assessment is based on personal communication with judges.
[40] 11/2014 IM rendelet Section 78.
[41] *Ibid.*

defendant and his or her family or dependants, which would be disproportionate, the court can allow payment in instalments. The court can also order a stay in the execution of the fine, for a maximum of three months, which can be extended once for a further three months (Law on the Execution of Criminal Sanctions Section 42 (1)–(2)).

The defendant can either apply right after the sentence becoming final, or after receiving the notification. The sentencing judge decides in both cases (Code of Criminal Procedure Section 672 (2)).

These payment instalments are not the same as the instalment payments ordered by the sentencing judge. Rather, this is an additional, corrective and procedural option. What follows from this is that even if the sentencing judge is making the decision, the latter does not constitute the reopening of the judgment, which remains final (so-called simplified review, 'egyszerűsített felülvizsgálat', Code of Criminal Procedure Sections 672–5). This means that this procedural option cannot be used to alter the amount of the instalment if it was already ordered in the judgment, nor is it possible to apply for a stay in the payment of the first instalment.[42] What also follows from this is that – this being technically a review of a final sentence – the decision is final and cannot be applied (Law on the Execution of Criminal Sanctions Section 44 (4)).

8.2.4.3 Non-payment

In Hungarian law a civil enforcement of the judgment is not possible. This is because dogmatically speaking (as opposed to back taxes, for example) a day fine meted out as a sanction for a crime cannot be considered as an enforceable (civil) claim of the state. Instead, a fine not paid is commuted to imprisonment. There are two exceptions from this general rule: day fines imposed against juveniles and, under certain circumstances, if assets seized during the investigation or the trial can cover the fine.

COMMUTATION OF THE NON-PAID FINE TO IMPRISONMENT If the defendant does not pay either the fine or any of the instalments within the set deadline, the day fine (or the remaining part of it) is commuted to imprisonment. One daily unit equals one day of imprisonment (Criminal Code Section 50 (4)). The imprisonment in such cases can be lower than the legal minimum of thirty days. The imprisonment is executed in the lowest security prison ('fogház'), except the cases where the day fine was imposed together with a fixed-term executable imprisonment (in case of crimes committed for

---

[42] 84. BK vélemény.

pecuniary gain), in which case it is executed at the security level imprisonment.[43] In the latter case, if the imprisonment is suspended, then the commuted imprisonment is added to the time of suspension (thus this too, is suspended).[44] If the fine is paid any time before the commencement of or during the imprisonment, the defendant shall be freed at once.[45]

ENFORCEMENT OF DAY FINES AGAINST JUVENILES Should a juvenile not pay the fines by the fifteen-day deadline, the court shall first attempt to enforce it as a civilian claim. To this procedure the Law on Judicial Execution applies. The execution is undertaken by the court bailiff ('törvényszéki végrehajtó').[46] Should the bailiff fail to execute it as a civil claim, the fine is commuted to community service or imprisonment.

8.3 PRACTICAL IMPLEMENTATION

In practice, the Hungarian system of criminal sanctions remains in practice heavily tilted towards imprisonment. Of the total number of sanctions imposed following a trial, only an average of 30 per cent are day fines in the last four years from which statistics are available.[47] A slight increase since the introduction of the new Criminal Code (which, as elaborated above, lowered the minimum of the amount of the daily unit) is apparent, yet it is too early to say whether this is due to normal fluctuation or the sign of an emerging trend.

The number of daily units in Hungarian criminal law can go from low to relatively high. Yet, it appears that in practice the higher range of daily units is relatively rarely used. The majority of daily units consistently fall between 100 and 150 days. As Figure 8.1 shows, this is one fifth of the highest possible number. This is consistent with the general practice in Hungarian criminal justice where for more serious crimes, imprisonment is imposed and likely indicates a belief that imprisonment, even if suspended, is considered to be a more serious sanction than a day fine.

The range of the amount of the daily unit is also fairly broad in Hungarian criminal law, yet, likewise to the number of daily units, the distribution of it is

---

[43] Law on the Execution of Criminal Sanctions Section 66 (1).
[44] *Ibid.*, Section 66 (4).
[45] *Ibid.*, Section 66 (2).
[46] 11/2014 IM rendelet Section 79.
[47] Due to the structure of the database, the table only includes sanctions meted out in a judgment establishing criminal liability following a trial. The data do not include foregoing the trial (lemondás a tárgyalásról), expedited trial (bíróság elé állítás) and agreement on the admission of guilt (egyezség a bűnösség beismeréséről).

TABLE 8.1 *Number and percentage of day fine sanctions per year*

Year	N	% of all sanctions	Total N of sanctions
2013	15,665	23	67,277
2014	19,664	28	70,919
2015	20,075	30	67,216
2016	21,529	32	67,550
2017	22,790	35	65,004
Total	99,723	30	337,966

Source: National Office of the Judiciary

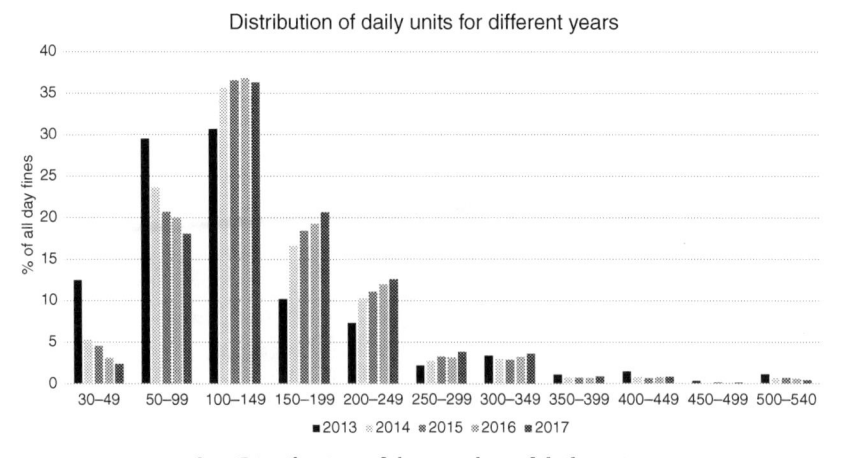

FIGURE 8.1 Distribution of the number of daily units per year
Source: National Office of the Judiciary

somewhat one-sided. Most of the daily units fall in the lower and middle of the range (Figure 8.2).[48]

Given the fact that the largest number of day fines falls into the lower section of the range, both for the number and the amount of the daily units, it is not a surprise that the total amount of day fines also remains relatively low (Figure 8.3).

As discussed above, day fines are a compulsory complementary punishment to imprisonment in Hungarian criminal law for crimes committed with the special intent of gaining pecuniary gain. These include, in statistical terms, insignificant

---

[48] The spike in 2013 is due to the change of the law. The new Criminal Code entered into force in 2013 and – on the initiative of the judiciary, the representatives of which found the lowest amount too high – the lower end of the range was lowered from 2,500 to 1,000 HUF (see above). As it is apparent from the statistical data the practice immediately adjusted.

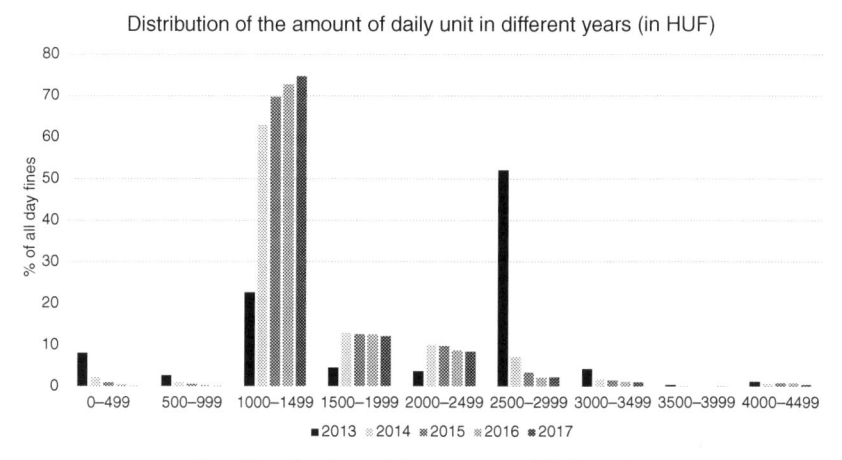

FIGURE 8.2 Distribution of the amount of daily units per year
Source: National Office of the Judiciary

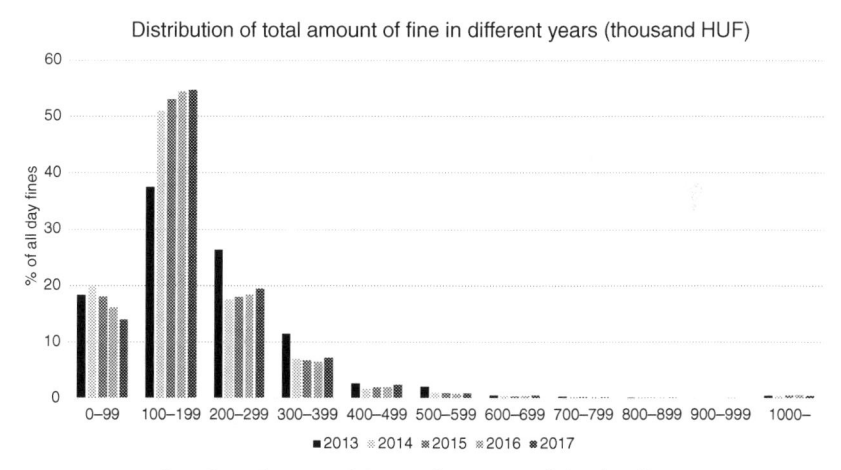

FIGURE 8.3 Distribution of the total amount of the day fines per year
Source: National Office of the Judiciary

offences, basic economic crimes such as falsification of documents and economic fraud. If the legislative intent here was a compulsory pecuniary sanction for offences committed with pecuniary gain, this option is not completely exploited by the courts: there is hardly any difference to the day fines imposed for crimes committed without such a special intent (Table 8.2). This might be due to the fact that under this rule day fines are a compulsory additional sanction

TABLE 8.2 *The amount and number of daily units of day fines imposed for offences with the special intent of Pecuniary Gain in 2017*

Aim pecuniary gain			Number of daily units	Amount of daily unit	Total amount of fine
No	N		96,017	96,017	96,017
	mean		135	1,440	180,584
	median		120	1,000	150,000
Yes	N		3,706	3,706	3,706
	mean		160	1,527	242,176
	median		140	1,000	175,000
Total	N		99,723	99,723	99,723
	mean		136	1,443	182,873
	median		120	1,000	150,000

Source: National Office of the Judiciary

to imprisonment and thus the combination of the two shall be considered as a total sanction. This also means, however, that judges do not tend to lower the imprisonment only to counterbalance it with a higher fine. If that were the case, the difference to crimes without this special intent would be larger.

Day fines thus remain an alternative sanction for minor offences in the Hungarian criminal justice system. In 2017, most day fines were imposed for battery causing minor bodily harm, theft and public nuisance, followed by fraud and battery causing serious bodily harm (Table 8.3).

As no empirical, qualitative studies to date have been conducted on the day fine practice of Hungarian judges why the broad range available under the law is not utilised for more serious crimes, especially serious economic crimes remain a mystery. We initially hypothesised that the use of criminal forfeiture, which is often applied in cases concerning serious economic crimes and which is an in effect much more serious sanction, might be responsible. We theorised that judges regard criminal forfeiture as a quasi-pecuniary sanction (which it is not) and forego day fines in cases when sizeable forfeiture is ordered. This hypothesis, however, was not supported by our data, which showed no significant correlation between the two.

8.4 CONCLUSION

All in all, it can be argued that the institution of the day fine fulfils a function as an alternative to (executable) imprisonment for minor offences and misdemeanours. Day fines constitute around 30 per cent of all imposed sanctions

TABLE 8.3 *Offences with the highest percentage of day fines among the total number of imposed sanctions and most frequent alternatives to day fines in 2017*

Criminal offence	No				Percentage			Most frequent other sanctions
	Fine	Other sanction	No sanction	Total	Fine %	Other sanc-tion %	No sanc-tion %	
battery causing minor bodily harm	2,532	1,552	306	4,390	58	35	7	Imprisonment (14%), Community service (10%)
theft	1,755	38,499	5,932	46,186	4	83	13	Imprisonment (37%), Community service (27%)
public nuisance	1,500	33,195	8,866	43,561	3	76	20	Community service (26%), Imprisonment (24%)
fraud	741	7,363	2,498	10,602	7	69	24	Imprisonment (46%), Community service (15%)
battery causing serious bodily harm	622	9,644	1,881	12,147	5	79	15	Imprisonment (56%), Community service (16%)
possession of narcotics	565	4,845	2,087	7,497	8	65	28	Community service (34%), Imprisonment (10%)
causing a road accident	366	1,150	2,928	4,444	8	26	66	Driving ban (30%), Imprisonment (10%)
driving under the influence of alcohol	349	12,071	45,606	58,026	1	21	79	Driving ban (92%), Community services (11%)
forgery of administrative documents	339	6,082	3,921	10,342	3	59	38	Community service (13%), Imprisonment (11%)
forgery of private documents	250	2,404	415	3,069	8	78	14	Community service (14%), Imprisonment (5%)

TABLE 8.3 *(continued)*

| Criminal offence | No | | | | Percentage | | | Most frequent other sanctions |
	Fine	Other sanction	No sanction	Total	Fine %	Other sanction %	No sanction %	
harassment	172	2,308	825	3,305	5	70	25	Community service (17%), Imprisonment (16%)
embezzlement	158	1,695	930	2,783	6	61	33	Imprisonment (32%), Profession ban (14%)
use of a forged private document	90	2,254	1,196	3,540	3	64	34	Community service (10%), Imprisonment (7%)
vandalism	70	867	335	1,272	6	68	26	Community service (24%), Imprisonment (14%)
conspiracy to commit excise violation	29	544	299	872	3	62	34	Community service (16%), Imprisonment (16%)
larceny of a motor vehicle	25	887	334	1,246	2	71	27	Imprisonment (40%), Driving ban (40%)
breach of accounting regulations	22	154	286	462	5	33	62	Imprisonment (11%), Profession ban (6%)
criminal offence with individual identification	21	1,667	1,378	3,066	1	54	45	Community service (15%), Imprisonment (12%)
unlawful conveyance of operating a vehicle	6	211	349	566	1	37	62	Driving ban (33%), Community services (15%)
offence against transport security	3	269	365	637	0	42	57	Driving ban (17%), Community services (4%)

Source: National Office of the Judiciary

and this is in Central East-European comparison a relatively high number. There is no larger pattern discernible from the statistical data in the day fine practice in crimes where it is regularly applied. However, this is probably at least partly due to the complexity of the Hungarian sanction system that allows a high level of individualisation.

With that said, it is also clear that the institution of day fines is not used to its full potential, especially for serious economic crimes. The available range would allow much more considerable total fines than the ones imposed by judges. The reasons for this is not entirely clear, but most likely due to a view among judges that imprisonment is the most serious sanction and they prefer to apply the latter for serious economic offences. The same might also explain why there is no significant difference between day fines as an elective sanction and compulsory day fines for offences committed for pecuniary gain, among others fraud; judges might deem it to be disproportionate to impose significant fines on top of a potentially significant executable imprisonment. Another likely explanation might be the compulsory forfeiture for pecuniary gains from criminal offences, which might also be viewed as a sufficient enough pecuniary sanction that makes day fines less prominent among the sanctions imposed for serious economic crimes.

Questionable practices also remain in the everyday implementation of day fines that might raise issues concerning human rights and fundamental constitutional principles. These include imposing day fines on defendants with no income and assets and the lack of monitoring as to who actually pays the fine. These might warrant further empirical investigations.

REFERENCES

LEGISLATIVE ACTS AND ADMINISTRATIVE REGULATIONS

1978 évi IV. Törvény a Büntető Törvénykönyvről (Act No. 4 of 1978 on the Criminal Code)

2012 évi C. Törvény a Büntető Törvénykönyvről (Act No. 100 of 2012 on the Criminal Code

2013 évi V. Törvény a Polgári Törvénykönyvről. (Act No. 5 of 2013 on the Civil Code)

2013 évi CCXL. Törvény a büntetések, az intézkedések, egyes kényszerintézkedések és a szabálysértési elzárás végrehajtásáról (Law on the Execution of Criminal and Administrative Sanctions)

11/2014. (XII. 13.) IM rendelet a fogvatartott személy esetében a büntetőeljárás lefolytatása során, továbbá a büntetőügyekben hozott határozatok végrehajtása során a bíróságokra és egyéb szervekre háruló feladatokról (Decree of the Minister of Justice on the Execution of Judgments and Decisions in Criminal Cases)

JUDICIAL DECISIONS

25. Büntető Kollégiumi Vélemény
84. Büntető Kollégiumi Vélemény
Kúria Bfv.II.1523/2014/10
Kúria Bfv. II. 538/2014/19

COMMENTARIES

Mészáros, R. 2018. 'A pénzbüntetés', in Kónya, I. (ed.). *Kommentár a Büntető Törvénykönyvhöz*. Budapest: HVG-ORAC.

ARTICLES

Tóth, M. 2003. 'A pénzbüntetés kiszabásának gyakorlata', *Jogi Továbbképző Intézet*. Budapest.
Pápai-Tarr, Á. and Sipos, F. 2019. 'A pénzbüntetés fejlődésének hazai mérföldkövei'. *Miskolci Jogi Szemle* 14(2), 315–30.

9

Day Fines in France

Bruno Deffains and Jean-Baptiste Thierry

The day fine sentence was created by Law No. 83–466 of 10 June 1983 and was contained in Articles 43–8 to 43–11 of the former Criminal Code. This law also created the sentence of community service. The day fine and community service were created to replace the usual sentencing solutions. Today, these sentences are said to be alternatives. They are, more particularly, both considered as alternatives to the prison sanction.

The inspiration for the day fine system came from other countries. In 1979, a report was prepared for the Ministry of Justice by Mr Robert Schmelck, Attorney General at the Court of Cassation.[1] It is in that report that the day fines were proposed. The idea was, however, not new. The *Société générale des prisons et de législation criminelle* had already studied the day fine sentence in 1954.[2] A government task force had also accepted the principle of day fines in 1973. However, the Criminal Code Revision Commission did not incorporate the day fine in its proposals.[3] This working group, composed mainly of magistrates, focussed on the principle of pecuniary punishment[4] and gave a number of recommendations regarding the scope of this sentence and its recovery. Among many important ideas put forward in the report of Schmelck, the report noted the problematic character of the prison sanction as it does not stimulate the reintegration of the convicted into society:

---

[1] Schmelck, *Rapport sur la peine pécuniaire des 'jours-amendes'*.
[2] *Rev. pén.*, 1954, p. 11.
[3] *Supra* note 1, p. 8.
[4] Although the Schmelck report draws on several foreign examples (Finland, Sweden, Denmark, Federal Republic of Germany, Austria, Argentina, Brazil, Canada), the main existing publications in French have looked at the German system.

custodial sentences no longer benefit the favour they have long benefited. It is now agreed that imprisonment, if it retains its value of punishment and remains the essential means of protection against dangerous offenders, responds very poorly to the function of social rehabilitation of the convicted person which modern criminal law has assigned to the punishment.[5]

The idea of the working group was to hit the offender in his wallet. According to the report, the fine has a number of advantages: it does not lead to a corruption of the convicted, restoration is possible in the event of a judicial error and a fine provides money to the state instead of merely costing money (like in the case of imprisonment). The authors of the report consider that the alternative of imprisonment might have a negative impact on the resocialisation of the offender. However, the report equally noticed several disadvantages of the traditional fining system: it is not sufficiently dissuasive, because it does not intimidate the rich or insolvent offenders; it violates the principle of equality as the fine will have different effects depending upon the wealth of the offender; and finally, it violates the principle of the individualisation of the punishment, as the payment of a fine is often executed by the family members of the convicted. The report further noted that although a fine should in principle be proportional to the convicted persons' wealth, judicial decisions did not really reveal the extent to which an adjustment of the fine to the offenders' wealth actually took place. It was even often not clear whether the amount of the fine depended on the seriousness of the offence.[6]

In its conclusions, the report considered that the day fine could 'stop the increase in mass delinquency, the most important in terms of the number of crimes committed, but also the least serious when considered in terms of individual guilt'. The desire to fight particularly mass delinquency explains why the day fine cannot be applied for '*crimes*', being the most serious criminal offences in French law. Crimes can lead to an imprisonment of fifteen years or to a life sentence. To ensure the success of the day fine, the Schmelck report

---

[5] *Supra* note 1, p. 3. '*les peines privatives de liberté ne jouissent plus aujourd'hui de la faveur dont elles ont longtemps bénéficié. L'on s'accorde maintenant à reconnaître que l'emprisonnement, s'il conserve sa valeur de châtiment et reste l'indispensable moyen de protection à l'égard des délinquants dangereux, répond très mal à la fonction de reclassement social du condamné que le droit pénal moderne assigne à la peine*'. The observation is almost ironic: the finding of the impasse in imprisonment is old and renewed and yet the prison sentences imposed remain numerous and the legislator fails to stem the increase in the prison population. The development of alternative sentences to imprisonment seems more to allow increased repression of offences which would not have been previously punished.

[6] *Supra* note 1, p. 6. Overall, the report is not based on statistical or criminological studies that tend to show the effectiveness or ineffectiveness of the fine.

also called for a wide information campaign aiming at awareness raising regarding this new sentence.

During the parliamentary debate on what would become Law No. 83–466 of 10 June 1983, the Senate had even proposed to repeal the fixed fine, replacing it with just the day fine penalty. The adoption of the new Criminal Code in 1992 did not call into question the existence of this penalty, which is now provided for in Articles 131–3 and 131–5 of the Criminal Code.[7] Since then, day fines have only been subject to technical adjustments.

Although the day fines sentence was considered as an alternative to short-term imprisonment, the scope of this sentence is particularly wide. There is no particular limit regarding the length of the imprisonment, as far as the question is concerned when the day fine can be used as an alternative to imprisonment.[8] In France, the maximum imprisonment is ten years and twenty years in case of recidivism. Alternative sentences in general and the day fine in particular, can in principle be pronounced irrespective of the duration of the prison sentence.

9.2 LEGAL FRAMEWORK FOR DAY FINES

In positive law, the penalty of day fines can be imposed in different criminal law cases and at different moments in the penal process: at the time of the court decision, or during its execution. As a result, there is considerable uncertainty about the legal nature of this sentence, which many describe as a kind of 'hybrid'. These uncertainties do not, however, prevent the relative success of this sentence, which is more often pronounced than, for example, community service.

Despite this success, the legislator does not attach great importance to this sentence. For example, the recent Law 2018–2022 concerning Programming and Reform of Justice of 23 March 2019 does not address day fines at all. This is striking as this Law is leading to many changes in the punishment system. In sum, the day fine can be imposed in various ways: either as an alternative for

---

[7] There are many other provisions of the Criminal Code and the Code of Criminal Procedure, which refer to the fine and its enforcement.

[8] The principle of the alternative penalty is that it replaces a prison sentence incurred for an offence. The maximum term of imprisonment for an offence is ten years imprisonment. Day fines can replace any prison sentence – up to ten years. Observe that alternative sentences – pronounced instead of imprisonment – include community service, penal coercion – which has been abolished in March 2020 – internships, sanction-reparation, private and restrictive penalties for Article 131–6 and the day fine.

the prison sanction, or as a complementary penalty, or during the execution of the sentence.

9.2.1 *Alternative Punishment*

The day fine can be applied to all offences. Article 131–3 of the Criminal Code lists the penalties that can be imposed when an offence is committed, being: imprisonment, home detention under electronic surveillance,[9] community service, fine, day fine, probationary sentences and privative or restrictive rights under Article 131–6, the penalty-repair. The day fine is therefore part of a large arsenal of sentences that can be pronounced by the trial court. As previously mentioned, crimes are not affected by this punishment.[10] Ticket fines (*contraventions*) are also excluded. The reason is simple: because of the non-execution of the penalty-day sanctioned by the incarceration of the convicted person, it is not possible to apply this penalty for 'contraventions' as these offences cannot give rise to a prison sanction. The day fine cannot, in principle, be imposed in addition to a prison sanction (see exceptions in the next section). Nor can it be pronounced in cumulation with a fixed fine.[11] Article 131–5 of the Criminal Code considers the imposition of a day fine only for offences punishable by imprisonment. This excludes the day fine when an offence is only punishable with a fine. In addition, the day fine may be suspended.[12] The day fine is not applicable to legal persons, nor to minors. The exclusion is logic for legal persons as in France the day fine is considered an alternative to the prison sanction. However, the exclusion of the day fine in case of minors is more questionable. When the day fine is imposed as an alternative sanction, it is pronounced by the district court (*tribunal correctionnel*).[13]

---

[9]   This is a punishment created by the law of 23 March 2019, loi de programmation 2018–2022 et de réforme pour la justice. Strictly speaking, this sentence is not new, since it only repeats what previously existed: placement under electronic surveillance, which was an adjustment to the prison sentence.

[10] It refers to crimes which incur a sentence of seclusion, cannot be subject to the fine penalty. As this is an alternative penalty, it only applies to offences (which is specific to our tripartite classification of offences). To these penalties must be added the additional penalties, pronounced in addition to the main penalties and which are specifically provided for by the texts punishing offences.

[11] Code pénal, Article 131–9.

[12] Code pénal, Article 132–31.

[13] The district court can decide collectively (sitting in a bench of three judges), but also as a single judge, in normal adversarial proceedings. The decision could, however, also be made in writing, at the end of a non-adversarial procedure: the criminal order. The penalty can also

9.2.2 *Complementary Punishment*

The nature of the day fine in France is peculiar as it can be pronounced as an alternative to the prison sanction, as just discussed. It can, however, also be imposed in addition to the prison sanction, in which case it becomes a complementary punishment.[14] The day fine can be imposed as a complementary penalty (to imprisonment), for example, in case of an unlawful use of narcotics[15] or for several infringements to traffic laws.[16] The privileged field of this additional penalty therefore concerns the offences provided for by traffic laws. When the sentence of day fine is pronounced as additional penalty, it is also pronounced by the district court (*cour correctionnel*).

9.2.3 *Instalments*

When the day fine sentence is pronounced, it can be split. Article 132–28 of the Criminal Code provides that the court may, for serious medical, family, professional or social reasons, decide that the day fine shall, for a period not exceeding three years, be executed in instalments. However, the possibility of splitting *ab initio* a day fine penalty can be puzzling[17] since it already contains an instalment.

9.2.4 *Execution of a Sentence*

The penalty of day fine can finally be decided by the judge of application of the sentences.[18] Several provisions make it possible to convert a prison sentence or other sentence into a day fine. Article 132–57 of the Criminal Code, for example, provides that where the sentence of imprisonment is less than or equal to six months, the penalty enforcement judge may decide that the convicted person will be sentenced to a day fine. It is also provided that in the event of partial execution of a community service, the penalty

---

be proposed by the public prosecutor within the framework of the procedure of appearance on preliminary recognition of guilt: it will then have to be approved by a judge.

[14] Some authors therefore consider the day fine as a hybrid fine: Roure, 'Les jours-amendes: une sanction à redéfinir', p. 64.

[15] Code de la santé publique, Article L. 3421–7.

[16] See *e.g.*: Code de la route, Article L. 211–26 (la conduite sans assurance); Article L. 221–2-1 (conduite sans permis); Article L. 224–18 (fausse déclaration pour obtenir le permis); Article L. 236–3 (rodéos motorisés).

[17] Bioy, 'Le jour-amende en droit pénal français', p. 92.

[18] The judge in charge of the execution of the sentences pronounced by the courts.

enforcement judge may order the conversion of the non-executed part into a day fine. According to Article 741–1-1 of the Code of Criminal Procedure, the judge responsible for the enforcement of sentences may, *ex officio*, at the request of the person concerned or at the request of the public prosecutor, order by reasoned decision to substitute for community service a penalty of day fine.

The penalty enforcement judge therefore has the power to convert one sentence (for example imprisonment) into another sentence (for example a day fine). The same possibility is provided for in Article 733–1 of the Code of Criminal Procedure, which allows the judge to apply penalties to transform the sentence of community service into a day fine penalty. Whether the day fine is imposed by the district court as an alternative or additional sanction, or at the execution stage by the penalty enforcement judge (whereby the prison sanction is converted into a day fine), the day fine still has the same objective and definition.

9.2.5 *Definition*

Article 131–5 of the Criminal Code prescribes that the convicted person pays to the Treasury an amount whose total value results from the setting by the judge of a daily contribution for a given number of days. The amount of each day fine is determined considering the resources and the charges of the defendant; it cannot exceed 1,000 euros. The number of day fines is determined taking into account the circumstances of the offence; it cannot exceed 360. The originality of this penalty is therefore that it is not fixed according to the maximum foreseen for the offence, but according to two elements: the number of day fines, on the one hand and the amount of the daily fine, on the other hand.

Article 131–25 of the Criminal Code provides that the total amount is due upon expiry of the total number of day fines pronounced. However, Article R. 55 (4) of the Code of Criminal Procedure grants a reduction to the convicted person who would pay the total amount of the fine days before the expiry of the time limit: if he/she pays within one month of his/her conviction, he/she benefits from a 'discount' of 20 per cent. Finally, non-performance may result in imprisonment corresponding to the number of unpaid days.

The hybrid nature of the day fine has led to questions in legal doctrine. Although it is used by the courts, it was considered as 'unclassifiable' into particular categories of the law of punishment.[19] It follows that there are

---

[19] Classification refers here to the French typologies of fines (principal, secondary, complementary . . .). The day fine system is independent from these typologies.

uncertainties concerning the exact nature of this penalty. Those uncertainties did not give rise to any particular dispute. So far the French Court of Cassation never had to decide on the particular nature of the day fine. This is to some extent surprising as penalties normally correspond to a particular typology. A practical consequence of this uncertainty is that it may be difficult to determine the correct nature of the day fine. As a result it is often difficult to obtain information on the motivation of particular decisions which pronounce the day fine[20] or on the decision of the penalty enforcement jurisdiction, which are often not publically available. However, as noted by Jacques-Henri Robert,

> the quite paradoxical result of this situation is that, thirteen years after the entry into force of the Criminal Code, the Court of Cassation has never been led to clarify the ambiguities of the law 'since' when pronouncing day fines, the judges are very careful not to pronounce convictions of which the motivation or arrangement could raise questions of law relating to the legal nature of the day fine.[21]

9.2.6 *Determination of the Day Fine*

The penalty of day fine must take into account the resources and charges of the convicted person. However, there is no specific device allowing the judge to know precisely these resources and charges. Apart from the fact that there is no legal definition of these terms, there are no specific guidelines regarding sentencing either. When the judge determines the income, costs can in principle not be deduced. The information upon which the judge bases his/her decision is to be provided by the defendant. Therefore, when an individual is summoned to appear before the criminal court, it is specified that he/she must provide his/her proof of income and his/her tax assessment or non-taxation notice. This obligation to provide information concerning income is rather weak, as a result of which 'far from the exact appreciation of the convict's economic reality, the judge often has only a rough and global idea'.[22] In the context of the immediate appearance (*comparution immédiate*), it is often impossible to obtain information on the defendant's financial situation. This procedure of immediate appearance is often applied when the defendant was caught red-handed and that therefore is an emergency condition. It is de facto applied when the defendant is not represented by a counsel. It is the case

---

[20] The decisions rendered by the criminal courts are not accessible on the existing databases.
[21] Robert, 'Jours-amende', p. 4.
[22] *Supra* note 17, p. 86.

where the defendant is summoned to court immediately after the offence took place. In that particular case there is often no information on his/her financial information and often systematically a prison sanction will be imposed. The result of these types of accelerated procedures is often the imposition of a prison sanction. In those cases of an immediate appearance after a red-handed offence, day fines become de facto irrelevant.

9.3 PRACTICAL IMPLEMENTATION OF DAY FINES

In 2017, out of 557,762 convictions for offences, 23,607 included a day fine (around 4 per cent).[23] In the same period 180,088 nominal or fixed fines were imposed. Day fines appear to be less often pronounced when an offender is convicted for several offences.[24] The fact that 23,607 day fines were imposed shows that the penalty is surely not insignificant. It is all the more surprising that there are almost no disputes concerning the application of this day fine to be found in case law. The fact that discussions related to day fines never reach the Court of Cassation is probably related to the relatively small amounts involved. Decisions of the penalty enforcement judge are not published. As a result, there is no information about the amount of the day fine, the type of offences concerned, etc. Although the sentence is not negligible, the record of its use is disappointing.

> The day fine seems today to represent a nebula, to which however few studies are devoted. . . . Its regime, its functioning and its empirical reality are the subject of little interest . . . This sanction is often overlooked by justice professionals . . . Some statistical data exist, however, but they generally only show the data relating to the pronouncement of the day-fine by the trial courts and the known official publications do not report the reality of the execution of this sentence either.[25]

Judges do not seem to have strong incentives to impose a day fine as there are often difficulties in practice to recover the small amounts of the fine.[26] One

---

[23] 14,738 community services were pronounced, 180,088 fixed fines and 286,377 prison sanctions.
      www.justice.gouv.fr/art_pix/Stat_Annuaire_ministere-justice_2017_chapitre6.pdf.

[24] 16,672 day fines in case of a single offence; only 6,935 day fines in case of multiple offences.

[25] *Supra* note 17, p. 18. '*Le jour-amende semble aujourd'hui représenter une nébuleuse, à laquelle pourtant peu d'études sont consacrées. . . . Son régime, son fonctionnement et sa réalité empirique font l'objet de peu d'intérêt . . . . Cette sanction est souvent méconnue par les professionnels de la justice . . . . Certaines données statistiques existent pourtant, mais elles n'exposent généralement que les seules données relatives au prononcé du jour-amende par les juridictions de jugement, et les publications officielles connues ne font pas davantage état de la réalité de l'exécution de cette peine*'.

[26] See Saas, Lorvellec, Gautron, 'Les sanctions pénales, une nouvelle distribution', p. 159. One magistrate mentions in that respect: '*on nous avait par exemple demandé . . . de ne plus*

can also observe that since day fines can only be imposed on people who have at least some means, one important aspect that probably plays a role are the benefits that people get from the state and whether they are high enough to at least allow the imposition of a minimal day fine. However, these benefits are difficult to evaluate considering the absence of data.

9.4 STATISTICAL ELEMENTS

There is no empirical investigation of the effectiveness of day fines in France. No empirical studies were conducted. The only statistical information is descriptive. So, it is impossible to derive a clear conclusion regarding the effectiveness of these fines compared to the fixed fines or other sanctions. There are equally no data concerning the public or professional perceptions of the day fine system.

As we can observe in Table 9.1, there is an increase in the number of convictions and a corresponding increase in the number of day fines. Clearly, one can notice that the courts increasingly favour monetary sanctions.[27] One can notice an increase in the number of day fines, but the respective increase is not proportional. One can only notice that the day fine was more frequently pronounced.[28] When the day fine is used as a complementary punishment, it is, compared to all other additional penalties, almost not used at all.

Day fines are more frequently pronounced for traffic offences, simple thefts, drugs offences, outrages and non-performance of community service, as well as wilful violence. 'This sanction is more often pronounced, but the offences in repression which it intervenes seem very targeted ... are privileged offences having an object or causing material damage and the offences aimed at sanctioning the non-respect of a preceding sanction ordered by a public authority or aiming at this authority itself in the exercise of its function of control'.[29]

Regarding the amount, the average day fine imposed, in full and not per day, is between 500 and 600 euros.[30] The monetary value per day is

---

prononcer de jours-amendes parce que de toute façon, ils n'étaient pas suivis et depuis 2008, il n'y avait pas d'audiencement, c'est-à-dire que nous, on n'audiençait pas pour recouvrer les jours-amendes. De fait, ils se sont adaptés, ils ont moins prononcé de jours-amendes qu'ailleurs', p. 164.

[27] *Supra* note 17, p. 357.
[28] *Ibid.*, p. 359.
[29] *Ibid.*, p. 385.
[30] *Ibid.*, p. 390.

TABLE 9.1 *Penalties imposed 2006–17*

	2006	2007	2008	2009	2010	2011	2012	2013	2014	2015	2016 (hors TP)	2017P (hors TP)
Fine	170,715	174,676	175,478	183,576	175,422	170,767	178,749	177,946	179,285	176,150	181,976	177,666
Partially susspended	159,271	163,491	163,893	171,125	163,832	159,872	167,311	166,748	169,109	166,372	172,567	168,456
Totally suspended	542	706	539	736	518	501	505	502	510	645	483	466
Alternative penalty	11,444	11,185	11,585	12,451	11,590	10,895	11,438	11,198	10,176	9,778	9,409	9,210
Suspension of drivers licence	61,024	59,518	59,211	62,387	59,712	60,303	62,718	63,827	60,943	61,762	59,589	60,962
Prohibition of drivers licence	19,818	17,711	14,489	12,938	11,656	13,838	14,755	15,577	8,495	6,978	7,618	7,201
Revocation of drivers licence	1,976	2,046	2,033	2,054	1,675	1,426	1,375	1,482	1,092	845	778	632
Community service	14,519	14,301	14,208	16,385	15,653	14,607	15,505	15,944	15,874	16,173	15,148	14,682
Day fine	19,971	20,292	22,099	23,377	23,963	24,001	24,705	24,526	22,962	23,014	22,863	23,607
Exile from French territory	885	795	843	569	328	236	174	60	34	29	16	22
Prohibition to write checks	32	25	15	12	13	11	14	12	6	3	7	5
Others	3,823	4,348	5,524	7,052	6,424	6,184	6,191	6,226	12,480	14,720	13,159	14,813

Source: www.justice.gouv.fr/art_pix/Stat_Conda_Cr_Del_Contrav_2017p.ods.

relatively low: around 8.50 euros. The overall recovery rate appears to be satisfactory (around 70 per cent).

9.5 EVALUATION

According to Law and Economics scholars, the day fine system may be considered as superior to the alternative models of punishments such as the 'Beckerian maximal fines' or 'fines equal to harms' models:

> The criminal law usually consists of a great range of offences that vary in their severity and harm. Similarly, society consists of many potential offenders who differ in their income and their blame-worthiness for committing a wrong. Therefore, in theory, a system that is able to tailor the sentence in a systematic way to fit all the relevant features may achieve better general and marginal deterrence.[31]

The main argument is that the fine might achieve efficient general deterrence from committing crimes since it threatens the offender's entire wealth. Nevertheless, it is doubtful whether fines can satisfy the requirement of marginal deterrence. The economic perspective is that fines should reflect the harm caused by the offence. In that case, the fine may achieve marginal deterrence for at least a part of the population, since the magnitude of the punishment increases with the severity or the harm of the offence. However, a risk of under-deterrence may follow for those offenders for whom the fine is insignificant. Furthermore, it does not achieve a complete marginal deterrence since the group that cannot afford to pay the fine is incentivised to commit more severe crimes.[32]

In practice, a day fine is calculated by assigning a numeric penalty unit to each offence based on its seriousness. The penalty unit is then multiplied by the defendant's adjusted daily income to determine the day fine amount. The result is an economic sanction adjusted to the seriousness of the offence and simultaneously graduated to the defendant's financial condition. From this perspective, the Law and Economics view argues that the day fine model combines the advantages of the above-mentioned models but avoids their shortcomings:

> The underlying feature of the day fine system is that it imposes an equal relative burden on all offenders with respect to the crime they commit and regardless of their wealth. On the one hand, it considers the severity of the

[31] Kantorowicz-Reznichenko, 'Day Fines: Should the Rich Pay More?', 481.
[32] *Ibid.*, 493.

crime by changing the number of day fines accordingly. On the other hand, it takes into account the financial capacity of the offender through the unit of fine. Those two steps assure that the fine is high enough to generally deter potential offenders from committing crimes, irrespective of their wealth. Furthermore, in case some criminals are not deterred from committing all crimes, it sets different expected costs for different offences to prevent the severer crimes.[33]

However, the process of planning the introduction of day fines implies that some conditions should be met. We suggest to consider each of those conditions and to evaluate whether they are met in the case of France. First, the Criminal Code ought to allow for payment of the fine by instalments. If the total amount of the fine must be paid at once, the day fine would lose the advantage of potentially increasing the payment rate since low-income offenders might not have the full amount (and they would certainly not be punished in such a way by the courts). Indeed, in France the day fine system allows for a payment in instalments.

The second important provision for an efficient application of day fines should include sufficiently detailed guidelines for calculating the fine, which is not the case in France. In order to prevent the undesirable situation of non-uniform fines across different judges, the law ought to provide precise instructions of what should be taken into account in calculating the amount of the day fine. From this point of view, the French system could be improved by introducing clear guidelines regarding the application of the day fine. Apart from the very imprecise reference to resources and charges: even if the principle of individualisation of the sentence is fundamental, the fact remains that some additional clarifications should be made.

In addition, to avoid under-deterrence the amount of the fine should encompass the entire wealth of the offender and not only his/her personal income. If only the personal income is included, persons with profits from other assets would be under-deterred since the daily unit would underestimate their wealth. The French system currently does not take into account wealth or other sources of income of the offender.

The third legal element is the lack of an upper limit on the daily unit. Whenever the law sets a limit to the daily unit that may be imposed on the offender, it allows for under-deterrence of certain high-income offenders. This practice introduces the disadvantage of the fixed fine, even though the model of day fines strives to encompass all offenders regardless of their

---

[33] *Ibid.*, 494.

wealth. One can observe that the French day fine model does not satisfy precisely such a condition because there is an upper limit of the daily unit (which is 1,000 euros).

Finally, in order to achieve an efficient use of financial information regarding the offender, the legal system should allow access to this information. The question concerns the limit that the authorities imposed from obtaining certain fiscal data, thus hindering the possibility to correctly assess the offender's wealth. Concerning fiscal data, there is nothing special in the French system: during the procedure, the accused has to come with his/her tax notice, without further special inquiry. The authorities could have access to all the necessary elements but, in fact, it remains a purely declarative operation.

The day fine system implies that the amount of the fine is tied to an offender's daily earnings. In France, the use of this system seems to be quite limited in practice. This is probably the case because fines have traditionally been based on the individual crime rather than on the individual offender's ability to pay. However, through the introduction of day fines, it is possible that judges become more comfortable with the monetary penalties when the amounts can be adjusted to individual cases and circumstances. The day fine approach has also the potential added benefit of raising total collected fine revenues. Using a two-step procedure to set fine amounts so that they systematically reflect the gravity of offences and offenders' means eliminates most of the objections usually raised about monetary penal sanctions. The door may now be open to wider acceptance and use of monetary sanctions in France.

REFERENCES

Bioy, H. 2016. *Le jour-amende en droit pénal français*. Dalloz, Bibliothèque de la Justice.

Code de la santé publique, Article L. 3421–7.

Code pénal, Article 131–9.

Code pénal, Article 132–31.

Code de la route, Article L. 211–26 (la conduite sans assurance); Article L. 221–2-1 (conduite sans permis); Article L. 224–18 (fausse déclaration pour obtenir le permis); Article L. 236–3 (rodéos motorisés).

Kantorowicz-Reznichenko, E. 2015. 'Day Fines: Should the Rich Pay More?', *Review of Law and Economics* 11: 481.

Robert, J.-H. 2008. 'Jours-amende', *Juris-Classeur Pénal: Article 131–25*, fasc. 20, p. 4.

Roure, D. 1996. 'Les jours-amendes: une sanction à redéfinir', *Recueil Dalloz*, 64.

Saas, C., Lorvellec, S. and Gautron, V. 2013. 'Les sanctions pénales, une nouvelle distribution', in Danet, J. (ed.), *La réponse pénale: dix ans de traitement des délits*, Presses universitaires de Rennes.

Schmelck, R. 1979. *Rapport sur la peine pécuniaire des 'jours-amendes'*. Ministry of Justice.

Société générale des prisons et de législation criminelle 1954. *Revue pénitentiaire et de droit pénal (Rev. pén.)*, 11.

10

Day Fines in Portugal

Maria Fernanda Palma and Helena Morão

10.1 HISTORICAL DEVELOPMENT OF THE DAY FINE MODEL IN PORTUGAL

10.1.1 *Legislative-Historical Process and General Reason behind the Day Fine System*

The introduction of the day fine model in Portugal, in Article 47 of the Portuguese Penal Code, goes back to the first version of the 1982 Penal Code. The Explanatory Memorandum mentions the fact that this system allows for a configuration of the day fine, taking a simultaneous account of, on the one hand the severity of the offence and the guilt of the offender, and, on the other, of the economic status of the latter.[1]

The previous criminal sanctions system was established by the 1852/1886 Penal Code (actually, the 1852 Penal Code which, having undergone the 'Newest Penal Reform' of 1884, gave rise to the formally new Penal Code of 1886). In fact, that system, not being a pure system of fixed fines, only accepted variations of the pecuniary amount between an upper and a lower limit, in proportion to the offender's disposable means (Article 41 of the 1852 Penal Code and Article 67 of the 1886 Penal Code). However, after the 1954 reform, Articles 63 and 84 of the 1886 Penal Code clearly established a system of variable fines based on the offender's guilt, while also maintaining fixed fines and lump sum fines.

Even before the establishment of the democratic regime in Portugal with the Revolution on 25 April 1974 (Carnation Revolution) and the passing of the 1976 Constitution, a long period of discussion about criminal reform had already begun with the presentation in 1963 of a Project of a General Part of

---

[1] About the legal history of the day fine system in Portugal, see Dias, *Direito Penal Português – Parte Geral II – As consequências jurídicas do crime*, p. 114.

the Penal Code, followed by the presentation of a Project of a Special Part in 1966.[2] These Projects were elaborated by Eduardo Correia, the only Full Professor of Criminal Law at the Law Faculty of the University of Coimbra and one of the two Full Professors of Criminal Law in Portugal at the time.

Eduardo Correia's project was very innovative, but never came into force, first of all due to the historic and political background of its presentation (in a regime which did not recognise political rights). His project aimed at a decrease in the maximum limit of the imprisonment term (the maximum general limit was ten years, by the terms of Article 46), favouring a criterion which linked guilt to special prevention, seen as guilt for personality development. On the other hand it was underpinned by a general view on the grounds and goals of punishment, thus highlighting the fine as a substitutive sanction for imprisonment that did not imply deprival of freedom, as well as an alternative or even exclusive penalty in certain cases.

In the aftermath of the Revolution on 25 April 1974 and the coming into force of the 1976 Constitution, Eduardo Correia was to preside over a Revision Committee that worked out the project underlying the 1982 Penal Code, drawing inspiration from the very projects he had brought forward in 1963 and 1966.

The core idea of the 1982 Penal Code (that entered into force in 1983) was that fine sentencing should meet criteria that, on the one hand took simultaneously into account the severity of the offence and the culpability of the offender and on the other hand (adopting an egalitarian view) had regard for the economic status of the perpetrator. In order to grasp the scope and the autonomy of the above-mentioned criteria, it is worth emphasising that the prohibition of *reformatio in peius*, in case of an appeal to the exclusive benefit of the defendant, does not rule out the increase of the daily amount of the fine, whenever a significant improvement in the offender's economic and financial status takes place during the pendency of the appeal (Article 409 (2) of the Code of Penal Procedure).

Such equity concern introduced criteria of distributive justice in the criminal sanctions system. As a matter of fact, the quantitative variation of the fine, entailing patrimonial sacrifice and the corresponding restriction of freedom, must be set in proportion to the severity of the offence and the level of guilt, therefore allowing, in the cases where a substitution of imprisonment by a fine takes place, for the conversion of a model based on imprisonment days into one based on fine days with the current general limits of 10 (minimum) and

---

[2] See *Actas das Sessões da Comissão Revisora do Código Penal – Parte Geral*, Vol. I and II (Lisbon: AAFDL, n.d.).

360 days (maximum). But that conversion would be unfair if automatic and disregarding the offender's economic status, levelling the sacrifice imposed on persons with different disposable income. The underlying logic is, thus, of a sacrifice made proportionate to the offender's economic status, on the basis of a distributive criterion, which necessarily mitigates a certain 'compensatory' effect of the crime's harm inherent in the fine. Consequently, the court sets the daily amount of the fine, which in the case of singular persons has to the present day the general limits of 5 euros (minimum) and 500 euros (maximum).

From 1995 onwards, with the revision undertaken by the Act 48/95 delivered on 15 March (formally giving rise to the 1995 new Penal Code, whose changes had, in the first place, drawn inspiration from the 1966 *Alternative-Entwurf eines Strafgesetzbuches*), the possibility of cumulating imprisonment and fine in sentencing was discarded. Instead the solutions of the alternative fine, of the exclusive fine in limited cases and of the substitutive fine were pursued. Following the rise of the fine upper limit from 360 to 600 days, it became possible to substitute an up to five years imprisonment term by a fine.

Hence, in the Portuguese legal system, the day fine system consistently developed to appear as an alternative solution to the prison sentence, according to a logic of protection of legal interests and special prevention, in compliance with the punishment goals stated in Article 40 of the Penal Code.[3] And in the cases where the fine is applicable as alternative sanction, a certain correspondence is established to the imprisonment term, which is only capable of expressing the concrete measure of patrimonial freedom restriction if related to a daily amount of the fine set between a maximum and a minimum limit.

10.1.2 *The Framing of the System Evolution As a Solution in Terms of Criminal Policy, Including Some Critical Issues*

The adoption of a system largely hospitable to the day fine, mainly after 1995, results from a concern to seek alternatives to the prison sanction, not only because of the advantage, generally accepted, of reducing the prison population, but above all, due to the understanding that, in certain cases, the imprisonment penalty would be more criminogenic than a factor of

---

[3] 'Article 40 (Aims of penalties and security measures)
  1 – The application of penalties and security measures aims at the protection of legal interests and the agent's reintegration in society.
  2 – The penalty should in no case exceed the extent of the guilt'.

rehabilitation. Consequently, it should be avoided as *ultima ratio* of the state criminal policy, in accordance with the principle of minimal criminalisation, as provided in Article 18 (2) of the Constitution of the Portuguese Republic.[4]

However, the option made was not prone to a large expansion of cases covered by a compulsory substitution of the imprisonment term by a fine. This solution was reserved, in line with the Portuguese tradition prior to the 1982 Penal Code, for the offences punishable with up to one year imprisonment term, whenever the aims of special and general prevention are secured. That applies not only to the substitution by a fine, but also by any other penalty not involving freedom deprival, in accordance with Article 45 of the Penal Code.[5]

As mentioned above, the 1995 revision of the Penal Code enhanced the possibility of implementation of the day fine as an alternative to the prison sanction, through increasing the number of fine days, with the intent of altering the prior situation of scarce court sentencing of fines as well as establishing the respective correspondence to the imprisonment term.

This clear preference for the day fine met with criticism from some scholars, who argued in favour of a more relevant role for other alternative penalties, also dismissive of freedom deprival, but more directly promoting rehabilitation.[6]

In fact, the basically insoluble problem about day fines is that its variability in terms of adjustment to the economic status of the offender impairs its general preventive character and is permeable to manipulations by a third party who is to bear the patrimonial weight of the fine. Thus, it becomes necessary to impose specific conditions to avoid any assistance from a third party or, conversely, any prejudice to relatives dependent on the offender's upkeep.[7]

The aim of this critical viewpoint about the fine model is to discuss the controversial defence of society by means of a patrimonial sanction not only for the wealthier offenders, who have a larger availability to compensatory mechanisms, but also for the ones with a lesser income. Without prejudice to

---

[4] 'The law may only restrict rights, freedoms and guarantees in cases expressly provided for in the Constitution and such restrictions must be limited to those needed to safeguard other constitutionally protected rights and interests' (dre.pt/constitution-of-the-portuguese-republic).

[5] 'Article 45
    Substitution of imprisonment by fine
        1- Imprisonment for a period not exceeding one year shall be substituted for a fine or other non-custodial penalty, except when imprisonment becomes necessary to prevent future offences'.

[6] Palma, 'As alterações reformadoras da parte geral do Código Penal na revisão de 1995 – Desmantelamento, reforço e paralisia da sociedade punitiva', pp. 31–51.

[7] Antunes, *Penas e Medidas de Segurança*, p. 27.

their right of a penalty not involving restriction of freedom, the feeble eco-nomical means of the latter make it hardly possible for this fine model to have a rehabilitation effect. Moreover, it often worsens situations of destitute social opportunities. The retributive character of the fine prevails, in many occasions, over its preventive function, thus becoming, at this essential level, a strictly negative feature, that is, not criminogenic and of minute relevance to a rehabilitation procedure, that is the positive character of special prevention.

On the other hand, it has become increasingly obvious – or we could say that it is a logical evidence – that where the fine model could act as a deterrent, for instance in cases concerning patrimonial infractions or the management of public property, the requirements of the positive general prevention and the punishing approaches pervading our society are not a fertile ground for the implementation of these sanctions.

Finally, the fact that the pecuniary administrative sanctions imposed on the so-called regulatory offences concerning data protection or to which the corporations of the economic, financial and environmental sectors are liable are extremely high, tends to weaken the effectiveness of the extant penal fines in terms of economic costs for the offender. The same applies to the day fine system itself, unable to address the fundamental issue of crime deterrence, from the offender's cost-benefit viewpoint. Thus, for potential agents the fine is generally not dissuasive enough and from a criminal policy perspective the use of pecuniary administrative sanctions that do not have the maximum limit, restrictions of fines become more effective.

10.1.3 *Conclusions of the Legislative Historic Process*

Therefore, a number of conclusions are to be drawn from the historic development of the day fine model in Portugal.

First: The adoption of this system aimed at a sheer restrictive effect on prison sentences: as substitutive fine, it was intended to avoid the crim-inogenic consequences of short-term imprisonments.

Second: The preference for this system has been associated to minor and moderate offences where the need for general prevention is less compelling.

Third: The fine only pursues an indirect preventive effect, having prima facie a retributive quality.

In spite of this retributive quality, the day fine has not proved adequate in economic, financial, environmental or political criminality, where retribution and positive general prevention usually require, according to public opinion, an exemplary punishment.

Also in sectors of economic and financial activity as well as in areas covered by the recent EU dispositions about data protection, fines and the day fine model are not appropriate to counterbalance, as a deterrent, the offender's cost-benefit equation related to the aforementioned offences. In fact, fines are not as high as to have such a deterrent effect as imprisonment in certain cases.

The fine as primary or even exclusive penalty is thus reserved for offences where a somewhat symbolic punishment will suffice, as it is the case of crimes of private prosecution or, in recent times, discrimination offences.

The day fine model has the advantage of tailoring the penalty according to offence and guilt criteria, somehow analogous to the tailoring of the imprisonment term.

The day fine model also proportions the restriction of the convicted offender's patrimonial rights to his disposable income, according to distributive justice logic in what concerns sanctions.

The day fine model is, however, an impediment to the effectiveness of preventive modalities associated with a cost-benefit calculation of the offender. The General Law Governing Regulatory Offences, that does not follow the day fine system and allows for the increase of the maximum limit of the pecuniary sanction up to the amount of the economic benefit derived from the administrative offence (Article 18), can certainly have a general and special preventive effect in a number of sectors of economic, financial and environmental criminality. Fines, as a translation of the length of imprisonment, will never be sufficient, because of its maximum limits, to achieve this compensatory effect on the most economically lucrative offences.

10.2 THE LEGAL FRAMEWORK OF DAY FINES

Fines are currently established in the Portuguese criminal law system both as a primary and a substitutive sanction within the framework of a criminal policy option for penalties which do not imply deprivation of liberty, as long as they are imposed for less serious offences (Article 70 of the Penal Code), in accordance with the constitutional principle of minimal criminalisation (Article 18 (2) of the Constitution).[8]

As a primary sanction (Articles 47–9 of the Penal Code), fines are directly mentioned in the incriminating norm and in most cases, as an alternative to

---

[8] *Supra* note 1, pp. 74 *et seq.*, 89 *et seq.*, 114 *et seq.* and 358 *et seq.*; *supra* note 7, pp. 16, 20–1, 24 *et seq.*, 47 *et seq.*, 76 *et seq.* and 105 *et seq.*

the imposition of an imprisonment sanction (alternative fine). For instance, Article 137 (1) punishes involuntary manslaughter with 'imprisonment up to three years or a fine'. However, only in negligible cases are fines the single primary sanction imposed, as it is, for instance, the case with the offence of alimony default (Article 250 (1)). In addition to the sanction of dissolution, fines are also a primary punishment applicable to legal persons (Article 90 (A) (1)).

As a substitutive sanction (Article 45), fines can be imposed in lieu of a primary sanction of imprisonment to the extent that the latter does not exceed one year, even if the incriminating norm does not establish it directly (substitutive fine).

The choice of the alternative fine is subject to an assessment whether the sanction is adequate and sufficient to meet the punishment purposes (Article 70).[9] By the terms of Article 40, sentencing pursues the protection of legal interests and the re-socialisation of the offender, whereby it shall not outdo the level of guilt. However, the legal doctrine holds a different view about this provision, setting different prevalence relations between the above criteria, within the ambit of the theories of punishment. Therefore, there are authors who argue that culpability plays a role as a restraining principle of prevention, even if the sanction should not be set below a minimum limit of positive general prevention; others, conversely, consider prevention as a restraining principle of culpability and consequently do not endorse the application of preventive punishment when guilt is of small scale.[10]

With regard to the substitutive fine, the legislator seems to be more accurate in his statement that the fine should be applied whenever possible, except for the cases where imprisonment becomes necessary to prevent recidivism (Article 45 (1)), though it remains controversial whether this criterion is autonomous of the one stated in the Articles 70 and 40.[11]

At a first stage, the fine is set in daily units, usually ranging from a minimum limit of 10 up to a maximum of 360 days (Articles 47 (1) and 45 (1)). Some

---

[9] The Decision of the Constitutional Court 61/2006, www.tribunalconstitucional.pt, judged unconstitutional a number of norms in the Penal Code and in the Code of Penal Procedure, viewed as not enforcing a rationale for the dismissal of a non-deprivation of liberty penalty.

[10] See, on one side, Rodrigues, 'O modelo de prevenção na determinação da medida concreta da pena', pp. 147 *et seq.*; and Dias, *Direito Penal – Parte Geral*, pp. 89 *et seq.*; and on the other side, Palma, *Direito Penal – Conceito material de crime, princípios e fundamentos – Teoria da Lei Penal: interpretação, aplicação no tempo, no espaço e quanto às pessoas*, pp. 107 *et seq.*

[11] See the discussion in Monteiro, Santos and Carneiro, 'A pena de multa de substituição no actual Código penal português – Algumas considerações de natureza política e jurídico-criminal', pp. 235 *et seq.*; and *supra* note 7, p. 76.

incriminating norms specify different upper limits of 60, 90, 120, 240 or 600 daily units. Notwithstanding, the law tends to equate 60 days of fine to 6 months' imprisonment, 120 days of fine to 1 year imprisonment, 240 days of fine to 2 years' imprisonment, 360 days of fine to 3 years' imprisonment and 600 days of fine to 5 years' imprisonment.[12] As to cases involving multiple offences, the fine shall not exceed 900 daily units (Article 77 (3)). With regard to legal persons, an equal number of fine days are applicable; otherwise, if legal provisions imposing fines as the primary sanction are unavailable, to one month of imprisonment correspond ten days of fine (Article 90(B) (1–4)).

The number of daily units is set, taking into account the guilt level of the offender and the prevention needs (Articles 47 (1) and 71).[13] Nevertheless, the particular relevance ascribed to each of these factors differs according to the interpretation of the aforementioned Article 40. If compensation for the harm caused by the crime has been made and a primary fine above 240 days should not be imposed on the offender, this pecuniary sanction can be converted into an admonition (Article 60). And if a fine above 600 days should not be imposed on a legal person, it can be replaced by an admonition, a bail for good conduct or judicial supervision (Articles 90 (C), (D) and (E)).

At a second stage and in the name of the equality principle, the amount of the daily unit, ranging from 5 to 500 euros, is determined 'taking into consideration the economic and financial circumstances of the convicted offender, along with his personal obligations' (Articles 47 (2), 45 (1) and 90 (B) (5)). The law does not clarify whether the setting of this daily amount should solely consider the defendant's income or include his assets.[14] However, case law has been holding the view that 'the punishment should not deprive the offender of a basic living allowance, extensive to those whose upkeep they are responsible for'.[15]

These economic and financial circumstances are investigated by the sentencing court, who has the competence to order the production of further evidence for this particular purpose, as well as to request a social report or

---

[12] *Supra* note 7, p. 28.

[13] If there were any doubts concerning the substitutive fine, they were elucidated in the Decision of the Supreme Court of Justice to Standardize Case Law 8/2013, www.dgsi.pt: 'The fine resulting, by the terms of the current Articles 43 (1) and 47 of the Penal Code, from the conversion of the imprisonment term, provided the latter is not longer than 1 year, shall be set in accordance with the criteria established in Article 71 (1) and not necessarily for an equal or proportional period of time to the one established for the converted imprisonment term'. See Fidalgo, 'Pena de multa de substituição', pp. 149 *et seq.*

[14] *Supra* note 1, pp. 128 *et seq.*; *supra* note 7, pp. 47–9.

[15] Albuquerque, *Comentário do Código Penal à Luz da Constituição da República e da Convenção Europeia dos Direitos do Homem*, p. 298.

additional information from the re-socialising services (Articles 369–71 of the Code of Penal Procedure). It applies, in this domain, the general rules of evidence that govern the criminal procedure. Nevertheless, it is not common practice of the judicature to order an autonomous inquiry on the aforementioned conditions, considering, however, of relevance the statements made by the defendant or the elements of proof already in the proceedings records.

In fact, due to its nature of criminal sanction and its liability to conversion or reversal to imprisonment, fines can only be imposed by judicial conviction and after *res iudicata*, in accordance with Articles 27 (2) and 32 (2) of the Portuguese Constitution.

Nonetheless, the legislator was concerned to adopt some measures in order to avoid fine default and its conversion or reversal to imprisonment (Articles 49 and 45 of the Penal Code),[16] allowing for a certain flexibility when fixing the date of payment and payment in instalments (Article 47 (3–4)), payment in days of community work at the instance of the convicted offender (Article 48)[17] and the suspension of the subsidiary imprisonment if subject to compliance with non-pecuniary duties or rules of conduct (Article 49 (3)).[18] In addition, provisions are laid down to enforce assets execution, which is ordered by the Public Prosecutor (Articles 49 (1) and 90 (B) (4) of the Penal Code and Article 491 (1–2) of the Code of Penal Procedure). Moreover, the Supreme Court of Justice standardised case law in the sense that the substitutive fine may also be executed in days of community service, a previously controversial issue.[19] At

---

[16] In cases of conversion of a primary fine the subsidiary imprisonment is imposed for the corresponding time reduced to two thirds (Article 49 (1)) and in cases of reversal of a substitutive fine into imprisonment the primary imprisonment stated in the sentence is enforced (Article 45 (2)).

[17] On the equivalence of day fines and days of community service, see the Decision of the Supreme Court of Justice for the Standardization of Case Law 13/2013, www.dgsi.pt: 'The correspondence between the fine and the community service which results from the replacement of a fine, by the terms of the Article 48 (2) of the Penal Code, is the one established in the article 58 (3) of the same statute, that is, a day of fine corresponds to an hour of work'.

[18] See Leite, 'Algumas considerações em torno do art. 49.°, n.° 3, do CP', pp. 171 *et seq.*

[19] Decision of the Supreme Court of Justice for the Standardization of Case Law 7/2016, www.dgsi.pt: 'In the case of a fine which has been sentenced as substitute sanction, by the terms of Article 43 (1) of the Penal Code, the defendant may, after *res iudicata* and under the provision of Article 48 of the Penal Code, request to serve the punishment in days of work'. Agreeing: Rodrigues, 'Cumprimento da pena de multa de substituição', pp. 191 *et seq.*; and Antunes, 'Execução da pena de multa de substituição através de prestação de dias de trabalho', pp. 501 *et seq.* Disagreeing: Leite, 'Efectividade e credibilidade da pena de multa de substituição', pp. 293–344. On the contrary, the Decision of the Supreme Court of Justice for the Standardization of Case Law 12/2013, www.dgsi.pt, states that: 'After *res iudicata* of the sentence of execution of imprisonment as consequence of the non-payment of the fine to which the former sanction was converted . . . it is of no relevance the subsequent payment of

last, where the substitutive fine comes to be reverted in imprisonment, the latter may be served as house arrest under electronic monitoring (Article 43 (1) (c) of the Penal Code).

Fixed fines no longer exist in the Portuguese criminal law system, although the suspension of imprisonment can be subjected to pecuniary duties, including the payment of a lump sum (Article 51 (1) (c)). On the other hand, the punitive administrative sanctions of pecuniary nature imposed by administrative authorities do not follow the day fine model. Furthermore, Article 18 of the General Law Governing Regulatory Offences allows for the increase of the maximum limit of the pecuniary sanction up to the amount of the economic benefit derived from the administrative offence, as long as this increase does not exceed one third of the legal limit.

10.3 THE PRACTICAL IMPLEMENTATION OF DAY FINES

During the first decade in which the present Portuguese Penal Code (1982) was in force, there was no relevant increase in the imposition of fines.[20] Even though no empirical studies were conducted on the deterrence effect of day fines, the 1995 reform of the Penal Code, enlarging the extent covered by the alternative fine to a broader range of offences, along with an increase of the maximum limit on the number of day fines as well as on the daily amount, urged a remarkable expansion in the imposition of the primary fine, which became, since then, the most frequently imposed criminal sanction in Portugal.[21] Between 2005 and 2009, the only groups of cases where the imposition of day fines did not prevail were the ones regarding offences against property or related to narcotic drugs and psychotropic substances.[22] As to the second group of offences, this tendency has been somewhat mitigated until 2017, according to the data supplied for this study by the Portuguese Directorate-General for Justice Policy (Ministry of Justice).

Until 2006, the imposition of fines undergoes thus an increase to reach a 75 per cent out of the total convictions. From the 2007 Penal Reform onwards, which updated the minimum daily amount of the fine from one to five euros and altered the extent to which the fine can substitute an

the fine as to avoid the execution of imprisonment, since the provisions made by Article 49 (2) of the Penal Code do not apply to the case in question'.

[20] *Supra* note 1, pp. 151–2.

[21] Permanent Observatory for Portuguese Justice/ Centre for Social Studies, *As Tendências da Criminalidade e das Sanções Penais na Década de 90 – Problemas e bloqueios na execução da pena de prisão e da prestação de trabalho a favor da comunidade – Relatório Preliminar*, pp. 43–8 and 60; and *A Justiça Penal – Uma reforma em avaliação*, pp. 479–80.

[22] *Supra* note 21, pp. 485–7.

imprisonment term from six months to one year, this rate goes down to levels just above 60 per cent. This decrease results, however, from the greater adoption of other penalties, which do not involve the deprivation of freedom, such as the suspension of imprisonment or the community service and not from a reduction in the imposition of fines.[23] According to the figures made available for this study by the Portuguese Directorate-General for Justice Policy, this trend continues between 2013 and 2017, while convictions resulting in effective imprisonment stand around 8 per cent (although between 2005 and 2009 they came close to 5 per cent).[24]

The cases of fine payment in days of community work and of suspension of the subsidiary imprisonment are not statistically very significant. However, global statistical data concerning the number or the amount of the daily units set for the fine, as well as its default rate, are not available.

It is important to note that the fine is the most applied sanction in Portugal even if on the one hand, the Portuguese criminal law establishes several non-pecuniary alternatives to imprisonment and several alternatives to the payment of fines, and on the other hand by 2019 the minimum wage did not exceed 635 euros and according to the National Institute of Statistics, the average salary has not reached more than 951 euros.

Additionally, the Portuguese social security system provides various welfare benefits dependent on different requirements often related to an indexing reference of social support (IAS), such as:

- family benefits for children and young persons, maternity, paternity and adoption benefits and benefits to meet other family expenses relating to disability and dependency;
- health benefits that include access to the National Health System and to the National Network for Long-term Integrated Care, as well as sickness benefits;
- invalidity benefits: disability pension, benefits in case of occupational disease, special protection during disability and social inclusion benefit;
- old-age pensions, including a social old-age pension and survivors' benefits;
- unemployment benefits, including allowances for self-employed workers and a social unemployment benefit;
- a social integration income for persons in financial need with a monthly maximum amount of 189.66 euros in 2019.

---

[23] *Ibid.*, pp. 501–3.
[24] *Ibid.*, p. 485.

Whereas the law does not establish a connection between these benefits and the day fine system, the setting of the daily amount of the fine should not deprive the offender of a basic living allowance as seen in the previous section.

10.4 PUBLIC PERCEPTION OF DAY FINES

Although no study about the general level of acceptance of the fine has so far been conducted among us, the Portuguese doctrine is quite hospitable to it, in addition to the fact that it is often sentenced in courts.

In the academic literature is on the one hand emphasised, as a criminal policy advantage of the fine, the avoidance of the de-socialising, stigmatising and criminogenic effects associated to imprisonment, the reduction of the costs implied by the penitentiary system and the possibility to allocate the collected sums to a compensation for the harm caused by the offence.[25]

On the other hand as to the inconveniences usually brought forward against fines, such as the inequality of the effort for the poor and the rich, the possibly unfair consequences for the offender's family as well as the lesser preventive effectiveness of this sanction, it is argued that they can be mitigated within an appropriate legal regime as to setting the fine, namely by way of adjusting its daily amount to the offender's economic and financial status and that such disadvantages are, in any case, comparatively inferior to the ones caused by the execution of a sentence involving deprivation of freedom.[26]

Under the constitutional principle of equality, it is otherwise unacceptable that the fine might be ruled out due to the offender's insufficient income. In such circumstances, the court shall fix it in the legal minimum, convert it in a subsidiary imprisonment and proceed to the concomitant suspension of the subsidiary imprisonment on the condition that non-pecuniary obligations are fulfilled.[27]

Furthermore, the fine may not be paid by a third party, under pain of incurring an offence against the administration of justice (Article 367 (2) of the Penal Code)[28] – although the help from close relatives is not punished, according to Article 367 (5) (b) – neither is permitted its coverage under any insurance contract by the terms of Article 14 (1) (a) of the Insurance Contract Statute.

---

[25]   *Supra* note 1, pp. 120–1; *supra* note 7, pp. 24–5.
[26]   *Supra* note 1, pp. 121–2; *supra* note 7, p. 25.
[27]   *Supra* note 7, pp. 49, 108.
[28]   *Supra* note 1, pp. 118–19; *supra* note 21, p. 26.

10.5 CONSTITUTIONALITY CHALLENGES

Article 8 (7) of the General Statute of Tributary Offences used to state the *joint* liability of the corporate leaders who wilfully contributed to the offence for the fines imposed on legal persons, irrespective of their autonomous responsibility for the offence. Such rule, allowing for the payment of the fine to be directly and entirely claimed on the joint liable party, came, however, to be declared unconstitutional by the Constitutional Court in 2014, for violating the principle of non-transferability of penalties (Article 30 (3) of the Portuguese Constitution),[29] a decision with generally binding force. In the view of the Constitutional Court, the need to guarantee the payment of the fines applied on corporations and the effectiveness of criminal prevention do not justify that the legal person may elude the execution of the fine or that the State thereby renounces the exercise of *ius puniendi*.

Still, this decision of unconstitutionality did not include the case of *subsidiary* liability of corporate leaders for the fines imposed on legal persons 'due to acts carried out during their term of office or to previous acts whenever it was their fault that the corporate assets became insufficient for the payment' (Article 8 (1) (a) of the General Statute of Tributary Infractions). The Constitutional Court held the view that, in this circumstance, at stake was a liability of civil nature for an autonomous own act which causes damage to the Public Revenue and not a transfer of criminal responsibility.[30] Despite the general adoption of this rule by Article 11 (9) of the Penal Code it remains controversial to view the non-payment of an amount set for sanctioning reasons of prevention and culpability related to the legal person as civil damage.[31] However, this argument was not taken into account by the Constitutional Court.

REFERENCES

Actas das Sessões da Comissão Revisora do Código Penal – Parte Geral, Vol. I and II. Lisbon: AAFDL.

Albuquerque, P. P. 2015. *Comentário do Código Penal à Luz da Constituição da República e da Convenção Europeia dos Direitos do Homem*. Lisbon: Universidade Católica Editora.

Antunes, M. J. 2016. 'Execução da pena de multa de substituição através de prestação de dias de trabalho', *Revista Portuguesa de Ciência Criminal* 26, 501–47.

Antunes, M. J. 2017. *Penas e Medidas de Segurança*. Coimbra: Almedina.

[29] Decision of the Constitutional Court 171/2014, www.tribunalconstitucional.pt.
[30] Decision of the Constitutional Court 249/2014, www.tribunalconstitucional.pt.
[31] Viana, 'A (in)constitucionalidade da responsabilidade subsidiária dos administradores e gerentes pelas coimas aplicadas à sociedade', pp. 201 *et seq.*

Dias, J. F. 1993. *Direito Penal Português – Parte Geral II – As consequências jurídicas do crime*. Lisbon: Aequitas.

Dias, J. F. 2019. *Direito Penal – Parte Geral*, Vol. I (Questões fundamentais – A doutrina geral do crime). Coimbra: Gestlegal.

Fidalgo, S. 2010. 'Pena de multa de substituição', *Revista Portuguesa de Ciência Criminal* 20-1, 149–61.

Leite, A. L. 2015. 'Algumas considerações em torno do art. 49.º, n.º 3, do CP', *Revista do Ministério Público* 142: 171–91.

Leite, A. L. 2016. 'Efectividade e credibilidade da pena de multa de substituição', *Ab Instantia* 6: 293–344.

Monteiro, F. C., Santos, M. and Carneiro, A. T. 2014. 'A pena de multa de substituição no actual Código penal português – Algumas considerações de natureza política e jurídico-criminal', in Monte, M. F. *et al.* (eds.), *Estudos em comemoração dos 20 anos da Escola de Direito da Universidade do Minho*. Coimbra: Coimbra Editora.

Palma, M. F. 2004. 'As alterações reformadoras da parte geral do Código Penal na revisão de 1995 – Desmantelamento, reforço e paralisia da sociedade punitiva', in Palma, M. F. *et al.* (eds.), *Casos e Materiais de Direito Penal*. Coimbra: Almedina.

Palma, M. F. 2019. *Direito Penal – Conceito material de crime, princípios e fundamentos – Teoria da Lei Penal: interpretação, aplicação no tempo, no espaço e quanto às pessoas*. Lisbon: AAFDL.

Permanent Observatory for Portuguese Justice/ Centre for Social Studies, 2002. *As Tendências da Criminalidade e das Sanções Penais na Década de 90 – Problemas e bloqueios na execução da pena de prisão e da prestação de trabalho a favor da comunidade – Relatório Preliminar*. University of Coimbra, opj.ces.uc.pt.

Permanent Observatory for Portuguese Justice/ Centre for Social Studies, 2009. *A Justiça Penal – Uma reforma em avaliação*. University of Coimbra, opj.ces.uc.pt.

Rodrigues, A. M. 2002. 'O modelo de prevenção na determinação da medida concreta da pena', *Revista Portuguesa de Ciência Criminal* 12-2, 147–82.

Rodrigues, H. R. 2012. 'Cumprimento da pena de multa de substituição', *Revista do Ministério Público* 131: 191–212.

Viana, J. M. 2009. 'A (in)constitucionalidade da responsabilidade subsidiária dos administradores e gerentes pelas coimas aplicadas à sociedade', *Revista de Finanças Públicas e Direito Fiscal* II-2, 199–210.

CASE LAW

Decision of the Constitutional Court 61/2006, www.tribunalconstitucional.pt

Decision of the Constitutional Court 249/2012, www.tribunalconstitucional.pt

Decision of the Constitutional Court 171/2014, www.tribunalconstitucional.pt

Decision of the Supreme Court of Justice to Standardize Case Law 8/2013, www.dgsi.pt

Decision of the Supreme Court of Justice to Standardize Case Law 12/2013, www.dgsi.pt

Decision of the Supreme Court to Justice to Standardize Case Law 13/2013, www.dgsi.pt

Decision of the Supreme Court of Justice to Standardize Case Law 7/2016, www.dgsi.pt

Day (Unit) Fines in England and Wales

Valsamis Mitsilegas and Foivi Sofia Mouzakiti

Gilbert and Sullivan were no doubt right to expect that the punishment should fit the crime, but it has also to fit the criminal. While we must all be equal before the law, what we seek is equality of justice, not equality of treatment.[1]

Compared to other European countries, such as Finland, Sweden and Denmark, the legislature in England and Wales was late to adopt a system of income related fines – and very quick to abandon it. These fines, known as 'unit fines', were introduced in October of 1992 by the Criminal Justice Act of 1991 and abolished a mere seven months later, in a move that has been described as 'perhaps the most astonishing and unjustified *volte face* in the history of the English criminal justice system'.[2] This is all the more surprising, because the adoption of unit fines was preceded by a prolonged nationwide debate, which climaxed with a series of unit fine experiments in magistrates' courts that produced very positive results.

In the following sections, we first examine the rationales that led to the adoption of unit fines, before we look more closely to the structure and operation of the scheme and finally, to the reasons that led to its abrupt repeal. As we will see, it was not for a lack of support of them as a pecuniary sanction that unit fines failed to take roots in England and Wales; rather, it was for a lack of political willingness to choose construction instead of destruction and resolve the faults that emerged out of their initial implementation. One of those faults stemmed from the system's failure to provide sentencers with a level of flexibility in determining the amount of the fine – something that the current fining structure in the UK provides ample room for.

---

[1]   HL Deb 12 March 1991, vol. 527, cols. 102–3.
[2]   Cavadino and Dignan, *The Penal System: An Introduction*, p. 128.

11.1 HISTORICAL DEVELOPMENT OF DAY FINES IN ENGLAND AND WALES

The national conversation over the introduction of day fines dates back to 1970. In May of that year, the Advisory Council on the Penal System published a report which examined, among other things, the (well-established) Swedish day fine system and considered whether the UK could follow a similar approach.[3] The members of the Council, however, concluded that the complications associated with introducing day fines in the UK would outweigh the benefits. As such, they only went so far as to endorse the principle of determining fines by looking separately into the seriousness of the offence and the offender's ability to pay.[4] They urged courts to adopt this principle in their fining practices and suggested that the question of day fines should be re-examined in the future.[5] A few years later, faced with the increasing prison population in the UK, the Expenditure Committee of the House of Commons recommended that the question be explored again – so did the Parliamentary All-Party Penal Affairs Group.[6] But the defining moment for day fines in the UK came at the turn of the 1980s; by that time, support for them had grown significantly and several organisations associated with criminal justice advocated for their introduction.[7]

While these developments were unfolding, the Conservative party was re-elected.[8] Its manifesto was laconic when it came to criminal justice measures, but it nonetheless promised that the Government would give the lead in the fight against crime by, among others, 'building the prisons in which to place those who pose a threat to society – and by keeping out of prison those who do not'.[9] The ever-increasing prison population of England and Wales was a key concern for the new government,[10] and for a good reason; at the dawn of the

---

[3] Home Office, *Non-Custodial and Semi-Custodial Penalties: Report of the Advisory Council on the Penal System*, pp. 5–8.

[4] *Ibid.*

[5] *Ibid.*, at vi.

[6] Parliamentary All-Party Penal Affairs Group, *Too Many Prisoners: An Examination of Ways of Reducing the Prison Population*.

[7] These included the National Association for the Care and Resettlement of Offenders, the Prison Reform Trust, Justice and the Penal Affairs Consortium. See Nacro, *Fine Default: Report of a Nacro Working Party*; Justice, *Sentencing: A Way Ahead*; Penal Affairs Consortium, *Means-Related Fines*; Prison Reform Trust, *Tackling Fine Default*.

[8] In 1987.

[9] *1987 Conservative Party General Election Manifesto: The Next Moves Forward*, available at www.conservativemanifesto.com/1987/1987-conservative-manifesto.shtml.

[10] HC Deb 20 March 1988, vol. 130, cols. 1083–97; Faulkner, *Servant of the Crown: A Civil Servant's Story of Criminal Justice and Public Service Reform*, pp. 123 et seq.

1990s, more than 50,000 people were in custody,[11] a figure that put the country 'very high in the league table of punitiveness for Council of Europe states'.[12] The Green Paper on 'Punishment, Custody and the Community' that was published in 1988 argued that 'imprisonment is not the most effective punishment for most crimes. Custody should be reserved as punishment for very serious offenses, especially when the offender is violent and a continuing risk to the public'.[13] And while there was consensus that the increased use of fines by the courts could contribute to the reduction of the prison population, the government was well aware that the use of fines had been in decline for several years.[14] 'Because of the difficulty of imposing "realistic" fines on people with limited means, for example single parents and those living on benefits', the courts opted for probation or community service orders instead.[15] To avert further increase in the prison population, the Home Office embarked on the discussion over sentencing policies.[16]

In October of 1989, Douglas Hurd, the Home Secretary at the time, was preparing his speech for the upcoming Conservative Party Conference. His draft speech[17] read: 'too often people think that a sentence passed by a court is not proportionate to the crime committed'. He moved on: 'We need to make sense of sentencing. Detailed proposals will be laid before parliament soon, but the guiding principle is plain. Every convicted criminal should receive his *just deserts*'.[18] As his speech denotes, it was the theory of 'just deserts', originally developed by von Hirsch,[19] that informed the government's sentencing policies at that time and provided the fertile ground for the eventual introduction of day fines.[20] The proponents of that theory advocated a system of sentencing that places the principle of proportionality at the forefront – in other words, the severity of sentences should reflect the gravity of the offence.[21] Custodial

[11]   Sturge, 'UK Prison Population Statistics', 5.
[12]   HL Deb 30 November 1988, vol. 502, col. 365.
[13]   Home Office, *Punishment, Custody and the Community*.
[14]   Junger-Tas, *Alternatives to Prison Sentences: Experiences and Developments*, p. 24.
[15]   *Supra* note 10, Faulkner. See also Crow and Simon, *Unemployment and Magistrates' Courts*.
[16]   Whitehead, *Reconceptualising the Moral Economy of Criminal Justice: A New Perspective*, pp. 48–9.
[17]   The National Archives, PREM 19/2716 (011.jpg) http://discovery.nationalarchives.gov.uk/details/r/C16329001.
[18]   *Ibid.* (emphasis added).
[19]   Von Hirsch, *Past or Future Crimes: Deservedness and Dangerousness in the Sentencing of Criminals*.
[20]   Ashworth and Wasik, 'Fundamentals of Sentencing Theory: Essays in Honour of Andrew Von Hirsch', p. 1; Newburn, '"Tough on Crime": Penal Policy in England and Wales', 425–70.
[21]   Von Hirsch, 'Proportionality in the Philosophy of Punishment', 55–98. Ashworth, 'The New English Sentencing System', 759 *et seq.*

sentences should be reserved for the most serious of offences, whereas the less serious offences should be dealt with by punishment in the community. The fine, as the most commonly used penalty, was of particular interest to the government, who was keen to maximise its effectiveness. And means-related fines, the argument was, would represent a move towards fairer fining, underpinned by the principle of equal impact. It was in this context that the Home Office put in motion a pilot scheme for unit-fines. If it proved successful, the government planned to place day fines on a statutory footing.

The experiment, which ran between 1988 and 1989 in four magistrates' courts (Basingstoke, Bradford, Swansea and Teesside)[22] provided that the court would set the fine by following a two-stage process. At first instance, it would determine the seriousness of the offence by reference to a specific number of weekly 'units'. Measuring the units by reference to weeks instead of days (as it happened in continental systems) was considered preferable because on the one hand, courts were 'accustomed to assessing disposable weekly income in determining payments' and on the other hand, individuals rarely think in terms of daily income.[23] This is why in England the system became known as 'unit fines'.[24] The higher the number of 'units', the more serious the offence was; for example, the Basingstoke magistrates' courts reserved eight units for careless driving and ten to fifteen units for actual bodily harm.[25] At second instance, the cash value of those units would be calculated by reference to the offender's weekly disposable income.[26] The disposable income was determined by looking into an individual's income and then setting a weekly allowance on the basis of that income.[27] It must be noted, however, that the experiment had one limitation: the courts could lower fines for offenders of limited means, but due to legality doubts,[28] they could not increase them for affluent offenders.[29]

By introducing unit fines, the government sought to address three problems.[30] The first was the inconsistency of the courts' fining practices,

---

[22] Moxon, Sutton and Hedderman, *Unit Fines: Experiments in Four Courts.*

[23] *Ibid.*, p. 4.

[24] As opposed to day fines, which is the most commonly used term.

[25] Gibson, 'Unit Fines – Punishment and Proportionality'.

[26] HC Deb 20 February 1991, vol. 186, cols. 404–5.

[27] *Supra* note 22, p. 6.

[28] At that time, the principle that a fine can be reduced but not increased stemmed from the Court of Appeal's judgment in *R. v Prince Alfred Fairbairn* [1981] *Crim. L.R.* 190: 'The amount of a fine should be determined in relation to the gravity of the offence for which it is imposed and only then should the offender's means be considered to decide whether he has the capacity to pay such an amount'.

[29] *Ibid.*

[30] HC Deb 29 June 1993, vol. 227, cols. 905–20; Peggie, 'Justice for the Poor?', *Criminal Justice Matters*, 9.

a phenomenon mostly prevalent in the magistrates' courts.[31] The second was the inequality of the fining system; among the people that were fined for the same offence, some individuals suffered excessively from the fines imposed on them, because of their financial circumstances.[32] In other words, their inability to pay the fine was not taken into account. The third problem, closely interlinked with the second, was that of fine defaulters.[33] Too many individuals were imprisoned for defaulting on their fines; in 1991, the number of people that were incarcerated for that reason was estimated at 19,000.[34] Ninety per cent of them were unemployed. In respect of their potential to tackle these three problems, the results of the pilot scheme were promising.[35] First of all, the disparities between courts in fines imposed on low income offenders were significantly reduced.[36] Second, the fine amount imposed on those offenders was set at a more realistic level and the proportion of fines that were paid on time increased.[37] Finally, in three out of four magistrates' courts, the rate of individuals imprisoned for fine default fell between 24 and 27 per cent.[38]

The two-decade long discussion over the introduction of unit fines in England and Wales culminated in 1990 with the publication of the White Paper 'Crime, Justice and Protecting the Public: Proposals for Legislation' – the precursor of the Criminal Justice Act 1991. In this paper, the government put forward 'a more consistent approach to sentencing, so that convicted criminals receive their "just desserts". The severity of the sentence of the court should be directly related to the seriousness of the offence. Most offenders can be punished by financial penalties – by paying compensation to their victims and by *fines*'.[39] Fines, in turn, should take into account the offenders' means; 'those who are poor should be made to pay at least something, those better off a lot more, so both get their just desserts'.[40] The government, after receiving positive feedback from the magistrates' involved in the pilot schemes, was finally convinced that a system of unit fines was in the interest of justice; if sentences were to impose fairer fines, the argument

---

[31] HC Deb 29 June 1993, vol. 227, col. 911.
[32] *Ibid.*
[33] *Ibid.*
[34] *Ibid.*; HC Deb 20 June 1988, vol. 135, cols. 931–42.
[35] Evans, 'Fairer Fines Pay Off for Courts', *The Times* (1 May 1989).
[36] *Supra* note 22.
[37] *Supra* note 26.
[38] *Supra* note 22, p. 20. The fourth court (Basingstoke) hardly ever imprisoned anyone for fine default even before the pilot scheme took place.
[39] Home Office, *Crime, Justice and Protecting the Public: The Government's Proposals for Legislation*, para. 1.6. (emphasis added).
[40] *Ibid.*, para. 2.10.

was, this would expand the use of fines and facilitate their enforcement.[41] And so, the Bill for the Criminal Justice Act 1991 was introduced and was swiftly adopted by Parliament. The Act came into force on 1 October 1992.

11.2 THE LEGAL FRAMEWORK OF UNIT FINES

Now that we have an overview of the background that led to the adoption of unit fines in England and Wales[42] under the Act, let us take a closer look into the statutory framework. First of all, Section 18 (1) of the Act provided that magistrates' courts should fix fines by reference to 'units' only when they imposed fines on individuals – and not companies. Second, the unit fine system only applied in cases where the offence was punishable by a fine not exceeding a level on the standard scale,[43] or not exceeding the statutory maximum on summary conviction.[44] Finally, the system was not extended to the Crown Court, where the amount of fines imposed was higher.

Similarly to the pilot experiment, courts would calculate the fine by multiplying the *number* of units (a number which represented the seriousness of the offence) with the *value* of each of those units, which reflected the offender's 'spare' income.[45] The first order of business for the court was, therefore, to determine the number of units for the offence. Section 18 (4) of the Act prescribed, on a range from one to fifty, the maximum number of units for each level of offence; for example, the court could give up to ten units for a level 3 offence and up to fifty units for a level 5 offence. To determine the seriousness of the offence, the court had to take into account all the circumstances of the offence, including any aggravating or mitigating factors.[46] And, to mitigate the amount of a unit fine, it could set a smaller number of units than it would have if there were no mitigating circumstances.[47]

After deciding how many units reflected the seriousness of the offence, the second order of business for the court was to assess the value of each unit. That value signified how much the offender could spare to pay, depending on his or her circumstances – in other words, his or her *disposable weekly income*. According to the Home Office Guide to the 1991 Act, this did not involve

---

[41] *Ibid.*, para. 5.2.
[42] The unit fines provisions did not apply to Northern Ireland and Scotland.
[43] Section 18 (1)(a) of the Criminal Justice Act (hereinafter CJA) 1991. For an overview of the standard scale, see Section 17 (1) of the CJA 1991. Level 5, the higher level of the scale, corresponded to a fine amount of £5,000.
[44] Section 18 (1)(b) of the CJA 1991.
[45] *Ibid.*, Section 18 (2)(a)(b).
[46] *Ibid.*, Sections 18 (3), 28 (3) and 29.
[47] *Ibid.*, Section 28 (3).

a thorough examination of all of the offender's 'income, outgoings, savings and liabilities'.[48] It simply involved a judgment on how much he or she could afford to pay without suffering undue hardship. To make that judgment, the court had to be aware of the offender's financial circumstances. To ensure that this information duly reached the court, the Magistrates' Courts (Unit Fines) Rules 1992 called on clerks to supply defendants with a means enquiry form.[49] The Act also empowered courts to issue an order to that effect – but only following a conviction.[50] The means enquiry form provided magistrates with all the necessary information – weekly income, savings, state benefits, dependants and housing costs.[51] If the offender did not provide the information ordered by the court, the latter was free to determine the disposable income as it saw fit.[52] Not only that, but failure to comply with the order without a reasonable excuse carried a maximum penalty of a level 3 fine, while making (knowingly or recklessly) a materially false statement, or knowingly failing to disclose such a statement, carried a sentence of maximum three months' imprisonment or a level 4 fine.[53]

That said, the value that could be attached to each unit was not unconstrained; the Act specified a minimum (4 pounds) and a maximum (100 pounds) limit.[54] These limits ensured that the fine imposed was not so low so as to be derisory, or so high so as to surpass the sentencing powers of the magistrates' courts. So, when the court found the disposable weekly income of an offender to be lower than 4 pounds or higher than 100 pounds, it had to adjust it to reflect the statutory limits. It follows that, for the most serious offence (50 units), the maximum fine that could be imposed amounted to 5,000 pounds (50 x 100).

So, how did courts calculate the disposable weekly income in practice? The Act did not set out any rules on that, but it empowered the Lord Chancellor to do so.[55] These rules – the Magistrates' Courts (Unit Fines) Rules 1992 –

[48] Home Office, *Criminal Justice Act 1991: Fines and Other Financial Penalties* (1991), p. 2.
[49] Rule 3 of the Magistrates' Courts (Unit Fines) Rules 1992.
[50] Section 20 (1) of the CJA 1991.
[51] For an overview of the means enquiry form, see schedule 1 of the Magistrates' Courts (Unit Fines) Rules 1992.
[52] Section 18 (8)(b) of the CJA 1991.
[53] *Ibid.*, Section 20 (2) and (3).
[54] Under Section 18 (5), the amount corresponded to 1/50th of the cash ceiling for a level 1 and level 5 offence. Section 18 (6) provided for reduced limits in the case of fines imposed on underage individuals. If, however, a parent or guardian was required to pay the unit fine, then the disposable income would be calculated on the basis of the latter's means – see Section 57 (3) (a).
[55] Section 18 (2)(b) of the CJA 1991.

provided that (unless the offender has already done so) the court must, before sentencing, invite him or her to inform the court on all matters specified in the means inquiry form.[56] Within the parameters of the Act, the court would then calculate the disposable weekly income by subtracting the offender's *appropriate expenditure levels* from his or hers net weekly income,[57] and then dividing the result by three.[58] Schedule 2 of the Rules called on magistrates to determine the amount of reasonable weekly expenditures in their area.[59] These 'deemed expenditure levels' would, in turn, assist in the calculation of the offender's 'appropriate expenditure levels' referred to in the above formula.[60] The result of this process was that only a fraction (one third) of the disposable weekly income was taken into account for setting the value of each unit.

The question as to whether to take all, or a proportion, of the offender's disposable weekly income into account to determine the unit value was intensely discussed in the course of the pilot experiment.[61] Two approaches were proposed at the time. The first was in favour of taking into consideration all the disposable weekly income above a basic rate; according to its proponents, this was a simpler and more equitable approach.[62] Those who objected to this approach suggested that 'in taking every additional pound up to a given level the system bore too heavily on additional income until the norm was reached'.[63] And while the upper limits in the pilot were set on the low side (the higher limit, set by Basingstoke magistrates' court, was 20 pounds), the 100 pounds statutory limit was quite higher. The second approach, therefore, sought to address this concern by suggesting a way to calculate the unit value which would bear more *progressively* on the offender's disposable weekly income.[64] Two solutions, which were not mutually exclusive, were proposed. One was to include only the very basic expenditures in the calculation, but to take a proportion of the

---

[56]   Rule 4 (3) of the Magistrates' Courts (Unit Fines) Rules 1992.
[57]   The offender's net weekly income included any income from overtime, commissions and bonuses, minus (a) any tax payable on that income, (b) any contributions payable under the Social Security Acts and (c) any contributions paid to an occupational or personal pension scheme under the relevant legislation. See Schedule 2(1) of the Magistrates' Courts (Unit Fines) Rules 1992.
[58]   Rule 4(1) and Schedule 2 of the Magistrates' Courts (Unit Fines) Rules 1992.
[59]   *Ibid.*, Schedule 2 (2).
[60]   *Ibid.*, Schedule 2 (3).
[61]   *Supra* note 22, p. 24.
[62]   *Ibid.*
[63]   *Ibid.*
[64]   *Ibid.*

remaining (spare) income.[65] This approach had been adopted by the magistrates' court in Swansea, which during the experiment introduced a system whereby it took one pound for every additional five pounds of disposable income. The other proposed solution advocated expanding the list of expenditures to be considered, so as to gain a more accurate reflection of one's disposable income.[66] The drafters of the statutory framework opted for the second approach; they expanded the list of expenditures that were taken into account (compared to the one that was used during the pilot) but also introduced a divider (one third), so that only a part of the disposable weekly income was considered in setting the value of the unit.

To understand how this system worked, let us take the example of three offenders (A, B and C) who commit, say, careless driving.[67] First of all, the magistrates would decide how many units they would assign to this offence: for example ten units. Then, they would have to look into the offenders' disposable weekly income. A's disposable weekly income amounted to 240 pounds, B's to 120 pounds and C's to 9 pounds. Divided by three, as the above formula dictates, their disposable income would amount to eighty pounds, forty pounds and three pounds respectively. C's disposable income is below the statutory minimum and therefore would have to be adjusted upwards (four pounds). Therefore, A will pay 800 pounds (10 x 8), B will pay 400 pounds (10 x 40) and C will pay 40 pounds (10 x 4). The intention for the calculation to bear progressively on the offender's spare income is evident here; were it not for the one-third divider, A and B would have both paid a similar amount – the maximum of 100 pounds.[68]

The Act provided for three instances where the court could set the value of the unit at a different level than the one arrived at following the calculation.[69] First, in cases where a compensation order was made in addition to the fine, but the offender did not have the means to satisfy both, the court was entitled to reduce the amount of the fine, so that the offender could pay the compensation order.[70] Second, in the case of fixed penalty offences under the Road Traffic Offenders Act 1988, the court was empowered to increase the amount of the unit fine, so that the amount of the fine was not lower than that of the fixed penalty.[71] This was necessary to deter motor offenders of limited means

[65] *Ibid.*
[66] *Ibid.*
[67] For more examples, see *supra* note 48, pp. 7–8.
[68] Gibson, 'Unit Fines – Punishment and Proportionality'.
[69] Section 18 (7) of the CJA 1991.
[70] *Ibid.*, Section 18 (7)(a).
[71] *Ibid.*, Section 18 (7)(b).

from challenging the fixed penalty before the court (in hope of securing a lower fine), instead of paying it on the spot.[72] Third, in the case of a fine imposed for TV licence evasion, the court could increase the fine amount, in order to ensure that the fine is not cheaper to purchasing a TV licence.[73]

Unit fines were calculated by reference to weeks, but that does not mean that their payment was also weekly. On the contrary; if the offender could gather the amount, he/she had to pay the fine in a single instalment. That said, one could still pay a fine in instalments[74] – particularly in cases such as that of offender C above, where the offender's disposable weekly income was lower than the designated value of the unit. However, if repaying the fine within twelve months would bring him or her undue hardship, the court was empowered to remit the fine – in whole or in part.[75] If an offender was in income support, the magistrates' courts could recover the fine amount by ordering that the amount be deducted from the state benefits paid to him or her and be paid to the court.[76] The purpose of this was to minimise the risk of the offender defaulting – and perhaps imprisoned as a result.[77]

But what if someone defaulted on a fine? In this case, he or she was liable to imprisonment.[78] The maximum length of the imprisonment was calculated by reference to the number of the units that were attached to the offence – not to the offender's means.[79] But if the offender had paid part of the fine, then the maximum period of imprisonment would be reduced to reflect that – as long as it did not fall below seven days.[80]

11.3 PRACTICAL IMPLEMENTATION OF UNIT FINES

The statutory system of unit fines was remarkably short-lived; in fact, it remained into effect just long enough for us to tell the story of its demise. Before we delve into this, it is worth looking into the first (and only) available data that shed light on its impact on the magistrates' sentencing practices.

---

[72] *Supra* note 48, p. 8.
[73] Section 18 (7)(c) of the CJA 1991.
[74] Section 75 (1) of the Magistrates Courts Act 1980; (1983) 5 Cr. App. R. (S.) 203.
[75] Section 21 (2) of the CJA 1991.
[76] *Ibid.*, Section 24 (1). See also Fines (Deductions from Income Support) Regulations 1992/2182.
[77] Moxon, Hedderman and Sutton, *Deductions from Benefit for Fine Default*.
[78] Section 22 (1) of the CJA 1991.
[79] *Ibid.*, Section 22 (2). Up to 2 units resulted in a maximum of seven days' imprisonment, three to five units to a maximum of fourteen days' imprisonment, six to ten units to a maximum of twenty-eight days' imprisonment, eleven to twenty-five units to a maximum of forty-five days' imprisonment and more than twenty-five units to a maximum of three months' imprisonment.
[80] Section 22 (3) and (4) of the CJA 1991.

In the months that followed its implementation, a team of researchers carried out a study of four magistrates' courts in North England.[81] Perhaps unsurprisingly, the study identified some inconsistencies in the manner in which magistrates chose to impose unit fines.[82] For example, in one of the courts covered by the study, the magistrates specified the number of units, but failed to spell out the value of the unit – causing some confusion among offenders, who mistook the unit number for the fine amount.[83] In another court, they did not follow the two-step procedure for setting the unit fine, but instead specified the amount of the fine and left it up to the clerks to convert it into units.[84] These initial problems, however, were quickly resolved and the majority of magistrates welcomed the underlying principle of the new system, which brought about significant changes in their sentencing practices.

As one might expect, the unit fine scheme resulted to an increase in the use of fines by the magistrates' courts; before the Criminal Justice Act 1991 came into effect, 42 per cent of indictable offences were dealt with by a fine – a percentage which rose to 45 per cent in the quarter that followed the introduction of unit fines.[85] But the most significant rise occurred in the use of the fines among the unemployed, particularly with regards to the offence of theft and handling stolen goods, where the percentage rose from 31 per cent in the summer of 1992, to 48 per cent in the beginning of 1993.[86] This was an important development, given that the majority of the offenders sentenced by magistrates courts were unemployed[87] and that, as we discussed in section 1, the rise in unemployment at that time was one of the main reasons why the use of the fines was in decline. The scheme also impacted the amounts of the fines imposed; within the same period, the average fine amount for employed offenders increased from 140 pounds to 230 pounds, while the average amount for the unemployed decreased from 90 pounds to 70 pounds.[88]

---

[81] Crow, Cavadino, Dignan, Johnston and Walker, *Changing Criminal Justice: The Impact of the Criminal Justice Act 1991 in Four Areas of the North of England*; Crow, Johnston, Dignan, Cavadino and Walker, 'Magistrates' Views of the Criminal Justice Act 1991', 37–40.

[82] Cavadino and Crow, *Criminal Justice 2000: Strategies for a New Century*, p. 164.

[83] *Ibid.*

[84] *Ibid.*

[85] Home Office Statistical Bulletin, 'Cautions, Court Proceedings and Sentencing – England and Wales 1992' Issue 24/93 (September 1993), Table 8.

[86] Home Office Statistical Bulletin, 'Monitoring of the Criminal Justice Act 1991 – Data from a Special Data Collection Exercise' Issue 25/93 (September 1993), p. 5.

[87] *Ibid.* In early 1993, 14 per cent of them were employed and 69 per cent unemployed.

[88] *Ibid.*, p. 6.

Despite these positive developments, on 13 May 1993, less than one year after the introduction of unit fines, the Home Secretary at the time, Kenneth Clarke, made the following announcement:

> I am quite satisfied that courts should continue to have regard to the particular circumstances of individual offenders – in particular, to their means to pay – when fixing the level of a fine. I have been equally clear for some time and I have frequently said, that we should not require magistrates' courts to go through the mechanistic provision currently required under the unit fine arrangements. My hon. Friend the Member for Fylde (Mr. Jack), Minister of State in my Department and I have been seeking for some time modifications that we might make to the rules of the unit fines scheme to produce better results. We have now concluded that it is not possible to do so.
>
> Accordingly, I now propose to abolish the unit fines system and replace it with provisions which will require magistrates fully to consider an offender's means when imposing a fine but which will not require them to fine by application of any mathematical formula. . . . I get the sense that this change will be widely welcomed, not least by magistrates outside the House.[89]

So, what caused such an abrupt abolition of unit fines, so soon after they came into effect? First of all, some magistrates opposed the system for being too rigid[90] and unworkable;[91] in April 1993, when the House of Lords discussed the application of the system, some expressed concerns that 'many magistrates are extremely distressed by what is happening. Far from having the flexibility that they previously enjoyed, while taking people's means into account, they are now forced into a system which they regard as too rigid. They are being forced to hand out fines which are totally disproportionate to the crime or misdemeanour that has been committed'.[92] The problem was that magistrates were not accustomed to thinking in terms of units; instead, they thought in terms of 'set worth'; offence A is worth X amount of money – irrespective of the offender.[93] In other words, magistrates felt that the system interfered (unnecessarily) with their judicial discretion.

---

[89] HC Deb 13 May 1993, vol. 224, cols. 939–40.
[90] Dyer, 'You Finish up with Silly Fines and are Left with no Discretion', *The Guardian* (7 April 1993).
[91] Ashworth, 'Legislature Vs. Judiciary: The Struggle for Supremacy in English Sentencing', 275; *supra* note 2, p. 128.
[92] HL Deb 1 April 1993, vol. 544, cols. 1003–5.
[93] Ministry of Justice Criminal Justice Policy Group, *Review of Monetary Penalties in New Zealand* (June 2000) as cited in The Law Reform Commission, *Report on the Indexation of Fines: A Review of Developments* (July 2002), pp. 25–6.

As it turned out, it was not a lack of support in the underlying principle of the system that caused its demise, but rather its practical operation. One of the main sources of concern stemmed from the fact that the maximum value for each unit in the statutory framework was set at a considerably higher level (100 pounds) compared to the pilot experiment (20 pounds) – at a time where the UK was experiencing a severe economic recession.[94] Disposable income, too, was set at a higher level compared to the pilot.[95] Magistrates argued that the system had failed to take into account that one's expenses, such as hire-purchase repayments on cars, rose along with income.[96] As a result, when courts determined expenditure levels that were more suitable for low-income offenders and used them as a starting point to calculate the disposable income of someone with average income, the maximum unit value was easily reached. This arrangement disproportionately affected middle-class offenders, who were often fined at the maximum amount.[97] As a magistrate explained at the time, 'people are getting to 100 pounds per unit far too quickly. When the system was invented, they seemed to think that people would be a lot wealthier than they are'.[98]

But this was not the only cause for concern. According to the above-mentioned study, the main obstacle to the smooth operation of the scheme stemmed from the occasional difficulty to obtain information on the offenders' means.[99] When faced with this problem, certain courts decided to set the disposable weekly income at a guideline rate – accepting that this could be too low for some offenders.[100] Certain other courts, however, adopted a diametrically opposite approach, by setting the unit value at the maximum rate.[101] This observation was soon confirmed nationwide; it also produced some unusually high fines,[102] which were picked up by the press and sparked a lot of public controversy.[103] As Ashworth remarked at the time, 'the practical power of a couple of newspaper editors far outstrips the influence of a hundred criminologists'.[104]

---

[94] The Treasury insisted for this increase. See Ashworth, 'Sentencing by Numbers?'; Dunbar and Langdon, *Tough Justice: Sentencing and Penal Policies in the 1990s*, p. 96.

[95] HC Deb 29 June 1993, vol. 227, cols. 914–15.

[96] Sage, 'Means-Related Fines Likely to be Curbed', *The Independent* (8 March 1993).

[97] HC Deb 29 June 1993, vol. 227, cols. 906–7.

[98] *Ibid.*

[99] *Supra* note 81, 37–40.

[100] *Supra* note 82.

[101] *Ibid.*

[102] HC Deb 15 April 1993, vol. 222, cols. 943–4.

[103] '£9000 Parking Fine', *The Herald* (1 May 1993).

[104] *Supra* note 94.

11.4 PUBLIC PERCEPTION OF UNIT FINES

A lack of public education about the principle of equal impact that underpins unit fines left the scheme exposed to severe criticism from the media.[105] Immediately after they came into effect, the press portrayed the scheme as though it was penalising the rich; '£2,000 fine for a Rothchild heir as barman pays online £84', read a headline from the Evening Standard in October of 1992.[106] Of course, this was precisely what unit fines were meant to achieve. The press, however, ignored the fact that the system strived for fairness through equality of impact. Instead, several newspapers chose to compare and contrast the (very different) fines imposed on offenders for the same offence, without highlighting the justification for it. It has often been suggested that if courts declared the fines by referring to the number of units, instead of the total amount, unit fines would have been better received by the public.[107] That is because focus would shift from the monetary aspect of the fine to the fact that a similar punishment is indeed imposed for similar offences. This is what happens in Sweden, where newspapers only publish the number of days of the day fine and not the amount.[108]

But the beginning of the end for unit fines can be traced back to the famous 'crisp packet' incident. When an officer observed Mr Watkins, a young unemployed man, throwing a crisp packet out of his car, he cautioned him and asked him to pick it up. Mr Watkins, however, declined to do so and swore repeatedly at the officer – an incident which resulted in his arrest. His offence (taking into account the aggravating circumstances) amounted to twelve units – but Mr Watkins failed to fill in the means enquiry form. As a result, the magistrates' court assumed his disposable income to be the maximum (100 pounds) and gave him a fine of 1,200 pounds (100 x 12).[109] He later filled in the necessary forms and the fine amount was reduced to forty-eight pounds – but the publicity damage had already been done. The event made headlines at several newspapers, who made a mockery of the unit fine system.[110]

---

[105] Warner, 'Equality before the Law and Equal Impact of Sanctions: Doing Justice to Differences in Wealth and Employment Status'.

[106] '£2,000 fine for a Rothchild heir as barman pays online £84', *The Evening Standard* (27 October 1992).

[107] *Ibid.*; Ashworth, *Sentencing and Criminal Justice*, p. 234.

[108] Eriksson and Goodin, 'The Measuring Rod of Time: The Example of Swedish Day-Fines', 131.

[109] 'Man is fined pounds 1,200 for litter offence', *The Independent* (7 April 1993).

[110] Ramesh, 'Crisp Pounds £1,200 Fine Rubs Salt in Wound for Litter Bug', *The Guardian* (7 April 1993); Doran, 'Justice for the Middle Classes'; Clarke Responds to Public Outrage with a Fairer System of Fines', *Daily Mail* (4 May 1994).

The growing displeasure with the system prompted magistrates to call for reform.[111] In May 1993, they suggested 'that the maximum disposable weekly income figure should be at least halved and preferably reduced by more than that; and the subordinate legislation should be altered to allow for a sliding scale of allowances to take account of the fact that the commitments of defendants tend to rise with their income'.[112] To that Mr Clarke initially responded that unit fines would be retained, subject to amendments. But a few days later he succumbed to pressure from inside and outside the government and announced that they would be abandoned all together.[113]

Unit fines were officially abolished by Section 65 of the Criminal Justice Act 1993, which provided that courts should 'inquire into the financial circumstances of the offender' before setting a fine and that the fine should reflect the seriousness of the offence. To that end, the majority of the magistrates' courts followed the Sentencing Guidelines published by the Magistrates' Association. Still, 17 per cent of the magistrates' courts chose to retain an informal unit fine system,[114] although it is not clear for how long they did so. Under the new system, magistrates continued to lower fine amounts for low income offenders, but when it came to wealthy offenders their approach was less homogenous; some of them supported the idea of increasing the fine to reflect the offender's wealth, but some did not.[115] Therefore, depending on the court before which he/she appeared, a wealthy offender could either receive an increased fine or not.[116] In circumstances such as these, the principle of equality before the law is clearly violated.

Such inconsistencies were, perhaps, inevitable given the abolition of unit fines, which prescribed a clear formula for calculating the fine. Another inevitable consequence, however, was the immediate decline in the use of the fine by the magistrates' courts – especially among the unemployed; while 43 per cent of unemployed offenders were fined for indictable offences after unit fines came into force, once they were abolished, this figure fell to 32 per cent.[117] Unemployed offenders were more likely to receive a conditional discharge, because magistrates knew that they could not afford to pay a fine.[118]

[111] Sage, 'Magistrates to Seek Reform of Unit Fines', *The Independent* (4 May 1993).
[112] HC Deb 29 June 1993, vol. 227, cols. 914–15.
[113] HC Deb 29 June 1993, vol. 227, cols. 915–16.
[114] Charman, Gibson, Honess and Morgan, *Fine Impositions and Enforcement Following the Criminal Justice Act 1993*.
[115] Flood-Page and Mackie, *Sentencing Practice: an Examination of Decisions in Magistrates' Courts and the Crown Court in the mid–1990s*, p. 52.
[116] *Ibid.*, p. 53.
[117] *Ibid.*, p. 48.
[118] *Ibid.*

That said, research by the Home Office revealed that the imprisonment of fine defaulters rose – once again.[119] In 1994, 27 per cent all receptions under sentence consisted of fine defaulters – an overwhelming majority of which were unemployed.[120] In other words, it was not long before the same concerns that prompted the adoption of unit fines in the first place resurfaced.

This did not go unnoticed; in 1995, the Penal Affairs Consortium, concerned about the above developments, suggested that means-related fines should be re-introduced on the basis of 'the best aspects of the unit fines scheme'.[121] The discussion over unit fines, however, was not revived until 2003, when the Carter review of correctional services commented on the fall in the use of the fine and suggested, among other things, that a *day* fine system be introduced in England and Wales.[122] In its response, the government acknowledged that this suggestion would require primary legislation and promised to explore the matter further.[123] A year later, the government put forward a proposal to introduce 'daily income fines' – but the parliament was prorogued and the legislation did not go forward.[124] In 2006, the (Labour) government announced its commitment to introduce day fines by 2009 – but soon after there was a change in government and this never materialised.[125]

11.5 SPECIAL CHALLENGES

England is not the only common law county that has an uneasy relationship with the concept of unit fines. In fact, they have been considered – and rejected – by several other common law countries, including Australia and New Zealand.[126] Warner suggests that one of the reasons why these countries have failed to embrace a system of unit fines is the belief that increasing fines for the wealthy is at odds with the principle of proportionality;[127] while equality of impact seeks to ensure that the sentence (in our case, a fine) has an equal impact on offenders of different financial circumstances, the principle of proportionality seeks to ensure that the sentence is commensurate to the

---

[119] Moxon and Whittaker, *Imprisonment for Fine Default.*
[120] *Ibid.*
[121] *Supra* note 82.
[122] Carter, 'Managing Offenders, Reducing Crime: A New Approach', 27.
[123] Home Office, 'Reducing Crime – Changing Lives' (2004), para. 35.
[124] Section 43, Management of Offenders and Sentencing Bill, available at https://publications .parliament.uk/pa/ld200405/ldbills/016/2005016.pdf.
[125] Home Office, 'A Five Year Strategy for Protecting the Public and Reducing Re-offending' (February 2006, Cm 6717), pp. 19, 33.
[126] *Supra* note 105.
[127] *Ibid.*, 233–4.

seriousness of the offence. Therefore, the argument goes, these two pursuits are at odds with each other. As Warner rightly explains, however, this argument is unfounded; proportionality is only relevant to the determination of the offender's culpability and the seriousness of the offence.[128] Therefore, when courts set the number of the units by looking into the seriousness of the offence and *then* proceed to adjust the value of each unit by reference to the offender's income, the principle of equality does not conflict with that of proportionality.[129]

Unit fines may have been abandoned in England and Wales, but the principle of equal impact continues to play an important role when it comes to sentencing. The current legislation provides that the amount of the fine should reflect the seriousness of the offence and that, in fixing a fine, the court must take into account the financial circumstances of the offender – whether this results in reducing or increasing the fine.[130] The aim of the fine, according to the Magistrates' Court Sentencing Guidelines, is 'to have *an equal impact* on offenders with different financial circumstances'.[131] To aid in this, the Guidelines distinguish fines according to bands – from band A to band F – which reflect the seriousness of the offence.[132] And, in order to take into account the financial circumstances of the offender, the Guidelines set out a percentage of the relevant weekly income as a 'starting point', as well as a percentage 'range'.[133] For example, for a band A fine, the starting point is 50 per cent of the relevant weekly income and the percentage range is 25 per cent–75 per cent of it.[134] For a band B fine, the starting point is 100 per cent of the relevant weekly income, within a range of 75 per cent–125 per cent of that income; for a band C fine, the starting point is 150 per cent of the relevant weekly income and the range is 125 per cent–175 per cent – and so on.[135] The starting point provides the sentencer with a yardstick as to the severity of the penalty, while the 'range' enables him or her to take into account any aggravating or mitigating factors.[136] So, the current fining process is as follows: first, the court determines the appropriate fine band, depending on the offence; then, it decides where to place that offence within the

---

[128] *Ibid.*

[129] *Ibid.*

[130] Section 164 of the CJA 2003.

[131] Sentencing Guideline Council, 'Magistrates' Court Sentencing Guidelines' (May 2014), p. 148 (emphasis added).

[132] *Ibid.*

[133] *Ibid.*

[134] *Ibid.*

[135] *Ibid.*

[136] *Ibid.*, 16–17.

designated range for that particular fine band; finally, it moves on to examine the financial circumstances of the offender in order to calculate his or hers 'relevant weekly income'.[137] The approach of the Sentencing Guidelines is, as Ashworth points out, 'an attempt to combine structure with flexibility'.[138]

Equality of impact may be embedded in the Sentencing Guidelines, but that does not mean that it is achieved in practice. On the contrary; empirical research on the sentencing practices of courts in the UK has demonstrated that '*proportionality* seems to matter most to sentencers in determining levels of fine imposition, rather more so than *equity*'.[139] In particular, when the researchers assigned magistrates throughout the UK with a series of fictitious case studies and asked them to determine a fine, they found that when the magistrates applied the Sentencing Guidelines strictly, they were unhappy with the result of the fine – because it resulted, in their view, to some inappropriately high fines. They also expressed concern as to 'how some such fine levels might be viewed by the public at large and about the risk to the reputation and credibility of the courts of disproportionate fines'. Indeed, many of the participants made reference to their (mostly unhappy) experiences with 'unit fines' some fifteen years earlier and summed up their perspectives on the methodologies that they had been testing by dubbing them as 'unit fines by the backdoor'.[140] This brings us back to Warner's observation; proportionality and equality of impact do not always reconcile, at least in the minds of the sentencers.

11.6 CONCLUSION

Unit fines may have failed to take roots in England and Wales, but the framework that replaced them is not akin to the traditional fixed fine system either.[141] While the latter is only concerned with the severity of the offence, the Criminal Justice Act 2003 introduced a system that, as we saw above, mandates sentencers to take into account the offender's financial circumstances when setting a fine. We could, therefore, describe it as a system that sits in the middle of a spectrum with fixed fines on the one end and unit fines on the other. At the

---

[137] *Ibid.*, 148–9. The Sentencing Council has included a 'fine calculator' in its website to assist sentencers in this process. See www.sentencingcouncil.org.uk/fine-calculator/.
[138] *Supra* note 107, p. 333.
[139] Raine and Dunstan, 'How Well Do Sentencing Guidelines Work?: Equity, Proportionality and Consistency in the Determination of Fine Levels in the Magistrates' Courts of England and Wales', 13–36.
[140] *Ibid.*, 31.
[141] Kantorowicz-Reznichenko, 'Day-Fines: Should the Rich Pay More?', 481–501.

same time, the new system ensures that sentencers enjoy a greater level of discretion when setting a fine compared to the limited discretion they enjoyed under the (more prescriptive) unit fine scheme. This was, after all, one of the main reasons why part of the judiciary met unit fines with hostility, argued for its abolition – and won.

And while the idea of reintroducing unit fines has floated several times after they were abandoned, it is arguably not a priority for policy-makers. This is, at least to some extent, attributable to the fact that the number of individuals imprisoned for fine default has decreased significantly since 1995;[142] following the *Crowley* judgment, which called upon courts to consider all other enforcement procedures before committing a fine defaulter in prison,[143] the courts have been addressing the matter in alternative ways – for instance, through community service orders. In other words, one of the main problems that the unit fines scheme set out to address in the early 1990s no longer exists and so, there is little incentive to revisit the issue.

REFERENCES

Ashworth, A. 1991. 'The New English Sentencing System', *UC Davis Law Review* 25: 755–71.

Ashworth, A. 1993. 'Sentencing by Numbers?', *Criminal Justice Matters* 14: 6–7.

Ashworth, A. 1997. 'Legislature Vs. Judiciary: The Struggle for Supremacy in English Sentencing', *Federal Sentencing Reporter* 10: 275–77.

Ashworth, A. and Wasik, M. 1998. *Fundamentals of Sentencing Theory: Essays in Honour of Andrew Von Hirsch.* Oxford: Oxford University Press on Demand.

Ashworth, A. 2015. *Sentencing and Criminal Justice.* Oxford: Cambridge University Press.

Carter, P. 2003. 'Managing Offenders, Reducing Crime: A New Approach', *Strategy Unit*, 11 December.

Cavadino, M. and Crow, I. 1999. *Criminal Justice 2000: Strategies for a New Century.* Winchester: Waterside Press.

Cavadino, M. and Dignan, J. 2007. *The Penal System: An Introduction.* London: Sage.

Charman, E., Gibson, B., Honess, T. and Morgan, R. 1996. *Fine Impositions and Enforcement Following the Criminal Justice Act 1993.* London: Home Office.

Criminal Justice Act 1991.

Criminal Justice Act 2003.

Crow, I. and Simon, F. 1987. *Unemployment and Magistrates' Courts.* London: NACRO.

Crow, I., Cavadino, M., Dignan, J., Johnston, V. and Walker, M. 1994. 'Magistrates' Views of the Criminal Justice Act 1991', *Justice of the Peace* 158: 37–40.

---

[142] Ministry of Justice, 'Guide to Offender Management Statistics: England and Wales', p. 19.
[143] [1996] 2 W.L.R. 681.

Crow, I., Cavadino, M., Dignan, J., Johnston, V. and Walker, M. 1996. *Changing Criminal Justice: The Impact of the Criminal Justice Act 1991 in Four Areas of the North of England*. University of Sheffield, Centre for Criminological and Legal Research.

Default, F. 1981. *Report of a Nacro Working Party*. London: NACRO.

Doran, A. 1994. 'Justice for the Middle Classes; Clarke Responds to Public Outrage with a Fairer System of Fines', *Daily Mail*, 4 May.

Dunbar, I. and Langdon, A. 1998. *Tough Justice: Sentencing and Penal Policies in the 1990s*. Oxford University Press.

Dyer, C. 1993. 'You Finish up with Silly Fines and are Left with No Discretion', *The Guardian*, 7 April.

Eriksson, L. and Goodin, R. E. 2007. "The Measuring Rod of Time: The Example of Swedish Day-Fines', *Journal of Applied Philosophy* 24: 125–36.

Evans, P. 1989. 'Fairer Fines Pay Off for Courts', *The Times*, 1 May.

Faulkner, D. 2014. *Servant of the Crown: A Civil Servant's Story of Criminal Justice and Public Service Reform*. Winchester: Waterside Press.

Flood-Page, C. and Mackie, A. 1998. *Sentencing Practice: an Examination of Decisions in Magistrates' Courts and the Crown Court in the mid-1990s*. London: Home Office.

Gibson, B. 1991. 'Unit Fines – Punishment and Proportionality', *New Law Journal* 141: 750–51.

HC Deb 20 March 1988, vol. 130, cols. 1083–97.

HC Deb 20 June 1988, vol. 135, cols. 931–42.

HC Deb 20 February 1991, vol. 186, cols. 404–5.

HC Deb 15 April 1993, vol. 222, cols. 943–4.

HC Deb 13 May 1993, vol. 224, cols. 939–40.

HC Deb 29 June 1993, vol. 227, cols. 905–20.

HL Deb 30 November 1988, vol. 502, col. 365.

HL Deb 12 March 1991, vol. 527, cols. 102–3.

HL Deb 1 April 1993, vol. 544, cols. 1003–5.

Home Office. 1970. *Non-Custodial and Semi-Custodial Penalties: Report of the Advisory Council on the Penal System*. London: HMSO.

Home Office. 1988. *Punishment, Custody and the Community*. London: HMSO.

Home Office. 1990. *Crime, Justice and Protecting the Public: The Government's Proposals for Legislation*. London: HMSO, para. 1.6.

Home Office. 1991. *Criminal Justice Act 1991: Fines and Other Financial Penalties*. London: HMSO.

Home Office. 2004. *Reducing Crime – Changing Lives*. London: HMSO.

Home Office. 2006. *A Five Year Strategy for Protecting the Public and Reducing Re-offending*. London: HMSO.

Home Office. 1993. 'Cautions, Court Proceedings and Sentencing – England and Wales 1992', *Home Office Statistical Bulletin* Issue 24, Table 8.

Home Office. 1993. 'Monitoring of the Criminal Justice Act 1991 – Data from a Special Data Collection Exercise', *Home Office Statistical Bulletin*, Issue 25, p. 5.

Junger-Tas, J. 1994. *Alternatives to Prison Sentences: Experiences and Developments*. Amsterdam/New York: Kugler Publications.

JUSTICE (British Section of the International Commission of Jurists), 1989. *Sentencing: A Way Ahead*. London: JUSTICE.

Kantorowicz-Reznichenko, E. 2015. 'Day-Fines: Should the Rich Pay More?', *Review of Law & Economics* 11: 481–501.

Magistrates' Courts (Unit Fines) Rules 1992.

Ministry of Justice, Criminal Justice Policy Group. 2000. *Review of Monetary Penalties in New Zealand.*

Ministry of Justice. 2018. *Guide to Offender Management Statistics: England and Wales.*

Moxon, D., Sutton, M. and Hedderman, C. 1990. *Deductions from Benefit for Fine Default.* London: Home Office.

Moxon, D., Sutton M. and Hedderman, C. 1990. *Unit Fines: Experiments in Four Courts.* London: Home Office.

Moxon, D. and Whittaker, C. 1996. *Imprisonment for Fine Default.* London: Home Office.

Newburn, T. 2007. '"Tough on Crime": Penal Policy in England and Wales', *Crime and Justice* 36: 425–70.

Parliamentary All-Party Penal Affairs Group, 1980. *Too Many Prisoners: An Examination of Ways of Reducing the Prison Population.* Chichester: Rose.

Penal Affairs Consortium, 1990. *Means-Related Fines.* London: Penal Affairs Consortium.

Prison Reform Trust and United Kingdom, 1990. *Tackling Fine Default.* London: Prison Reform Trust.

Raine, J. W. and Dunstan, E. 2009. 'How Well Do Sentencing Guidelines Work?: Equity, Proportionality and Consistency in the Determination of Fine Levels in the Magistrates' Courts of England and Wales', *The Howard Journal of Criminal Justice* 48: 13–36.

Ramesh, R. 1993. 'Crisp Pounds £1,200 Fine Rubs Salt in Wound for Litter Bug', *The Guardian* 7 April.

Sage, A. 1993. 'Means-Related Fines Likely to be Curbed', *The Independent* 8 March.

Sage, A. 1993. 'Magistrates to Seek Reform of Unit Fines', *The Independent* 4 May.

Sturge, G. 2018. 'UK Prison Population Statistics', House of Commons Briefing Paper, Number CBP-04334 (23 July).

The National Archives, PREM 19/2716 (011.jpg), http://discovery.nationalarchives.gov.uk/details/r/C16329001.

Von Hirsch, A. 1986. *Past or Future Crimes: Deservedness and Dangerousness in the Sentencing of Criminals.* Manchester: Manchester University Press.

Von Hirsch, A. 1992. 'Proportionality in the Philosophy of Punishment', *Crime and Justice* 16: 55–98.

Whitehead, P. 2015. *Reconceptualising the Moral Economy of Criminal Justice: A New Perspective.* London: Springer/Palgrave Macmillan.

Warner, K. 2012. 'Equality before the Law and Equal Impact of Sanctions: Doing Justice to Differences in Wealth and Employment Status'. In Zedner, L. and Roberts, J. V. (eds.), *Criminal Justice: Essays in Honour of Andrew Ashworth.* Oxford: Oxford University Press.

Day Fines in Slovenia

Mitja Kovac

12.1 INTRODUCTION

The imposition of day fines and related questions on the optimal punitive policy have been for the last few decades one of the most extensively debated issues in the Slovenian criminal law scholarship. This chapter offers a thorough analysis of day fines in Slovenia and critically comments on the current unacceptably low percentage of day fines in the overall punitive structure.

The chapter offers an overview of the historical development of day fines in Slovenia, provides a thorough discussion on its current regulatory structure, investigates its main sources of inefficiencies and problems of daily implementation, explores the issues of public perception of day fines and identifies the main obstacles, roadblocks and special challenges that lay ahead on the path towards the optimal implementation of day fines in Slovenia.

The main findings are: (1) the current provisions of the Slovenian Criminal Code provide day fines as an exclusive monetary remedy (besides imprisonment, driving ban and expulsion of a non-citizen from the country); (2) the Slovenian legal system is characterised by the downgrading of petty offences to simple administrative procedures; (3) legal scholarship has been for decades arguing in favour of the day fine system and has been constantly pointing out the suboptimal structure of de facto punitive policies; (4) the introduction of day fines into the newly established, independent Slovenian legal system was based upon scholarly arguments suggesting that day fines have an enormous advantage over the classical system by eliminating the main failure of fines – by eliminating its social injustice; (5) the main driving force behind the reintroduction of day fines into the Criminal Codes of 1994 and of 2008 was an extensive scholarly push, based on comparative assessment (legal transplants) of the most successful and advanced legal systems and on the position of the

Slovenian legal system as part of the German legal family and on the grounds of fairness and effectiveness; (6) the current, shockingly low percentage of day fines is unacceptable; yet in 2017 a structural break with significant increase in the percentage of day fines occurred; (7) the public discourse (and also public prosecutors and judges) perceive day fines as inefficient, unjust, ineffective and non-retributory; (8) the main reason for the low percentage of day fines is the non-existence of the priority rule, absence of active promotion of alternative sanctions and the fact that day fines are actually not requested by prosecutors; and (9) the current 'ignore-day-fine' practice by public prosecutors is merely an excuse for insisting on old practices (status quo bias).

Two caveats should be made. The first caveat is that not in all issues discussed in this chapter consensus has been reached. I summarise the most important features of the day fine system in Slovenia. On some of these findings a consensus has been reached; on others, further empirical investigation is needed in order to provide substantive insights. The second caveat is related to the scope of this chapter. Since it is not possible to cover the entire penal policy and penology, the chapter merely focuses on the most striking and significant insights related to the use of day fines in Slovenia.

12.2 HISTORICAL DEVELOPMENT OF DAY FINES IN THE COUNTRY

Slovenia gained its independence in 1991 and, hence, its criminal law, jurisprudence and the system of day fines is still in its adolescent stage. However, the issue of day fines, discussions related to a proper system of such fines and its relevance in criminology sparked an intensive scholarly debate that can be traced even back to the times of ex-Yugoslavia.

Namely, Slovenia's unique position in the former Socialist Federal Republic of Yugoslavia (hereinafter SFRY) can also be illustrated with distinctive debate on the proper scope, content and rationale of criminal sanctions.[1] The old Yugoslavian criminal jurisprudence advanced the so-called 'pluralistic approach', where every sanction serves its own purpose, as

---

[1] One should note that although Yugoslavia had its general criminal law each of its federal socialist republics have also their own criminal codes. Thus, the Federal Criminal Code of Yugoslavia was enacted on 28 September 1976 (*Kazenski Zakonik SFRJ, Uradni list SFRJ, No. 44/1976*) and the Criminal Code of the Socialist Republic of Slovenia (federal unit) was enacted 26 May 1977 (*Kazenski Zakonik SR Slovenije, Uradni list SR Slovenije, No. 12/1977*). See *e.g.* Bavcon *et al.*, 'Kazensko Pravo Splošni Del', 78–81; Bačić, 'Krivično pravo: opći dio', 91–104; and Jovanović and Jović, *Krivično pravo: opšti deo*, pp. 113–15.

the leading theoretical principle.[2] The classification of criminal sanctions (including monetary fines) was in the exclusive domain of the Federal Criminal Code of Yugoslavia,[3] which organised sanctions in four main categories: (a) sanctions; (b) conditional conviction and judicial reminder; (c) security measures; and (d) educational measures.[4] However, the enforcement modality of different criminal sanctions has been in the exclusive domain of the Criminal Codes of different Federal Republics.[5] Insightfully, already in the late 1980s Slovenian scholars have extensively studied different criminal law systems and related sanctions and openly debated different theoretical concepts of sanctions.[6] Moreover, the issue of the proper version of monetary sanctions triggered an intensive scholarly debate that can even rival the one on the abolishment, or de facto non-enforcement of the death penalty.[7] Article 34 of the Criminal Code of SFRY[8] of 1976 on criminal sanctions offered four different types of potential sanctions: (a) death penalty; (b) imprisonment; (c) monetary fine; and (d) confiscation of property. One of the main novelties introduced by this Criminal Code of 1976 is the decrease of potential penalties/sanctions from twelve different sorts of penalties contained in the Criminal Code of SFRY from 1947, to seven in the Criminal Code in 1951, to five in the 1959s updated version and finally to four in 1976.[9] Moreover, the Criminal Code of SFRY from 1976 specifically stated in Article 33 that the purpose of sanctioning is threefold: (a) prevention of criminal activity and perpetrators' re-engagement and re-socialisation; (b) educational influence on others not to commit crimes; and (c) to strengthen the morale of socialist self-governing societies and to influence the development of social responsibility and discipline of citizens.[10]

From the early 1950s the monetary fines mentioned in Article 34 of the Criminal Code of SFRY[11] of 1976 have been subject of intensive scholarly debate. One of the main criticisms of fines derived from the fact that fines (as

---

[2] *Ibid.*, Bavcon *et al.*, 269.

[3] Kazenski Zakonik SFRJ, *Uradni list SFRJ*, No. 44/1976.

[4] Bavcon, *Kriminalna Politika in njene Tendence v Socialistični Družbi*, pp. 16–17; Frank, *Teorija Kaznenog Prava Op*, pp. 202–6.

[5] *Supra* note 1, Bavcon *et al.*, 270.

[6] For example, there was an extensive debate on the optimal theoretical rationale, on the metaphysical, idealistic, normative, sociological and contractual concepts of punishment and related sanctioning. See e.g. Kobe and Bavcon, 'Kazenski zakonik s pojasnili', 37–44.

[7] *Ibid.*, 40–4. See also *supra* note 1, Jovanović and Jović, pp. 239–58.

[8] *Supra* note 3.

[9] *Supra* note 1, Bavcon *et al.*, 280.

[10] Article 33, 'Kazenski Zakonik SFRJ', *Uradni list SFRJ*, No. 44/1976.

[11] *Ibid.*

conceptualised in 1976) do not affect all people equally.[12] Moreover, critics advanced the fact that the fine is also not only affecting the convict, but also the other members of his/her immediate family who in some cases de facto pay for a financial penalty (fine) and who are due to such payment afterwards financially worse off.[13] Furthermore, some Yugoslavian scholars even argued that fines are not particularly effective and that their effect may be even lower than anticipated, since a fine may be paid by someone else instead of the sentenced person.[14] However, Slovenian scholars, while defending the effectiveness of fines, provided a counterargument and in late 1980s for the first time suggested that fines should be calculated in relation to the convict's wealth.[15] Insightfully, Bavcon and Šelih, influenced by the German and Austrian legal theory, actually employed a comparative analysis of several western states and argued that fines should be calculated in relation to the convict's daily earning (i.e. day fines).[16] Thus, Bavcon and Šelih in their encyclopaedical book 'Kazensko pravo' from 1987,[17] while stating that day fines are the most common remedy in all advanced, western legal systems, actually coined the concept of day fines into the Slovenian (and at that time also Yugoslavian) jurisprudence. In addition, they also suggested that day fines are the most effective replacement for inefficient short-term sanctions of imprisonment.[18]

However, Article 39 of the Criminal Code of SFRY of 1976 merely allowed monetary fines (in absolute amounts) and provided that 'a fine may be a major or secondary penalty'. As the main one, it can be pronounced only when it is prescribed for an individual offence. However, it can also be pronounced as a secondary sentence even if it is not prescribed. This can be done in instances of crimes that are committed out of self-interest, if the court pronounced imprisonment as the main sanction.[19] According to Article 39 (1) of the Criminal Code[20] the fine has been prescribed in the range from the general minimum to the general maximum. Furthermore, Article 41 of the Criminal Code also provided that when assessing fines, the court had to take into

---

[12]   The ones with a worse financial situation have to carry a disproportionately higher burden than the ones with more financial assets; see *e.g.* Srzentić, Stajić and Lazarević, *Krivično pravo Socialističke Federativne Republike Jugoslavije*, pp. 316–67.

[13]   *Ibid.*, pp. 340–67.

[14]   See *e.g.* Srzentić, Stajić and Lazarević, *Krivično pravo Socialističke Federativne Republike Jugoslavije*, pp. 316–67.

[15]   *Supra* note 1, Bavcon *et al.*, 284.

[16]   *Ibid.*

[17]   *Supra* note 1, Bavcon *et al.*

[18]   *Ibid.*, 284.

[19]   *Supra* note 10, Article 39.

[20]   *Ibid.*

account the convict's financial situation, whereas Article 39 (2) of the Criminal Code provided that in justified cases, the court may determine that the fine is repayable in instalments, but these instalments should not exceed two years.[21] In addition, if the sentenced person failed to pay the fine, within the fixed time-limit, the court could recover the amount forcibly (executive order).[22] If the executive order remained unsuccessful, however, the court could according to Article 39 (4) change the penalty payment into imprisonment by setting one day of imprisonment for each initial 500 dinars.[23]

After the independence in 1991 the discussions on the feasibility of day fines again took the ground and the ideas of day fines, advocated for several years by Bavcon and Šelih, otherwise esteemed and highly influential Slovenian law professors, finally found their way into the lawmaking process. The draft version of the new Slovenian Criminal Code[24] introduced, among other modern instruments, also the concept of day fines. Šelih, for example, discussed (and advocated) the proposed day fines and suggested that the essence of the novice is that the court should first define how much of the daily amounts will be deducted from the perpetrator's income and then, determines the amount of that income per day and calculates a fine that the perpetrator has to pay.[25] She also offered the system of day fines in Finland as the prime example of successful adoption of day fines and also advanced the comparative legal perspective, suggesting that all advanced western legal systems employed day fines for the last twenty years.[26] Moreover, Šelih advocated the introduction of day fines into the newly established, independent Slovenian legal system by suggesting that day fines have an enormous advantage over the classical system by eliminating the main failure of fines: social injustice.[27] Namely, day fines eliminate social injustice that is caused by the fact that ordinary (fixed amount) fines affect those who have higher incomes less than those whose income is lower.[28]

In line with scholarly suggestions the first Criminal Code in the independent Slovenia has been enacted in 1994[29] and has indeed contained a provision on day fines. Article 38 (1) (day fines) of the Criminal Code of 1994

---

[21] *Ibid.*
[22] *Ibid.*
[23] *Ibid.*
[24] Delovni osnutek Kazenskega Zakonika Republike Slovenije in njegove usmeritve, Vlada Republike Slovenije.
[25] Šelih, 'Problemi kazenskih sankcij', 474–9.
[26] *Ibid.*
[27] *Ibid.*
[28] *Ibid.*
[29] *Kazenski zakonik Republike Slovenije – KZ, Uradni list RS*, št. 63/94 z dne 13.10.1994.

introduced day fines as an exclusive monetary remedy (besides imprisonment, driving ban and expulsion of a non-citizen from the country) and provided that the fine is imposed in daily amounts and amounts to at least 5 and up to a maximum of 360 daily amounts and for crimes of self-interest of up to a maximum of 1,500 daily amounts.[30] In addition, Article 38 (2) of the Criminal Code provided also that courts determine the daily amount by taking into account the amount of the perpetrator's daily earnings in relation to his/her three-month salary and his/her other income and family obligations.[31] According to commentators such provisions ensure that the fines affect all perpetrators in the same way regardless of their financial position.[32]

However, the amended Criminal Code of 2004 (KZ-UPB1)[33] in its Article 38 (1) added to the day fines also the possibility of a certain, one-time fixed amount. Namely, Article 38 (1) of the Criminal Code of 2004 provided that a fine is imposed in daily amounts. However, if this is not possible, then also in a certain, fixed amount.[34] Of course, this refers to cases where courts, for example, could not find information on the income of the offender. Moreover, Article 38 (2) of the same Code also provided that if a fine is imposed in daily amounts, it may amount to at least 5 and up to 360 daily amounts, for offences committed up to a maximum of 130 times the daily amount. If a fine is fixed at a certain amount, the minimum amount must not be less than 30,000 Slovenian tolars (SIT), the highest being not more than 3,000,000 SIT and for crimes of mercilessness not higher than 9,000,000 SIT.[35] In addition, the number of daily amounts of fines shall be determined by the court in accordance with the general rules on the assessment of the penalty. The amount of the daily amount is determined by the court by taking into account the amount of the perpetrator's daily earnings in relation to his/her three-month net salary and his/her other income and his/her family obligations. When determining the amount of the daily amount, the court shall rely on data which are not older than one year at the time the sentence is pronounced.[36]

[30] *Ibid.*, Article 38 (1).

[31] *Ibid.*, Article 38 (2).

[32] Bavcon *et al.*, 'Kazenski Zakonik Republike Slovenije z Uvodnimi Pojasnili', 42–3, 131–2.

[33] 'Zakon o spremembah in dopolnitvah Kazenskega zakonika', KZ-B, Uradni list RS, št. 40/04 z dne 20.4.2004.

[34] 'Kazenski zakonik (uradno prečiščeno besedilo)', KZ-UPB1, Article 38 (1), Uradni list RS, No. 95/2004, z dne 27.8.2004.

[35] *Ibid.* Exchange rate for the Slovenian tolar to euro was at the time of the adoption of the euro in Slovenia fixed to: 239.64 SIT = 1 euro.

[36] *Ibid.*, Article 38 (2).

However, the newest Criminal Code of 2008 (*Kazenski zakonik* – KZ-1, Off. Gaz. No. 55/08) and as amended of 2017[37] contains again day fines as an exclusive monetary remedy. This shift back to the day fines as an exclusive monetary sanction (no fixed amount possible) has been advocated and founded in the Slovenian long-standing belonging (and influence) to the German legal family and via extensive comparative analysis, where the system of day fines in Germany, Austria and Finland have been taken as prime examples upon which the Slovenian Criminal Code should be designed.[38]

In relation to these constant shifts the literature notes that the setting of fines in daily amounts was introduced for the first time by the Criminal Code of 1994.[39] However, since the courts did not accept and utilise this form of fines, a legislative change of 1999 amended this solution by determining the possibility of pronouncing both modalities of fines. This sceptical attitude towards day fines may be explained by the lack of knowledge, lack of needed information and simple behavioural phenomena of status quo bias. The Criminal Code of 2008 then reintroduced the imposition of a fine in the form of daily amounts, at least 10 and a maximum of 360 daily amounts and for committing acts done out of illegal gain-seeking interest, no more than 1,500 daily amounts.[40]

The literature also emphasises the comparative success of day fines in Finland, Austria, Germany, France and also other Scandinavian countries and the fairness of day fines in cases of different material status of convicts and its resistance to the issues of inflation. Bavcon *et al.* also emphasise that day fines are now one of the most important and commonly used penalties, familiar in all modern criminal laws and they also represent the most effective replacements for short-term imprisonments.[41]

To sum up, the main driving force behind the re-introduction of day fines into the Criminal Codes of 1994 and of 2008 was an extensive scholarly push, based (a) on comparative assessment (legal transplants) of the most successful and advanced legal systems; (b) on the position of the Slovenian legal system as part of the German legal family; and (c) on the grounds of fairness and effectiveness. Moreover, Jager and Markelj even provided a Law and

---

[37] 'Kazenski zakonik', *Uradni list RS*, št. 50/12 – uradno prečiščeno besedilo, 6/16 – popr., 54/15, 38/16 in 27/17.
[38] See e.g. Vlada Republike Slovenije, *Predlog Kazenskega Zakonika*, Ljubljana, 17.01.2008.
[39] *Supra* note 32, 370–1.
[40] *Ibid.*, 371.
[41] *Ibid.*, 370.

Economics analysis offering a set of economic arguments in favour of day fines that have been afterwards incorporated in the legislative process.[42]

12.3 THE STRUCTURE OF THE FINE

The current Criminal Code of 2008 and as amended of 2017,[43] as already stated, provides in Article 47 day fines as an exclusive monetary sanction.[44] It reintroduced the imposition of a fine in the form of daily amounts, at least 10 and a maximum of 360 daily amounts and, for committing acts of mercy, no more than 1,500 daily amounts. Namely, Article 47 (fines) of the current Criminal Code provides that a financial penalty shall be imposed by multiplying a certain number of daily amounts that the perpetrator must pay in the judgment by the amount of the daily amount determined by the court in relation to the economic situation of the perpetrator.[45] The number of daily amounts may not be less than 10 and not more than 360 and for acts committed to seek illegal financial gain, not more than 1,500.[46] Moreover, the court determines day fines by observing the general rules on the imposition of penalties, with the exception of circumstances relating to the financial situation of the perpetrator.[47] Article 47 (3) also states that the court should determine the amount of the day fines according to the financial situation of the perpetrator on the basis of information on his/her earnings, other income, the value of his/her assets, the average cost of his/her maintenance and his/her family obligations.[48] However, the Criminal Code in Article 47 (3) also contains a specific provision limiting the daily amount and provides that the daily amount (of day fines) cannot be higher than 1,000 euros.

Furthermore, the Criminal Code in its Article 47 (4) contains a specific provision with the exact instructions to the courts on how and which data courts should take into account when employing day fines. Namely, Article 47 (4) states that when the court is deciding on the amount of the day fine that

---

[42] Jager, *Ekonomska analiza kazenskega prava in kriminalitetne politike*, p. 1635; and Markelj, *Ekonomska analiza kazenskih sankcij*, pp. 456–81.

[43] *Kazenski zakonik, Uradni list RS*, št. 55/08, 50/12, 6/16, 54/15, 38/16 and 27/17.

[44] The Criminal Code (KZ-1F, Off. Gaz. No. 27/2017, from 2.6.2017) in Article 43 states that for criminal offences, the perpetrators may be sanctioned by the following sanctions: (a) jail; (b) day fine; (c) driving ban on motor vehicles; and (d) expulsion of a non-citizen from the country.

[45] Article 47 (1), Criminal Code, KZ-1F, Off. Gaz. No. 55/08, 50/12, 6/16, 54/15, 38/16 and 27/2017, from 2.6.2017.

[46] *Ibid.*, paragraph 2.

[47] *Ibid.*

[48] *Ibid.*, paragraph 3.

should be imposed, the court shall take into account data that are not older than one year when the sentence is pronounced. If the court cannot obtain data for determining the amount of the day fine or if its acquisition would be linked to disproportionate problems or delay or if it is a criminal offence (gathering of data), the amount of the day fine is determined on the basis of the data at the court's disposal and otherwise by the court's established circumstances regarding the financial situation of the perpetrator.[49]

In addition, the same Article 47 (5) also states that in a judgment, the court should set a time limit for the payment of a day fine which should not be less than fifteen days and not longer than three months.[50] However, in duly justified cases, the court may allow the sentenced person to pay a day fine in instalments, with the payment deadline not exceeding two years.[51] Moreover, if the perpetrator is late with the payment of an individual instalment, the court may order an immediate payment by a court order (executive order) within a time limit not exceeding three months.[52]

Commentators note that when imposing a day fine, courts essentially carry out two operations: first they determine the number of amounts, then they calculate the amount of the day fine.[53] The number of daily amounts means the criterion for determining the amount of the penalty and determines the glare for the proportion between the severity of the crime and the degree of guilt. The next operation carried out by the court is to determine the amount of the day fine, in such a way that it takes into account the amount of the perpetrator's daily earnings in relation to the official data of the tax authority (directly from the Financial Administration) and the perpetrator's family obligations.[54] The data on the perpetrator's daily earnings, on his/her monthly income, on his/her financial assets and on his/her income flow are provided by the Financial Administration of the Republic of Slovenia, an administrative body within the Slovenian Ministry of Finance which collects all financial information on any income of Slovenian citizens.[55] Insightfully, the previous Criminal Code, however, contained a specific provision that if such

---

[49] *Ibid.*, paragraph 4.
[50] *Ibid.*, paragraph 5.
[51] *Ibid.*
[52] *Ibid.*
[53] *Supra* note 1, Bavcon *et al.*, 371.
[54] *Ibid.*
[55] The main tasks of the Financial Administration of the Republic of Slovenia are: assessment, calculation and collection of taxes and duties; customs clearance of goods; financial supervision; financial investigation; gaming supervision; cash controls on entering or leaving the EU; control of admission, removal and transit of goods subject to special measures due to interests of the safety and protection of the health and lives of people, animals, plants, environmental

information cannot be obtained, the daily amount is taken as 1/30 of the last official average monthly net earnings of the employed person.[56]

The family obligations of the perpetrator are, in particular, his/her maintenance obligations (for example, obligations arising from a house loan).[57] When determining the amount of the daily unit, the court shall, as already emphasised, rely on data which are not older than one year at the time when the fine is imposed. If the sentenced person fails to pay the day fine within the prescribed time limit, the court forcibly recovers the amount (executive order).[58]

Moreover, if the execution (executive order) proves to be ineffective the court enforces the day fine in such a way that it determines one day of imprisonment for each two day fines imposed.[59] The confinement in which the unpaid fine is changed does not have the nature of a prison sentence. Thus, this imprisonment may last for less than fifteen days, and these types of confinements, cannot cause legal consequences for the convict, nor is such imprisonment subject to the provisions on conditional release.[60]

Article 87 of the Criminal Code (Method of execution of a day fine)[61] actually precisely prescribes the method of how day fines should be executed. Namely, Article 87 states that if the fine is not imposed or enforced, it shall be executed by the court in such a way that one day of imprisonment is determined for each two day fines imposed, with the imprisonment not exceeding six months.[62] Commentators emphasise that this also implies that day fines of

---

protection, as well as protection of the cultural heritage, intellectual property and commercial policy measures; recovery; deciding in other administrative procedures according to regulations in the competence of the Financial Administration; deciding in the minor offence proceedings according to supervision regulations in the competence of the Financial Administration; implementation of foreign trade and common agriculture policy measures in the competence of the Financial Administration; storage, sale and destruction of seized, confiscated, abandoned or found goods and supervision of destruction of goods; and co-operation and exchange of data with EU bodies, competent bodies of the EU Member States and with competent bodies of other states; co-operation with international organisations and professional associations; Ministry of Finance, Financial Administration of the Republic of Slovenia, General Financial office, *About the Financial Administration: Organization and Tasks*, Financial Administration, 2019. Available at: www.fu.gov.si/en/about_the_financial_administration/#c338.

56   *Supra* note 42, Markelj, p. 7.
57   *Supra* note 1, Bavcon *et al.*, 371.
58   *Ibid.*, 372.
59   *Ibid.*
60   *Ibid.*
61   Article 87, Criminal Code, KZ-1F., Off. Gaz. No. 255/08, 50/12, 6/16, 54/15, 38/16 and 7/2017, from 2.6.2017.
62   Article 87 (1), Criminal Code, KZ-1F., Off. Gaz. No. 255/08, 50/12, 6/16, 54/15, 38/16 and 7/2017, from 2.6.2017. See also *supra* note 1, Bavcon *et al.*, 372.

more than 360 days may become unrecoverable.[63] However, those high day fines can only be imposed if the offence has been committed out of a self-interest.[64]

Yet, if the sentenced person pays only part of the day fine, his/her residue shall be changed proportionally to the confinement and if he pays the remaining sum, the execution of the prison sentence should be terminated.[65] Evidently, if the sentenced person dies, the fine is not executed. Furthermore, in Slovenia a day fine up to 360 daily amounts may also be executed in such a way that a convicted person performs work for general benefit without compensation in a period of no more than one year instead of paying a fine.[66] The scope of work is determined by replacing one daily amount by one hour of work. In relation to the potential issues that are not covered by the explicit provision of Article 87, the provisions of the eighth to thirteenth paragraphs of Article 86 (Method of executing a prison sentence) of the Criminal Code shall apply *mutatis mutandis*.

Finally, day fines are imposed exclusively by judges (prosecutors and police have no authority) and the collection of fines is operationalised and performed by the special executive departments of the courts themselves. The 2008 Criminal Code also explicitly disregarded the previous possibility that fixed fines could be used in cases where the information on the financial status of a convict was not available.[67] Currently, day fines in Slovenia are thus the exclusive monetary remedy – fixed fines are not used at all.[68]

12.4 PRACTICAL IMPLEMENTATION

Historically, the courts in Slovenia most often imposed monetary fines in the 1980s, when the proportion of monetary fines was about 35 per cent of all imposed sanctions. Since 1990 its use began to decrease; in 1994 and 1995 it was only around 9 per cent of all sanctions; after 1995 (when the CC-94

---

[63] *Supra* note 1, Bavcon *et al.*, 372.

[64] *Ibid.*

[65] Article 87 (2), Criminal Code, KZ-1E, Off. Gaz. No. 255/08, 50/12, 6/16, 54/15, 38/16 and 7/2017, from 2.6.2017. See also *supra* note 1, Bavcon *et al.*, 372.

[66] Article 87 (4), Criminal Code, KZ-1E, Off. Gaz. No. 255/08, 50/12, 6/16, 54/15, 38/16 and 7/2017, from 2.6.2017.

[67] See e.g. *supra* note 42, Markelj, p. 7.

[68] However, the obsolete Criminal Code of 2004 (*Kazenski zakonik, Uradni list RS, št.* 95/04), actually contained in Article 38(a) provision enabling courts in instances when the information for determining the daily amount is unknown to him and when the defendant did not submit such information to the end of the main hearing, to impose a fixed fine. See also *supra* note 42, Markelj, p. 7.

entered into force) the amount of day fines was at 7 per cent; after 1999 (when the changes of the KZ-94 came into force) it first dropped to 5.5 per cent (2000) and then rose to 6.7 per cent (2001).[69]

This low percentage of day fines (for all crimes) could be explained by the provision in the Criminal Code of 1994 (KZ-UPB1) that in its Article 38 (1) added to the day fines also the possibility of a certain, one-time fixed amount. This possibility for the court, under the obsolete KZ-UPB1, that when the data for the determination of the day fine are not known and when the convict does not submit them to the end of the imprisonment, to impose a fine in a certain amount has been extensively criticised. For example, Markelj, in his Law and Economics assessment of the Slovenian system of criminal sanctions emphasised that such a low percentage of day fines is unacceptable.[70] He also argued that such a low percentage of day fines also causes additional costs, if a convicted person is unable or unwilling to pay the fines and the compulsory exemption is not successful, the fine is converted into an imprisonment.[71]

Moreover, the National Resolution on the Crime Prevention Act of 2007 (Off. Gaz. No. 40/2007)[72] suggested the increased employment of day fines as one of the most promising institutions that could decrease the criminality rate. One has to note that the available data in the period from 1991 to 2007 (official statistics) due to the omitted variable bias, endogeneity and reverse causality problems (independence from the previous Yugoslavia, reform of the entire judicial system, organisation change of the entire police force, shift from socialism to capitalism etc.) cannot offer reliable substantive insight on the reasons (causality) and the consequences of the partial introduction of day fines and the related legislative impacts. However, data show that the amount of reported criminal acts in 1995 (36,587) increased to 90,354 in 2006,[73] and that courts are increasingly willing to impose more severe sanctions.[74]

In 2007 (one year before the amendment of the Criminal Code) courts issued 9,863 decisions out of which day fines amounted to 9 per cent, 14 per cent were imprisonments and 74 per cent were conditional convictions.[75] In 2009 the proportion of day fines then increased to 10 per cent (out of all sanctions, for all crimes). This fact could be partially related also to the adoption of the new

---

[69] *Supra* note 1, Bavcon *et al.*, 372.
[70] *Supra* note 42, Markelj, p. 7. See also Bošnjak, 'Rezultati analize kazenskih postopkov'.
[71] *Ibid.* See also Florjančič, 'Izbira, odmera in izrek kazenskih sankcij', 18–22.
[72] Resolucija o Nacionalnem programu preprečevanja in zatiranja kriminalitete za obdobje 2007–2011, Uradni list RS, št. 40/2007.
[73] Ministrstvo za notranje zadeve – Policija: Statistični podatki s področja kriminalitete za leto 2007.
[74] Marinko, 'Kakšne sankcije izrekajo sodišča v kazenskem postopku?', 28–30.
[75] Vrhovno državno tožilstvo RS: Skupno poročilo o delu državnih tožilstev, 2007.

Criminal Code of 2008 that in Article 47 re-introduced day fines as an exclusive monetary sanction,[76] and partially to the increased scholarly push towards increased employment of day fines.[77]

One has to note that the Slovenian Ministry of Justice each year (from 2009 onwards) publishes an extensive 'judicial statistics' report containing a vast amount of statistical variables (each year report is more than 500 pages long) on all possible sorts of judicial (per court) performance measures.[78] However, these reports do not contain any data on the employment of the day fines and thus any systematic analysis on the practical implementation of day fines in Slovenia after 2010 is unfeasible and may be done only on a very general level.

However, the official statistics on the criminal offences and different sorts of employed sanctions of the Statistical Office of the Republic of Slovenia (hereinafter SORS) for the 2014–17 period reveals an insightful trend. Namely, the rate of criminal offences is steadily decreasing, as well as the rate of imprisonment, whereas the rate of day fines has been decreasing from 2014 to 2016 and suddenly increased in 2017 to, for Slovenian circumstances, a staggering 459 cases. The trend continues, since in 2018 there were 503 cases where day fines have been imposed (Table 12.1). Moreover, also the total rate of adults against whom the criminal procedure before the criminal court has been finished by criminal offences steadily decreasing.[79]However, analysis also reveals that despite the indemnified increase in the employment of day fines in the year 2017, the percentage is still very low in comparison to the advanced western legal systems and represents merely 7.4 per cent and in 2018 represents 8.2 per cent of all imposed sanctions (Table 12.1).[80]

The data also show[81] that there were several day fines imposed for criminal offences against property; a considerable amount of day fines in 2015 for criminal offences against economy; two in 2014 and one in 2015 for criminal offences against legal transactions; two in 2015 for criminal offences against official obligation and public authority; there was a fair amount of day fines imposed for criminal offences against the administration of justice (twenty in 2015, fifteen

---

[76]　The Criminal Code (KZ-1E, Off. Gaz. No. 27/2017, from 2.6.2017) in Article 43 states that for criminal offences, the perpetrators may be sanctioned by the following sanctions: (a) jail; (b) day fine; (c) driving ban on motor vehicles; and (d) expulsion of a non-citizen from the country.

[77]　See *e.g.* Šelih, *Načelo sorazmernosti in kazenske sankcije*, pp. 1357–68.

[78]　These reports are available at: www.mp.gov.si/si/obrazci_evidence_mnenja_storitve/uporab ni_seznami_imeniki_in_evidence/sodna_statistika/.

[79]　SORS, May 2019, available at: https://pxweb.stat.si/pxweb/Dialog/SaveShow.asp.

[80]　*Ibid.*

[81]　The criminal offence classified according to the Penal Code KZ-1, which was used between 2008 and 2012.

TABLE 12.1 *Annual amount of criminal offences and day fines (convicted adults)*

Year	2014	2015	2016	2017	2018
Criminal offences	9,410	7.926	6,687	6,252	6,098
Imprisonment	8,925	7,468	6,276	5,689	5,490
percentage of imprisonment	94.8	94.2	93.8	90.9	90
Suspended imprisonment	6,987	5,620	4,880	4,419	4,139
Security measures	35	44	33	48	51
Day fines	374	348	332	459	503
percentage of day fines	3.7	4.4	5	7.4	8.2

Source: Statistical Office of the Republic of Slovenia, May 2019, available at: https://pxweb.stat.si/pxweb/Dialog/SaveShow.asp.

in 2016 and sixteen in 2017); for criminal offences against public order and peace; for criminal offences against life and body (three in 2014, thirty-two in 2015, twenty-three in 2016 and forty-four in 2017); for criminal offences against human rights and liberties (three in 2014, five in 2015, twenty-seven in 2016 and sixty-two in 2017); several each year for criminal offences against honour and good name and also an increasing amount of fines for criminal offences against environment and traffic safety.[82] One should also note that the majority of imprisonment sanctions are actually suspended ones (conditional).

To sum up, the percentage of cases in which fines are imposed (out of all imposed sentences) was in 2017 at 7.4 per cent and in 2018 raised further to 8.2 per cent.[83] The percentage indeed increased after the reform in 2008. However, this increase could not be attributed solely to the adoption of the new legislative provision and is still far behind the target ratio. From a Law and Economics perspective such a low percentage of day fines is simply unacceptable and inefficient. Moreover, the percentage of cases in which imprisonment sentences (including conditional imprisonment) are imposed (out of all sentences) was in 2017 still a staggering 90.9 per cent. The percentage is slowly decreasing from 2014 onwards.

Finally, one should note the particular 'Public attorney's' newly published data for 2019 which actually do show a further increase in day fines. Namely, according to this data set in 2019 there were 6,606 convictions, 487 acquittals and 599 dismissal judgments were issued against juvenile offenders.[84]

[82] SORS, Statistical Office of the Republic of Slovenia, 2019.
[83] *Ibid.*
[84] Vrhovno državno tožilstvo republike Slovenije, 'Statistični podatki za leto 2018 kažejo večjo učinkovitost državnih tožilstev', 21.1.2019. Available at: www.dt-rs.si/novica/statisticni-podatki-za-leto-2018-kazejo-vecjo-ucinkovitost-drzavnih-tozilstev.

Moreover, there were 1,517 penalties and 777 day fines imposed, which amounts to 11.8 per cent of day fines and confirms the increasing trend of imposed day fines (a 3.6 per cent increase in day fines in comparison to previous year 2018).[85] As a warning sanction, in 2019 Slovenian courts imposed 4,588 suspended sentences. In comparison with the previous years, also the percentage of cases in which a prison sentence was imposed is decreasing.[86]

Insightfully, the Supreme State Prosecutor's Office agrees that instead of a number of conditional prison sentences (in particular), day fines are often a much more effective remedy for minor offences.[87] Therefore, the prosecutors have been directing for a long time to request more financial penalties for minor sins, but most of the district prosecutor's offices have not yet taken those guidelines.[88] The Supreme State Prosecutor's Office also held that courts should impose day fines more often – and the main reason they do not is that day fines are actually not requested by prosecutors.[89]

Last but not the least, if an offender has really no means to pay the fine and if the execution (executive order) proves to be ineffective the court enforces the day fine by imposing a financial penalty in such a way that it determines one day of imprisonment for each two day fines.[90]

One may wonder whether such a low percentage of day fines is caused by the Slovenian structure of welfare benefits. Namely, one could argue that day fines could only be imposed on people who have at least some means. Therefore, too low welfare benefits might impede the possibility to employ day fines as a sanction. Such an argument might indeed be part of the explanation. Yet, Slovenia is a social welfare state, with extensive welfare benefits, consisting of cash payment and other in kind contributions (e.g. housing). For example, unemployment benefit amounts to: 80 per cent of the basis (which is the average monthly salary received by an insured person during the eight months prior to unemployment, including compensation of salary, health insurance, family protection insurance, old-age and invalidity insurance) for the first three months; 60 per cent for the following nine months; and 50 per cent of the basis after twelve months.[91] Benefits may not be lower than 350 euros gross and may not exceed 892.50 euros gross.[92] An insured person is entitled to benefit from

---

[85] *Ibid.*
[86] *Ibid.*
[87] Lovšin, 'Za več denarnih in manj pogojnih kazni', Dnevnik, 14.10.2013.
[88] *Ibid.*
[89] *Ibid.*
[90] *Ibid.*
[91] European Commission, 'Your Social Security Rights in Slovenia', Directorate-General for Employment, Social Affairs and Inclusion.
[92] *Ibid.*, p. 36 *et seq.*

the day following the termination of compulsory insurance, if the insured person has submitted the unemployment documentation and a request for benefit within thirty days of terminating the compulsory insurance.[93]

Persons are entitled to social assistance and income support if they are not able to assure their own physical safety as a result of circumstances which they are unable to change. Social assistance is intended to provide resources so that minimum living requirements are met. Income support is intended to cover long-term living expenses (accommodation expenses, etc.) and expenses for meeting minimum living requirements.[94]

In addition, the OECD member with the lowest income equality measured by the Gini coefficient is Denmark, which is actually followed by Slovenia, Slovakia and Norway, according to the latest data available to the OECD.[95] The Sustainable Governance Indicators (SGI) show that Slovenia ranks third (after Iceland and Slovakia), followed by Norway in 2017.[96]

In the Republic of Slovenia, social security is defined as an individual's right to be insured against the following contingencies: illness, unemployment, old age, injury at work, disability, maternity, maintenance of children and benefits to family members after the person who provided for the subsistence dies and rights regulated by the Social Assistance Act (Off. Gaz. No. 23/2007) as amended of 2018.[97] Pursuant to the provisions of the Constitution of the Republic of Slovenia,[98] the state must regulate compulsory health, pension, disability and other social insurance and ensure its proper functioning. At the same time, it must protect the family, motherhood, fatherhood, children and young people and create the necessary conditions for such protection.

Pursuant to the Social Assistance Benefits Act of 2010 and as amended of 2018 (Off. Gaz. No. 73/2018),[99] financial social assistance provides the users with means for meeting minimum needs in the amount guaranteeing their subsistence. Subsistence is considered to be provided if the entitled person

[93] *Ibid.*

[94] *Ibid.*

[95] Available at: data.oecd.org/inequality/income-inequality.htm.

[96] Available at: www.sgi-network.org/2018/Policy_Performance/Social_Policies/Social_Inclusio n/Gini_Coefficient.

[97] Zakon o socialnem varstvu, Uradni list RS, št. 3/07 – uradno prečiščeno besedilo, 23/07 – popr., 41/07 – popr., 61/10 – ZSVarPre, 62/10 – ZUPJS, 57/12, 39/16, 52/16 – ZPPreb-1, 15/17 – DZ, 29/17, 54/17, 21/18 – ZNOrg in 31/18 – ZOA-A).

[98] Ustava Republike Slovenije, Uradni list RS, št. 33/91-I, 42/97 – UZS68, 66/00 – UZ80, 24/ 03 – UZ3a, 47, 68, 69/04 – UZ14, 69/04 – UZ43, 69/04 – UZ50, 68/06 – UZ121,140,143, 47/ 13 – UZ148, 47/13 – UZ90,97,99 in 75/16 – UZ70a.

[99] 'Zakon o socialno varstvenih prejemkih', *Uradni list RS*, št. 61/10, 40/11, 14/13, 99/13, 90/15, 88/ 16, 31/18 in 73/18.

receives income, after deduction of taxes and compulsory social security contributions, amounting to the minimum income.

From 1 August 2017 the basic minimum income amounts to 297.53 euros. The persons who are entitled to receive social assistance do not have any income or receive income below the above stated amount. In case of no income, the entitled persons receive the full stated amount; otherwise, they are entitled to receive the difference between own income and the above stated amount.[100]

When assessing the eligibility, account is taken of the ceiling as well as of the fact whether an individual or family has assets enabling subsistence, whether all other rights were exercised (social assistance is the last of the rights within the system, eligible when all other subsistence options are exhausted) and whether the person concerned is active in seeking solutions to his/her problem. The latter is of particular importance to all who can work and must be registered with the Employment Service of Slovenia, participate in offered programmes of active employment policy and actively seek employment.[101]

The amount of financial social assistance to entitled persons who do not have their own income pursuant to the Social Security Act[102] is set in the amount of the minimum income. Twice a year, namely in January and July, the basic amount of the minimum income, set forth in the Act, is adjusted to the rise in consumer prices according to the data of the Statistical Office of the Republic of Slovenia.[103]

The amount of financial social assistance to other entitled persons is determined as the difference between the minimum income to which the eligible person is entitled and his/her income determined in the manner specified by the Social Security Act.[104] The amount of cash financial assistance to a family is determined as the difference between the sum of minimum incomes to which individual eligible persons or family members are entitled and the incomes of all the family members.[105]

12.5 PUBLIC PERCEPTION OF DAY FINES

According to official statistics there were 3.2 convicted persons per 1,000 inhabitants.[106] Lobnikar, Prislan and Modiec performed an extensive analysis

---

[100] Ministry of Labour, Family, Social Affairs and Equal Opportunities, 'Social Welfare Programs', 2019. Available at: www.mddsz.gov.si/en/areas_of_work/social_affairs/social_assistance/.

[101] *Ibid.*

[102] *Supra* note 93.

[103] *Supra* note 94.

[104] *Supra* note 93.

[105] *Ibid.*

[106] SORS 2019, available at: www.stat.si/StatWeb/Field/Index/10/60.

of public perception of enforcement policy and their results, carried out on a random sample of inhabitants in ten local environments in Slovenia, that shows that the population is relatively favourably assessing the efforts of the Slovene police.[107] In general, Slovenians are not afraid to become victims of crime and they are also satisfied with the community's connection in the environments where they live.[108] Moreover, the inhabitants in Slovenia on average feel highly secure and their study also emphasised the high community connection of the inhabitants in rural and urban environments. The inhabitants perceive the police as effective and even friendly.[109] Unfortunately, there was no scientific study performed assessing the public perception of fines. However, the public perception, boosted/generated/ reinforced/channelled by daily media (aggressive, tendentious reporting), news, opinion makers and public discourse perceives day fines as inefficient, unjust, ineffective and non-retributory. Consequently, the public perception generally favours imprisonment over day fines.[110] This perception is then followed by public prosecutors and judges.

Lazslo and Sotlar, for example, show that Slovenian perception of private security ranking received 94 points which makes it equal to Belgium that holds the first place among twenty seven EU countries.[111] Plesničar argues that the basis of the Slovenian sentencing system is the concept of individualisation of punishment, where proportionality is of the utmost importance and is set first by legislation determining sentencing ranges for specific offences and then by the judiciary aiming to narrow the ranges to an appropriate sentence in individual cases.[112]

However, it should be emphasised that legal scholarship has from the 1980s onwards advocated the employment of day fines and other alternative sanctions as the main alternative to imprisonment.[113] Petrovec emphasised two consequences of introducing alternative methods of punishment: the enforcement of a less violent form of punishment and thus creating a new perspective

---

[107] Lobnikar, Prislan and Modic, 'Merjenje uspešnosti implementacije policijskega dela v skupnosti v Sloveniji', 89–110.

[108] *Ibid.*, 106.

[109] *Ibid.*, 107.

[110] See e.g. Petrovčič, 'Pogojno veselje Po liniji najmanjšega odpora v pravosodju trije od štirih obsojencev s sodišča odidejo svobodni'; Felc, 'Denarna kazen dolgoročno ni učinkovita'; Repovž, 'Bodo visoke kazni za delo na črno učinkovite?'.

[111] Christián and Sotlar, 'Private Security Regulation in Hungary and Slovenia – A Comparative Study Based on Legislation and Societal Foundations', 143–62.

[112] Plesničar, 'The individualization of punishment: Sentencing in Slovenia', 462–78.

[113] See e.g. Hacin, 'Pregled slovenskega penološkega raziskovanja od sredine petdesetih let dvajsetega stoletja', 235–52.

for treating offenders and finding new ways of punishing, recognising that traditional prison is inadequate.[114] Petrovec also drew attention to the unsuccessful implementation of the pronouncement of alternative criminal sanctions in the Republic of Slovenia and the lack of a network of organisations that would be used to deal with community service.[115] At the same time, he proposed setting up an inventory of alternative sentences and monitoring their performance.

12.6 SPECIAL CHALLENGES

Despite tremendous scholarly efforts during several decades the percentage of day fines and their daily employment remains disproportionately low, even minor. Namely, continuous scholarly discussions that date back to the 1980s have materialised or, one may argue, succeeded in legislative change. The new Criminal Code of 2008 and as amended of 2017,[116] as already stated, provides in Article 47 day fines as an exclusive monetary sanction.[117] It reintroduced the imposition of a fine in the form of daily amounts, at least 30 and a maximum of 360 daily amounts and for committing acts of mercy, no more than 1,500 daily amounts. Thus, the legislation is in place, yet the de facto employment of day fines is far from the optimal level.

The main identified challenge that should be addressed by policy-makers is actually how to convince public prosecutors and consequently also the judges to request/insist/apply day fines more often. Namely, as stated, the prosecutors have been directing for a long time to request more financial penalties for minor sins, but in most of the district prosecutor's offices those guidelines have not yet been taken. The Supreme State Prosecutor's Office also held that courts should impose day fines more often – and the main reason for the low employment is that day fines are actually not requested by prosecutors. Hence, the Kranj district public prosecutors' employment of day fines should be used as a positive example. As stated, the current 'ignoring' practice of day fines by public prosecutors is merely an excuse for insisting on old practices (status quo bias). The example of the Carniolan district prosecutor's office, which is several times more effective in imposing day fines than the average

---

[114]　Petrovec, 'Alternativne zaporne kazni', 50–9.
[115]　Petrovec, 'Alternativno kaznovanje v slovenski zakonodaji in praksi', 345–50.
[116]　*Supra* note 43.
[117]　The Criminal Code (KZ-1E, Off. Gaz. No. 27/2017, from 2.6.2017) in Article 43 states that for criminal offences, the perpetrators may be sanctioned by the following sanctions: (a) jail; (b) day fine; (c) driving ban on motor vehicles; and (d) expulsion of a non-citizen from the country.

Slovenian prosecutor, could be taken as an implicit evidence of such a *status quo* bias. Namely, if prosecutors at the state level on average reach only 4 per cent of fines, Kranj has a much more successful 18 per cent share of fines.[118]

As an illustration one may quote the head of the Kranj County Prosecutor's Office, Irena Kuzma, who argues that she does not have a special recipe for improving the efficiency of Gorenjska prosecutors except for perseverance, as she says that for many years the prosecutors in Kranj have been trying to change the punitive policy and have purposefully proposed monetary fines on several occasions.[119] Only suggestion is not enough; the public prosecutor should actually insist on the employment of the day fine. 'I must point out that the changed penal policy of the courts can be achieved only by persistently proposing fines and lodging complaints, when the court does not pronounce the sentences that we have proposed'.[120] In addition, from the institutional point of view the introduction of the priority rule (as existing in Germany) should be considered while novelising, amending the existing Criminal Code.

12.7 CONCLUSIONS

This chapter has identified the most striking principles and insights that relate to the perplexing issue of day fines in Slovenia. The chapter argues that the legislative infrastructure (provisions of the Criminal Code) is in place for an optimal implementation of day fines. Yet, its de facto imposition is far behind the percentage in the developed western legal systems. The current, shockingly low percentage of day fines is actually unacceptable and represents sources of inefficiency, injustice and unfairness. Ironically, the public discourse and also public prosecutors (and judges) also perceive day fines as inefficient, unjust, ineffective and non-retributory. Identified, a contradictory perception of day fines between the legal scholarship and judiciary/public prosecutors is also the main driving force behind the staggeringly low percentage of imposed day fines. However, one may argue that the main reason for the low percentage of day fines is that day fines are actually not requested by prosecutors. The current 'ignore-day-fine' practice by public prosecutors is merely an excuse for insisting on old practices (status quo bias) and represents the main challenge for the Slovenian policy-maker on the path towards the optimal penal policy and de facto implementation of day fines.

---

[118]   *Supra* note 103.
[119]   *Ibid.*
[120]   *Ibid.*

REFERENCES

Bačić, F. 1980. 'Krivično pravo: opći dio', *Informator* 91–104.

Bavcon, L. 1958. *Kriminalna Politika in njene Tendence v Socialistični Družbi.* Univerza v Ljubljani, Pedagoška fakulteta.

Bavcon, L., *et al.* 1994. 'Kazenski Zakonik Republike Slovenije z Uvodnimi Pojasnili', *ČZ Uradni list, Ljubljana*, 42–3, 131–2.

Bavcon, L. *et al.* 2003. 'Kazensko Pravo Splošni Del', *Uradni list Republike Slovenije*, 78–81.

Bavcon, L. and Kobe, P. 1970. 'Kazenski zakonik s pojasnili in sodno prakso', *Uradni list SR Slovenije*, 37–44.

Bošnjak, M. 2004. 'Rezultati analize kazenskih postopkov', *Pravna praksa* 36: 15–17.

Christián, L. and Sotlar, A. 2018. 'Private Security Regulation in Hungary and Slovenia – A Comparative Study Based on Legislation and Societal Foundations', *Journal of Criminal Justice and Security* 2: 143–62.

Criminal Code, Article 87, KZ-1E, Off. Gaz. No. 255/08, 50/12, 6/16, 54/15, 38/16 and 7/2017, from 2.6.2017.

Delovni osnutek Kazenskega Zakonika Republike Slovenije in njegove usmeritve, 1993. Vlada Republike Slovenije.

European Commission, 2018. *Your Social Security Rights in Slovenia*, Directorate-General for Employment, Social Affairs and Inclusion.

Felc, M. 2011. 'Nedelo: Denarna kazen dolgoročno ni učinkovita', *Delo* 4(4).

Florjančič, D. 2006. 'Izbira, odmera in izrek kazenskih sankcij', *Pravna Praksa* 19–1: 18–22.

Frank, S. 1951. *Teorija Kaznenog Prava Po, Krivinom zakoniku od godine.* Sveuciliste Zagreb.

Hacin, R. 2015. 'Pregled slovenskega penološkega raziskovanja od sredine petdesetih let dvajsetega stoletja', *Revija za kriminalistiko in kriminologijo* 66: 235–52.

Jager, M. 2002. *Ekonomska analiza kazenskega prava in kriminalitetne politike*, p. 1635.

Jovanović, L. and Jović, M. 2004. *Krivično pravo: opšti deo. Viša škola unutrašnjih poslova.* Sveuciliste Zagreb Viša škola unutrašnjih poslova.

'Kazenski Zakonik SFRJ', *Uradni list SFRJ*, No. 44/1976.

'Kazenski zakonik', *Uradni list RS*, št. 50/12 – uradno prečiščeno besedilo, 6/16 – popr., 54/15, 38/16 in 27/17.

'Kazenski zakonik (uradno prečiščeno besedilo)' KZ-UPB1, *Uradni list RS*, No. 95/2004, z dne 27.8.2004.

'Kazenski zakonik Republike Slovenije' KZ, *Uradni list RS*, št. 63/94 z dne 13.10.1994.

Lobnikar, B., Prislan, K. and Modic, M. 2016. 'Merjenje uspešnosti implementacije policijskega dela v skupnosti v Sloveniji', *Revija za kriminalistiko in kriminologijo* 67: 89–110.

Lovšin, P. 2013. 'Za več denarnih in manj pogojnih kazni', *Dnevnik*.

Marinko, J. 2002, 'Kakšne sankcije izrekajo sodišča v kazenskem postopku?' (What Are The Penal Sections Pronounced In Criminal Cases?), *Pravna praksa* 33–34: 28–30.

Markelj, L. 2008. 'Ekonomska analiza kazenskih sankcij' in K. Zaic (ed.), *Ekonomska analiza prava v Sloveniji.* Uradni List.

Ministrstvo za notranje zadeve – Policija: Statistični podatki s področja kriminalitete za leto 2007.

Petrovčič, P. 2011. 'Pogojno veselje Po liniji najmanjšega odpora v pravosodju trije od štirih obsojencev s sodišča odidejo svobodni', *Mladina* (29 July).

Petrovec, D. 1999. 'Alternativno kaznovanje v slovenski zakonodaji in praksi', *Revija za kriminalistiko in kriminologijo/Ljubljana* 50: 345–50.

Petrovec, D. 2015. 'Alternativne zaporne kazni', IUS Software, GV Založba, 50–9.

Plesničar, M. M. 2013. 'The Individualization of Punishment: Sentencing in Slovenia', *European Journal of Criminology* 10: 462–78.

'Resolucija o Nacionalnem programu preprečevanja in zatiranja kriminalitete za obdobje 2007-2011', *Uradni list RS*, št. 40/2007.

Repovž, E. 2010. 'Bodo visoke kazni za delo na črno učinkovite?', *Delo* (16 November).

Šelih, A. 1993. 'Problemi kazenskih sankcij', *Podjetje in delo* 5–6: 474–79.

Šelih, A. 2009. 'Načelo sorazmernosti in kazenske sankcije', *Podjetje in delo* 6: 1357–68.

Statistical Office of the Republic of Slovenia, 2019.

Vlada Republike Slovenije, *Predlog Kazenskega Zakonika*, Ljubljana, 17.01.2008.

Vrhovno državno tožilstvo RS: Skupno poročilo o delu državnih tožilstev, 2007.

'Zakon o spremembah in dopolnitvah Kazenskega zakonika' KZ-B, *Uradni list RS*, št. 40/04 z dne 20.4.2004.

'Zakon o socialno varstvenih prejemkih', *Uradni list RS*, št. 61/10, 40/11, 14/13, 99/13, 90/15, 88/16, 31/18 in 73/18.

13

Day Fines in Spain

Jesús Barquín Sanz

13.1 INTRODUCTION: FINES IN SPANISH CRIMINAL LAW

Fines, applied in most cases through the day fine model, are currently the only financial penalty in Spanish criminal law. Other historical penalties of an economic nature no longer exist. Such is the case of the confiscation of goods once it was banned by the Spanish Constitution of 1812; and also of the 'caución' after it was repealed by the current CP (Spanish Penal Code) in 1995 (or 1996, if we place greater emphasis on its entry into force).[1] This was sort of a bond designed for communities in which a person of respect or patriarch would take responsibility for ensuring that one of its members would comply with the law; it had been very rarely applied and was clearly out of date in the second half of the twentieth century. The forfeiture of assets stopped being formally considered a penalty also in 1995. Thus, when the CP lists the different typologies to classify penalties, it does not include a generic section of 'financial penalties' but it directly places the *multa* (fine) as a separate category in itself, at the same level as the other two subclassifications: 'custodial penalties' (prison, house arrest. etc.) and 'penalties restricting other rights' (community service, restraining order, disqualifications, etc.).[2]

It could be argued that the penalty consisting of a ban on applying for subsidies or public aids and loss of the right to obtain tax or social security benefits or incentives, established by Articles 302, 305 and 308 CP has an essentially financial content.[3] However, it seems reasonable to disagree with

---

[1] The Ley Orgánica 10/1995, 23 November, of the Penal Code entered into force on 24 May 1996.

[2] Article 32 CP: 'The penalties that may be imposed pursuant to this Code ... are custodial, restricting other rights and fines'. ('Las penas que pueden imponerse con arreglo a este Código ... son privativas de libertad, privativas de otros derechos y multa.')

[3] Roca Agapito, *El sistema de sanciones en el Derecho penal español*, p. 262. This author also rejects that its nature is that of a criminal penalty.

this approach: regardless of its economic repercussion, this is one of the penalties restraining other rights within the varied set of disqualifications ('inhabilitaciones') and suspensions. Some financial loss is inherent to practically all penalties restraining or depriving of other rights; hence this cannot be the ground for discerning the nature of any of these penal sanctions in particular.

In Spanish criminal law, another model for applying a fine coexists along with the predominant model of day fines: the proportional fines, which are never linked to the person's income or wealth nor are expressed in terms of days or months, but calculated as a multiple of the damage caused by the criminal conduct, the earnings obtained or expected or the amount of the fraud, among other parameters. These should in principle be reserved for offences regarding which the legislator considers that the deterrent efficacy of the amounts inherent to day fines is not enough. This is easy to assume in offences where the expectation of financial benefit is considerable, for example production and trafficking of drugs (Article 368 CP) or currency counterfeiting (Article 386 CP). However, it does not seem so reasonable when the benchmark is the damage caused, as for instance in computer crimes (Articles 264 and 264 bis CP), because, among other reasons, in the Spanish legal order there is a model of *ex delicto* civil liability that is closely linked to the criminal justice system. For urban planning offences (Articles 319 and 320 CP) the proportional fine was introduced only as recently as 2010; before this, day fines, particularly in the way these are implemented in Spain – without enquiry into the real financial situation of the accused and routinely applying the daily minimum sums – proved inefficient in preventing urban planning offences, where the potential benefits of infractions are substantial.[4]

In 2010, criminal liability of legal entities was introduced in the Spanish criminal law as a subsystem. Within this system the proportional fine plays an important role.[5] This made this type of fines gain weight in the criminal justice system as a whole. As a preliminary note of a general nature, it is important to underline that this chapter will, however, be focused on the *traditional* criminal law system, where the liable persons are the individuals. Everything that will be said will therefore relate by default to the penal fines assigned to natural persons, particularly of course to day fines. There certainly are particular provisions (an entire punitive subsystem, in fact) for fines addressed to legal persons. These will also be dealt with in the present work, albeit secondarily and making clear in each case the specificity of this regulation.

---

[4] Garcés Peregrina, 'El enjuiciamiento de los delitos urbanísticos en la provincia de Málaga', 147.
[5] Ley Orgánica 5/2010, of 22 June, amending the 1995 CP; entered into force on 23 December 2010.

13.2 HISTORICAL DEVELOPMENT OF DAY FINES IN SPAIN

In the Spanish historical penal legislation there are precedents of individualisation of the fine according to the economic situation of the convict both in the *Partidas* (thirteenth century) and in other medieval laws (*Fueros*).[6] The codification meant the end of the validity of these norms, so that it can be said that, in the last two centuries, the history of day fines in Spain is short. Well-known and praised by Spanish academic criminal lawyers throughout the twentieth century, this system of calculating fine penalties was not incorporated in positive legislation until the entry into force of the current CP in 1996. Previously, the model in force was the so-called amount system, in which the law does not set the fine in temporary terms prima facie as in the day rate system, but directly in terms of a financial amount. So, it was established in the Spanish penal codes previous to 1995–6 by means of a minimum and a maximum. There has always been a proportional system as well. This was present in the previous Penal Code of 1973 and it has been part of the list of sentencing options in Spanish criminal law ever since the beginning of codification in 1822,[7] through an arithmetic operation based on a specific pecuniary parameter associated with the offence: ¼ of x, ½ of x, x^*2, x^*10, etc.

After the restoration of the rule of law and constitutional democracy in Spain in 1978, there were several attempts to produce a new penal code, which would still need a further two decades while the old one kept being adapted and updated. All those initiatives for a new CP throughout the 1980s and 1990s included day fines, also known as the Nordic or Scandinavian model. In fact, the earlier drafts (1980 and 1983) went one step further in contemplating the obligation of delayed payment following precisely the temporal instalments decided by the court: daily, weekly or monthly sums. This was a model suggested by the German Alternative Draft ('Alternativ-Entwurf') of 1966,[8] a scholarly draft penal code of great influence on recent generations of academic criminal lawyers in Spain. In any case the day fine model, in either version, never faced any opposition or major criticism and thus it was not at all controversial when it was finally introduced in the 1995 CP.

---

6 Roldán Barbero, *El dinero, objeto fundamental de la sanción penal: un estudio histórico de la moderna pena de multa*, p. 216; Mapelli Caffarena, *Las consecuencias jurídicas del delito*, p. 216.

7 Article 89 CP 1822 provides it for bribes in general, while Article 767 focuses specifically on cheating at gambling. Regarding the CP 1850, see for instance Article 314 CP on bribery.

8 Mir Puig, *Derecho penal. Parte general*, p. 752; Cano Paños, '50 años del Proyecto Alternativo del Código Penal Alemán (1966–2016)', 102; Baumann, 'Was erwarten wir von der Strafrechtsreform?', p. 30.

The dominant opinion on day fines since the decades before their introduction in the Spanish penal system until today seems to be that we live in a society where a financial penalty on those responsible for criminal deeds is sufficiently punitive and therefore potentially dissuasive.[9] For this to be effective it is of paramount importance to adapt the sum of the fine to the financial means of the offender, which would also allow a reduction in the long-standing abuse of prison penalties. That is why day fines were added to the Spanish CP in 1995. The problem is that the real-life application of these fines has never met the expectations. As we shall see below, the implementation of these fines follows, with few exceptions, a model closer to the traditional system of total amount fines.

Recent years have witnessed a diminishing trust in the legal system's capacity to act individually on each offender. This is connected with the probably definitive abandonment in practical terms of the ideal of material adaptation of fine sums depending on the financial circumstances of the offenders (except perhaps in the most extreme cases of the destitute and conspicuous millionaires). At the same time, the proportional fine has expanded at the expense of the day fine as a punitive alternative. The most significant impulse to the proportional fine came after 2010, with the approval of regulations concerning the legal responsibility of the legal entity, where the proportional fine is privileged by legislators as the punitive resource of choice. The generalisation of this type of fine is unambiguously indicative of the fact that today's political-criminal orientation is the opposite of that which in its day led to the adoption of a model of day fines in the Spanish legal system.

13.3 LEGAL FRAMEWORK

13.3.1 *The Number of Days*

A question as simple as which are the minimum and maximum number of fine days that can be imposed in Spanish criminal law does not admit a similarly simple answer.

---

[9] Díez Ripollés, 'La evolución del sistema de penas en España: 1975–2003', 08–07, 24. Similar terms are used by the majority of academic criminal lawyers devoted to these matters. Compare representative positions before and after the reform of the CP: Morillas Cueva, *Teoría de las consecuencias jurídicas del delito*, p. 124; Gracia Martín, Boldova Pasamar and Alastuey Dobón, *Lecciones de consecuencias jurídicas del delito*, p. 92. The latter, doubtless bearing in mind the practicalities of the application of day fines in Spain, underlines that the advantages of day fines are of a theoretical nature and that their real-life implementation meets numerous difficulties.

13.3.1.1 Minimum

In particular, some problems arise regarding the minimum number of days. There are weighty arguments to establish it in either thirty days or one day; or even in ten days, although the latter case is based on a weak and purely formalistic foundation.

(a) Ten days is assumed to be the minimum term for a day fines penalty, since this is what the CP formally proclaims in its Article 50.3: 'its minimum duration will be ten days'. But this sounds like empty rhetoric since, as shown below, the special part of the CP consistently fixes a month as the minimum period for day fines. Additionally, Article 71 CP states that this ten days limit is irrelevant in case of reduction of the penalty in application of the sentencing rules (as for accomplices, attempts, mitigating circumstances, etc.), while the eleventh transitory provision sets one day as the minimum for the conversion of the fine penalties provided for offences in the special criminal or procedural laws prior to the 1995 Penal Code. Thus, it seems indisputable that the aforementioned legal reference to a minimum of ten days for the fine penalty lacks actual content. It is a *flatus vocis* that does not have any legal implication.

(b) The thirty days option does have sufficiently solid basis as this is the minimum duration consistently contemplated in the CP for fines for any offence. In none of the approximately 300 cases where the CP provides a day fine is the minimum period under thirty days. In fact, this minimum of one month (to be computed as thirty days following Article 50.4 CP) appears in at least twenty-seven cases,[10] all of them associated to minor offences by individuals. Not one single case deserves a shorter period. Above this minimum, the following in the frequency scale (some twenty times) is three months and a minimum of two months has practically no presence in the code (exclusively in Article 244.1 CP and only as an alternative penalty).

(c) One day. If, instead of focusing on the punishment assigned by CP to the different offences in their standard formulation (provided for the author of the crime committed, without mitigating or aggravating circumstances, in which case the minimum would be thirty days as has just been explained), we consider the minimum number of day fines that

[10] Articles 147.2 and 3, 171.7.1 and 2, 172.3.1 and 2, 173.4, 203.2, 234.2, 236.2, 246.2, 247.2, 249.2, 252.2, 253.2, 254.2, 255.2, 256.2, 263.1.2, 270.4.2, 274.3.2, 337.4, 337 bis, 386.3, 389.2, 402 bis and 556.2 CP.

can be the object of a sentence for someone convicted of an offence, then the minimum extreme can indeed be as low as one day.

On the one hand, starting with the typical minimum of thirty days, reaching the absolute minimum of one day requires merely a reduction of four degrees – that is, successively halving the minimum penalty four times, which is unlikely in real life but theoretically possible: for example, in an attempted minor theft (Article 234.2 CP: fined from one to three months) where there may concur mitigating circumstances (such as an partial defence) the penalty could be reduced hypothetically up to four degrees and therefore the minimum limits would be fifteen days (one-degree reduction), seven days (two-degree reduction), three days (three-degree reduction) all the way to one day (four-degree reduction).[11]

On the other hand, the already mentioned eleventh transitory provision establishes a minimum of one day for the conversion of fines assigned by special laws to minor offences. For example, the exotic and never used minor offence in Article 67 of the Air Navigation Penal and Procedure Act of 1964 (Ley 209/1964, Penal y Procesal de Navegación Aérea).

Neither case is remotely likely, but they make the question 'can a sentence be reduced to a one-day fine?' demand a positive answer. And, since the day is an indivisible unit to the effects of punishment calculation (Article 70.2 CP), it seems reasonable to consider the one day as the minimum sensible duration of a day fine penalty, even though we should not forget that the minimum punishment effectively assigned by the CP is thirty days for a completed offence.

As for the punitive subsystem of legal persons, the minimum duration of day fines is six months (Articles 52.4.c, 197 quinquies, 258 ter, etc. CP).

13.3.1.2 Maximum

Greater consistency can be observed regarding the maximum duration of penalties concerning day fines in the Spanish CP. The terms established in Article 50.3 for both individuals and legal entities correspond with those established in the provisions of the special part: two years (almost invariably expressed in months: twenty-four months)[12] and five years, respectively. Both are, incidentally, limits

---

[11] Bear in mind that in its current formulation, Article 66.2 CP establishes that the only calculation guidelines for penalties that do not apply to minor offences are specifically those of Article 66 CP itself; nothing is said about Articles 62, 63 or 68 CP, among others.

[12] Exceptions: Article 189 CP, as well as Article 50 and all fines of this duration for legal persons. In any case, it is established that for fine penalties, months last 30 days and years 365 days, so this exception is merely of a formal sort and has no practical consequences. Regarding prison sentences, the criteria are less clear and often months are counted as 30 days long and years as 365 days and thus 2 convictions of 6 months would be 5 days shorter than one of one year. This

that the CP uses frequently: the legislation often establishes for particular offences committed by both individuals and legal persons maximum limits of day fines that coincide with the absolute maximum penalties.

Two subtleties apply, though:

(a) A maximum of thirty months can be reached by raising the penalty in those cases where the CP so states. This is a provision applicable to cases of virtually no real incidence in the judicial practice, such as, for instance, Article 323.2 CP (particularly serious damages to cultural objects of artistic, historic or archaeological value).

(b) In case of suspension of a prison penalty, the combination of Articles 84.1.2ª and 80.2.2ª CP allows the judge to impose as a condition for the suspension that the convicted should pay a day fine. The fine may reach a maximum of two years and eight months, that is, the equivalent to one year and four months of prison, since the conversion rate is two daily fees for each day of imprisonment.[13] This derives from the reform of the CP in 2015 and is not currently being applied.[14]

13.3.2 *The Daily Unit*

Currently and since 2004,[15] the amount is fixed at a minimum of 2 euros and a maximum of 400 euros. Previously, between the entry into force of the CP in 1996 and 2004, the minimum limit was 200 pesetas and the maximum 50,000 pesetas, equivalent to 1.20 euros and 300.50 euros respectively. Formally, the types of wealth that should be assessed by the judicial bodies in order to determine the daily unit covers the whole financial situation of the convicted, including not only his/her regular personal income but also property and other assets, debts, other sources of income, family obligations and other personal circumstances.

For corporations, the minimum is 30 euros and the maximum 5,000 euros. These limits have not changed since the introduction of the specific regulation in matters of criminal responsibility of legal entities in 2010.[16]

---

is not the case of fine penalties, where 24 months and 2 years amount to the same number of days, 720.

[13] Gracia Martín, Boldova Pasamar and Alastuey Dobón, *Lecciones de consecuencias jurídicas del delito*, p. 94.

[14] On the risk of the replacement of short custodial sentences with fines as a source of social redistribution of prison sentences, see Killias, Aebi and Kuhn, *Précis de criminologie*, p. 509.

[15] Ley Orgánica 15/2003, 25 November, amending the 1995 CP; entered into force on 1 October 2004.

[16] Ley Orgánica 5/2010, 22 June, amending Ley Orgánica 10/1995, 23 November, of Código Penal, entered into force on 23 December 2010.

13.3.3 *The Authority That Can Impose Day Fines*

In the Spanish legal system, the competence to impose any penalty, fines included, belongs exclusively to the judges in exercise of their jurisdictional[17] powers according to the law. Neither the police nor the prosecution can, under any circumstances, impose a fine. This applies to criminal law. Things are different in sanctioning administrative law, where fines can be imposed by the different administrative authorities (for example, traffic or taxes) but always subject to judicial supervision in the form of an eventual appeal. And these are never day fines, which in Spain exist only in criminal law.

13.3.4 *Access to Financial Information*

Judicial bodies gain access to financial information regarding the offender via an inter-agency communication network called Judicial Neutral Point (*Punto Neutro Judicial*). Authorised agents, usually belonging to the judicial body, which is led by the clerk of the court (whose official name in Spain was actually clerk of the court or 'secretario judicial' until 2015, but now lawyer of the judicial system or 'letrado de la Administración de Justicia'), can access an ample variety of information available from virtually all bodies of the public administration, among them the Directorate of Police, the Directorate of Traffic, the State Agency of the Tax Administration (work-related tax collection, bank accounts, requests for return, tax on economic activities, pension plans), the National Institute of Statistics, the Treasurer's Office of Social Security, the Secretariat for Penitentiary Institutions, the Offenders Registry, the Land Registry, the Central Mercantile Registry and the bank where the defendants deposit their bails.

It is, however, important to clarify that in practice this type of enquiry is only performed systematically in the execution of sentences, be it concerning the payment of fines or civil liability. Sometimes the Judicial Neutral Point is used in the context of the investigating process by way of a separate civil liability proceedings ('pieza de responsabilidad civil') according to Articles 589 and 590 LECr (which should actually be called pecuniary responsibilities proceedings ('pieza de responsabilidades pecuniarias') since it should also involve the future payment of a possible fine or provisions regarding the forfeiture of certain goods and assets). But in practice this is only done in certain cases in

[17] Also of a jurisdictional status are fines imposed by judicial bodies in the procedural context (for example, Article 247 LEC on procedural bad faith, Articles 175 and 661 LECr on default of appearance by witnesses or experts): STS 4 November 2014 (ECLI:ES:TS:2014:4504).

order to secure the eventual civil liability that the offender may have incurred. However, if only the evaluation of the financial situation of the defendant in view of the imposition of a fine is at stake, in practice those types of proceedings will not be instituted.

13.3.5 *Authorities in Charge of Collecting the Information and Enforcing Court Decisions*

Again, it is judges and courts who have competence here to access the information available by the Judicial Neutral Point and especially in the enforcement of the court decisions. This information can also be accessed by the public prosecutor and in fact the public prosecutor (and, in case there is one, the private prosecutor) should primarily impulse the investigation into the defendant's financial situation. But in practice the prosecution virtually never does that type of inquiry in order to fix the daily unit to be requested for a day fine.

13.3.6 *What Happens in Case of Fine Default?*

There is a system of subsidiary liability fixed in Article 53 CP: one day of either prison or house arrest ('localización permanente', only for minor offences) or community service for every two daily fees defaulted. Even if there is an established system for replacing the payment of the fine with other penalties, paying is not optional for the convicted since the judicial body must try to execute the fine by seizing their goods, if there be any, before attempting an alternative penalty.

13.4 PRACTICAL IMPLEMENTATION

As suggested by certain previous statements, the fundamental fact about the practical implementation of day fines in Spain that must be taken into account above any theoretical consideration is that seldom anybody does conduct a serious early enquiry into the defendant's financial situation. And this despite the widespread, hitherto unchallenged belief that such is precisely the essence of day fines. Simply put, the most necessary step is dispensed with. Instead, judicial bodies all over Spain resort to standardised sums that have changed little since the minimum and maximum limits of 2 euros and 400 euros (still applied today) were introduced in 2004 and even since the courts began to apply the new system introduced by the 1995 CP, when the fee was still expressed in pesetas. In the early stages of the day fine implementation, regional variation of criteria could be detected across Spain, but today application criteria seem consolidated and standardised. This is our conclusion after a contrastive survey of sentences from different Provincial Courts ('Audiencias Provinciales') and personal interviews with judges and magistrates from Granada, Málaga, Huelva, Pontevedra, Barcelona, Gerona, Segovia, Madrid and Bilbao, conducted specifically for this publication. As a rule, the standard payment by default is established at 6 euros per day (exactly 1,000 pesetas, which was the Spanish currency before the euro), which can then be modified downwards or upwards by the judicial body in those cases where the procedure contemplates an evaluation of the financial circumstances of the defendant. Typical examples of the above are cases of parents who owe child support, on the one hand, and corporate fraud on the other. It could be said that, in general, judges reach final decisions on the sums to be imposed following their impressions after the indictment and the oral hearing. In general, those sums bear as reference the daily 6 euros that is commonly used by default. Six euros per day is also the most common amount found in a study by Garcés on urban planning offences in the province of Málaga:[18] 12 months at 6 euros, totalling 2,160 euros; the second most frequent fine being 10 euros per day (12 months at 10 euros, totalling 3,600 euros). This actually coincides with what the Supreme Court suggested as reasonable in the absence of specific investigation already twenty years ago, at the beginning of the application of the day fines in Spain, when the CP was still establishing 200 pesetas and 50,000 pesetas as minimum and maximum limits respectively: STS 20 November 2000 (ECLI:ES:TS:2000:8430), STS 11 July 2001 (ECLI: ES:TS:2001:6031). The reasoning of this latter judgment basically coincides with the one that can currently be read in many court judgments: for higher daily units a more thorough investigation of the financial situation of the defendant is mandatory, but a fee barely above the minimum like 1,000 pesetas or 6 euros can be imposed without any further verification than just checking that the person is not indigent, for whom the absolute minimum is reserved.[19]

---

[18] Garcés Peregrina, 'El enjuiciamiento de delitos urbanísticos', 134.

[19] STS 11 July 2001 (ECLI:ES:TS:2001:6031), Fifth Legal Ground: 'Para cuotas elevadas es absolutamente necesario que se contrasten datos más completos sobre la situación económica del acusado. Pero para la imposición de cifras levemente superiores al mínimo, como la cuota de 1,000 ptas diarias impuesta en el caso actual, es suficiente con que, por la profesión o actividad a que se dedica el acusado o por sus circunstancias personales, se constate que no se encuentra en la situación de indigencia que es la que debe determinar la imposición del nivel mínimo absoluto de 200 ptas'.

The reasoning is similar in recent decisions, such as for instance STS 9 September 2016 (ECLI:ES:TS:2016:3974), 32nd Legal Ground.

From an operational point of view, it is also important to highlight the importance of the accusatory principle for this matter, as no judicial body can impose a daily fine higher than that requested by the prosecution (most often the public prosecutor but occasionally a private prosecutor).[20] The main consequence of this from a technical legal perspective is the revocation by a higher court of any sentences where the judicial body has imposed a higher sum than that requested by the prosecution. A procedural consequence is that a judge no longer feels responsible for investigating the financial situation of the defendant. After all, it is the prosecution who places a request for a fine in the first place and also the one who must argue and present evidence in the trial why a particular amount of the fine is requested. This in turn enables the defendant to argue their defence.[21]

From this angle, the judicial body is expected to decide on the basis of the information presented by both parties and in case the prosecution does not offer information concerning the financial situation of the defendant it would be unfair to reproach the judge when in fact it may not even be legal for them to do it. On the other hand, this is the kind of activity that falls within the duties of an investigating judge ('juez de instrucción') via the abovementioned civil liability proceedings. The simplest way to actually examine the financial situation of the defendant would be to institute such proceedings by default in all cases involving a probable day fine penalty, for which no legal modification would be needed, just a change of mindsets and habits that often prove to be more complicated to accomplish than a penal reform. Another theoretically viable option would be by way of a separate examination by the enforcing judge once the sentence is definitive, but this would certainly require a legal reform. There is no prospect of such change in the application of day fines in Spain in the near future. This is related to two main reasons: one, as we have seen, is the weight of habit in a field such as the administration of justice that is eminently conservative, and two, the work saturation of the judicial bodies in Spain that makes expectations about their performance to be mainly concerned with productivity in terms of numbers of sentences and cases closed. The immediate future will be focused exclusively on measures aimed at speeding up processes and lightening the load of outstanding issues, such as the plea bargain. In this context, the opening of a specific separate proceedings ('pieza separada') for the calculation of the minimum daily rate of day fines

---

[20] This was decided by the Penal Section of the Supreme Court on a Non-Jurisdictional Agreement of 20 December 2006, as a general rule for all types of sentences. A recent application can be checked at SAP Ourense 22 April 2019 (ECLI:ES:APOU:2019:176), 6th Legal Ground.

[21] Some nuances on this matter can be read in the STS 23 January 2019 (ECLI:ES:TS:2019:91), 14th Legal Ground.

would not be welcomed by anybody; even less so at a time when, as we shall study statistically in the coming sections, the application of day fine penalties has increased significantly.

In the daily activity of a single-judge criminal court a large number of issues is often resolved by means of plea bargains, in which case it is not rare for the prosecution and defence to agree on even lower daily rates. In those cases the prosecution (generally the public prosecution) frequently agrees on a daily rate of four euros, unless the financial situation of the defendant is ostensibly buoyant and may sometimes even go as far down as three euros without a specific enquiry. Conversely, the absolute minimum of two euros is usually reserved for people in the worst cases of destitution: the homeless and other individuals surviving thanks to the aid provided by social services and charity organisations, such as, for example, immigrants popularly known as 'manteros' (street hawkers with a sheet set-up) who live on the income generated through the sales of fake brands and illegal copies of CDs and DVDs.

It must be remarked that this minimum of two euros as daily fee is absolute and cannot be exempted in any event, not even for people without any income or personal assets at all. The structure of welfare benefits in Spain includes free healthcare and access to social institutions for eating, as well as occasional provision of a place to sleep for the homeless. There is also the possibility of accessing a small regular amount of money as subsidy, but this is not always easy to obtain, particularly for those who live in the margins of society. In such cases, a sensible judge could fix the daily fee at the minimum of two euros. In addition, the judge could impose community service for the (very likely) case of non-payment. But in practice, a homeless person sentenced, especially if recurrently, to a day fine would quite probably end up in prison as an ultimate and subsidiary consequence of the conviction.

From a technical-legal viewpoint, the almost systematic absence of research into the material resources of a convict demands, in all reason, that the daily rate should not be established far above the minimum of two euros. It is a constitutional imperative as well as a demand inherent to the due process that every court decision must be sufficiently reasoned and it is here that courts find it convenient to be able to resort to default parameters that demand little argumentation. Usually this parameter is 6 euros, a sum that is very close to the absolute minimum of two euros – the latter being reserved for the destitute. The segment between three and five euros per day is allotted to people to whom free legal aid has been granted, convicts without financial means and the unemployed. The amount of six euros, perhaps all the way up to ten euros, is assigned to people of a standard financial situation, with regular income and some property such as a modest house (maybe two) and a car.

Any sum above those would usually demand serious justification by means of specific proceedings of pecuniary responsibilities or by way of information provided by the prosecution – which, as stated before, is very rarely done.

All this contains ample generalisations because the absence of solid legal foundations allows room also for isolated decisions that may be perfectly unreasonable or at least far removed from the criteria of the majority of judges and courts. These are, therefore, approximate data and it should not be difficult to find examples that do not fit. Particularly, in the larger and more expensive cities such as Madrid and Barcelona, for a few years during the early stages of the implementation of day fines, some judicial bodies displayed a tendency toward higher daily rates than in other areas of lower cost of living. But even that was done in the absence (except for truly exceptional cases) of a serious enquiry concerning the financial situation of the convict. In recent years, the jurisprudence of the Spanish Supreme Court ('Tribunal Supremo') has exerted a homogenising influence, even though its resolutions on the matter are not exempt of exceptions and discrepancies, the analysis of which exceeds the scope of this paper.

For a short sampler of recent sentences sourced from different geographic areas across Spain see, for example:

- SAP León of 12 March 2019 (ECLI:ES:APLE:2019:277), where the daily rate is raised in appeal from two to six euros with no argumentation whatsoever;
- SAP Soria of 11 March 2019 (ECLI:ES:APSO:2019:61), which simply argues that the minimum of two euros is reserved for the destitute and that six euros is sufficiently close to the minimum and, therefore, (the implication seems to be) the resolution does not require any further justification or the opening of formal enquiries as to the financial situation of the convict;
- SAP Barcelona of 8 February 2019 (ECLI:ES:APB:2019:3017), where the daily rate is reduced in appeal from six to four euros on the grounds that the judge had justified the original rate on a fact that is not proved, namely that the convict owned a bar;
- SAP Madrid of 16 January 2019 (ECLI:ES:APM:2019:1132), which reduces the daily rate from ten to six euros out of respect for the accusatory principle and on the grounds that six euros is a suitable rate in the light of 'the convict's financial means, considering the trade she was in and the fact that six is toward the minimum limit of the range allowed by the law'.

Exceptionally, there are some sentences where the maximum rate is imposed, or at least a close one, even in the absence of a proper financial enquiry. These are cases where the convict's material resources are notoriously high. A good example would be the court conviction of January 2019 against a famous Real Madrid soccer player for several tax offences (SAP Madrid of 22 January 2019, ECLI:ES:APM:2019:1473). Even though the fine established by the CP is of the proportional kind, in this case a calculation was made for the daily rate as a substitution for the prison sentence. The rate for the fine was determined at 250 euros per day, a much higher daily rate than is habitual, but still far from the absolute maximum of 400 euros per day. It is significant that this was the result of a plea bargain. It could be argued that, had the sum been calculated by the judicial body in its executive powers, the rate would have been higher, likely very close to the absolute maximum. On the other hand, the weight of habit is determinant here and in practice the routine rates of six, ten, maybe twenty euros are still applied even for notoriously wealthy persons.

Recent, well-known decisions of the Spanish Supreme Court convicting politicians can provide arguments in favour of each of the two hypotheses just mentioned. On the one hand, two decisions on offences of gross disobedience committed by an authority or public officer for which several members of the regional Government of Catalonia were convicted: STS 22 March 2017 (ECLI:ES:TS:2019:91) and STS 23 January 2019 (ECLI:ES:TS:2019:91). In them, the daily fee was settled to 200 euros and 100 euros, respectively, the latter not directly by the Supreme Court but as a ratification of the daily fine fixed by the judging court in Barcelona. In both cases, the concise grounding was the economic capacity of the convicts, evidenced by their academic formation and their positions as President and Counsellors of the Regional Government in Catalonia, as well as in other political offices.

Illustrative of the usual mechanisms in the matter on the part of the Spanish courts, are the two judicial decisions that solved the case of the Black Credit Cards illegitimately used by a number of counsellors of the Spanish savings bank Caja Madrid, among them the former Spanish Minister of Economy and the Treasury.[22] Several significant issues can be identified in them: the prosecutors mechanically requested a fee of either 300 euros (public prosecution) or 15 euros (both private prosecutions) for each and every one of the defendants, without any reasoning to support one or other request and, above all, without discriminating according to the personal situation of each particular defendant. The decisions fixed a twenty euros daily fine to each of the convicts, again without stopping to argue their decision, not even in the most succinct way, which the Supreme Court justified with the already known argument that the daily

---

[22] SAN 23 February 2017 (ECLI:ES:AN:2017:271) and STS 3 October 2018 (ECLI:ES:TS:2018:3253).

fee was low, much closer to the minimum than to the maximum, which made it unnecessary to ground it thoroughly.[23] The Supreme Court also argued that, although the fee was higher than usual, the convicted happened to be bank counsellors, all of whom are supposed to have a comfortable economic situation. However, it was public knowledge that, even if all of them were persons belonging to the political power circles of Madrid, some of them were trade unionists or members of political parties without particular economic support behind, while others possessed enormous personal assets. The really relevant fact here is not the daily fee, which anyway seems low for counsellors of one of the biggest banks of the country, nor the lack of investigation or reasoning on the daily unit, which is customary, but the homogeneity of the amounts for each one of the more than fifty persons sentenced to a day fine. This is of course connected to the absence of any inquiry. It seems obvious that the financial situation of all those defendants could not be exactly the same.

In short, this manner of doing things has been adopted by practically all judges and courts whereby an eventual fine is most likely to be determined by a daily rate as close as possible to the minimum rate. This is why we can affirm that the day fine penalty in the Spanish legal system does not represent a way of taking wealth seriously, but rather, on the contrary, of taking income lightly. From the viewpoint of their practical implementation, day fines are not very different from the old system of global fines that was operative in Spain for almost two centuries and the reason may rest partly in a certain inertia on the part of the legal system. This is also probably the reason why successive reforms of the CP are giving increasing importance to proportional fines, as previously explained.

13.4.1 *For Which Categories of Offences Day Fines Can Be Used De Jure and in Which Cases It Is Used De Facto*

De jure, day-fines is a ubiquitous penalty in the CP. It is established for offences belonging to almost all the possible categories, even for certain offences against life (involuntary manslaughter) and certain offences of

---

[23] STS 3 October 2018 (ECLI:ES:TS:2018:3253), 52nd legal ground: 'Es cierto que no se explican las razones de fijar la cuota de multa en 20 euros diarios. Pero, como ya hemos señalado en ocasiones, la ley fija un mínimo de 2 y un máximo de 400 euros, por lo que la cuantía fijada se encuentra mucho más próxima a la cuantía mínima, lo que debilita la necesidad de fundamentación. De otro lado, de la propia sentencia se desprende que la cuantía no es desproporcionada con la posición económica de quien ha sido miembro del consejo de administración de una Caja de Ahorros'.

abortion; the only exception as a group are the offences against the international community (genocide and others), where prison is the only possible penalty, occasionally together with disqualifications for public office. Actually, in the statistics for fines imposed in 2017, fines are represented almost everywhere and where they are not,[24] this is due to the scarcity (sometimes absence) of sentences on the matter. Thus, there was not a single sentence for offences related to genetic manipulation and there was only one for offences against the national defence and another one for offences regarding the Air Navigation Penal and Procedure Act, neither of them involving a fine.[25]

This means, on the other hand, that they are de facto imposed for almost every possible type of offence, of course more often on those which are more frequently committed and prosecuted.

13.4.2 *Statistical Facts*

The relevance of fine penalties in the Spanish legal system has indeed fluctuated over time. It is worth noticing, though, that the introduction of day fines in 1995–6 did not boost the presence of fines in the legal system, rather the contrary: from 1997 and especially 1998, which is when the effects of the new CP became observable, a precipitous decline of the percentage of cases in which fines are imposed out of all imposed sentences can be noticed. This has been studied by Díez Ripollés[26] and is represented in Table 13.1 and Figure 13.1, showing how the percentage that used to be more than 50 per cent by 1975 (when dictator Franco died), started to drop slowly along the following years, so that it was 46 per cent in 1985 and 35 per cent in 1990; then it increased up to 43 per cent in 1995 and plummeted from 37 per cent in 1997 to 19 per cent in 1998, 14.5 per cent in 1999 and 12 per cent in 2001; in 2002 it recovered up to 14 per cent and then grew to 21 per cent in 2003.

Along the period between 2004 and 2007 some data can be obtained via the statistics published by the INE (National Statistics Office; www.ine.es); however, the methodology for this data is not consistent with the one that produced the statistics for 2008 onwards.[27] Bearing in mind that this data should be read as approximative at best, the percentage of fines out of all imposed sentences

---

[24] Statistics on sentences according to type of sentence and offence provided by the INE (Spanish Statistical Office): www.ine.es/jaxiT3/Tabla.htm?t=25714&L=1.

[25] Statistics on offences according to type provided by the INE.: www.ine.es/jaxiT3/Datos.htm?t=25997&L=1.

[26] Díez Ripollés, 'La evolución sistema penas', 15–16.

[27] See Barquín Sanz and Luna del Castillo, 'En los dominios de la prisión: distribución numérica de las penas en el código y en la justicia penal', 10.

TABLE 13.1 *Portion of fine sentences of total sentences (1975–2003)*

	1975	1978	1980	1983	1985	1988	1990	1993
fine sentences	50.9 %	48.1 %	46.7 %	48.7 %	46.0 %	40.8 %	35.2 %	38.8 %
	1995	1997	1998	1999	2000	2001	2002	2003
	43.0 %	37.0 %	18.9 %	14.5 %	13.0 %	12.1 %	14.1 %	21.0 %

Source: Díez Ripollés, 'La evolución sistema penas' (2006), 15–16.

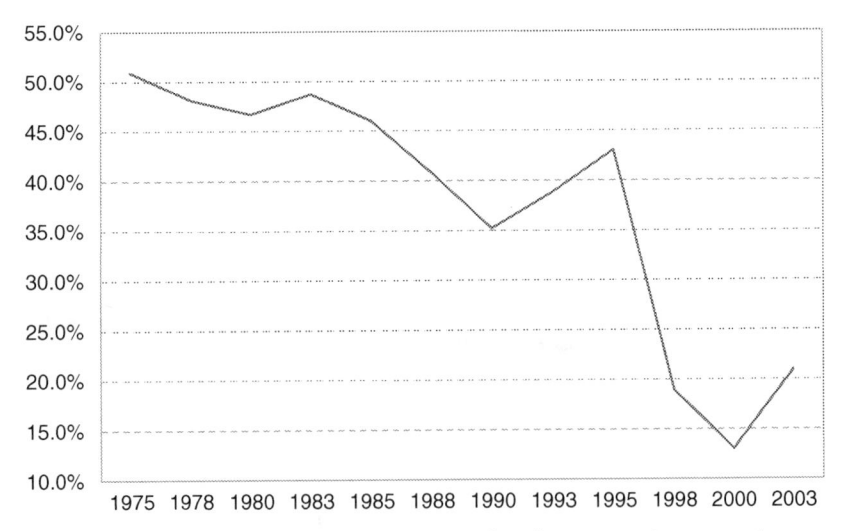

FIGURE 13.1 Portion of fine sentences of total sentences (1975–2003)
Source: author, based on data from Díez Ripollés, 'La evolución sistema penas'
(2006) 15–16.

stood in the range of 22 per cent–29 per cent: 24.9 per cent in 2004,[28] 26.3 per cent in 2005,[29] 28.9 per cent in 2006,[30] and 21.8 per cent in 2007.[31]

After 2008 the INE provides reliable and homogeneous data that enable a solid reading of the evolution of fine penalties in the decade 2008–17, which is the most recent and, therefore, more interesting for our purposes here.[32] Before

[28] www.ine.es/jaxi/Datos.htm?path=/t18/p466/a2004/l0/&file=02f003.px.
[29] www.ine.es/jaxi/Datos.htm?path=/t18/p466/a2005/l0/&file=01003.px.
[30] www.ine.es/jaxi/Datos.htm?path=/t18/p466/a2006/l0/&file=01003.px.
[31] www.ine.es/jaxi/Datos.htm?path=/t18/p466/a2007/l0/&file=05001.px.
[32] An analysis of this data for the period 2008–11, as well as methodological explanations about the system used to exploit data offered by the INE for those years can be found in Barquín Sanz and Luna del Castillo, 'En los dominios de la prisión', 10–20, 46–50.

engaging in the presentation of the statistical data available, it must be clarified that these do not discriminate between day fines and proportional fines. It must be presumed, though, that the recurrence of the latter is much smaller, even if it has recently gained presence in the CP, because it is not commonly applicable in the most frequent offences, on which detailed data will be offered later (offences against property, bodily harm offences and offences against freedom).

Percentage data offered by the INE over the total number of sentences imposed for all kinds of offences in Spain between 2008 and 2017 are offered in Table 13.2. Between 2008 and 2015, both included, fine sentences represented between 19 per cent (peaks in 2011 and 2012) and 25 per cent (peak in 2009) to boost in 2016 (31.0 per cent) and 2017 (33.4 per cent).[33] The strong rise in the use of fines during the last phase of this period can be described as a veritable explosion linked to the conversion of misdemeanours ('faltas') into minor felonies ('delitos leves'). Also a change in the attitude of judicial bodies toward the use of prison sentences has occurred, largely because they have become increasingly aware of the heavy financial burden implied for the national economy.[34] This argument is reinforced by the drop in the number of the prison population in Spain since 2010.[35]

In parallel, throughout the decade, prison sentences became initially the dominant type of penalty[36] between 2010 and 2015, both included, to then relinquish this position in favour of fines in 2016 and 2017, as can be seen in Table 13.2. This descent in the second half of the decade has gone from 25.5 per cent in 2012 to 19.8 per cent in 2017. The evolution of both penalties along these ten years is graphically represented in Figure 13.2. The next penalties in terms of percentual presence in sentences of 2017 are disqualifications for jobs and positions (15.5 per cent), deprivation of the right to drive (8.4 per cent) and the prohibition to approach the victim (5.9 per cent).[37]

If we analyse the data according to types of offence, it is noteworthy that in these five years the imposition of fine penalties has climbed significantly for frequently committed offences; for example, offences against property (from 2.6 per cent of the total number of penalties imposed in 2013 to 12.2 per cent in 2017, which is a multiplying factor of 4.8); bodily harm offences (2013: 0.6 per cent; 2017: 5.2 per cent; a factor of 8.6), offences against freedom

---

[33] www.ine.es/jaxiT3/Datos.htm?t=25714.
[34] Similarly, Dünkel, 'European Penology: The Rise and Fall of Prison Population Rates in Europe in Times of Migrant Crises and Terrorism', 644.
[35] See Brandáriz García, 'La evolución del sistema penitenciario español, 1995–2014: Transformaciones de la penalidad y modificación práctica de la realidad penitenciaria', 19–23; Barquín Sanz, Cano Paños and Calvo Alba, 'Resocialización y encuestas de calidad de vida penitenciaria', 254–5.
[36] See Barquín Sanz and Luna del Castillo, 'En los dominios de la prisión', 47, 50–2.
[37] www.ine.es/jaxiT3/Datos.htm?t=25714&L=1.

TABLE 13.2 *Portion of fine sentences and prison sentences of total sentences* (2008–17)

	2008	2009	2010	2011	2012	2013	2014	2015	2016	2017
fine sentences	22.9 %	25.2 %	20.2 %	19.0 %	19.4 %	20.0 %	20.3 %	22.5 %	31.0 %	33.4 %
prison sentences	20.6 %	22.3 %	22.7 %	24.6 %	25.5 %	25.3 %	25.5 %	24.8 %	20.9 %	19.8 %

Source: www.ine.es.

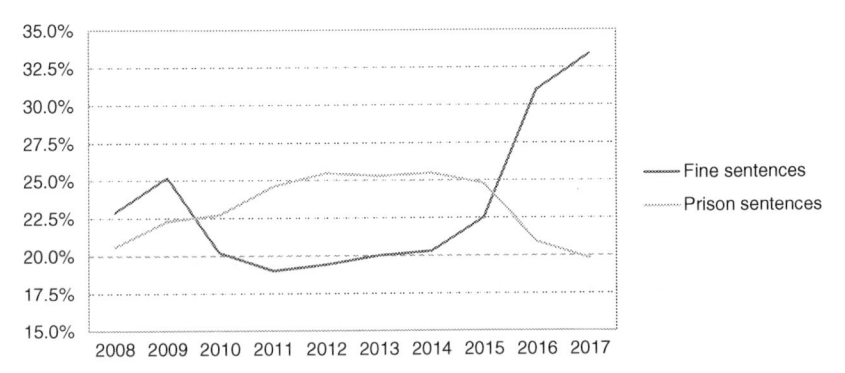

FIGURE 13.2 Portion of fine sentences and prison sentences of total sentences (2008–17)
Source: author, based on data from *www.ine.es.*

(2013: 0.07 per cent; 2017: 1.7 per cent, a factor of 24.6). In parallel, the percentage over the total number of imposed prison sentences for the same offences has diminished: offences against property (2013: 8.7 per cent; 2017: 7.5 per cent); bodily harm offences (2013: 3.5 per cent; 2017: 2.3 per cent), offences against freedom (2013: 0.37 per cent; 2017: 0.31).[38]

In order to interpret this data correctly one must bear in mind that a sudden variation of percentages occurred between 2015 and 2017. This does not correspond to a simple process of replacement of prison sentences with fine sentences, as the reduction of the former is much smaller than the rise of the latter. Comprehensive data concerning the total number of penalties imposed are illuminating in this regard. Table 13.3 shows a moderate descent of 7.8 per cent in prison sentences between 2014 (156,799) and 2017 (145,494),

---

[38] All this data is also accessible at www.ine.es/jaxiT3/Tabla.htm?t=25714&L=1.

while simultaneously there is a rise of a significant 134 per cent in fine sentences between 2011 (104,783) and 2017 (245,265). In other words, if we compare homogenous date periods (always versus 2017 as the last year in which there is available data), prison sentences rose 7.2 per cent since 2011, rose 2.1 per cent since 2012, descended 5.5 per cent since 2013, descended 7.2 per cent since 2014 and descended 4.9 per cent since 2015; whereas fines rose 134 per cent since 2011, 126 per cent since 2012, 101 per cent since 2013, 96 per cent since 2014 and 77 per cent since 2015.

This explosion in the imposition of fines occurred specifically between 2015 and 2016, and this trend persisted, albeit in moderation, in 2017. Notice how the total number of prison sentences in 2013 was 153,950, versus 145,494 in 2017, with figures for the years 156,799 (2014), 152,937 (2015) and 145,577 (2016); equivalent figures for fines are 121,971 (2013) and 245,265 (2017), with results for the years 125,223 (2014), 138,927 (2015) and 215,288 (2016). Total figures for convictions for those last five years range between 608,901 (2013) and 734,919 (2017) and the years yield 615,640 (2014), 617,696 (2015) and 695,013 (2016). As can be observed from Table 13.3 and is graphically clear from Figure 13.3, there is almost exact correspondence between the rise in the number of fine sentences and the rise in the number of total convictions in those same years. Also, there is correspondence between this last graphic representation and Figure 13.2 presented above.

Finally, it is relevant to state that to this day, to the best of our knowledge, no empirical studies have been conducted to examine the relative effectiveness of day fines in Spain, which anyway makes sense given the 'peculiar' application of them, in which wealth is not really taken into consideration.

13.5 PUBLIC PERCEPTION

In the Spanish social and political landscape, it cannot be said that there is a clear perception concerning the day fine system by the general population. Unlike other countries, there has never been a debate about the appropriateness of discriminating the daily fee of fines depending on the financial situation of the convict, as established for criminal offences. In the cases affecting people with large economic means (athletes, artists, businessmen, politicians), usually related to corruption or tax evasion crimes and with wide repercussion in the media, naturally there is practically no one who considers the fines imposed excessive, but it is also true that in such cases the penalties are more frequently of a proportional fine type rather than a day fine type.

TABLE 13.3 *Fine sentences, prison sentences and total sentences (2008–17)*

	2008	2009	2010	2011	2012	2013	2014	2015	2016	2017
fine sentences	145,819	158,250	126,199	104,783	108,373	121,971	125,223	138,927	215,288	245,265
prison sentences	129,890	139,663	141,849	135,713	142,444	153,950	156,799	152,937	145,577	145,494
total sentences	630,980	627,752	624,599	551,387	557,793	608,901	615,640	617,696	695,013	734,919

Source: www.ine.es.

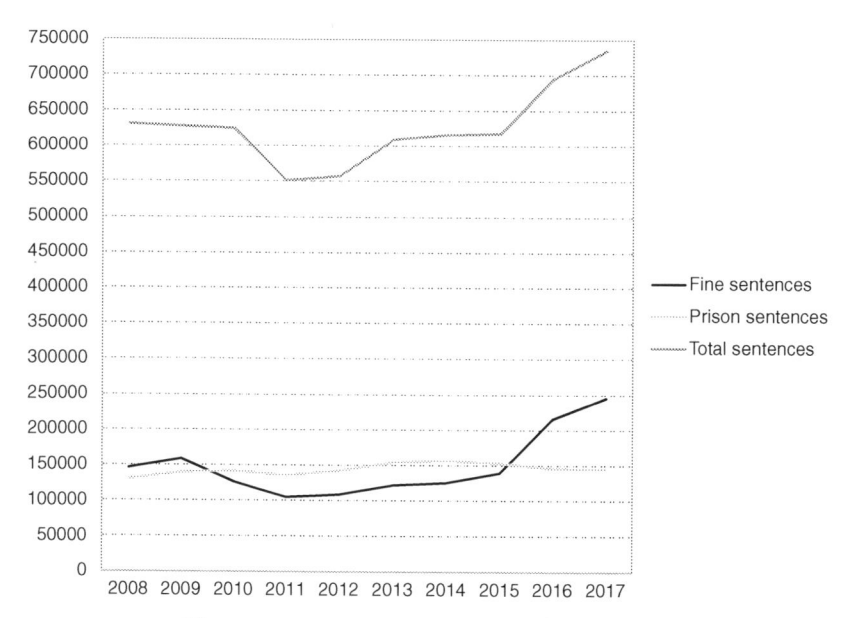

FIGURE 13.3 Fine sentences, prison sentences and total sentences (2008–17)
Source: author, based on data from *www.ine.es.*

It is interesting, on the other hand, that there is not a similar debate concerning non-criminal unlawful conducts, which, since the day fine model is exclusive of criminal law in Spain, are calculated on a general basis regardless of, or with merely a weak link to the patrimony and the income of the convict and despite the fact that the fines for them are usually higher or much higher than penal fines.

It seems reasonable, therefore, to conclude that there is at least a tacit general agreement over day fines as the suitable model for applying fine sentences. However, the fact that the practical implementation of day fines in Spain falls quite short in terms of assessing the financial capacity of the defendant, then convicted, should be taken into account in this regard, since one could hardly say that the day fine model is actually being implemented as such in the Spanish justice system.

On the other hand, it might seem reasonable to extract from these pages the image that the Spanish population in general trusts its criminal justice system, but this would be an audacious conclusion. In fact, the perception of criminal justice is often detected as weak against crime, despite the data of low crime and high incarceration rates offered by Spain in comparison with neighbouring countries. The focus is on the prison penalty, whereas the fine is likely not perceived by the citizens as a material part of the criminal justice system, but rather as a circumstantial addition that does not merit special attention. This is despite the fact that, as we have seen, in recent years the application of fine sentences by judges and courts has increased remarkably.

13.6 OTHER CHALLENGES

In Spain, there is personal liability for non-payment of a fine, whereby the absence of payment can be compensated by the completion of a prison term, residential detention or community services, calculated on the basis of a day of subsidiary liability for every two units of fine, although with certain limits. In this field, unlike what has been previously seen for the determination of fees for day fines, there is a wide diversity of criteria on the part of different judicial bodies. This is largely due to the imprecision of the regulations in force, which leave a significant margin of appreciation in the hands of judges and courts. It is important to remark, in the first place, that the judicial bodies usually grant generous instalments, of a minimum of 100 or even 60 euros per month, for the payment of the fine. And, secondly, that mere will contrary to the payment of the fine is not enough to declare the default, but the judicial body competent for execution (usually, the same that imposed the sentence) must make an equity inquiry on the condemned and, if applicable, seize the necessary assets to collect the penalty. If the forced execution takes place, the sentence is fulfilled. It is only once verified that the convict does not have assets on which to execute the fine when the judicial body has to decide about the eventual subsidiary enforcement through either prison, residential detention or community services. In any event, subsidiary liability cannot be imposed on individuals who have been sentenced to prison for more than five years. This implies that in particular cases the judicial body may not be able to enforce a fine. This could frequently be the case, due to a lack of sizeable goods owned by the convicted. If a fine has been imposed on someone sentenced to more than five years of prison and this sentence is still partially or totally pending, then this implies that an unpaid fine can no longer be converted into imprisonment, house arrest or community service. In other words, in that particular case the fine will simply not be collected and no alternative sanction is imposed either.

The INE statistics stopped separately offering the figures for subsidiary personal liability for non-payment of a fine as of 2012, so that there is no updated data available on those studied by Suárez López, from which it can be inferred that the percentage of application of this subsidiary liability ranged between 6 and 7 per cent of the total fines for the years 2009, 2010 and 2011.[39] In view of the notable increase of fines along with the downward evolution of the Spanish prison population in recent years, it seems reasonable to assume that the rates of imposition of subsidiary personal liability through prison have not increased since 2012.

REFERENCES

Barquín Sanz, J. and Luna del Castillo, J. D. 2012. 'En los dominios de la prisión: distribución numérica de las penas en el código y en la justicia penal', *Revista Electrónica de Ciencia Penal y Criminología* 14–16: 1–52.

Barquín Sanz, J., Cano Paños, M. Á. and Calvo Alba, M. Á. 2018. 'Resocialización y encuestas de calidad de vida penitenciaria', *Revista de Derecho Penal y Criminología* 20: 251–85.

Baumann, J. 1968. 'Was erwarten wir von der Strafrechtsreform?', in Baumann, J. (ed.), *Programm für ein neues Strafgesetzbuch*. Frankfurt am Main: Fischer Bücherei.

Brandáriz García, J. A. 2015. 'La evolución del sistema penitenciario español, 1995–2014: Transformaciones de la penalidad y modificación práctica de la realidad penitenciaria', *Crítica Penal y Poder* 9: 1–31.

Cano Paños, M. Á. 2016. '50 años del Proyecto Alternativo del Código Penal Alemán (1966–2016)', *Cuadernos de Política Criminal* 119: 73–120.

Cardenal Montraveta. S. 2020. *La pena de multa. Estudio sobre su justificación y la determinación de su cuantía*. Madrid: Marcial Pons.

Díez Ripollés, J. L. 2006. 'La evolución del sistema de penas en España: 1975-2003', *Revista Electrónica de Ciencia Penal y Criminología* 08–07: 1–25.

Dünkel, F. 2017. 'European Penology: The Rise and Fall of Prison Population Rates in Europe in Times of Migrant Crises and Terrorism', *European Journal of Criminology* 14: 629–53.

Faraldo Cabana, P. 2015. 'Novedades en la pena de responsabilidad personal subsidiaria por impago de multa (arts. 35 in fine y 53.1)', in J. L. González Cussac (ed.), *Comentarios a la Reforma Penal de 2015*. Valencia: Tirant lo Blanch.

Faraldo Cabana, P. 2017. *Money and the Governance of Punishment. A Genealogy of the Penal Fine*. London and New York: Routledge.

Garcés Peregrina, J. M. 2014. 'El enjuiciamiento de los delitos urbanísticos en la provincia de Málaga', *Jueces para la Democracia* 81: 126–51.

García San Martín, J. 2015. *Las medidas alternativas al cumplimiento de las penas privativas de libertad: adaptado a las reformas del Código penal y de la Ley de Enjuiciamiento Criminal de 2015*. Madrid: Dykinson.

González Tascón, M. M., Loredo Colunga, M., Roca Agapito, L., Villa Sieiro, S. V., Albuerne Gutiérrez, M. A. and Bravo Arteaga, A. 2015. 'Aproximación a la pena de trabajos en beneficio de la comunidad a partir de la evidencia empírica: la

---

[39] J. M. Suárez López, 'Multa', in L. Morillas Cueva and J. Barquín Sanz (eds.), *La aplicación de las alternativas a la pena de prisión en España* (Madrid: Defensor del Pueblo, 2013), p. 309.

aplicación judicial de la pena', *Revista Electrónica de Ciencia Penal y Criminología* 17–08: 1–26.

Gracia Martín, L., Boldova Pasamar, M. Á. and Alastuey Dobón, C. (eds.) 2016. *Lecciones de consecuencias jurídicas del delito*. Valencia: Tirant lo Blanch.

Killias, M., Aebi, M. A. and Kuhn, A. 2012. *Précis de criminologie*. Bern: Stämpfli.

Mapelli Caffarena, B. 2011. *Las consecuencias jurídicas del delito*. Pamplona: Civitas.

Martínez-Buján Pérez, C. 1997. 'La regulación de la pena de multa en el Código Penal Español de 1995. (Los días-multa y la multa proporcional, con referencia a la responsabilidad personal subsidiaria en caso de impago)', *Estudios penales y criminológicos* 20: 225–86.

Mir Puig, S. 2016. *Derecho penal. Parte general*. Barcelona: Reppertor.

Moliné, J. C. and Larrauri Pijoan, E. (eds.) 2002. *Jueces penales y penas en España. Aplicación de las penas alternativas a la privación de libertad en los juzgados de lo penal*. Valencia: Tirant lo Blanch.

Morillas Cueva, L. 1991. *Teoría de las consecuencias jurídicas del delito*. Madrid: Tecnos.

Morillas Cueva L. and Barquín Sanz, J. (eds.) 2013. *La aplicación de las alternativas a la pena de prisión en España*. Madrid: Defensor del Pueblo.

Roca Agapito, L. 2007. *El sistema de sanciones en el Derecho penal español*. Barcelona: J.M. Bosch.

Roldán Barbero, H. 1982. *El dinero, objeto fundamental de la sanción penal: un estudio histórico de la moderna pena de multa*. Madrid: Akal.

Suárez López, J. M. 2013. 'Multa', in L. Morillas Cueva and J. Barquín Sanz (eds.), *La aplicación de las alternativas a la pena de prisión en España*. Madrid: Defensor del Pueblo,

Varona Gómez, D. 2004. 'El arresto de fin de semana: lecciones a aprender de su breve historia. (Sobre las razones y excusas para su reforma)', *Revista de Derecho Penal y Criminología* 13: 47–80.

14

Day Fines in Poland

Dawid Marko and Sławomir Steinborn

14.1 HISTORICAL DEVELOPMENT OF DAY FINES IN POLAND

In Poland, the day fine models previously adopted in Finland, Sweden, Denmark, Austria, Germany and Hungary have not gone unnoticed. Since the late 1970s Polish criminal literature broadly discussed the above-mentioned solutions and pointed to the positive trends of the main assumptions of this model, claiming the desirability of implementing day fines into the Polish legislation.[1] However, it should be noted that Polish criminal law in the post-war period was characterised by a high level of repression and deterrence, which emanated from the ideology and goals defined by the communist regime. This was due to the fact that criminal law was treated as a useful instrument to pursue the political and economic goals of the new authority. Therefore, the fine imposed as an autonomous sanction did not play a significant role, giving way to custodial sentences combined with a mandatory or facultative cumulative fine imposed on a perpetrator regardless of his/her financial situation. Although the need to overcome the approach of recognising deprivation of liberty as the sole measure to prevent minor offences was already understood, the instruments adopted for that effect in the Criminal Code of 1969, enabling much wider fine imposition than before, had in practice a relatively minor impact.[2]

Social movements during the first half of 1980, with the creation of 'Solidarity', generated momentum for a change, especially towards reducing

---

[1] Thornsted, 'System grzywien dniówkowych w Szwecji', 61; Szumski, 'Grzywna dniówkowa', 10; Horvat, 'Nowy węgierski kodeks karny', 94; Spotowski, 'Grzywna dzienna', 11; Wojciechowska, 'O grzywnie w ujęciu austriackiego kodeksu karnego', 108–14; Melezini, 'Czy system stawek dziennych przy wymiarze grzywny', 116–19; Grebing and Spotowski, 'Kara grzywny według systemu stawek dziennych w prawie karnym RFN', 166–75.

[2] Grześkowiak et al., 'Kara grzywny', pp. 98–108.

excessive repressiveness. It is when the proposal for the adoption of day fines into the Polish legislation appeared for the first time – in the draft amendments to the Criminal Code of 1981. However, the imposition of martial law in 1981 brought an end to this trend for nearly a decade. Conditions for fundamental reform of the criminal law arose after political transformation after 1989. The principal objective during the work on a new Criminal Code was the rationalisation of the penal policy and significant reduction of the prison population.[3] Thus the basic assumption was to create a system of penalties and penal measures, in which the imprisonment penalty would be treated as *ultima ratio* in relation to crimes of low or medium seriousness – for which the primary measure of penal reaction should be the fine, restriction of liberty (community service) or conditionally suspended imprisonment.[4] In the new Criminal Code of 1997[5] (which entered into force on 1 September 1998) special attention was paid to the role played by the fine. The priority character of this penalty was reflected in the new arrangement of the catalogue on penalties foreseen in Article 32 CC, in which the fine was placed in the first position, in the construction of alternative sanctions in a special part of the Criminal Code, wherein the fine was ranked first, as well as in the newly established directive of the primacy of non-custodial measures of penal reaction (Article 58 (1) CC).[6] Moreover, according to the doctrine's proposals,[7] the authors of the project of the new Criminal Code decided to adopt the day fine model. It was therefore concluded that this model was to be regarded as more appropriate to the above-mentioned objectives of the fine assigned in the new codification. In support of this move, the authors of the project indicated that this system has no disadvantages, which would not equally apply to the fixed fines system, but would at the same time have many advantages. The central point of the project promoters was to enable an individualisation of the fine in relation to the severity of the offence and the material status of the perpetrator as well as elimination of the perpetrator's financial situation impact on the ailment of the fine imposed on perpetrators of the same offences and the

---

[3] *Ibid.*, pp. 109–14.

[4] Zoll, 'Założenia polityczno-kryminalne kodeksu karnego w świetle wyzwań współczesności', 47–8.

[5] The Act of 6 June 1997 – The Criminal Code (consolidated text: Journal of Law of 2018, item 1600, as amended, hereinafter also referred to as 'CC').

[6] *Supra* note 2, p. 115.

[7] Cieślak, 'Zagadnienia reformy prawa karnego', 49; Kunicka-Michalska, 'Grzywna na miarę kieszeni', 7; Marek, 'Co to znaczy postępowe i nowoczesne', 5; Szumski, 'O celowości recepcji systemu grzywien stawek dziennych', 72–9; Melezini, 'W sprawie reformy kary grzywny', 16–17; Majewski, 'Grzywna w projekcie nowego kodeksu karnego', 75–91; Melezini, 'System wymiaru grzywien w nowym Kodeksie karnym', 89–92.

associated emphasis on the fundamental right of equality before the law. Equally significant was constituting an obligation imposed on the court to thoroughly examine all conditions involving the material and family situation of the perpetrator and the simplified procedure of adjudication of the alternative sentence, because the calculating mechanism is envisaged by law without an element of discretion.[8]

In the original wording of the Criminal Code of 1997 the fine, as an autonomous self-existent penalty, could be imposed when it was included in the sanction of the provision as a punishment for committing a specific offence, as well as a result of the commutation or extraordinary mitigation of punishment. In Poland, the fine coexists with the restriction of freedom or the restriction of freedom and imprisonment of up to one year (often – twenty-nine provisions), up to two years (most often – sixty-six provisions), up to three years or for a period from three months to five years. It is noteworthy that the number of sanctions containing a fine increased from 41 in the Criminal Code of 1969 to 105 in the current, which constitutes almost one-third of the sanctions envisaged by this Code.[9] Notwithstanding the foregoing, the Code provided for a penalty of the fine beside the penalty of imprisonment (cumulative fine) and as part of the conditional suspension of imprisonment (accessory fine). Further considerations are mostly devoted to the fixed fine.

The current shape of the statutory regulations regarding the fine underwent a substantial modification in 2015[10] (entered into force on 1 July 2015). It resulted from the fact that a newly adopted penal philosophy was not adequately reflected in the practice of justice, which, despite the wide range of applicability of the fine, took completely the wrong direction, what led to a significant exceeding of the reasonable limits of imprisonment with the conditional suspension of its execution.[11] Therefore, this amendment was intended to radically change the structure of imposed sentences by extending the scope of applicability of the fine at the cost of the conditional suspension of imprisonment. For that purpose several amendments were made, in particular the priority of fine over the conditional suspension of imprisonment received further statutory strengthening in Article 58 (1) CC. Furthermore, a new

---

[8] *Ibid.*

[9] *Supra* note 2, p. 117 and literature cited therein.

[10] The Act of 20 February 2015 amending the Act: the Criminal Code and certain others acts. (Journal of Law of 2015, item 396.)

[11] Zoll, 'Komisja Kodyfikacyjna Prawa Karnego wobec problemów związanych z represją karno-prawną', pp. 26–32; 'Uzasadnienie rządowego projektu ustawy o zmianie ustawy – Kodeks karny oraz niektórych innych ustaw z projektami aktów wykonawczych z 15 V 2014, druk sejmowy nr 2393', pp. 1–5, see also mentioned in this document 'Ocena skutków regulacji', pp. 102–41, within statistical facts, www.sejm.gov.pl/Sejm7.nsf/druk.xsp?nr=2393.

provision (Article 37(a)) was inserted in the Criminal Code, according to which a fine may be imposed instead of the penalty of imprisonment if a statute provides for the penalty of deprivation of liberty not exceeding eight years as the upper limit of a statutory penalty. Moreover, Article 58 (2) CC was repealed, what created the possibility of ruling a fine regardless of the financial situation of the perpetrator, which provision was recognised as the dam for fine adjudication. From 1 July 2015 on the mere lack of factual basis did no longer preclude the imposition of a fine (with the minimum daily unit). Currently, only in the special part of the Criminal Code a mere 220 offences are included for which day fines may be imposed.[12]

14.2 THE LEGAL FRAMEWORK OF DAY FINES

In Poland, the rules governing the limits of the fine imposed for offences are stated by Article 33 CC. According to its paragraph 1, the fine is imposed in terms of a daily unit, setting out a number of daily units and the amount of one unit. Unless a statute provides otherwise, the number of daily units shall not be lower than 10 and not exceed 540. Originally, the upper limit of unit numbers was 360, which was changed in the amendment of 2009[13] (entered into force on 8 June 2010). In justification of this amendment, the Polish Ministry of Justice pointed at the fact that it will cause a potential increase in the number of persons to whom the court will be able to impose a fine as a penalty corresponding to the degree of social harmfulness of the offence and the degree of guilt, in line with the assumptions of the directive of imprisonment as a penalty *ultima ratio*. Nonetheless, this move was widely criticised as not referring to empirical studies and leading to super-fluous repression.[14]

The Criminal Code and other statutes provide specific provisions concerning the number of daily units. It is worth to mention four of them. In 2017, the exception to the rule that 540 is the maximum number of daily units was introduced. Namely, for certain types of offences a fine may be imposed up to 3,000 units (Article 277(b) and 309 CC). Secondly, when the Criminal Code provides for the possibility of extraordinary aggravation of a penalty, the fine may entail to 810 units (Article 38 (3) CC). The same limit applies when the fine is imposed as a cumulative penalty (Article 86 (1) CC). Lastly, the day fine

---

[12]   Małecki, 'Ustawowe zagrożenie karą i sądowy wymiar kary', pp. 284–9.

[13]   The Act of 5 November 2009 amending the Acts: the Criminal Code, the Code of Criminal Procedure, the Executive Criminal Code, the Criminal Fiscal Code and certain others acts (Journal of Law of 2009 No. 206, item 1589, as amended).

[14]   *Supra* note 2, pp. 122–4.

model is also adopted in the Criminal Fiscal Code[15] with regard to fiscal offences. The general upper limit of the daily units' number is higher than in the Criminal Code – it shall not exceed 720 units when a fine is imposed for a fiscal offence (Article 23 (1) CFC) and maximum 1,080 units when it is imposed as a cumulative penalty (Article 39 (1) CFC).

Pursuant to Article 33 (3) CC, the amount of one daily unit may not be lower than 10 PLN[16] and not more than 2,000 PLN (from circa 2.30 euros to 455 euros). Thus, in principle, in Poland a fine may be imposed for an offence in the amount from 100 PLN to 1,080,000 PLN (from circa 23 euros to 245,455 euros). It should be noted, however, that the amount of a daily unit remained unchanged since the adoption of the Criminal Code in 1997, as in 2010 only the maximum number of daily units was increased from 360 to 540. This means that due to the devaluation of money for over twenty years, the repressiveness of the fines has been reduced, especially in relation to wealthier people, for whom a high unit may be determined. Due to the principles of the imposition of the fine in the system of daily units, the increase in the number of fine units in 2010 does not compensate for the reduction of the real amount of the daily unit. If the inflation rate were taken into account when determining the upper limit of the daily unit, it should amount to over 3,700 PLN in 2013.[17]

Different rules regarding the amount of the day fine unit are foreseen in the Criminal Fiscal Code. It is based on the so-called parametric system. Namely, the daily unit shall not be less than one-thirtieth of the minimum wage,[18] nor exceed it 400 times (Article 23 (3) CFC). Currently, the limits of one daily unit of fine imposed for a fiscal offence range from 93.33 PLN to 37,333.33 PLN. This means that a fine for a fiscal offence may be imposed in the amount from 933.33 PLN to 26,880,000 PLN.

A fine for a fiscal offence may be imposed only by the court, even if criminal proceedings are ended on the basis of an agreement between the prosecution and the defence. The imposition of the fine in the system of daily units takes place in two stages: at the first stage, the court determines the number of daily units. This decision is based on judicial discretion, subject to general principles of the imposition of penalties, set forth in the Criminal Code. The second stage consists of determining the amount of one daily unit. This decision is based on the specific principles regarding the calculation of the

---

[15] The Act of 10 September 1999 – The Criminal Fiscal Code (consolidated text: Journal of Law of 2018, item 1958, as amended, hereinafter also referred to as 'CFC').
[16] The average 1 euro exchange rate in 2020 is 4.4 PLN.
[17] Dudek, 'Inflacja pieniądza a prawo karne', 79–80.
[18] The minimum wage is fixed by the government and in 2021 was fixed at 800 PLN.

daily unit. These stages are disjunctive and are, in principle, based on the consideration of different circumstances. However, it is not excluded to take into account the same factual circumstances at both stages, in particular those relating to the perpetrator (e.g. diminished sanity of the perpetrator), but from a different angle – first from the point of severity of the sentence and then from the perspective of the perpetrator's earning potential.[19]

When determining the number of daily units of a fine, the general principles concerning the imposition of penalties should be followed. The main directives are set out in Article 53 CC: the severity of the penalty shall not exceed the degree of guilt, the court shall also take into account the degree of social harmfulness of the offence,[20] as well as preventive and educational aims which a penalty should achieve with regard to the sentenced person and the need to develop legal awareness in society. The court should also take into account different circumstances, that is, the perpetrator's motivation and manner of conduct, the type and the extent of negative consequences of the crime, the characteristics and personal conditions of the perpetrator, the perpetrator's way of life prior to the crime and his/her behaviour after the crime. Especially important are his/her efforts to redress the damage or to satisfy the public perception of justice in any other form, as well as the victim's conduct, but also the positive results of the mediation between the victim and the perpetrator or the settlement they have reached during the proceedings held before a court or a public prosecutor. Furthermore, it is noted that the assessment should also consider the material benefit that the perpetrator gained or intended to gain from the crime, because it is a circumstance that co-determines the load of social harmfulness of a given behaviour.[21]

According to Article 33 (3) CC, the court, while determining the amount of the daily unit, takes into consideration the perpetrator's income, personal and family conditions, financial situation and income perspectives. The starting point is to estimate the income of the perpetrator, which includes all income regardless of their source (e.g. employment or another kind of paid engagement, pensions, rental income, bank deposits, royalties, income from participation in profits of legal entities, income from owned movable or immovable

---

[19] Majewski, in *Kodeks karny. Część ogólna. Komentarz*, p. 697.

[20] According to Article 115 (2) CC, while determining the degree of the social harmfulness of an act, the court takes into consideration the type and nature of the infringed legal interest, the extent of inflicted and anticipated damage, the manner and the circumstances of the commission of the act, the importance of duties violated by the perpetrator, as well as the form of the intent, the perpetrator's motivation, the type of violated safeguard rules and the degree of such violation.

[21] Kolasiński, 'Kara grzywny w kodeksie karnym', 18.

property or revenues from paid disposal of property or property rights). Although it is not strictly specified by the law, in judicial practice the sum will be deduced with relevant costs, such as tax-deductible expenses, contributions for mandatory social and health insurance and expenses for the justified needs of the perpetrator and other members of his/her family. Other liabilities, for example the repayment of a loan or tax arrears, may be relevant only in the enforcement proceedings (spreading into instalments, deferral of payment).[22] Further must be assessed the perpetrator's personal conditions (e.g. age, education, qualifications, physical and psychological predispositions), family conditions (e.g. the total number of the perpetrator's dependants and duties stemming from it), the financial situation (all movable and immovable assets and possessed funds) and income perspectives (basically whether the perpetrator takes full advantage of his/her income opportunities, e.g. the perpetrator initially does not take up any form of employment or the perpetrator derives his/her assets before the hearing). The above-mentioned circumstances are important for determining the amount of the daily unit and should be present at the moment of adjudication by the first instance court, not at the moment of committing the offence.

The above-described, extensive catalogue of the prerequisites examined before the imposition of the fine, requires the ability to effectively obtaining evidence of the perpetrator's financial situation. Hence, Article 213 (1) of the Code of Criminal Procedure[23] introduces in criminal proceedings an obligation to collect the perpetrator's personal background information, including inter alia the age of the perpetrator, his/her family and property relationships, level of education, profession, sources of income and the Taxpayer Identification Number (NIP). Moreover, pursuant to Article 213 (1)(a) CCP (added by the amendment of 2015) where necessary, the prosecutor, another authority conducting the pre-trial proceedings or the court shall obtain information from electronic databases of the Ministry of Finance concerning the property relations and sources of income of the perpetrator, including pending and completed fiscal proceedings, on the basis of up-to-date data available in the database. Information obtained from the above-mentioned databases should allow the formation of a proper sanction in relation to the perpetrator and to facilitate the enforcement of the fine, other financial penalties and the costs of proceedings, albeit that obtaining information from this database is not mandatory. In practice, the problem is on the one hand that the information contained

---

[22] Dadak, *Grzywna samoistna w stawkach dziennych*, pp. 278–83.
[23] The Act of 6 June 1997 – The Code of Criminal Procedure (consolidated text: Journal of Law of 2018, item 1987, as amended, hereinafter also referred to as 'CCP').

in the database often is not comprehensive and on the other hand the fact that this database does not include people operating outside the tax system (in the so-called 'grey zone'). Furthermore, if a need arises, according to Article 214 (1) CCP the court or the prosecutor (in pre-trial proceedings) orders a social background report to be carried out, which outcomes should include, in particular, a concise description of the life of the suspect until present and precise information about his/her environment, including family ties, school or professional environment and also information about the financial and family situation, as well as income sources. It should also be mentioned that if the suspect has been charged with committing a criminal offence for which the fine can be imposed, the execution of that ruling may be secured *ex officio* on the property of the suspect, where there is a justified concern that without such security the execution of the ruling will be impossible or significantly impeded. In that case the police may affect a provisional seizure of the movables of the suspected person (up to seven days), provided that there is a justified concern that the person might conceal them.

In practice, the above-mentioned personal information is collected by the authority conducting pre-trial proceedings (primarily by the police) directly after the presentation of charges, in particular to the protocol of the suspect's interrogation and then by the court, during the first interrogation after bringing the case to trial. Usually, this information is collected on the basis of the perpetrator's statements, as well as certificates from the employer or other organisations and institutions, in which the perpetrator's income is obtained. The authorities relatively rarely use social a background report and information from the database of the Ministry of Finance, typically only in case of the more serious offences. In contrast, freezing of the suspect's property is rather frequently applied. In the explanatory memorandum accompanying the draft of the amendment of 2015, it was recognised that the lack of proper practice of the judicial authorities in reliably establishing facts in the field of personal background information is one of the main causes of the low quota of the fine in the structure of the imposed sentences, as well as the low intensity of the imposed fines.[24] At present, there is a lack of up-to-date, comparable empirical research, hence this trend cannot be verified.

The fine should be paid by the sentenced person within thirty days of being summoned to pay. If this does not happen, the fine is compulsory enforced (Article 44 of the Criminal Enforcement Code).[25] The system of

---

[24] *Supra* note 11, 'Uzasadnienie rządowego projektu', p. 141.
[25] The Act of 6 June 1997 – The Criminal Enforcement Code (consolidated text: Journal of Law of 2019, item 676, as amended, hereinafter also referred to as 'CEC').

fine enforcement applicable in Poland is sometimes the subject of criticism. It is indicated that it is not enough flexible and often the only answer to the lack of assets and problems with paying the fine is its conversion into a substitute imprisonment.[26]

The fine may also be spread out in instalments up to one year, if its immediate enforcement would result in too serious consequences for the sentenced person or his/her family (Article 49 (1) CEC). In cases deserving special consideration and especially when the amount of the fine is significant, the fine can be spread out in instalments up to three years (Article 49 (2) CEC). The court takes into account the current situation of the sentenced person and his/her family, including data on his/her actual earnings, other incomes, family situation, health of the sentenced in conjunction with the possibilities of employment, his/her education and profession and job opportunities consistent with this education and learned profession and the existence of the property of the convicted and his/her spouse, which may be subject to execution.[27]

However, if the execution of a fine not exceeding 120 daily units turns out to be ineffective or the circumstances of the case show that it would be ineffective, the court may convert a fine into community service. It is then assumed that ten daily units are equivalent to a month of community service, rounded up to a full month. The court also determines the number of working hours – from twenty to forty hours for a month, taking into account the directives specified in Article 53 CC (Article 45 CEC). In the literature, it is pointed out that such low conversion rate of the fine for community service is unjustified and could lead to an extension of the process of the execution of the fine. Sometimes, it is more profitable for sentenced persons to serve a substitute imprisonment than to serve a community service. Therefore, it is postulated that the daily units of the fine should be converted only to the number of working hours, without specifying the period in which this work is to be carried out. Then it will depend on the convicted person and the employer when the fine will be considered to be replaced by the work done.[28]

The fine is converted into a substitute imprisonment if the execution of the fine has been ineffective or the circumstances of the case show that it would be ineffective and the convicted person declares that he/she does not agree to do community service determined according to Article 45 CEC or evades to do this service, as well as when the conversion of the fine for community service is

---

[26] Małolepszy, *Pomocniczy model wykonywania samoistnej kary pozbawienia wolności*, p. 7 *et seq.*
[27] Słupecki, *Kara grzywny samoistnej i jej wykonanie*, pp. 169–71.
[28] *Supra* note 26, pp. 38–9; *supra* note 22, p. 463.

impossible (for example due to the amount of a fine higher than 120 units or the incapacity of the sentenced person to work) or pointless. According to Article 46 (2) CEC one day of imprisonment is equivalent to two daily units of fine. At the same time, a substitute penalty can neither exceed twelve months of imprisonment, nor the upper limit of imprisonment for a given offence. If the law does not provide for a given offence of imprisonment, the upper limit of the imprisonment cannot exceed six months.

On the margins of these considerations it should also be pointed out that Polish criminal fiscal law provides for auxiliary liability for the (day) fine (Article 24 CFC). If an alternate of a corporate entity who conducts its affairs as a representative, administrator, employee or in any other capacity is held liable for a fiscal offence and sentenced to a fine, this corporate entity thereof may be held accountable in whole or in the part of this fine on the basis of auxiliary liability. In order to incur such liability, it is sufficient that the represented corporate entity gained or may have gained a material benefit from committing that fiscal offence. The auxiliary liability is obligatory in the current legal status. This means that the court is obliged to impose auxiliary liability whenever a fine is imposed on the perpetrator of a fiscal offence and there are subjective and objective prerequisites justifying such liability.

Although the Polish Criminal Code adopted the day fine model, it must be noted that in Polish criminal law the day fines occur alongside the conventional model of the fixed fine. Despite the fact that the intention of the Criminal Code of 1997 was to develop day fines in the whole area of criminal law, the legislator left a number of provisions containing offences envisaged in some other specific acts, to which a fixed fine model applies.[29] Moreover, this model is also foreseen for the contraventions and fiscal contraventions (petty offences). Fixed pecuniary penalty may also be imposed on the criminal liable collective entity – in the amount from 1,000 PLN to 5,000,000 PLN, which may not, however, exceed 3 per cent of the revenue earned in the business year in which the offence for which the collective entity is liable was committed.[30]

14.3 THE PRACTICAL IMPLEMENTATION OF DAY FINES

The day fine can be imposed as a self-existent penalty or as a cumulative penalty along with imprisonment. The Criminal Code provides for a fine as

[29] See Article 11 of the Act of 6 June 1997 – Regulations implementing the Act: the Criminal Code (Journal of Law of 1997 No. 88, item 554, as amended).
[30] See Article 7 of the Act of 28 October 2002 on Criminal Liability of Collective Entities for Punishable Offences (consolidated text: Journal of Law of 2019, item 628, as amended).

a penalty for minor offences. The fine is foreseen as a threatening penalty alternatively with a restriction of liberty or with a restriction of liberty and imprisonment (up to one, two, three or five years depending on the severity of the crime). Additionally, pursuant to Article 37(a) CC the fine may be imposed instead of imprisonment if the law provides for a specific offence imprisonment of up to eight years. It means that Polish law provides for broad possibilities of imposing a fine as a sole penalty. The Criminal Code foresees no possibility to conditionally suspend the execution of a fine. The fine can also be imposed along with imprisonment, as so-called 'cumulative fine'. This possibility is provided for by some special acts, for instance for drug offences. The cumulative fine can also be imposed if the perpetrator committed an offence in order to gain a material benefit or when he/she gained such benefit (Article 33 (2) CC). The fine in these cases complements the severity of the imposed sanction for elements of economic discomfort. The fine may also be imposed along with conditionally suspended imprisonment (Article 71 (1) CC). In this case, the fine is in fact the only real repression related to the conviction, what is important not only from the perspective of the perpetrator, but also the society, as it shows that the perpetrator is not left completely unpunished. In this situation the fine has an accessorial function, because in the case of ordering the execution of a conditionally suspended imprisonment, the fine is not enforced (Article 71 (2) CC).

In accordance with the assumptions of the Criminal Code of 1997, the fine was supposed to play a crucial role in penal policy. It was expected that its share in the structure of imposed sentences would increase up to 30–40 per cent.[31] Paradoxically, the entry into force of the Criminal Code of 1997 resulted in a radical reduction in the share of fines in the structure of imposed penalties. This share fell from 27.4 per cent in 1997 to 18.4 per cent in 1999 and 15.1 per cent in 2000. Thus, it decreased by almost half. In parallel, there was a noticeable increase in the percentage of conditionally suspended imprisonment. In 2001 this downward path was halted and the rate of fines rose to 20.5 per cent, which was the result of frequent adjudication of the fine for drunk (or drug) driving (Article 178(a) CC), which was criminalised as an offence in 2000.[32] According to data provided in Table 14.1, it should be stated that in the years 2001–14 this change led to the stabilisation of this percentage at around one-fifth of the total number of sentences.

When interpreting this situation, it should be pointed out that this does not indicate changes in the scope of the choice of the sentence in the case law

---

[31] Marek, 'Problemy regulacji prawnej i orzekania kary grzywny', 15–16.
[32] Błachut, 'Wpływ wprowadzenia Article 178a k.k. na obraz zjawiska przestępczości i prawnokarnej reakcji na nią', p. 304.

TABLE 14.1 *Adults validly sentenced by common courts by type of punishment in the years 1997 and 1999–2018*

Year	Fine (self-existent)		Restriction of liberty (community service)		Imprisonment (absolute)		Conditionally suspended imprisonment		Other		Total
	Absolute number	%	Absolute number	%	Absolute number	%	Absolute number	%	Absolute number	%	Absolute number
1997	57,689	27.4	10,934	5.2	25,752	12.2	116,159	55.2	12	0.0	210,600
1999	38,209	18.4	15,648	7.5	26,158	12.6	127,437	61.1	142	0.0	207,607
2000	33,699	15.1	14,796	6.6	30,741	13.8	143,497	64.4	75	0.0	222,815
2001	64,475	20.5	28,507	9.0	36,943	11.8	184,819	58.8	136	0.0	315,013
2002	75,698	20.7	39,156	1.7	35,790	9.8	214,485	58.8	89	0.0	365,326
2003	93,274	22.4	52,763	1.7	36,558	8.8	233,055	56.1	143	0.0	415,933
2004	111,491	21.7	71,887	1.0	48,993	9.5	278,338	54.3	2,565	0.5	513,410
2005	100,968	20.0	67,254	1.3	42,969	8.5	291,409	57.8	1,514	0.4	504,281
2006	88,407	19.1	57,918	12.5	42,421	9.3	272,653	58.8	1,410	0.3	462,937
2007	82,988	19.5	47,091	11.0	37,685	8.8	257,141	60.9	1,396	0.3	426,377
2008	89,011	21.2	40,643	9.7	38,495	9.1	250,774	59.6	1,806	0.4	420,729
2009	88,236	21.2	43,524	10.5	37,913	9.1	243,974	58.7	1,625	0.4	41, 272
2010	92,329	21.3	49,692	11.5	39,582	9.1	251,087	58.0	201	0.0	432,891
2011	93,571	22.1	49,611	11.7	40,947	9.7	239,076	56.4	259	0.1	423,464
2012	91,296	22.4	50,730	12.4	41,691	10.2	224,185	54.9	205	0.0	408,107
2013	76,759	21.7	41,287	11.7	39,684	11.2	195,348	55.3	130	0.0	353,208
2014	63,078	21.4	33,009	11.2	35,633	12.0	163,534	55.4	99	0.0	295,353
2015	61,461	23.6	31,096	12.0	33,952	13.0	133,076	51.2	449	0.2	260,034
2016	98,776	34.1	61,720	21.3	43,695	15.1	81,673	28.2	3,648	1.3	289,512
2017	84,721	35.1	53,854	22.3	44,527	18.4	54,819	22.7	3,515	1.4	241,436
2018[33]	81,433	30.3	80,196	29.8	50,751	18.9	53,164	19.8	3,177	1.2	268,721

Source: Statistical data collected by the Ministry of Justice and compiled by the authors.

[33] Statistical data for 2018 are unofficial and may differ from those that will be published.

practice, due to the above-mentioned criminalisation of drunk driving. Sentences imposed for this offence constituted almost one-fourth of all sentences, as well as almost half of the imposed fines.[34] Contrary to initial expectations, among the means of the penal reaction, instead of the fine, the dominant position was taken by the penalty of conditionally suspended imprisonment. The literature points to two crucial factors that have probably led to the halting of the trend to impose the fine at a wider scale. On the one hand, attention is drawn to the coincidence between the entry into force of the new codification and the rapid escalation of unemployment with the progressive pauperisation of society, what increased the group of perpetrators who were subject to the new directive on the fine (Article 58 (2) CC), which was a barrier to imposing the fine in cases where the fine is unenforceable. On the other hand, as a probable reason was indicated the new model of fine, which undoubtedly placed much more demands on the practice of justice in determining the financial status of the perpetrator and is based on more complicated rules. However, this issue is left unresolved in the absence of adequate empirical research.[35]

The aforementioned amendment of 2015 was intended to prevent the trend discussed above. As previously mentioned, in order to make the fine more broadly used as a penalty for the minor offences, since 1 July 2015 the fine may be imposed even more frequently, including regardless of the perpetrator's material status (what banned repealed Article 58 (2) CC). The fine also received formal priority over competing on the same field conditional suspension of imprisonment (Article 58 (1) CC). An analysis of the available data implies that, as a result of the amendment of 2015, the percentage of imposed fines increased by around 10 points (from 21.4 per cent in 2014 to 34.1 per cent in 2016, 35.1 per cent in 2017 and 30.3 per cent in 2018) but the upward trend was halted in 2018. Undoubtedly, the effect of the amendment is a substantial increase in the proportions of the sentences for the restriction of freedom and absolute imprisonment, what seems to be associated with the introduction of the commented amendment, the institution of simultaneous adjudication of imprisonment and a restriction of liberty (so-called 'combined penalty'). In this context it is interesting that the percentage of community service almost tripled (from 11.2 per cent in 2014 to 21.3 per cent in 2016, 22.3 per cent in 2017 and 29.8 per cent in 2018). It seems that community service (including 'combined penalty') in further years may effectively compete with the fine in the field of minor and medium severe offences. Moreover, the experience of the first years has shown that Poland successfully reduced the percentage of conditionally

[34] *Ibid.*
[35] *Supra* note 2, p. 156.

suspended imprisonment (from 55.4 per cent in 2014 to 28.2 per cent in 2016, 22.7 per cent in 2017 and 19.8 per cent in 2018). It remains to be seen in the upcoming years if new trends can be perceived as a success of the whole amendment and whether an intended effect is achievable. It is expected that the share of the fine in the structure of imposed sentences should constitute at least 60 per cent, whereby the self-existent fine should be an alternative not only for imprisonment of up to five years, but also of up to eight years.[36]

This goal still seems far off, especially in view of the intensity of the amounts of the imposed fines. The data in Table 14.2 (the published statistical materials, unfortunately, determines the sentence of the fine by the amount) shows that amounts are still within the lower limit. In the period of the analysed sixteen years the share of fines in the lower amount (100–500 PLN) decreased from 41.2 per cent in 2002 to 7.4 per cent in 2017 and in the second level (501–1,000 PLN) – from 43.7 per cent in 2002 to 31.9 per cent in 2017, while the share of the fines in the third level (1,001–2,000 PLN) increased from 11.6 per cent in 2002 to 35.1 per cent in 2017 and in the last level (2,001 and more PLN) from 3.6 per cent in 2002 to 20.1 per cent in 2017. In addition to the above, in the last group only 5,873 from 21,668 imposed fines exceeded the amount of PLN 5,000. The trend is upwards-moving, but the growth rate is much too low to replace more repressive sanctions. After all, the amount of fines imposed is relatively low, especially in comparison to the average national salary (4,271.51 PLN in 2017 and 4,585.03 PLN in 2018).

Unofficial statistical data for 2018 confirms above observations. In 2018, the day fines in the range of 10–20 PLN represented 83 per cent of all imposed fines (Figure 14.2). At the same time, fines in the amount of 200 daily units and more constituted only 4 per cent (Figure 14.1).

It is important to raise another matter. Namely, as mentioned above, after the amendment of 2015 the fine was supposed to be the basic penal reaction. Again, it should be underlined that the scope of applicability of the fine is currently very wide. However, in judicial practice these possibilities are not fully utilised. Analysis of the available data provided by the Ministry of Justice shows that nearly half of the imposed fines are adjudicated for only a few crimes – against safety in traffic (especially for aforementioned Article 178(a) CC).[37] The rest of the sentences imposing the fine concerns a narrow scope of the crimes, especially against property (in this area mainly Article

---

[36] *Supra* note 2, p. 162.
[37] Szymanowski, 'Orzecznictwo w sprawach karnych w Polsce w świetle statystyki sądowej za rok 1997 oraz lata 1999–2001', 23; Małecki and Tabora, 'Wymiar kary za popełnienie przestępstwa przeciwko bezpieczeństwu w komunikacji po najnowszych nowelizacjach Kodeksu karnego', 5–33.

TABLE 14.2 *Size of the fines imposed in the years 2002–17 by the amount*

Year	Total Absolute number	%	100 – 500 PLN Absolute number	%	501 – 1000 PLN Absolute number	%	1001 – 2000 PLN Absolute number	%	2001 and more PLN Absolute number	%
2002	75,698	100.0	31,156	41.2	33,049	43.7	8,801	11.6	2,692	3.6
2003	93,274	100.0	38,172	40.9	40,356	43.3	11,337	12.2	3,409	3.7
2004	111,491	100.0	42,201	37.9	50,258	45.1	14,467	13.0	4,565	4.1
2005	100,968	100.0	36,900	36.5	46,434	46.0	13,367	13.2	4,267	4.2
2006	88,407	100.0	26,962	30.5	41,801	47.3	14,793	16.7	4,851	5.5
2007	82,988	100.0	18,311	22.1	38,316	46.2	19,638	23.7	6,723	8.1
2008	89,011	100.0	18,947	21.3	41,659	46.8	21,414	24.1	6,991	7.8
2009	88,236	100.0	17,530	19.9	41,116	46.6	22,381	25.4	7,209	8.2
2010	92,329	100.0	16,996	18.4	42,782	46.3	23,713	25.7	8,838	9.6
2011	93,571	100.0	16,999	18.2	43,505	46.5	24,324	26.0	8,743	9.3
2012	91,296	100.0	16,243	17.8	41,951	46.0	23,940	26.2	9,162	19.0
2013	76,759	100.0	12,075	15.7	33,453	43.6	21,276	27.7	9,955	13.0
2014	63,078	100.0	7,367	11.7	24,307	38.5	19,834	31.4	11,571	18.3
2015	61,461	100.0	6,613	10.8	23,010	37.4	19,433	31.6	12,330	20.1
2016	98,776	100.0	9,101	9.2	36,220	36.7	33,141	33.6	20,230	20.5
2017	84,721	100.0	6,237	7.4	27,019	31.9	29,720	35.1	21,668	25.6

Source: Statistical data collected by the Ministry of Justice and compiled by the authors

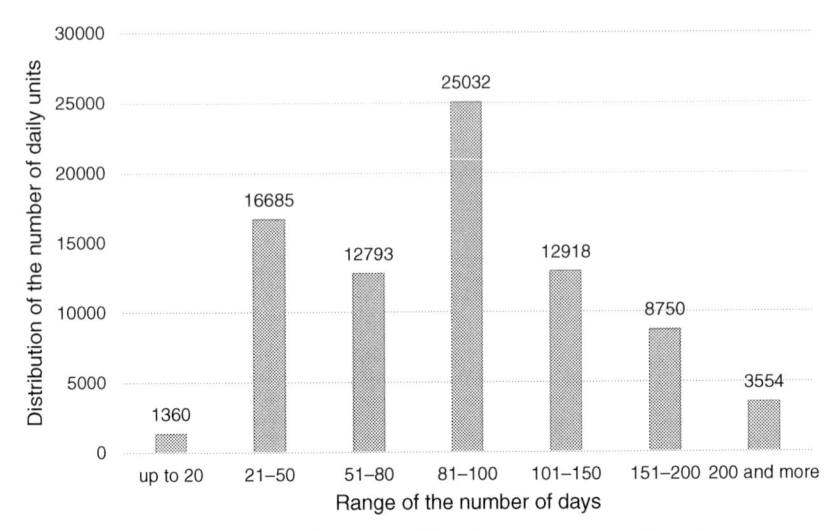

FIGURE 14.1 Day fines in 2018 by the number of daily units
Source: Non-official statistical data collected by the Ministry of Justice
and complied by the authors

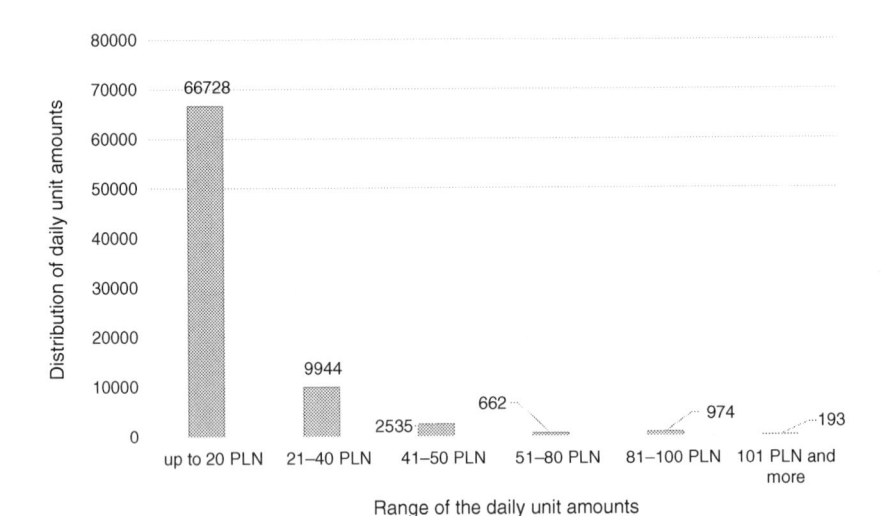

FIGURE 14.2 Day fines in 2018 by daily units
Source: Non-official statistical data collected by the Ministry of Justice
and complied by the authors

278 (1) CC – theft and Article 286 (1) CC – fraud), economic activity, the
credibility of the documents and drug crimes (especially personal drug
possession). Nevertheless, for fiscal crimes imposing the fine is the rule

(slightly over 90 per cent of the total imposed sanctions). In comparison to before the amendment of 2015, the extent of the categories of offences for which day fines were imposed has practically not grown. Bearing in mind Article 37(a) CC, there are a lot of crimes which are never or hardly ever punished in this way.

Summarising, Poland is still aiming at disseminating and rendering day fines as the basic penal reaction. As mentioned above, directly after the adoption of day fines in the Polish criminal system the desired objectives were not reached. Hence it became necessary to make significant amendments to the Criminal Code (amendment of 2015). The coming years will therefore be decisive in demonstrating whether the aforementioned amendment will bring the expected results in the structure of imposed sentences. The first two full years since the date of entry into force provide a good prediction. However, it seems that if this is to happen, the intensity of the amount of imposed fines should increase, and justice practitioners should more thoroughly analyse the perpetrator's financial situation as well. At the same time, it must be mentioned that in Poland the problem with the collection of fines is not significant, which does not mean that there are no problems. Before the amendment of 2015 the index of enforceability was considered on a satisfactory level and the enforcement system was considered to operate efficiently. That led the legislator to the above-mentioned decision to repeal Article 58 (2) CC, which included the directive banning the imposition of an unenforceable fine.[38] The specificity of the model of the execution of the fine means that the enforcement proceedings usually take place in multiple stages. In most cases, the fine is enforced or just voluntarily paid, not uncommon after dividing the fine into instalments. Penal forms (conversion of the fine into imprisonment or community service) are used much less frequently. Remission represents only a very limited percentage. The exceptional character, which, according to the law, this institution has, is fully visible in the practice of the fine.[39]

In the literature, however, it is noticed that still too many sentenced persons serve a substitute imprisonment for a converted fine instead of paying a fine.[40] In 2013, 4,414 convicted persons served a substitute imprisonment for a fixed fine (which is approximately 5 per cent of persons yearly sentenced to this punishment) and 9,479 persons, which were sentenced to a cumulative fine.[41]

---

[38] *Supra* note 11, 'Uzasadnienie rządowego projektu', pp. 138–42.
[39] *Supra* note 22, pp. 117–29.
[40] In 1997 approximately 16 per cent self-existent fines and 24 per cent cumulative fines were converted to substitute imprisonment – see Szumski, 'Kara zastępcza za nieuiszczoną grzywnę (w świetle ustawodawstwa i praktyki sądowej)', 48.
[41] Małolepszy, 'Model wykonywania kary grzywny w polskim prawie karnym', pp. 118–19.

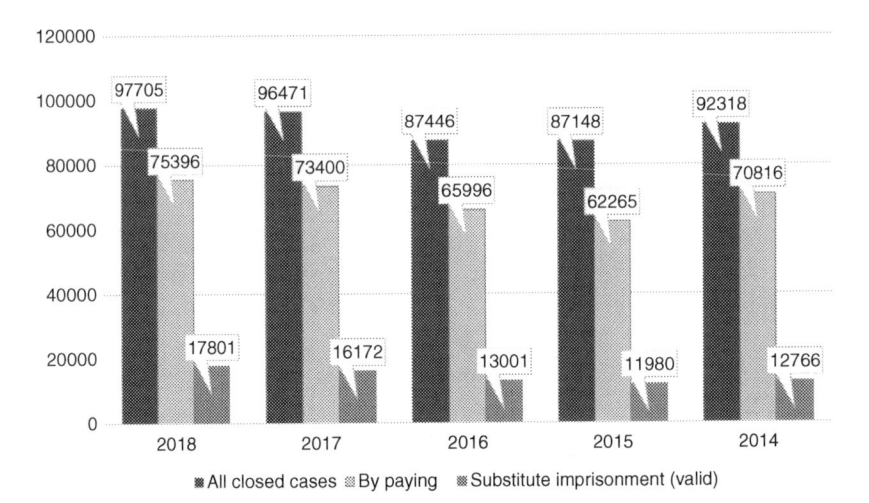

FIGURE 14.3 Enforcement of the fine – closed cases in the years 2014–18
Source: Non-official statistical data collected by Ministry of Justice and complied
by the authors

As shown in Figure 14.3, between 2014 and 2018, every year approximately 15 per cent of autonomous fines were converted to substitute imprisonment and the trend is still upwards (13.7 per cent in 2015, 14.9 per cent in 2016, 16.7 per cent in 2017 and 18.2 per cent in 2018). Therefore, a reform of the fine execution system is proposed. Also due to the inevitable increase of the number of substitute imprisonment fines it is important to evaluate what will be consequence of the increase in the total number of fines in relation to other penalties imposed.

After the repeal of Article 58 (2) CC, there are no formal obstacles any more to impose the fine on a person who has no assets. In the justification for the amendment of 2015 the necessity to separate the decision on imposing a fine from the assessment of the financial and economic situation of the perpetrator was emphasised, so that it can be imposed when, pursuant to Article 58 (1) CC, the court comes to the conclusion that it will be an adequate penalty in a given case.[42] Hence, the conclusion that the perpetrator has no assets affects only the rate, not the admissibility of imposing the fine. However, in such a situation, it is only possible to set a single rate at 10 PLN.[43] If later the fine cannot be collected even by enforcement, it shall be

[42] *Supra* note 11, 'Uzasadnienie rządowego projektu', p. 141.
[43] Górowski, 'Orzekanie kary grzywny po 1 lipca 2015 r.', 68.

converted into a substitute community service or imprisonment (Articles 45–8 CEC).

The above-mentioned rules also apply to recipients of social assistance benefits. There are no specific formal indications for such cases. The fine cannot be excluded due to the mere fact that the perpetrator receives one of the most common welfare benefits, such as family benefits (especially the benefit for bringing up a child, the so-called '500+' in the amount of monthly 500 PLN per child), disability benefits (inter alia disability pension – in 2021 minimum 250 PLN monthly), unemployment benefits (in 2021 1,200 PLN in the first three months and 942.30 PLN from the fourth month onwards) or social assistance benefits (in cash – average a few hundred PLN – or in kind) for persons and families whose income does not exceed the income criterion (in 2021 701 PLN monthly for a single person and 528 PLN monthly per person in the family). It appears that in practice the fact that the perpetrator is entitled to social benefits is taken into consideration at the rate assessment stage, with regard to the extent to which the fine will have a negative impact on the perpetrator's family.

14.4 THE PUBLIC PERCEPTION OF DAY FINES

The fine imposed in the system of daily units does not raise specific controversies in Polish society. Information on convictions in the media mostly indicates only general the amount of the fine, without differentiating between number of units and the amount of one unit. However, it should be noted that in view of the current strong populist tendencies in Poland, which affect the shape of the criminal law and its perception in society, one can observe the concentration of the public attention on imprisonment as the only means of combating crime. The advantages of fines as a means of reaction to petty and medium crime are virtually unnoticed.

On the other hand, both scientists and practitioners generally positively assess the system of day fines, because it allows the individualisation of the fine to be paid in relation to the severity of the crime and the payment possibilities for the sentenced person.[44]

It should also be noted that in Poland currently a fundamental review of the criminal law has been started. A proposal for a law from the Ministry of Justice has been drafted to amend the Criminal Code and is to be examined

---

[44] *Supra* note 2, p. 117; *supra* note 19, p. 687; Hryniewicz-Lach, in *Kodeks karny. Część ogólna. Komentarz*, p. 603.

by the Constitutional Court after the president's decision.[45] The amendment's ratio, as it is stated in the justification of the draft law, is to tighten penal repression, which is in line with a remarkable trend of an increasing punitivity and deterrence level that can be observed in Poland for some time now. From the perspective of this report, special importance gains the wording of the proposed Article 33 (1)(a) CC. The mentioned proposal, by determining the lower limit of the number of daily units depending on the statutory threat of the imprisonment for a given offence, which is punishable with both a fine and imprisonment (minimum 50 units in case of an offence carrying imprisonment up to one year and accordingly: minimum 100 units – up to two years, minimum 200 units – up to three years and minimum 300 units – over three years), in fact significantly raises the lower limit of the fine.

REFERENCES

Błachut, J. 2007. 'Wpływ wprowadzenia Article 178a k.k. na obraz zjawiska przestępczości i prawnokarnej reakcji na nią', in Błachut, J. (ed.), *Nauki penalne wobec problemów współczesnej przestępczości. Księga jubileuszowa z okazji 70. rocznicy urodzin Profesora Andrzeja Gaberle*. Warsaw: Wolters Kluwer.

Cieślak, M. 1988. 'Zagadnienia reformy prawa karnego', *Palestra* 5: 42–64.

Dadak, W. 2011. *Grzywna samoistna w stawkach dziennych*. Warsaw: LexisNexis Poland.

Dudek, P. M. 2014. 'Inflacja pieniądza a prawo karne', *Państwo i Prawo* 10: 68–84.

Grebing, G. and Spotowski, A. 1982. 'Kara grzywny według systemu stawek dziennych w prawie karnym RFN', *Nowe Prawo* 3–4: 166–76.

Górowski, W. 2015. 'Orzekanie kary grzywny po 1 lipca 2015 r.', *Palestra* 7–8: 65–75.

Grześkowiak, A. *et al.*, 2016. 'Kara grzywny', in Melezini, M. (ed.), *System prawa karnego: Kary i inne środki reakcji prawnokarnej*. Warsaw: C.H. Beck.

Horvat, T. 1979. 'Nowy węgierski kodeks karny', *Państwo i Prawo* 12: 93–98.

Hryniewicz-Lach, E. 2017. in Królikowski, M. and Zawłocki, R. (eds.), *Kodeks karny. Część ogólna. Komentarz*. Warsaw: C.H. Beck.

Journal of Law of 1997 No. 88, item 554.

Journal of Law of 2009 No. 206, item 1589.

Journal of Law of 2015, item 396.

Journal of Law of 2018, item 1958.

Journal of Law of 2018, item 1987.

Journal of Law of 2019, item 628.

Journal of Law of 2019, item 676.

Kolasiński, B. 1993. 'Kara grzywny w kodeksie karnym', *Prokuratura i Prawo* 3: 13–33.

Kunicka-Michalska, B. 1988. 'Grzywna na miarę kieszeni', *Gazeta Prawnicza* 5: 7.

---

[45]   See 'Projekt ustawy o zmianie ustawy – Kodeks karny oraz niektórych innych ustaw z 14 V 2019 r., druk sejmowy 3451', www.sejm.gov.pl/sejm8.nsf/druk.xsp?nr=3451.

Marek, A. 2003. 'Problemy regulacji prawnej i orzekania kary grzywny', *Państwo i Prawo* 2: 13–24.

Majewski, J. 1994. 'Grzywna w projekcie nowego kodeksu karnego', *Przegląd Sądowy* 11–12: 74–91.

Majewski, J. 2016. in Wróbel, W. and Zoll, A. (eds.), *Kodeks karny. Część ogólna. Komentarz.* Warsaw: Wolters Kluwer.

Małecki, M. 2015. 'Ustawowe zagrożenie karą i sądowy wymiar kary', in Wróbel, W. (ed.), *Nowelizacja prawa karnego 2015: komentarz.* Cracow: Krakowski Instytut Prawa Karnego.

Małecki, M. and Tabora, P. 2017. 'Wymiar kary za popełnienie przestępstwa przeciwko bezpieczeństwu w komunikacji po najnowszych nowelizacjach Kodeksu karnego', *Paragraf na drodze* 3: 5–33.

Małolepszy, M. 2014. *Pomocniczy model wykonywania samoistnej kary pozbawienia wolności.* Poznań: Wydawnictwo Nauka i Innowacje.

Małolepszy, M. 2015. 'Model wykonywania kary grzywny w polskim prawie karnym', in Małolepszy, M. (ed.), *Reforma systemu sankcji w Niemczech, Austrii i Polsce.* Warsaw: C.H. Beck.

Marek, A. 1988. 'Co to znaczy postępowe i nowoczesne', *Gazeta Prawnicza* 8: 5.

Melezini, M. 1982. 'Czy system stawek dziennych przy wymiarze grzywny', *Nowe Prawo* 3–4: 116–19.

Melezini, M. 1993. 'W sprawie reformy kary grzywny', *Przegląd Prawa Karnego* 9: 15–29.

Melezini, M. 1998. 'System wymiaru grzywien w nowym Kodeksie karnym', *Monitor Prawniczy* 3: 89–92.

Słu goclki, L. 1984. *Kara grzywny samoistnej i jej wykonanie.* Warsaw: Wydawnictwo Prawnicze.

Spotowski, A. 1981. 'Grzywna dzienna', *Gazeta Prawnicza* 15–16: 11.

Szumski, J. 1991. 'O celowości recepcji systemu grzywien stawek dziennych', *Państwo i Prawo* 2: 72–9.

Szumski, J. 1979. 'Grzywna dniówkowa', *Gazeta Prawnicza* 16: 10.

Szumski, J. 2000. 'Kara zastępcza za nieuiszczoną grzywnę (w świetle ustawodawstwa i praktyki sądowej)', *Państwo i Prawo* 11: 39–53.

Szymanowski, T. 2002. 'Orzecznictwo w sprawach karnych w Polsce w świetle statystyki sądowej za rok 1997 oraz lata 1999-2001', *Państwo i Prawo* 10: 21–36.

Thornsted, H. 1975. 'System grzywien dniówkowych w Szwecji', *Przestępczość na świecie* 5: 61.

Wojciechowska, J. 1981. 'O grzywnie w ujęciu austriackiego kodeksu karnego', *Państwo i Prawo* 8: 108–14.

Zoll, A. 1998. 'Założenia polityczno-kryminalne kodeksu karnego w świetle wyzwań współczesności', *Państwo i Prawo* 9–10: 40–50.

Zoll, A. 2013. 'Komisja Kodyfikacyjna Prawa Karnego wobec problemów związanych z represją karnoprawną', in Utrat-Milecki, J. (ed.), *Reforma prawa karnego: W stronę spójności i skuteczności.* Warsaw: Oficyna Naukowa.

15

Day Fines in Croatia

Maja Munivrana Vajda[*]

15.1 HISTORICAL DEVELOPMENT OF DAY FINES IN CROATIA

Like in many other countries, in Croatia fine as a punishment has a long tradition. Its written roots may be traced to old medieval statutes of Croatian towns.[1] Throughout the Middle Ages fines were fixed and with many features which are considered obsolete today.[2] The more modern forms of fines can be found in French and Austrian Criminal Codes of the nineteenth century, which were in force in this region during the nineteenth and the first three decades of the twentieth century.[3] In the former Yugoslavia fines continued to play an important role.[4] The 1976 Criminal Code, as the last federal Code enacted before the dissolution of Yugoslavia, prescribed fixed fines.[5] In the late 1970s and in the 1980s the fine was the second most frequently pronounced punishment in Croatia, imposed in approximately one third of all the cases.[6] In 1989, two years before Croatia declared independence, the share of fines reached 36.6 per cent.[7]

During the first few years of independence, the fine as a criminal punishment was governed by Articles 36 and 37 of the Basic Criminal Code of the

---

[*] This chapter was written as a part of the institutional scientific project 'New Croatian Legal System' at the Faculty of Law in Zagreb (for the year 2019).

[1] See, e.g. Radić, 'Zatvor u srednjovjekovnom trogirskom pravu', 88–9, who describes the Statute of the city of Trogir from 1322, in which a fine played a prominent role.

[2] For example, fines were prescribed in casuistic manner and their application depended on the social status of the defendant. *Ibid.*, pp. 88–9.

[3] Horvatić, Derenčinović and Cvitanović, *Kazneno pravo. Opći dio 1. Kazneno pravo i kazneni zakon*, p. 91.

[4] Croatia was a part of SFR Yugoslavia since 1945 until 1991, when Croatia declared independence. More about the legislative history and different Criminal Codes in force during this time frame in Horvatić and Derenčinović, *Criminal Justice Systems in Europe and North America*, p. 8.

[5] See Article 39 of the Criminal Code of the SFRJ, Official Gazette 44/76.

[6] The most frequent was suspended imprisonment with the share of slightly below 50 per cent. See Bedrač, 'Statistkički prikaz izbora vrste i mjere kazne u Republici Hrvatskoj', 925.

[7] Novoselec, 'Sustav dani-novčana kazna i njegova primjena u hrvatskom kaznenom pravu', 80.

Republic of Croatia (hereinafter: BCCRC). This was essentially the old federal Yugoslav Criminal Code, which was taken over by an act of Parliament as Croatian law, with only minor adjustments.[8] According to this law, fines were to be imposed in the amount ranging from 5,000.00 HRD to 2,000,000.00 HRD for ordinary offences whereas offences committed out of greed could have been punished more severely, up to 5,000,000.00 HRD.[9] While fines remained fixed, thus in essence not individualised in a way modern day fines are, when determining the exact amount of the fixed fine the judges were explicitly obliged to take into account the perpetrator's wealth, including his or her income, property and family obligations.[10] An unpaid fine was to be forcibly collected and, failing that, converted to imprisonment.[11]

Even though the structure of the fine and its essential features remained the same in Croatia as in the former Yugoslavia, its share in the overall age of criminal sanctions started to decrease significantly. While in 1989 a fine was pronounced in as much as 36.6 per cent of all the cases of convicted adults, already in 1991 the share of fines fell to 27.1 per cent and in 1997 it was only 16.8 per cent, with a steady decrease in between.[12] In part the decrease can surely be ascribed to the poor economic condition during the conflict and in its immediate aftermath.[13] In addition, it may be assumed that during this time frame, in which Croatian authorities faced considerable difficulties in prosecution of criminal offences, arising out of occupation of a substantial part of Croatian territory, the focus was on prosecuting more serious offences punishable only by imprisonment and not by fines, such as war crimes. Finally, the early 1990s have been characterised by a huge devaluation of money, with a yearly inflation rate of around 1,000 per cent,[14] quickly rendering the

---

[8] Official Gazette 53/91, 39/92 and 91/92, 31/93, 35/93, 108/95, 16/96, 28/96. The Amendments Form 1992, for example, introduced the new Croatian currency (Hrvatski dinar, hereinafter: HRD, Eng. Croatian dinar), instead of the old Yugoslav dinar and changed the minimum and maximum amount.

[9] It is extremely difficult to convert this amount to today's currency, in part due to extremely high inflation rates. Roughly, on 1 January 1992, 5,000.00 HRD amounted to what would constitute 45 euros today and 2,000,000.00 HRD would amount 17,937 euros. On 30 May 1994, the day when the new currency – hrvatska kuna (hereinafter: HRK) – was introduced, 5,000.00 HRD constituted less than a euro, i.e. 0.7 euros and 2,000,000.00 HRD only 279 euros. See www.kunalipa.com/katalog/povijest/hrvatski-dinar-4.php.

[10] See Article 37 (3) BCCRC.

[11] Every started 10,000.00 HRD were replaced by one day of imprisonment, Article 36 (3) BCCRC.

[12] These figures include both the unsuspended and suspended fine, with the latter rather weakly represented in the 1990s, with approximately 1 per cent. Bedrač, 'Statistički prikaz', 932–3.

[13] *Supra* note 7, 80.

[14] E.g. according to the inflation calculator of the Croatian Bureau of Statistics, from January 1992 to January 1993, the inflation rate was 1,078 per cent, www.dzs.hr/app/rss/stopa-inflacije.html.

execution of any fixed fine meaningless. All of this contributed to a general reluctance of Croatian judges towards imposing a fine as a punishment.

It was against this background that significant novelties in regulation of fines were introduced. In 1997, the entirely new Criminal Code was enacted.[15] This Code brought the concept of day fines to Croatia.[16] According to Article 51 (1) a fine was to be prescribed and imposed according to the daily income of the convicted person. The minimum number of daily incomes was set at 10 and the maximum at 300, with the exception of offences committed out of greed, for which the maximum fine was 500 daily incomes (Article 51 (2) CC97). The main reason behind the introduction of day fines, as stated in the explanatory report, was to harmonise the Croatian regulation of fines with the modern legal systems.[17] Other reasons given by Croatian scholars in support of the day fine system can be boiled down to perceived unfairness of the system of fixed fines and the desire to individualise the punishment of fines to correspond more closely to the actual (pecuniary) circumstances of each defendant.[18] Finally, one of the motives was the aspiration to affirm the fine as a punishment in Croatia and make its use more frequent, thus approximating the share of pronounced fines in Croatia to the high percentage of fines in some other European countries.[19] While at first glance it may seem that this goal was achieved since very quickly the percentage of fines rose (from 10 per cent in 1998, to 16.5 in 2000, reaching its peak of 19.6 per cent in 2002), a more nuanced view, taking into account statistical reports over the span of more than ten years, reveals that the percentage of pronounced fines soon started to decline again. In 2012, the year preceding the entry into force of the entirely new Criminal Code (hereinafter CC2011),[20] which significantly amended the legal framework of day fines as will be described in the next chapter, after several years of gradual decline the percentage of unsuspended fines reached the lowest point in the past thirty years.

---

[15] Hereinafter CC97. This Code is often labelled as the first Croatian Criminal Code, since the earlier Code was taken over from the old State. Official Gazette 110/97, 27/98, 50/00, 129/00, 51/01, 111/03, 190/03, 105/04, 84/05, 71/06, 110/07, 152/08, 57/11, 143/12. It entered into force on 1 January 1998.

[16] It is important to emphasise that the concept of day fines was introduced only for criminal offences whereas for misdemeanours (administrative offences) fines remained fixed.

[17] Horvatić, *Novo hrvatsko kazneno pravo*, pp. 116, 129.

[18] Voices in favour of the day fine system have been raised by some Croatian scholars even before the break-up of Yugoslavia, e.g. by Šeparović in 1988 according to Novoselec, *supra* note 7, 83. See also Bačić, *Krivično pravo, opći dio*, p. 464.

[19] *Supra* note 17, pp. 116–29.

[20] Official Gazette 125/11, 144/2012, 56/2015, 61/2015, 101/17 and 118/18. The so-called *vacatio legis* period between the enactment of the new law and its entry into force was much longer than the usual eight days – it lasted over a year – in order to enable the judiciary, practitioners and the general public to become familiar with the extensive changes to Croatian criminal law.

TABLE 15.1 *Percentage of unsuspended punishments 1998–2012*

Year	1998	2000	2002	2004	2006	2008	2010	2012
Unsuspended Prison	13.5	13	11.8	11.5	15.5	18.1	19.7	19.5
Unsuspended Fine	10.5	16.5	19.6	14.6	11.6	8.9	6.3	4.1

Source: own table based on a comparison of various sources, including Bedrač, 'Statistički prikaz', 925, 932–3; Kurtović Mišić, Milivojević and Strinić, 'Novosti u propisivanju, izricanju i izvršenju novčane kazne', 656 and data gathered from the Croatian Bureau of Statistics, www.dzs.hr.

An explanation can probably be found in socio-economic reasons and low standard of living of Croatian citizens as well as in the negative attitude of judges towards this type of punishment, which was shaped in the early 1990s in a period of huge inflation.[21] Another explanation perhaps lies in the complexity of the day fine system, which requires judges to undertake several steps and determine not just the number of daily incomes, but also the amount of the perpetrator's (daily) income.[22] In order to avoid these steps, it seems that the judges were more inclined to impose suspended imprisonment instead of fines whenever they thought that the purpose of punishment did not require sending the perpetrator to prison.[23] Finally, the low percentage of fines can possibly be explained by the imprecise wording and in general poorly conceived provisions regulating fines as a criminal punishment. The law itself did not define the notion of the daily income. Hence, it remained unclear if the judges should rely on gross or only net income, as well as if they should take into account only taxable income or other receipts not considered income according to the Income Tax Act (welfare benefits, family and disability pensions, etc.).[24]

[21] Kurtović Mišić, 'Novosti', 656.
[22] It is interesting to mention that already in 1879 it was discussed if the judges should be forced to examine and determine pecuniary circumstances of the offender when determining the amount of the (fixed) fine. See Derenčin, *Osnova novoga Kaznenoga zakona o zločinstvih i prestupcih za Kraljevine Hrvatsku i Slavoniju 1879*, p. 196. Derenčin himself was against it as he thought that such determination would not necessarily correspond to the truth. He also argued that a fine should correspond to culpability of the offender and that grounding it on the wealth of the perpetrator instead would deprive it of its essence as a punishment.
[23] During the same time frame the percentage of suspended prison sentences continuously grew and reached 74 per cent in 2012 (Croatian Bureau of Statistics, Adult Perpetrators of Criminal Offences by Type of Decision, 2012, www.dzs.hr).
[24] More on different possible interpretations of the word 'income' in Grozdanić, 'Kazne – nova rješenja u Kaznenom zakonu i njihova provedba u sudskoj praksi', 340–1.

These dilemmas have been solved indirectly by the Supreme Court – a body in charge of determining the average income in Croatia as a subsidiary unit of a fine,[25] in three cases described below. In doing so, the Supreme Court based its determination on the average monthly net income (average net salary in Croatia) – after calculating and deducting taxes and personal exemptions – divided by thirty.[26] The possibility to rely on the average daily income in the Republic of Croatia in order to calculate the fine was provided for by the Criminal Code itself. According to Article 51 (4) CC97 the courts were able to rely on the average daily income in Croatia instead of the daily income of the perpetrator, (a) when the perpetrator did not have any income;[27] (b) when determination of income would considerably prolong criminal proceedings; and (c) whenever a penal order was issued, based on credible information in the criminal complaint, without conducting a trial.[28] Although reliance on average daily income should have been an exception, as stated clearly in the explanatory material,[29] it can safely be said that the exception became a rule, turning the logic of day fines upside down. Reliance on the average daily income was neither fair in the cases of perpetrators without any income nor in the cases in which perpetrators had income, but its determination would have been complex and would have taken too long (e.g. because it was coming from various sources). The former scenario led to perpetrators being sanctioned more severely than they should have been, whereas the latter levelled wealthy perpetrators with those who had no income, which was equally unjust. Nevertheless, the research shows that in more than 50 per cent of all the cases in which fines were imposed judges relied on the average daily income in Croatia.[30] Finally, even when the judges did try to determine the real income of the perpetrator, the primary source of

---

[25] This was to be done on the basis of the official data of the State Bureau of Statistics every three months (Article 51 (6) CC97).

[26] This probably served as a guidance to lower courts, which took the same approach when determining the daily income of an individual perpetrator. *Supra* note 24, p. 341.

[27] In such cases, if the perpetrator was the owner of a property or property rights, the courts had to determine the daily income by a free estimate in accordance with the value of such property or property right (Article 51 (5) CC97). This provision was heavily criticised in Croatian literature for it is the income from property that should be the basis for a free estimate and not the value of the property as such. See *supra* note 7, 87.

[28] This possibility is open for the offences punishable by fines or imprisonment of up to five years. If a person convicted on the bases of a penal order complains, a regular trial is carried out. See Article 540 *et seq.* of the Criminal Procedure Act (hereinafter: CPA), Official Gazette 152/08, 76/09, 80/11, 121/11, 91/12, 143/12, 56/13, 145/13, 152/14, 70/17.

[29] *Supra* note 17, p. 250.

[30] Comp. Svedrović, 'Kriminalnopolitička opravdanost promjena kaznenih sankcija s osvrtom na uvođenje doživotnog zatvora i na sustav izricanja kazne', 389; *supra* note 24, 68.

information remained the convicted person and his or her account of received salary, without courts engaging into any real, detailed inquiry.[31]

All of this led some scholars to label the practical implementation of fines in Croatia as a negation of the day fine system.[32] Even though, nominally, the fine was composed as a day fine, due to reliance on the average Croatian income in reality not much has changed from the days in which the law prescribed fixed fines. Hence, it is not surprising that the new CC2011, among many other changes it introduced to the Croatian criminal justice system, significantly amended the legal framework of day fines – including by abolishing reliance on average daily income.

15.2 THE STRUCTURE OF THE FINE

Before explaining in detail the current legal framework of day fines, it is important to mention that despite the changes, the essence of the fine as a punishment remained untouched by the CC2011. This means foremost that the (day) fine remained one of the two principal punishments, alongside imprisonment, applicable to adult perpetrators of criminal offences only. A *contrario*, a fine is not a punishment for juvenile perpetrators of criminal offences,[33] and day fines can neither be imposed on legal entities nor on perpetrators of administrative offences (misdemeanours).[34] Furthermore, it

---

[31] The convicted person would simply state his or her monthly salary. Theoretically, it was also possible to require information from the employer as well as to calculate the daily income based on the yearly tax return submitted to Tax Administration, but this was not often done in practice; see *supra* note 24, 341–2. Furthermore, the courts usually did not take into account any other possible sources of income beside salary, even in situations in which it was clear that the perpetrator was a wealthy person, with various sources of income or/and lots of property. *Supra* note 7, 84.

[32] *Supra* note 7, 85. See also Turković, Novoselec, Grozdanić, Mišić, Derenčinović, Bojanić, Munivrana Vajda, Mrčela, Nola, Roksandić Vidlička, Tripalo and Maršavelski, *Komentar Kaznenog zakona*, p. 62.

[33] The only punishment, which can be imposed only exceptionally, is juvenile imprisonment and the main sanctions for juveniles are educational (correctional) measures. See Article 5 of the Juvenile Courts Act, Official Gazette 84/11, 143/12, 148/13, 56/15.

[34] In those cases, fines are applicable as fixed fines only. See Article 10 of the Act on Criminal Responsibility of Legal Persons, Official Gazette No. 151/03, 110/07, 45/11, 143/12 and Article 33 of the Misdemeanor Act, Official Gazette no. 107/07, 39/13, 157/13, 110/15, 70/17, 118/18. With respect to inapplicability of day fines to legal entities, the legislator gave only the following brief explanation: 'Monetary fine prescribed for legal entities must be different from the fine prescribed for natural persons; not only must it be higher for legal entities than for natural persons, but the daily income system provided for in the Criminal Code is also inapplicable to legal persons'. See the Explanatory Report from December 2002, vlada.gov.hr/UserDocsImages//2016/Sjednice/Arhiva//49022.%20-%201.pdf.

is important to clarify more generally that whereas imprisonment may be imposed only as the principal punishment, fines in Croatia traditionally may be pronounced both as the main (stand-alone) punishment – for all the offences for which the law prescribes a punishment of imprisonment of up to three years – and as ancillary punishment, together with imprisonment, for all the offences committed out of greed.[35] In those cases, when fine is an ancillary punishment, it is also pronounced and imposed as a day fine.[36] The rationale behind the decision to hold onto the system of day fines, despite apparent difficulties with its implementation, was the belief that the day fine system has proven to be the best contemporary model of determination of the fine, with the potential to 'adjust this pecuniary punishment to the pecuniary circumstances of the offender, so to equally affect a wealthy and a poor perpetrator'.[37]

15.2.1 *The Number of Days*

The new law increased both the minimum and the maximum number of days. According to Article 42 (1), the number of days should not be lower than 30 or higher than 360 daily units. The new CC2011 also kept the distinction for offences committed out of greed.[38] These offences, as well as those for which such punishment is expressly prescribed,[39] can be punished with a higher fine of up to 500 daily units. The law explicitly obliges judges to determine the number of days on the basis of circumstances guiding the determination of punishment, with the exception of those relating to the pecuniary circumstances of the perpetrator,[40] and to specify this number in the judgment

---

[35] In those cases, the fine is not prescribed by law or the law prescribes that the perpetrator is to be punished by imprisonment or by a fine, but the court pronounces imprisonment as the main punishment (Article 40 CC2011).

[36] In Croatian literature ancillary fines were recently heavily criticised due to the fact that in such cases the fine loses its nature of punishment alternative to imprisonment. Furthermore, one of the rationales of fine – that the perpetrator does not lose his or her job, is not applicable here. Finally, it is unclear how the convicted person can earn to personally pay the fine if he or she goes to prison. See Dragičević Prtenjača, 'Sporedna novčana kazna u hrvatskom kazne-nom pravu i praksi', 59–92 and Novoselec, 'Sudska Praksa: Visina dnevnog iznosa. Sporedna novčana kazna', 717–21.

[37] *Supra* note 32, *Komentar*, p. 61.

[38] This distinction can be traced back to the nineteenth century. See *supra* note 22, p. 196.

[39] The only such offence in the CC2011 today is international public defamation (Article 149).

[40] According to Article 47 of the CC2011, when determining the type and range of punishment, the court shall, starting from the degree of culpability and the purpose of punishment, assess all the circumstances affecting the severity of punishment by type and range (mitigating and aggravating circumstances).

(Article 42 (2) and (3) CC2011). Case law reveals that in reality the number of days is in general very low, on average in the lower third of the prescribed sentencing frame.[41] However, this practice only fits the more general sentencing practices of Croatian courts. In one of his recent reports, the Chief State Attorney warned about the very lenient overall sentencing policies in Croatia.[42] Research shows that the majority of all punishments in Croatia are pronounced in the lower third of the sentencing frame, or even below the statutory minimum.[43]

15.2.2 *The Daily Unit*

The most significant novelties in regulation of fine concern the concept of the daily unit. The legislator has obviously taken into account some of the scholarly criticism sketched above and reshaped the daily unit. First of all, although this may seem insignificant at first glance, the CC2011 changed the terminology from former 'daily income', the term originally belonging to tax law, to a specific new term 'daily unit' (or 'daily amount', Croat. *dnevni iznos*). Already by doing that the legislator indicated that the term should be interpreted autonomously in the context of criminal law, that is, determination of fine. This is further clearly stated in Article 42(4) CC2011, which specifies that the amount of the daily unit should be determined by taking into consideration not just the perpetrator's income, but also his or her property as well as the average costs necessary for supporting the perpetrator and his or her family.

The explanatory report clarifies that income should be taken in a broad sense – to include income from employment and self-employment, income from property and property rights (renting property, lease, share holds, dividends, interests), but even pocket-money, receipts from non-employment, social welfare, income in goods and, furthermore, potential income that the person failed to earn due to unjustifiable resignation.[44] From this explanation it is clear that property can serve as a source of income, which is why it is questionable whether property should have been mentioned separately in Article 42 (4) CC2011.[45] The intention of the legislator was not to let the

---

[41] *Supra* note 21, 663.

[42] State Attorney Report for 2016, A-561/16, Zagreb, April 2017, p. 47, repeated in Report for 2017, A-643/17, published on 23 April 2018.

[43] This is the conclusion of the annual conference of the Croatian Association for Penal Law in 2004. See the whole issue (2004) 11 *Hrvatski ljetopis za kaznene znanosti i praksu*, 381–1157.

[44] *Supra* note 32, p. 61.

[45] Some scholars were against it, arguing that basing the daily unit on property as such would amount to confiscation. *Supra* note 7, 87.

perpetrator benefit from the property he or she is not using or renting.[46] Those perpetrators are able to pay the fine even if they do not have a regular income. While this is true, it is doubtful if taking property which is not producing any income is compatible with the nature of the day fine as punishment based on daily income.[47] This debate, however, is largely theoretical – according to available case law, courts tend to disregard not just the value of the property itself, but even property as an additional source of income (e.g. rent, interests, dividends).[48] The amount of the daily unit is mostly based on reported salary alone.[49]

As far as 'the average costs necessary for supporting the perpetrator and his or her family' are concerned, the provision is manifestly modelled upon the Austrian regulation of the fine and the so-called 'loss principle'.[50] This means that when determining the amount of the daily unit the courts should take into consideration not just the perpetrator's daily income, but also the average living expenses necessary to support the perpetrator and his or her family. The law is clear – the living expenses left to the perpetrator and his or her family must be average, meaning that the wealthy perpetrator will not be left with the amount he or she was regularly spending for living expenses before the punishment.[51] What the law does not say is how to calculate the average living expenses (per capita). The starting point could be the existential minimum or the personal exemption, which is not taxable;[52] yet, this amount does not represent the average cost of living,

---

[46] *Supra* note 32, pp. 61–2. The commentary further discusses German case law which in such cases takes 3 per cent of the property value as income from that property.

[47] More about this dilemma in *supra* note 7, 87.

[48] Novoselec and Martinović, *Komentar Kaznenog zakona, I. Knjiga, Opći dio*, p. 307, citing the judgment of the County Court in Zagreb, I Kž-220/15.

[49] See, for example, recent media coverage of the day fine imposed on a well-known conservative activist Željka Markić, who was convicted in 2018 for intentional defamation of a lesbian writer. The court determined the amount of the daily unit at 100 HRK – just a half of the average daily income determined by the Supreme Court for the same trimester. That would mean that her monthly salary was exactly the minimum wage in Croatia, which the public found hard to believe, given that she was a director and an owner of a profitable company. The judgment was abolished in the meantime (for reasons not related to punishment) and the repeated trial is ongoing. www.jutarnji.hr/vijesti/hrvatska/zeljki-markic-kazna-kao-da-nema-t vrtku-sud-nije-uzeo-u-obzir-imovinu-odvjetnica-mime-simic-zalit-ce-se-na-iznos-kazne-cel nici-u-ime-obitelji/6952503/.

[50] *Supra* note 48, p. 307.

[51] *Ibid.*

[52] In Croatia in 2019 it amounts to 3,800.00 HRK per month. According to the Croatian National Bank currency exchange list, applied as of 20 July 2019, this amounts to approximately 515 euros.

but a living minimum and this could perplex the judges.[53] Another possibility would be to rely on the trade union's consumer baskets, but consumer baskets are not calculated regularly and the last one was calculated in 2011.[54] An open issue further is whether the courts should take into account regional differences (e.g. different costs of living in the capital and in rural areas) and personal circumstances (e.g. existing bank loans which need to be repaid monthly), or that the expenses should always be the same, the only difference resulting from the number of the members of the shared household that the perpetrator needs to sustain. There is no source of information on how the courts in fact determine 'the average costs necessary for supporting the perpetrator and his or her family', but the available case law indicates that this is actually not done in practice at all and that the courts still base their assessment of the daily unit on income, that is, to be more precise, dominantly on salary.[55]

Finally, the law specifies that the minimum amount of the daily unit should not be less than 20.00 HRK,[56] nor more than 10,000.00 HRK.[57] These minimum and maximum amounts have been set by comparing the minimum and maximum daily units in Austria, Germany, Switzerland and Poland.[58] The doors are no longer ajar for the courts to rely on the average daily income in Croatia.[59] However, it is still possible to freely estimate the amount of the daily unit when the exact determination would be linked with incommensurate difficulties as well as in the cases in which a penal order is issued (Article 42 (5) CC2011). This exception should not serve as a leeway to judges in order to avoid determination of the precise amount of the daily unit. Yet, preliminary research indicates that this is fairly often done in practice.[60]

---

[53] The word 'average' here is confusing. It is regrettable that the legislator did not explain, at least in the explanatory material, what was meant by the phrase 'average costs necessary . . .' and how these costs were to be calculated. *De lege ferenda*, the law should require the judges to deduct the 'minimum amount necessary to support the perpetrator and his or her family'.

[54] Other models could also be applicable – e.g. guaranteed minimum benefit according to the Social Welfare Act. Z. Babić, Emin Context Report Croatia, Developments in relation to Minimum Income Schemes, May 2017, eminnetwork.files.wordpress.com/2013/04/context-report_croatia.pdf.

[55] *Supra* note 48, 308. The same confirmed a judge of the Municipal Criminal Court of Zagreb in an interview.

[56] Amounting approximately to 2.7 euros, according to the latest currency exchange list.

[57] Amounting approximately to 1,355.00 euros, *ibid*.

[58] *Supra* note 32, p. 62.

[59] This remains a possibility for the few remaining cases prosecuted under the old CC97.

[60] An interview with a judge of the Municipal Criminal Court of Zagreb.

15.2.3 *Access to Financial Information and Institutions Involved in Imposing and Collecting Day Fines*

A fine as a punishment can be imposed only by a judge in criminal proceedings. Public prosecutors can file a motion for imposition of the fine in the proceedings for the issuance of a penal order, suggesting a fine from 30 to 100 daily units, but a judge must confirm.[61] In order to collect the financial information necessary to calculate the fine, the judges can request necessary information from banks and other financial institutions, state agencies and legal entities and all of them are under an obligation to provide requested information unless this information is classified as secret.[62] Relevant data should primarily be gathered through the personal identification number (OIB), set by the Tax Administration of the Ministry of Finance in 2009.[63] This number was created with a view to enable coordination between institutions and obtain insights into financial data about all Croatian citizens; however, so far it has not become entirely functional. It is advertised under a slogan – one key for many locks,[64] implying that with OIB various types of information are available at one place. This goal, however, has not been fully implemented in practice yet. It is true that the OIB, figuratively speaking, unlocks many locks, yet there are many doors to open and a lot of roads to get to these doors. The initial idea was to create an e-system in which all relevant data bases revealing different financial information about one person would be unified and connected. If that were the case, it would be sufficient for a judge to enter OIB electronically and get all the relevant information, but unfortunately this has not been achieved. To illustrate this point, the court can request information about reported income from the Tax Administration, information about real estate of the perpetrator from the Land Register, etc. This information must be officially requested in a written manner and it requires from the courts (or state attorneys in preparation of the case) to carry out a small investigation of pecuniary circumstances of the defendant,

---

[61] See Article 540 *et seq.* of the CPA.

[62] Article 264 of the CPA. Having in mind the general obligation to cooperate, the legislator decided that it was not necessary to prescribe a specific duty of cooperation in this context, stressing that these bodies cannot hide behind business or other secret, *supra* note 32, p. 63. However, at the same time Novoselec and Martinović, *supra* note 48, p. 308, explain that it is exactly because data may not be available due to the secrecy that the law prescribes the possibility to freely estimate the amount of the daily unit.

[63] Tax Administration Office, 'What is OIB and why it is introduced', www.porezna-uprava.hr /HR_OIB/Stranice/sto_je_OIB.aspx.

[64] See the official webpage of the Tax Administration Office, oib.oib.hr/SaznajOibWeb/fizick aOsoba.html.

which prolongs proceedings and is regularly circumvented in practice.[65] Hence, in reality judges either rely on whatever the defendant declares as his or her income or property,[66] or avoid the fine as a punishment all together.

15.2.4 *Payment of the Fine and Substitution for Unpaid Fine*

The perpetrator is normally required to pay the fine within the time limit which can regularly not be shorter than thirty days nor longer than six months, as determined by the court depending on the circumstances of each case. The perpetrator can also be ordered to pay the fine in instalments within a period not exceeding one year, but the court reserves the power to cancel the instalment payment scheme if the perpetrator fails to pay an instalment in an orderly manner (Article 42 (6) CC2011). In literature this provision has been criticised as being too lenient towards the convicted person, who if punished by a fine should as a consequence feel a palpable financial loss.[67] Yet, the law even further benefits the accused. Where the convicted person is unable to pay the fine in full or in part within the time period specified in the judgment due to a significant subsequent deterioration in his or her pecuniary circumstances, which occurred without his or her fault, the court may at the request of the convicted person extend the payment deadline for up to twenty-four months or determine payment in instalments within that period (Article 42 (7) CC2011). According to a leading commentary, this provision should be applied sparingly, only in cases of illness, loss of employment, etc.[68] Whether this is often applied in reality is difficult to tell as there has been no published research on this issue recently. An earlier research found that in the early 2000s the courts most commonly set the deadline for payment between thirty days and three months. These shorter deadlines have been set in almost 85 per cent of the cases.[69] Another research from the late 2000s on the other hand establishes a complete opposite – that the deadline for payment was set in between three and six months in more than 85 per cent of the analysed cases.[70]

---

[65] Conclusion from an interview with a judge of the Municipal Criminal Court of Zagreb and from a number of available judgments in which fines were imposed.

[66] Though the defendant is not even legally required to tell the truth.

[67] Novoselec, *Opći dio kaznenog prava*, p. 394.

[68] *Ibid.*, p. 395.

[69] *Supra* note 30, 391. Caution should be exercised when relying on this data due to the limited number of analysed judgments, only 32.

[70] *Supra* note 41. As with the previous research, the importance and the validity of the results is limited due to the relatively small number of analysed judgments (36) and narrow geographical reach (only judgments from the Municipal Court of Split had been taken into consideration).

In any case, the issue of subsequent deterioration of the pecuniary circumstances of the defendant should be separated from a similar, yet different case of a defendant who did not have sufficient means from the outset. Although this is not explicitly stated in the law, the prevailing opinion is that in such circumstances fine as a punishment should not be imposed in the first place as there are other alternatives to prison.[71]

If the convicted person fails to pay the fine in full or in part within the time limit specified in the judgment, the fine is forcibly collected. In 2011, the first version of the new Criminal Code explicitly tasked the Tax Administration of the Ministry of Finance with forcible collection. Yet, this provision was amended even before it entered into force.[72] The new provision more vaguely prescribes that forcible collection is done via an 'authorized institution according to a special law' (Article 43 (1) CC2011). According to the directly relevant Act on Execution of Enforcement on Financial Assets, these are a Financial Agency (known under the acronym of FINA), the Croatian National Bank and banks in general.[73]

Subsidiary, if the fine cannot be forcibly collected within a three-month period,[74] the court shall try to substitute it with community service, so that two hours of community service replace one daily unit, whereby community service cannot exceed 720 hours. The necessary prerequisite for this conversion is the convicted person's consent (Article 43 (2) CC2011). As a final step, only if the convicted person does not agree to community service or does not perform it,[75] the fine or community service shall be converted to imprisonment (Article 43 (3) CC2011). One day of imprisonment replaces one daily unit, where it is a direct substitute for a fine, or two hours of community service, where the fine was first substituted with community service. In any event imprisonment for default cannot exceed twelve months (Article 43 (4) CC2011).[76] If the convicted person pays the fine after the decision on

---

[71] *Supra* note 32, p. 63; *supra* note 30, 368.

[72] See Official Gazette 144/2012. See Article 2 of the Act, Official Gazette 68/18.

[73] *Supra* note 48, p. 311. See also Article 2 of the Act on Execution of Enforcement over Monetary Assets, Official Gazette 68/18. Banks carry out the forcible collection pursuant to an order from the Financial Agency (Article 3 (1) (10) and Article 9 of the Act).

[74] From the text of the provision it is not clear from which day this period is calculated. One reasonable solution would be to start from the expiry of the deadline determined by the court for payment of the fine, but the Supreme Court held that the period of three months starts running only when the Tax administration notifies the court about the (first) unsuccessful collection of a fine. See *supra* note 48, p. 311, citing VSRH I Kž-163/17.

[75] The exception is when community service cannot be performed due to permanent incapacity of the convicted person for any type of work. In those rare cases the courts should suspend the execution of the fine and could not replace it with imprisonment. *Supra* note 48, p. 311.

[76] Theoretically, without an explicit provision this could happen for intentional defamation and for offences committed out of greed, punishable by a maximum of 500 daily units.

substitution has become final, the execution of imprisonment or community service is suspended. In the case of partial payment, only the remainder of the punishments is executed (Article 43 (5) CC2011).

This three-step scheme,[77] in which first forcible collection is tried, then the fine is replaced by community service and only in the third step, if community service is not performed, imprisonment is imposed, treats imprisonment for fine default indeed as *ultima ratio*. However, the scheme does not apply to convicted persons without either a permanent or temporary place of residence in Croatia. In those cases, if the convicted person does not pay the fine within the time limit specified in the judgment, the court must immediately order imprisonment as a substitute for the fine (Article 43 (6) CC2011).

15.3 PRACTICAL IMPLEMENTATION OF DAY FINES

The practical implementation of day fines in Croatia reveals many problems, some of which have already been sketched above. Perhaps most importantly, the fine is imposed less and less frequently, to the extent that today in Croatia it may be seen as completely marginal punishment. This is so despite the fact that the number of offences for which a fine can be imposed is relatively high – fine as a principal punishment can be imposed for a little bit less than one third of all the offences prescribed by CC2011.[78] In fact, the percentage of offences for which a fine can be imposed is significantly higher than it used to be in the last decades of the former Yugoslavia and early years of independence, when the fine was imposed incomparably more often. While the ratio was approximately the same according to CC97 (31.4 per cent), under the BCCRC fine was an applicable punishment for only 9.3 per cent of all the offences.[79] Another interesting trend is that not only the number of suspended prison sentences is on the rise, but also the number of suspended fines. Since 2015 on, suspended fines continuously outnumber unsuspended fines, as shown in Table 15.2.

---

[77] The three-step scheme is highly problematic when it comes to a fine as ancillary punishment, pronounced together with imprisonment. In those cases, the law does not provide any guidance and even though the Supreme Court in one case approved conversion of the ancillary fine to imprisonment, this remains controversial, both from a theoretical and practical point of view. *Supra* note 48, p. 312.

[78] Roughly, it may be pronounced for approximately 280 offences, including mitigating and aggravating forms, whereas the CC2011 incriminates slightly more than 900 forms of conduct (as basic, mitigating or aggravating forms of offences).

[79] See *supra* note 24, 338; *supra* note 17, pp. 252–4.

TABLE 15.2 *Adult perpetrators: criminal complaints, convictions, punishments 2013–18*

Year	2013	2014	2015	2016	2017	2018
Criminal Complaints	55,924	51,134	57,688	60,194	58,181	54,070
Convicted Persons	16,617	14,888	12,552	13,412	12,091	11,866
Suspended Prison	12,183 (73.3 %)	10,568 (71 %)	9,642 (76.8 %)	10,559 (78.7 %)	9,340 (77.2 %)	9,501 (80 %)
Unsuspended Prison	3,594 (21.6 %)	3,719 (25 %)	2,345 (18.7 %)	2,375 (17.7 %)	2,352 (19.5 %)	2,008 (16.9 %)
Unsuspended Fine	509 (3.1 %)	335 (2.3 %)	141 (1.1 %)	138 (1 %)	106 (0.9 %)	89 (0.8 %)
Suspended Fine	79 (0.5 %)	74 (0.5 %)	252 (2 %)	209 (1.6 %)	175 (1.4 %)	155 (1.3 %)

Source: Data collected from yearly reports of Croatian Bureau of Statistics, www .dzs.hr.

One could assume that suspended fines are extremely efficient when the courts rely on them to such an immense extent. Yet, there is no official data or available research either on the rates of recidivism by type of criminal sanction or on the number of revoked suspended sentences.[80] Even though this is not an indication of the effectiveness of different sanctions, it is interesting to observe that according to the Report on conditions in and work of prisons, penitentiaries and juvenile reformatories for 2017, out of the total prison population on 31 December 2017, 17.23 per cent of the persons were previously sentenced to a suspended imprisonment or a fine and 42.87 per cent of the persons were previously in prison.[81] Furthermore, in his report for 2017, in light of the high rates of recidivism the State Attorney expressed concern regarding not just lenient sentencing practices in general, as already mentioned above,

[80]   According to Article 58 (1) CC2011 a suspended sentence must be revoked if the person is convicted of one or more criminal offences committed during the period of probation and sentenced to a term of imprisonment exceeding one year. For less serious offences, for which a prison sentence of up to one year is imposed, the revocation of a suspended sentence is optional (Article 58 (2) CC2011). The probation office monitors only a small portion of suspended sentences – if imposed together with supervision, security measure or a special obligation, which is done in only around of 5 per cent of the suspended sentences.

[81]   That means that around one third of the prison population were first time offenders. See p. 17 of the report, www.sabor.hr/hr/izvjesce-o-stanju-i-radu-kaznionica-zatvora-i-odgojnih-zavoda-za-2017-godinu-podnositeljica-vlada.

but also the high percentage of community service,[82] and in particular of suspended imprisonment.[83] As said by the Chief State Attorney, this practice sends a wrong message that crime does pay and cannot achieve the purpose of punishment.[84]

Fines can be applied to all categories of offences – as long as they are punishable by imprisonment of up to three years.[85] Most frequently a fine as a principal punishment is imposed on perpetrators of offences against safety in traffic, economy, property, personal freedom, etc.[86]

Additionally, a fine can be imposed for any other offence, if committed out of greed, as ancillary punishment, together with imprisonment. In fact, unlike the regular fine, the percentage of this 'special' type of fine has not been in decline, despite theoretical problems surrounding its application and execution.[87] Since ancillary fines are also structured as day fines, all the identified problems, in particular regarding the determination of the daily unit, are equally relevant here. This type of fine is most commonly imposed on perpetrators of offences against property and offences against people's health.[88]

As far as case law is concerned, in addition to problems identified in the previous section, regarding foremost disregard of other forms of income and of living expenses as well as undue reliance on free estimate, available judgments reveal another irregularity. Whereas property should be taken into account when determining the amount of the daily income, the judges instead seem to rely on it when determining the number of units. This is done despite the explicit wording of the law which instructs the judges against relying on pecuniary circumstances of the perpetrator when determining the number of days.[89]

---

[82] In Croatia community service is a substitute not just for an unpaid fine, as explained above, but also a general substitute for fine or imprisonment of up to one year. According to Article 55 (1) CC2011 in fact it should replace the prison sentence not exceeding six months as a rule, unless it would fail to achieve the purpose of punishment.

[83] State Attorney Report for 2017, A-643/17, published on 23 April 2018, p. 48.

[84] *Ibid.*

[85] *E.g.* failure to render assistance or (ordinary) bodily injury.

[86] In 2018 out of 244 fines – as the principal punishment (both suspended and unsuspended), 79 were imposed for offences against the safety in traffic, 29 for economy, 23 for property, 15 for personal freedom, 10 for life and limb, 7 for counterfeiting and public order each, 66 for other offences and 8 for offences prescribed by secondary legislation (German *Nebengesetze*). Croatian Bureau of Statistics, First Release, Adult Perpetrators of Criminal Offences by Type of Decision, 2018, Zagreb, 2 May 2019.

[87] See Dragičević Prtenjača, 'Sporedna kazna' and Novoselec, 'Sudska praksa', *supra* note 36.

[88] Croatian Bureau of Statistics, First Release, Adult Perpetrators of Criminal Offences by Type of Decision, 2018, Zagreb, 2 May 2019. See also the reports for previous years available, www .dzs.hr.

[89] For example, the County Court of Zagreb in one case on appeal noticed that the convicted person had a regular monthly salary of 11,000.00 HRK and that he and his wife were the owners

TABLE 15.3 *The total number and percentage of ancillary fines*

Year	Convicted Persons	Ancillary Fines	Percentage
2009	25,368	277	1
2010	24,430	164	0.7
2011	23,389	145	0.6
2012	20,548	70	0.3
2013	16,617	91	0.5
2014	14,888	337	2
2015	12,552	196	1.6
2016	13,412	257	1.9
2017	12,091	234	1.9
2018	11,866	264	2.2

Source: Yearly reports on adult perpetrators of criminal offences by type of decision, Croatian Bureau of Statistics, www.dzs.hr. See also *Supra note* 36, 81.

Finally, a word about imprisonment for fine default. Unfortunately, there is no readily available official data on the execution of a fine and the number of fines replaced by imprisonment. Official data published by the Prison System and Probation Directorate within the Ministry of Justice expose only the number of imprisonment for fine default in relation to fixed fines imposed in misdemeanour proceedings.[90] With respect to converted day fines imposed in criminal proceedings, a study monitoring the execution of thirty-six fines imposed by the Municipal Court of Split from 2004 to 2008 shows that default imprisonment for fine was not often carried out.[91] Even when the replacement of a fine with imprisonment was ordered by a court, and that was relatively often due to different regulation set by the CC97,[92] in 86 per cent of such cases

of several real estates, which the court explicitly took into consideration when determining the maximum number of daily units for that offence (180). The amount of the daily unit was calculated by dividing the monthly salary with the number of days in a month (30), so that the daily unit was set at 366.70 HRK, leading to a fine of 66,006.00 HRK. Zagreb County Court, Kž-220/15, 14 April 2015, as reported by A. Garačić, *Kazneni zakon u sudskoj praksi. Opći dio*, pp. 255–6.

[90] During 2017 the total number of those imprisoned for failing to pay the fine for a misdemeanour was 167, www.sabor.hr/hr/izvjesce-o-stanju-i-radu-kaznionica-zatvora-i-odgojnih-zavoda-za-2017-godinu-podnositeljica-vlada.

[91] *Supra* note 21, 670–1.

[92] In 31 per cent of fines imposed after a trial and in 62.5 per cent of fines imposed in a penal order. According to Article 52 CC97, a fine was immediately replaced by imprisonment (except for offences against honour), without measures such as forcible collection of fine and community service in between.

execution of imprisonment was cancelled because under a threat of imprisonment the convicted person paid the fine. It seems that the same trend continues today. In 2018 only four persons have served a prison sentence as a replacement for an unpaid day fine.[93]

15.4 PUBLIC PERCEPTION OF DAY FINES

There has been no comprehensive public debate on the scope or the role that a day fine should play within the Croatian criminal justice system. Some limited debate only revolves around the height of fixed fines for misdemeanours, in particular for road traffic offences.[94] Occasionally the media criticises the superficial approach of courts in the determination of daily units and the fact that wealthy offenders are sentenced to very low fines, with daily units estimated even below the average daily income.[95] As far as professional circles are concerned, the issue of day fines has also not triggered much attention recently, despite the obvious problems in the implementation of the concept in Croatia. Some voices of criticism appeared in the 2000s following the introduction of the day fine system, but these foremost challenged the lack of precision of the day fine regulation and not the concept as such.[96]

Public perception of day fines could also be discerned through studies on safety and crime. However, as noticed by Kovčo Vukadin and Ljubin Golub, fear of crime and related topics of victimisation have not been the subject of much systematic research in Croatia.[97] Most studies have been conducted using convenience samples (e.g. students of one faculty), while only a few used representative samples of Croatia or Zagreb; yet without focus on punishments.[98] Some more recent studies carried out on a student

---

[93] Data received from the Assistant Minister of Justice, head of the Prison System and Probation Directorate, Jana Špero.

[94] E.g. recently the government proposed a significant increase of fines for road traffic violations with the official explanation that higher fines would deter potential violators more efficiently, www.jutarnji.hr/vijesti/hrvatska/kazne-za-prometne-prekrsaje-skacu-i-do-500-posto-vec-kra jem-mjeseca-na-snagu-bi-mogao-stupiti-rigorozni-zakon-koji-je-u-javnosti-izazvao-veliku-bur u/9066062/.

[95] For such recent example see the already mentioned media coverage of criminal proceedings for intentional defamation against Željka Markić, *supra* note 49.

[96] See in particular *supra* note 30, 425, but also *supra* note 24, 344–5 and Bačić and Pavlović, *Komentar Kaznenog zakona*, p. 286.

[97] For an overview of existing studies see Kovčo Vukadin and Ljubin Golub, 'Fear of Crime in Zagreb, Croatia: Gender Differences in the Face of Incivilities and Prior Victimization', 441–2.

[98] See e.g. National Public Opinion Survey on Citizen Perception of Safety and Security in the Republic of Croatia carried out in 2009 by the UNDP in the Republic of Croatia and the

population,[99] do touch upon the issue of appropriate punishment, at the same time revealing a relatively high level of punitive attitudes in Croatia.[100]

15.5 SPECIAL CHALLENGES

From all of the above it can be concluded that although it was introduced more than twenty years ago, the concept of day fines has not taken roots in Croatia. The new legislative framework from 2011 can be seen as an improvement of the day fine regulation, but obviously it did not achieve the intended purpose – to make it easier for the judges to calculate the daily unit and, consequently, to apply the fine more often. In fact, the opposite occurred. The fine has completely lost its prominence as a punishment for criminal offences and there is no clear strategy on how to revive the system of day fines and its practical importance in Croatia. At first, this may not seem to be a problem since the main function of the fine as an alternative to prison has been fulfilled through other alternative sanctions, including the suspended prison sentence, which all together make approximately 85 per cent of all punishments.[101] Hence, the decrease of the use of fine has not led to increased rates of imprisonment. On the contrary, these rates have also been in slight but constant decline. Yet, what is worrying is the fact that there is no official data or research on the efficiency of applied sanctions, i.e. rates of recidivism with respect to different types of punishments and their modifications. It would be interesting and important to know if the extremely high share of suspended sentences is followed by low or high rates of recidivism.

The implementation of the day fine system in Croatia is yet another example of the limited influence legal transplants often have. Those studying the phenomenon will not be surprised as it is not uncommon that legal transplants turn into 'legal irritants'.[102] One of the reasons may be found in

---

Ministry of Interior of the Republic of Croatia, www.seesac.org/f/docs/SALW-Surveys/On-Citizen-Perception-of-Safety-and-Security-in-the-Republic-of-Croatia-EN.pdf.

[99] See, e.g. Kovčo Vukadin and Vukosav, 'Students' Attitudes towards Risk, Victimization and Punishment in Croatia', 379–99.

[100] Kovčo Vukadin, Kondor-Langer and Žakman-Ban, 'Punitivnost studenata Visoke policijske škole', 10. According to this research, a fine is seen as appropriate punishment for drunken driving (misdemeanour) and to an extent for some less serious forms of theft.

[101] As indicated in Table 15.2, the most frequent alternative sanction remains by far suspended imprisonment. The notion of alternative sanctions is understood to connote sanctions alternative to unsuspended imprisonment. Derenčinović, Dragičević Prtenjača and Gracin, 'Alternative kazni oduzimanja slobode', 109–30.

[102] Comp. Legrand, 'The Impossibility of Legal Transplants', 111–24 and Teubner, 'Legal Irritants: How Unifying Law Ends Up in New Divergences', 417–41.

disharmony between formal (laws and rules) and informal institutions (tradition, legal and social culture), that is, resistance of informal, deep-seated rules of behaviour towards new and changeable laws.[103] Along the same lines, one of the main challenges to successful implementation of the concept probably lies in a strong shadow economy in Croatia and inefficient public administration, due to which comprehensive files about pecuniary circumstances of the defendant are not readily available to courts. Calculating daily units is futile in a system in which a salary or its significant part is not reported and institutions are not interconnected. Furthermore, it is true that the provision itself could be improved or perhaps more precise. For example, when calculating the amount of the daily unit, defendants should be left with the minimum amount necessary to cover the costs of living, instead of 'average costs', as the provision stands now. The fine is a punishment and it must affect the quality of life of the perpetrator. Lack of explicit guidance on how to calculate these costs or gather relevant data could be bypassed through a more pragmatic approach of the judges who should see themselves as active factors in the process of formation of legal rules. Yet, in Croatian positivist and formalistic legal culture the courts are seen as mere applicators of legal rules;[104] the view which disregards that every legal rule leaves room for interpretation and that judicial creativity does not necessarily breach the principle of legality. However, due to all of the above, the determination of the daily unit was obviously perceived as an additional onerous task, which the judges have been keen to avoid.

REFERENCES

Babić, Z. 2017. Emin Context Report Croatia, Developments in relation to Minimum Income Schemes, May 2017, https://eminnetwork.files.wordpress.com/2013/04/context-report_croatia.pdf.

Bačić, F. and Pavlović, Š. 2006. *Komentar Kaznenog zakona*. Organizator Zagreb.

Bedrač, I. 2004. 'Statistkički prikaz izbora vrste i mjere kazne u Republici Hrvatskoj.' *Hrvatski ljetopis za kazneno pravo i praksu* 11: 923–946.

Croatian Bureau of Statistics, First Release, Adult Perpetrators of Criminal Offences by Type of Decision, 2018, Zagreb, 2 May 2019.

Derenčin, M. 1997. *Osnova novoga Kaznenoga zakona o zločinstvih i prestupcih za Kraljevine Hrvatsku i Slavoniju 1879*. Zagreb: Croatiaprojekt.

---

[103] Šimić Banović, 'From Promising Institutional Transplants to Legal Irritants: Some Institutional Aspects', 290–301.

[104] Kasap, Lachner and Žiha, 'Through Legal Education towards European Education Area', 261.

Derenčinović, D., Dragičević Prtenjača, M. and Gracin, D. 2018. 'Alternative kazni oduzimanja slobode', in Bejatović, S. and Jovanović, I. (eds.), *Alternativne krivične sankcije (regionalna krivična zakonodavstva, iskustva u primeni i mere unapređenja)*. Conference paper. Beograd: Organizacija za europsku sigurnost i suradnju – OEBS: 109–130.

Dragičević Prtenjača, M. 2016. 'Sporedna novčana kazna u hrvatskom kaznenom pravu i praksi - s posebnim osvrtom na njezino izricanje u postupcima koji su vođeni za kazneno djelo primanja mita', *Hrvatski ljetopis za kaznene znanosti i praksu* 23: 59–92.

Garačić, A. 2016. *Kazneni zakon u sudskoj praksi*. Rijeka: Libertin naklada.

Grozdanić, V. 2000. 'Kazne – nova rješenja u Kaznenom zakonu i njihova provedba u sudskoj praksi', *Hrvatski ljetopis za kazneno pravo i praksu* 7: 327–47.

Horvatić, Ž. 1997. *Novo hrvatsko kazneno pravo*. Zagreb: Organizator Zagreb.

Horvatić, Ž. , Derenčinović, D. and Cvitanović, L. 2016. *Kazneno pravo. Opći dio 1. Kazneno pravo i kazneni zakon*. Zagreb: Pravni fakultet Sveučilišta u Zagrebu.

Horvatić, Ž. , and Derenčinović, D. 2002. *Criminal Justice Systems in Europe and North America*. Helsinki: Heuni.

Kasap, J., Lachner, V. and Žiha, N. 2018. 'Through Legal Education towards European Education Area', in D. Duić and T. Petrašević (eds.), *EU and Comparative Law Issues and Challenges Series Issue 2*. Osijek: Pravos: 252–74.

Kovčo Vukadin, I. and Ljubin Golub, T. 2012. 'Fear of Crime in Zagreb, Croatia: Gender Differences in the Face of Incivilities and Prior Victimization', *Varstvoslovje: Journal of Criminal Justice & Security* 14: 435–59.

Kovčo Vukadin, I., Kondor-Langer, M. and Žakman-Ban, V. 2018. 'Punitivnost studenata Visoke policijske škole', *Kriminalističke teme* 1: 1–22.

Kovčo Vukadin, I. and Vukosav, J. 2011. 'Students' Attitudes towards Risk, Victimization and Punishment in Croatia', in Kury, H. and Shea, E. (eds.), *Punitivity International Developments: Insecurity and Punitiveness*, Bochum: Universitaetsverlag Dr. Brockmeyer: 379–99.

Kurtović Mišić, A., Milivojeviç, L. and Striniç, V. 2009. 'Novosti u propisivanju, izricanju i izvršenju novčane kazne', *Hrvatski ljetopis za kazneno pravo i praksu* 16: 629–86.

Legrand, P. 1997. 'The Impossibility of Legal Transplants', *Maastricht Journal of European and Comparative Law* 4: 111–24.

Novoselec, P. 2005. 'Sustav dani-novčana kazna i njegova primjena u hrvatskom kaznenom pravu', *Hrvatska pravna revija* 6: 80–89.

Novoselec, P. 2016. *Opći dio kaznenog prava*. Osijek: Pravos.

Novoselec, P. 2017. 'Sudska Praksa: Visina dnevnog iznosa. Sporedna novčana kazna', *Hrvatski ljetopis za kaznene znanosti i praksu*, 24: 717–21.

Novoselec, P. and Martinović, I. 2019. *Komentar Kaznenog zakona, I. Knjiga, Opći dio*. Zagreb: Narodne novine.

Radić, Ž. 2005. 'Zatvor u srednjovjekovnom trogirskom pravu'. *Hrvatski ljetopis za kazneno pravo i praksu* 12: 89–107.

Šimić Banović, R. 2017. 'From Promising Institutional Transplants to Legal Irritants: Some Institutional Aspects', in *Recent Advances in Information Technology, Tourism, Economics, Management and Agriculture*. Budapest, Hungary: ITEMA Conference Proceedings: 290–301.

State Attorney Report for 2016, A-561/16, Zagreb, April 2017.

State Attorney Report for 2017, A-643/17, published on 23 April 2018.

Svedrović, M. 2003. 'Kriminalnopolitička opravdanost promjena kaznenih sankcija s osvrtom na uvođenje doživotnog zatvora i na sustav izricanja kazne', *Hrvatski ljetopis za kazneno pravo i praksu* 10: 341–428.

Teubner, G. 2001. 'Legal Irritants: How Unifying Law Ends up in New Divergences', in Hall, P. and Soskice, D. (eds.), *Varieties of Capitalism: The Institutional Foundations of Comparative Advantage*. Oxford University Press.

Turković, K., Novoselec, P., Grozdanić, V., Mišić, A., Derenčinović, D., Bojanić, I., Munivrana Vajda, M., Mrčela, M., Nola, S., Roksandić, V., Vidlička, S., Tripalo, D. and Maršavelski, A. 2013. *Komentar Kaznenog zakona*. Zagreb: Narodne novine.

16

Day Fines in Switzerland

Martin Killias and Lorenz Biberstein

16.1 INTRODUCTION

In this chapter, we shall present the results of an evaluation of monetary penalties under the Swiss Criminal Code (SCC). In 2007, a new SCC became legally effective in which short prison sentences were to a large extent replaced by income-based day fines. In addition, flat fines (as fixed sums ranging from 1 to 10,000 Swiss francs) became more widely available as additional sanctions. Both fines and day fines are to be converted into custody if they remain unpaid. Several thousand defendants are affected by such a conversion every year, but virtually no data and no information has been collected on this phenomenon up to now. In order to fill this gap, the Department of Justice of the Canton of Zurich commissioned an evaluation on how often, under what circumstances and against whom (i.e. what type of defendants) monetary penalties are converted into custody. To this end, 447 case files settled between March 2017 and February 2018 were analysed and a sample of 106 defendants serving a monetary sanction in prison from April 2017 to February 2018 were interviewed. Staff members and officials of the services in charge of collecting debts resulting from monetary penalties were also interviewed. The results show that the majority of defendants serving monetary penalties in prison are confronted with multiple problems of integration. A second group are defendants who were sentenced to substantial amounts of flat fines or day fines that they or people from their networks are unable to pay.

16.2 MONETARY PENALTIES AS AN ALTERNATIVE TO CUSTODIAL SANCTIONS

16.2.1 *Criticism of Short Prison Sentences*

In the early twentieth century, monetary sanctions started to become a theoretical alternative to short prison sentences. From 1970 on, the idea of day fines received increasing attention and was implemented in many

Western European countries. The idea behind day fines is that sentencing judges fix a certain amount of days to be 'served' by the defendant.

The basic idea of this innovation had been widespread criticism of short prison sentences as they were widely used throughout Europe during the nineteenth century. Generally attributed to the German-Austrian penologist Franz von Liszt,[1] the idea that short-term imprisonment is damaging was first expressed by Arnould de Bonneville de Marsangy,[2] a French pioneer who reached these conclusions from doctors who, at a time when Europe was still and regularly harassed by epidemics, saw short-term hospitalisation increasingly critical. In their view, bringing a patient to a hospital for a short period may be unnecessary if outpatient treatment could be equally promising, or too short to treat more serious diseases, but potentially damaging due to the risk of contamination. Bonneville de Marsangy who, as many of his contemporaries, saw crime as a kind of a contagious disease, concluded through analogy that short-term imprisonment might be too short to cure a prisoner from serious criminal propensities, but long enough to bring him into contact with hard-core criminals and to make him worse than before. These debates and their influence on Swiss criminal law are described in detail in Killias, Markwalder, Kuhn and Dongois.[3]

The idea that prison is damaging became extremely popular among penologists after World War II. Although empirical studies never were able to confirm the damaging effect of custody in comparison to non-custodial sanctions once all relevant variables were taken into account,[4] the basic assumption that short-term imprisonment should be replaced remained widely unchallenged. The only reason why the system still relied, in Switzerland (until 2006) and elsewhere in Europe, on the widespread use of short-term imprisonment (either suspended or immediate) was the unavailability of a feasible alternative. Since the 1970s, however, more and more countries adopted day fine systems, as shown in the other chapters of this volume.

16.2.2 *The Implementation of Day Fines in Switzerland*

In Switzerland, the proposal to replace short-term imprisonment by day fines was initially submitted in a draft of a new penal code by Professor Hans

---

[1]   Von Liszt, 'Der Zweckgedanke im Strafrecht', 1–47.
[2]   Bonneville de Marsangy, *De l'amélioration de la loi criminelle en vue d'une justice plus prompte, plus efficace, plus généreuse et plus moralisante*, p. 260.
[3]   Killias, Markwalder, Kuhn and Dongois, *Grundriss des Allgemeinen Teils des Schweizerischen Strafgesetzbuchs*, pp. 223–50.
[4]   As shown by a Campbell systematic review of the literature, Villettaz, Gilliéron and Killias, *The Effects on Re-offending of Custodial versus Non-custodial Sanctions*.

Schultz,[5] prepared at the request of the Swiss Federal Government. Over almost two decades, governmental expert and parliamentary committees studied the issue. Finally, the Penal Law Reform Act, voted on by Parliament on 13 December 2002, became legally effective on 1 January 2007.

The day fine system, as advocated by Professor Schultz and the vast majority of professors of criminal law, made day fines ('peine pécuniaire', 'Geldstrafe') available as a new sanction for those who were found guilty of a crime ('crime', 'Verbrechen') or an offence ('délit', 'Vergehen'), no matter of what kind or seriousness. Flat fines ('amendes', 'Busse'), however, remained the only option for offenders found guilty of a misdemeanor ('contravention', 'Übertretung'). Unlike day fines, flat fines are fixed according to the judge's discretion and range from 1 to 10,000 Swiss francs (or approximately 9,000 euros, Section 106 (1) SCC). Although the judge is expected to consider the defendant's economic situation (Section 106 (3) SCC), there is no strict correlation between his or her income and the amount of the flat fine.

The day fine system, as advocated by experts and the Government,[6] underwent a few significant changes during the parliamentary debates. First, day fines can be imposed for up to 360 days,[7] that is, for relatively long sentences in international perspective. Second and perhaps most importantly, day fines – unlike flat fines – can be suspended, according to the same rules that had existed for decades in relation to prison sentences (Section 42 (1) SCC). As for other sanctions, the judge fixes a period of probation between two and five years (Section 44 SCC). Since basically all offenders without (or rather, without too many) previous convictions qualify for a suspended sentence, day fines become executable in case of reoffending only when the perspectives of rehabilitation seem seriously compromised from the onset (Section 42 (1)–(2) SCC), or in case of a new offence during the period of probation (Section 46 (1) SCC). Judges have very little discretion in this respect and consistently suspend sentences if the defendant has none or relatively few previous convictions.[8]

During the transitional period between 2002 and 2006, practitioners noticed that this system had a few critical shortcomings. For example, it was said that defendants of minor offences ('contraventions', 'Übertretungen') for whom

---

5   Schultz, *Bericht und Vorentwurf zur Revision des Allgemeinen Teils des Schweizerischen Strafgesetzbuches.*
6   Botschaft des Bundesrates zur Änderung des Schweizerischen Strafgesetzbuches, 1979.
7   From 1 January 2018, the maximum has been lowered to 180 days (Section 34 (1) SCC). This had no tangible effects on the number of defendants convicted to day fines.
8   Killias, Markwalder, Kuhn and Dongois, *Grundriss des Allgemeinen Teils des Schweizerischen Strafgesetzbuchs,* p. 243.

the only sanction available is an immediate flat fine, might fare worse than those found guilty of a felony ('crime'/'Verbrechen' or 'délit'/'Vergehen') who usually qualify for a suspended sentence. As an example, it was said that drivers with an intoxication beyond 0.8 (i.e. a 'délit') will be eligible for a suspended day fine, whereas those driving with a blood intoxication below this threshold (but beyond 0.5) will be subject to an unsuspended flat fine of, possibly, several thousand Swiss francs.

In order to correct for this inconsistency, the Parliament amended the Penal Law Reform Act even before its enactment by adding Section 42 (4) SCC according to which judges can add a flat fine to a suspended day fine (or any other suspended sentence). Since 2007, judges widely use this option. As a result, most offenders are, in practice, sentenced to a suspended day fine plus a flat fine of often substantial amounts. The obvious reason is that suspended day fines are not being taken seriously by many offenders – nor by the general public who sees suspended day fines as a threat of little credibility. By adding a substantial flat fine to a suspended day fine, judges can to some extent avoid this impression.

Further, the new criminal code provided, in Section 41 (1) SCC, for the possibility of an immediate custodial sanction of up to six months if the defendant seems unable to pay a day fine from the onset. In practice, this rule is widely used in case of defendants without an official address in Switzerland.

Regarding the estimate of the daily income (as a base for day fines), Section 34 (2) SCC remains rather vague. It is said that one day fine equals 30 to 3,000 Swiss francs.[9] In assessing the amount, the judge has to take into account the defendant's income (of whatever source) as well as his/her financial obligations and constraints, including the needs of dependent family members. The code specifies that the judge will have access to information provided by the internal revenue service and social welfare data (Section 34 (3) SCC). On the way the amount is to be fixed, however, the code remains silent and the existing guidelines do not standardise even common living cost factors. After all, judges are expected to set out an amount that it is hoped will correspond to the defendant's daily income, but they are widely left alone in this task.

In theory, such a system can be considered fair, since – as in a fiscal system with taxes that are proportionate to every taxpayer's income – monetary

---

[9] Before 1 January 2018, no minimum was set by the law and many defendants without (or rather without officially known incomes) got away with ridiculous amounts. In reaction to these criticisms, the Parliament introduced the minimal amount of thirty Swiss francs that can be lowered to ten Swiss francs in case of especially needy defendants.

sanctions are meted out according to the defendant's means. In practice, however, several shortcomings can be observed.[10] First of all, judicial guidelines for the determination of daily incomes are by far not as developed as those that are in use among taxation offices, even with respect to living costs of a family. Second, the guidelines for day fines do not consider an individual's assets, but only his or her income. In practice, however, the difficulty to pay a day fine may depend more on how much cash a defendant has at his/her disposal, either personally or through support from his/her network, than on the monthly income. Those who are, theoretically at least, most at risk of being unable to pay a day fine are probably those who have a substantial income (and, thus, risk to be sentenced to higher day fines) but limited cash at hands. On the other hand, defendants with substantial assets and low (known) incomes tend to be privileged under such a system.

16.2.3 *Conversion of Monetary Penalties into Custody*

Whatever the pros and cons may be, those who turn out to be unable to pay monetary penalties end up in prison where they serve the number of days that corresponds to the number of day fines fixed by the sentencing judge. This conversion of monetary sanctions into prison terms has been in practice all along the history of criminal law, since unpaid fines had always been converted into some other form of punishment (prison, forced labour or, possibly, corporal punishment). To this end, unpaid fines used to be divided by a flat amount that corresponded to one day imprisonment.

The conversion of day fines and flat fines follows the same principles. Flat fines, however, can be converted more easily. Indeed, the sentencing judge sets, in meting out the fine, also the number of days (of up to three months) that are to be served if, except in cases of duress, the defendant fails to pay the due amount (Section 106 (2) SCC). Day fines, however, are meted out as a fixed number of days, ranging from 1 day to a maximum of 180 days (and even 360 days before 2018), the amount per day ranging from 10 to 3,000 Swiss francs (Section 36 (1) SCC). A further difference is that roughly nine in ten sentences involving day fines are suspended and become payable only once a judge, usually in connection with a new conviction, changes a formerly suspended into an immediate day fine sentence. This happens in roughly 9 per cent of all day fine sentences (Federal Statistical Office 2019, Table T 19.03.03.02.01.10.01). Flat fines, however, cannot be suspended (Section 105 (1) SCC). Since, in cases of

---

[10] For details and examples, see *supra* note 8, pp. 230–5.

a suspended day fine, judges regularly impose, in addition, a flat fine (Section 42 (4) SCC) in order to make the defendant feel at least partially an immediate consequence, defendants with financial constraints will far more often be subject to a decision of conversion related to their flat fine. In contrast, day fines, left aside that they are suspended in about nine out of ten cases, will only be converted as a last resort. Indeed, authorities in charge of collecting debts will have to bring the case to court who alone can decide over the conversion. This will be done only after lengthy procedures of instalment[11] (for details, see Section 35 (1) and (3) and Section 36 SCC). Flat fines, in contrast, are payable at short notice and, in case of default, immediately convertible into custody for three months at most (Section 106 (2) SCC).

16.3 EFFECTS OF DAY FINES ON SENTENCING

16.3.1 *Short Custodial Sentences Disappeared – at First Sight*

Before the SCC reform introduced in 2007, some 10,000 to 12,000 defendants used to be sentenced to an immediate (unsuspended) custodial sentence of up to six months per year (Figure 16.1; see also Simmler 2016, 78). In addition, between 35,000 and 40,000 suspended prison sentences of up to six months had been handed down by judges in Switzerland. In 2007, the number of entries into prison for a term not exceeding six months had dropped to 3,741, down from 11,910 in 2006, that is, the last year before the new system became effective. At the same time, short suspended prison sentences had disappeared completely. Figure 16.1 illustrates this dramatic change in the sentencing landscape.

In 2013, the number of entries into prison reached almost pre-reform levels, with 9,253 recorded entries of defendants serving ordinary custodial sentences not exceeding six months. Over the years, the number of entries has stabilised at that level, that is, the intentions behind the Penal Law Reform Act of 2002 seem to have largely vanished within a few years.

This is illustrated by Figure 16.2 that gives the details by main sanction at the level of convictions over an extended period. Before 2007, suspended custodial sentences played a very significant role, but disappeared completely after the Penal Law Reform Act became effective. They were almost completely replaced by suspended monetary penalties (day fines). Unsuspended monetary penalties (day fines) played an increasing role once this system was introduced in 2007. Flat fines played a very significant role before and after 2007, but the

---

[11] *Supra* note 8, p. 253.

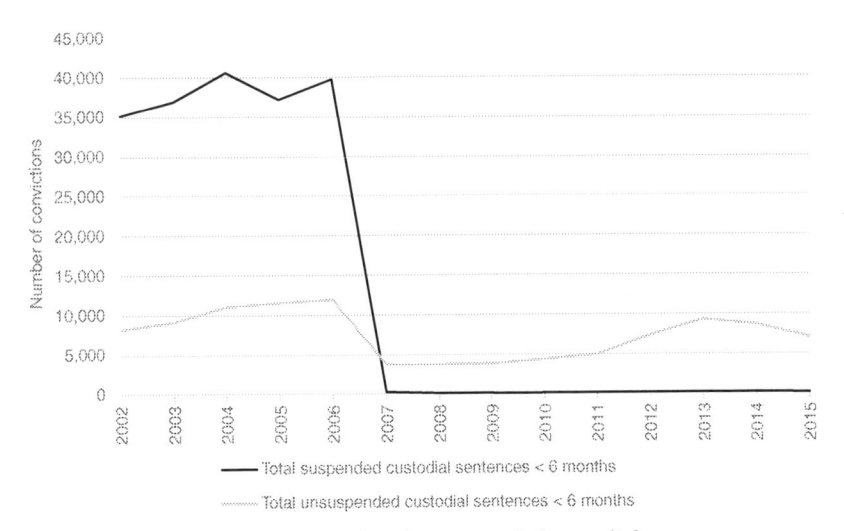

FIGURE 16.1 Total suspended and unsuspended custodial sentences not exceeding six months 2002–18, for all offences
Source: Federal Statistical Office, Table T 19.3.3.2.2.1.2

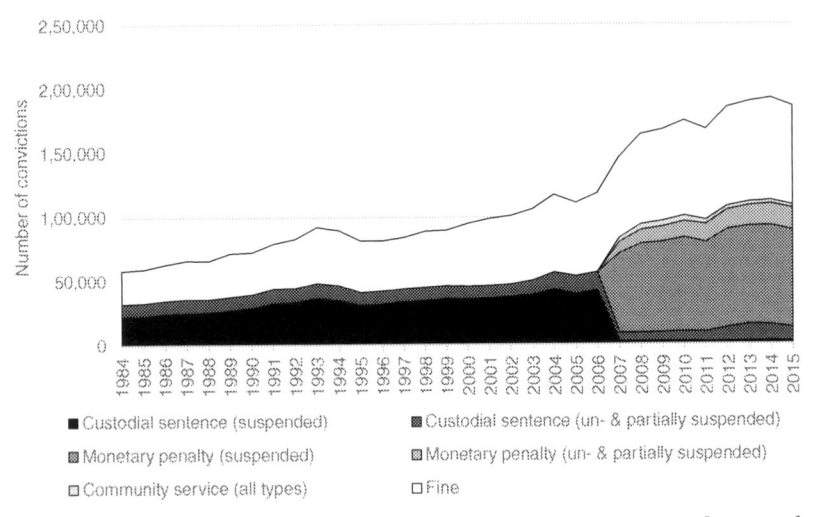

FIGURE 16.2 Convictions for misdemeanours and felonies[12] by type of principal sanction 1984–2014
Source: Federal Statistical Office, Table T 19.3.3.2.2.1.2

---

[12] Not all misdemeanours ('contraventions', 'Übertretungen') are recorded in the Register of Criminal Convictions, but only those with a fine exceeding 500 Swiss francs.

amounts have certainly increased in comparison to the pre-reform era, due to the newly introduced combination of suspended day fines with flat fines.

16.3.2 Day Fines and the Incarceration Rate

On a different level, the number of prison inmates ironically increased following the Penal Law Reform Act, as shown in Figure 16.3. This may be related to the fact that prisoners are, on average, serving longer sentences, often in connection with measures of treatment. In fact, the replacement of short prison sentences of up to six months, combined with the extension of the threshold for the suspension of custodial sanctions from eighteen to twenty-four and – in special cases[13] – even thirty-six months, may have pushed judges to opt for longer sentences, given the lack of judicial discretion whenever the defendant has too few previous convictions to justify an immediate custodial sentence. This observation is in line with the net-widening effect of many alternative sanctions.[14] It was equally made after previous legal reforms whereby the scope of alternative sanctions was widened.

The trend over time shows that, first of all, the number of inmates in confinement for the purpose of treatment (stationary measures)[15] has increased substantially over the years, in line with the increasing popularity of therapeutic approaches brought about with the Penal Law Reform Act. Whereas the number of inmates serving ordinary custodial sentences remained fairly stable over time, there was a clear drop in conversions of suspended custodial sentences into immediate custody, due to the massive decrease of suspended prison sentences and a reciprocal shift to day fines converted into custody. Flat fines converted into custody make up for a small minority among prisoners, but play an important role in other respects, as will be shown in the following sections.

16.3.3 Warning Voices Were Ignored

When the penal reform was debated, there were a few voices warning that, without appropriate precautions, the system could easily lead to a social redistribution of short custodial sentences rather than to their abolition.[16]

---

[13] According to Section 43 (1) SCC, judges can impose partially suspended custodial sentences for more than two years but not exceeding three years. For sentences up to twenty-four months, full suspension is the rule.
[14] Killias, Aebi and Kuhn, *Précis de criminologie*, pp. 453–5.
[15] In practice, this equals to indeterminate sentences to be served, in most cases, in an ordinary prison.
[16] See sources in *supra* note 8, p. 235.

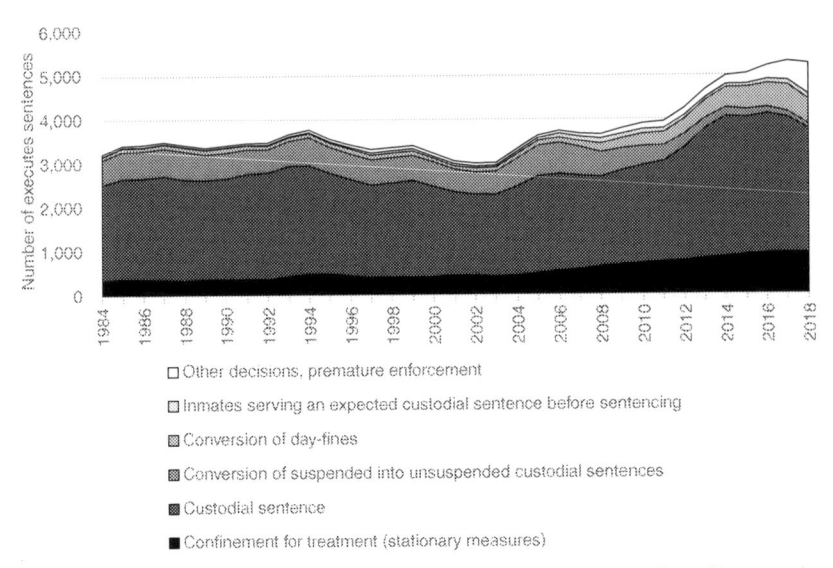

Other decisions, premature enforcement

Inmates serving an expected custodial sentence before sentencing

Conversion of day-fines

Conversion of suspended into unsuspended custodial sentences

Custodial sentence

Confinement for treatment (stationary measures)

FIGURE 16.3 Execution of sentences and measures: average number of inmates by principal sanction 1984–2018
Source: Federal Statistical Office, Table je-d-19.04.01.32

They were not taken seriously enough to redesign the system in a way to mitigate undesirable side effects. In the meantime, conversions of fines and day fines into custodial sentences have reached disturbing proportions.

Indeed, an increasing number of people are entering the custodial system in order to 'pay' for unpaid fines and day fines. Ironically and not untypical for a problem that is generally considered not to exist, no precise statistical data is collected to measure the extent of conversions of day fines into prison. According to data published by the Swiss Federal Statistical Office, some 1,500 persons are entering prison following the revocation of a suspended custodial or the conversion of a day fine sentence. Since, over many years, roughly 10 per cent of suspended prison sentences used to be revoked during the probation period and given the drop particularly of short custodial sanctions following the SCC reform, it is very unlikely that revocations make up for more than 500 cases per year after 2007. In sum, the number of day fines converted into custody can be estimated at about 1,000. To this number one should add 3,000–3,500 persons who are entering prison following the conversion of a flat fine (Figure 16.4).

More precisely, during the last year before the penal reform, in 2006, the number of persons entering prison following a decision of conversion of a fine

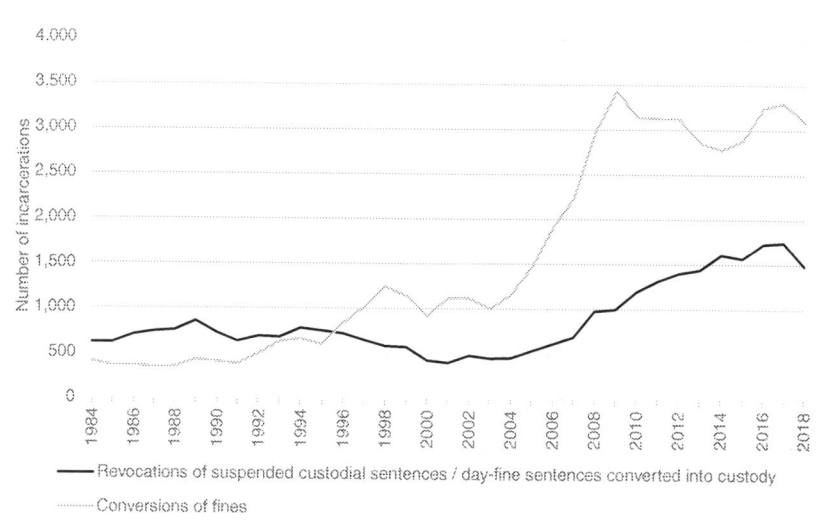

FIGURE 16.4 Prison admissions following the conversion of monetary sanctions into custody, 1984–2018
Source: Federal Statistical Office, Table je-d-19.04.02.32

was 1,907. By 2012, this number had increased to 3,115. In addition to the presumably 1,000 converted day fines, some 4,500 entries into the custodial system are due to unpaid fines and day fines. In view of the continued ignorance of the problem by federal policy-makers, the Department of Justice and Home Affairs of the Canton of Zurich mandated an evaluation of reconversions of flat fines and day fines[17] whose key results are presented in this contribution.

The main purpose of the evaluation was to assess the factual nature of such decisions and of the persons this concerned. How many day fines and flat fines are converted and how many persons are concerned? How many decisions of conversion are actually executed, or how many defendants successfully mobilised the necessary cash through friends or family networks to pay before the reconversion, or even after their admission to custody? What is the profile of those who end up in prison compared to those who avoided the ultimate consequence? What efforts were made preceding the conversion by the specialised agencies within the criminal justice system? How many fines remained unpaid because their execution through prison became time-barred?

---

[17]   Killias and Biberstein, *Ersatzfreiheitsstrafen im Kanton Zürich.*

16.4 A MAJOR PROBLEM DENIED: MONETARY PENALTIES
CONVERTED INTO CUSTODY

16.4.1 *The Present Study*

The present study is based on a sample of 447 cases that the authorities in charge of collecting fines and day fines in the county and city level had referred to the Department of Justice, because all reasonable efforts seemed exhausted to collect the due amount and which were settled between March 2017 and February 2018. In these cases, a conversion of a day fine or a fine into community service (possible at the defendant's request, under Section 79(a) (1) (c) SCC) was not feasible. The officials in charge of executing monetary sanctions on the county and city level were also interviewed in order to complete the picture. Beyond the analysis of official data, a survey among prisoners serving short custodial sentences following a decision of conversion was conducted to include the perspective of those concerned in the first place. Besides, we were able to obtain data from the Internal Revenue Service of the Canton of Zurich on prisoners serving time for unpaid monetary sanctions and their economic situation. Finally, the specialists of the correctional system assessed the costs associated with the execution of fines and day fines, on one hand and of executing such sanctions in prison, on the other hand.

The study concerned 447 case files involving 1,668 monetary penalties (of which 1,510 were fines and 158 were day fines).[18] The official data provided information on personal background, offence(s) the person had been found guilty of, sentences meted out against them and the way the case was settled (through payment, time-barred, execution of the custodial sentence instead of the monetary sanction and a residual category including deaths, early release etc.).

The survey among the inmates was based on a written, anonymous and standardised questionnaire that every inmate received at admission. 188 questionnaires were distributed to 185 persons (three persons having entered prison twice between October 2017 and February 2018). The response rate was 60 per cent (ninety-eight men and eight women). Data from the Internal Revenue Service were received in a form that allowed linking the data to the other information in our files while respecting data protection regulations. Beyond information on financial circumstances (including income, debts and assets), data on marital status, children and other dependent persons were

---

[18]   Readers should be aware that flat fines are very frequently imposed next to suspended day fines. Being always unsuspended, they are far more likely to be converted into custody than day fines.

obtained. The interviews with employees of the several offices in charge of collecting fines and debts from day fines included information on number of cases dealt with, sentences at stake, nature of offences and details on the management of the case. The data on the gross and net costs of converting monetary sanctions into custodial sentences were obtained through the accounting offices of the Justice Department. These costs include direct and indirect costs of staff as well as of consumables and infrastructures, of which the sums actually collected were deducted.

16.4.2 *How Many Monetary Sanctions Are Converted into Custody?*

A first finding concerns the number of penalties per person. The distribution is highly skewed, with 45 per cent of all persons in our sample having just one sanction to face. The other half have often experienced, however, multiple sentences, in two cases even twenty-five. A few persons are systematically sentenced to additional sanctions, such that the number of unpaid fines or day fines to be executed is constantly growing. Time-barred cases usually involve fines or day fines of persons without a known address in Switzerland (31 per cent with a known address versus 69 per cent without). The execution of monetary sanctions is time-barred after five years in the case of day fines (Section 99 (1)(e) SCC) and after three years in the case of flat fines (Section 109 SCC). In other words, the offices in charge of collecting debts are doing their job correctly in most cases. In the case of debtors without residence in Switzerland or without known address at all, the odds of collecting debts are fairly low in any case, even beyond monetary sanctions. If the amounts are relatively low, it can be suspected that the debt collectors often view the effort needed as disproportionate.

Day fines and flat fines can be paid (and prison avoided) even once all deadlines have expired (Section 36 (1) and Section 106 (4) SCC). Many persons concerned by a decision of conversion make use of this possibility. This was the case also among a substantial number of respondents in our sample. Of the total of 447 cases, 195 were settled last-minute, namely by complete payment in 155 cases and partial payment in 40 cases (these defendants had to 'pay' the unpaid sum in prison).

Successful payment clearly depends on the number of days to serve. Among those facing difficulties of payment (and, therefore, included in our sample), the average number of days was eight (and the median three) days among those who, in the end, successfully paid the amount due (and avoided prison), whereas those who were not successful faced on average 52 days (the median being 25), with an outlier serving 755 days. Even if the daily income has not

TABLE 16.1 *Kind of final settlement by type of monetary penalty*

	Flat fines		Day fines		Total	
	N	%	N	%	N	%
Amount paid	354	(97.0)	11	(3.0)	365	(100)
Execution time-barred	86	(94.5)	5	(5.5)	91	(100)
Other settlements	185	(84.5)	34	(15.5)	219	(100)
Conversion to custodial sentence	885	(89.1)	108	(10.9)	993	(100)
Total	1,510	(90.5)	158	(9.5)	1,668	(100)

Source: own table.

been overestimated by sentencing judges, the amounts to pay can rapidly reach staggering proportions as the number of days increases, the maximum being set at 180 days (Section 34 (1) SCC).

This is well reflected in our data: Among those who successfully paid their fine, the amount due was on average 120 Swiss francs, compared to 235 Swiss francs among those who went to prison. In the case of day fines, the gap is less clear, with both groups having a median due amount of 1,800 Swiss francs. On average, however, those who succeeded paying the amount due have outstanding fines of 1,700 Swiss francs, compared to 2,660 Swiss francs among those who went to prison. In sum, those who actually went to prison had, on average, higher amounts to pay that even their network could not easily afford coping with. In our sample, around 90 per cent of those who actually ended incarcerated faced an unpaid flat fine (Table 16.1), often of a substantial amount. By contrast, payment is more frequent among those who had to cope with flat fines (97 per cent) rather than a day fine (3 per cent).

Among those whose fine was converted, the prevailing offences for which they were convicted were either a traffic offence or repeated fare-dodging (riding in public transportation without a valid ticket).[19] Interestingly, among those who faced unpaid fines, those who actually paid in order to avoid custody had been convicted for a (serious) traffic offence in 59 per cent of the cases, compared to 44 per cent who had been convicted for fare-dodging. This difference probably reflects also the fact that traffic offenders may be better off than fare-dodgers who are indeed a more marginal population. They make up for 41 per cent of those who actually go to prison.

---

[19] Fare-dodging is usually not prosecuted, except in cases of persistent offenders, Section 57 (3) Law on Public Transportation.

Those who serve monetary sanctions in prison are, therefore, often convicted to high fines or a considerable number of day fines, often with substantial per day amounts. Next to this group, decisions to convert fines and day fines into custody often concern defendants with fairly trivial amounts. No less than 75 per cent of fines converted concern amounts of 350 Swiss francs or less and 25 per cent of no more than 100 Swiss francs. Thus, a substantial number of people serving fines in prison do so because of trivial amounts usually imposed for rather trivial offences. They must be faced with multiple problems of social integration (including previous incarceration) and often lack a social network that otherwise might support them in such situations. Those who ultimately succeed in avoiding prison by last-minute payments are typically better off in these respects.

16.4.3 *The Survey among Persons Entering Prison*

Shortly after their admission, persons actually entering custody were interviewed through a written, standardised questionnaire that included questions on the circumstances leading to their incarceration and previous experiences of this kind. Just over 80 per cent said having been unable to cope with the monetary penalty, 9 per cent said they were absolutely unwilling to pay and 12 per cent responded that they considered it easier to serve the time in prison rather than to pay (multiple responses were possible). This last result, that may come as a surprise, has to be seen in the context of often high debts resulting from day fines. Sums of around 30,000 Swiss francs (that are not unusual for day fines), may be hard to gain on the labour market, especially if, as a result of a former offence or of the conviction, a person with substantial revenues had lost his/her position.

Among those entering prison, 57 per cent had been arrested by the police, whereas 43 per cent entered on their own initiative. Compared to ordinary prison sentences, the proportion of unwilling entries seems relatively high, pointing, once more, to the probably problematic social integration of this population. Despite the fact that they are in prison to serve their monetary sentence, 39 per cent still hope being able to mobilise funds to pay the remaining amount and to get out of prison. Among these, 65 per cent hope that somebody belonging to their network might volunteer to pay the remaining amount. Among those who have a job, 48 per cent had informed their employers or colleagues about the reason of their immediate absence in advance. Finally, for 30 per cent the actual experience is the first incarceration in their lifetime – or, conversely, for 70 per cent prison has already been part of their history.

16.4.4 *Fiscal Data*

For obvious reasons, the internal revenue service was able to provide information only about persons with a known address in the Canton of Zurich. This included 57 per cent of the sample. The fiscal data provided covered the period 2013 to 2016.

According to the results, monetary sanctions that the authorities did not collect in time before they were time-barred concern mostly persons without a known address in Switzerland and on whom the tax offices do not have actual data. Defendants who paid the amount due before they were arrested typically had higher incomes than those who did not. As it seems, defendants who failed to pay rarely had children or other dependent persons to support. As it seems they disproportionately live in social isolation. They lack a network on whose support they can count in critical situations.

16.4.5 *Costs of Executing Monetary Penalties*

Collecting debts through various procedures and eventually converting them into prison terms brings substantial bureaucratic costs. The accounting office of the Justice Department was able to provide approximate estimates of the costs involved. Since the question is how much is to be paid and how much can be gained through the (often much delayed) collection of debts, two ways of handling this issue will be presented.

In both approaches, the 'cost estimate' will be a balance of payments received, minus costs of debt collection including the costs of converting monetary penalties into prison terms. If only direct costs are considered, that is, investments in collecting debts and having served days in prison, the net balance is positive, with a net profit per case of 113 and 143 Swiss francs, respectively, gained in 2017 and 2018. If indirect costs are included, such as the maintenance of the necessary infrastructure (offices, staff, prison facilities, etc.), the balance becomes negative, meaning that the net costs were seventeen and twenty-one Swiss francs, respectively, in 2017 and 2018. Per day served in prison, the balance of gains and costs is positive again, with 188 and 189 Swiss francs in both years 2017 and 2018. If indirect costs are included, the balance turns into a loss of twenty-eight and twenty-seven Swiss francs per day served in both years considered.

What does this mean? Of course, serving time in prison brings costs and only minimal profit. On balance, prisons operate, therefore, worldwide at considerable costs to the taxpayer. In the particular case of monetary penalties and their conversion into time to be served in custody, one should not ignore possible benefits through enforcing the payment of these particular kinds of debts. In sum, all cases included in our sample concern convicted defendants who had failed to pay the due amount within reasonable deadlines. It can, therefore, be presumed that without the pressure of having to serve the unpaid sanction in prison, the amounts ultimately collected would probably be more modest. From a bureaucratic point of view, the system of converting monetary sanctions into custody can hardly be seen as a failure. Even when all indirect costs are included (which is not obvious), it should be noted that the loss to the taxpayer is far more modest than with practically all other kinds of punishments.

16.5 POLICY IMPLICATIONS

Even if reasonable efforts are made to execute short prison terms resulting from the conversion of monetary penalties in a form that supports inmates' resources of coping with life in society, it must realistically be accepted that imprisonment, though not generally damaging as often claimed,[20] rarely produces positive effects. This does not mean that the continued use of prison is 'irrational', as often has been claimed. The present example of conversion of monetary penalties into custody offers a helpful illustration on this behalf. Indeed, if monetary penalties could remain unpaid without any serious consequences for defendants, it could be expected that many more defendants would simply ignore orders to pay. This would definitively undermine the legitimacy of monetary sanctions and, ultimately, of the criminal law itself since it relies upon such sanctions so widely. It should not be ignored that defendants who face difficulties paying the due amount are eligible for community service if they file such a request (Section 79(a) (1)(c) SCC). Only once authorities order the conversion into custody, community service no longer is an available option (Section 79(a) (2) SCC).

Even if the system of conversions operates with rationality and moderation, the fact remains that monetary penalties instead of formerly common short (and often suspended) custodial sentences leave a growing fraction of convicted defendants in custody. In other words, short prison sentences have not really been abolished. Rather, they were socially redistributed, hitting, in the first place, defendants with multiple problems of social integration including financial strain, as well as foreign defendants without (legal) residence in the country. These two groups continue to be targets of (short) immediate custody. This side effect was by no means unforeseeable. It was a deliberate decision of the legislator to save the middle class from custody, even under the form of

---

[20] *Supra* note 4.

suspended sentences, in connection with traffic and minor economic offences. The question, of course, remains whether this kind of sentencing system can be seen as fair, but we have to admit that this is, ultimately, a political decision.

As the data have shown, defendants who serve their monetary penalties in prison are not in all cases marginal persons without any resources. In some cases, day fines were meted out at a time when the defendant had a well-paid job that he/she may have lost after the hearing. Perhaps even more often, day fines were suspended in the first place and became payable after a new offence when the judge revoked the former suspension. Under such circumstances, it may well be that the amounts to pay are out of proportion with the defendant's current or foreseeable financial situation. In such cases, it may well be rational to spend a few weeks or months in prison, given that the income during the corresponding period might never reach the amount of the penalty.

In this connection, there remains also the question whether day fines and flat fines are being fixed with the necessary attention to the defendant's financial circumstances. For example, the real costs of having dependent children are often not handled with great attention. This, however, is just a simple and frequent situation, but neither the Parliament nor the Judiciary have ever cared about preparing more developed guidelines on how simple and frequent situations like these can be taken into account. Left alone with a few summary indications, judges are not really able to pay the necessary attention to these details during a short hearing centred on issues of guilt and fault. More precise guidelines, modelled along taxation offices' ways of handling frequent and typical life-circumstances, might be helpful in streamlining day fines and flat fines efficiently and more equitably.

All these problems are accentuated in Switzerland with its extremely high rate of suspended sentences. In a European comparison, based on data published regularly by the European Sourcebook of Crime and Criminal Justice Statistics,[21] Switzerland is among the countries where even serious offenders face fairly low risks of being sentenced to immediate custody, at least for a first or even a second conviction. This is not only true for traffic and minor offences, but includes serious crimes such as robbery, drug trafficking, serious bodily injury (i.e. aggravated assault) and even a majority of rapists. In light of this preference for suspended sentences, it should not come as a surprise that day fines are almost systematically suspended. This may lead judges to pay only superficial attention to the financial circumstances of the defendant, given that in nine out of ten cases, the amount will never be payable. However,

---

[21] Aebi, *et al. European Sourcebook of Crime and Criminal Justice Statistics 2014.*

the problem will be serious if the defendant relapses and if, following a subsequent conviction, the formerly suspended sentence is to be executed.

Furthermore, as explained above, flat fines can never be suspended. Since judges almost systematically add a flat fine to whatever sentence (monetary or custodial) they impose, these fines are more likely to be converted into prison. Although, in theory, even for meting out flat fines the defendant's financial circumstances should be taken into account, judges usually fix 'round' amounts that can be substantial. In addition, the conversion of flat fines is made easier because the judge indicates how many days the defendant has to serve in case he/she does not pay within the deadlines.

Finally, it is possible that the problems reported in this chapter are more serious in Switzerland than in other countries. To the authors' knowledge, in no other European country have short custodial sentences been so systematically replaced by monetary penalties, suspended or not. This means that monetary penalties are more than presumably anywhere else hitting defendants found guilty of even serious offences and often marginal profiles, combined with very limited financial resources.

REFERENCES

Aebi, M. F., *et al.* 2014. *European Sourcebook of Crime and Criminal Justice Statistics 2014*. Helsinki: European Institute for Crime Prevention and Control, affiliated with the United Nations (HEUNI).

Bonneville de Marsangy, A. 1864. *De l'amélioration de la loi criminelle en vue d'une justice plus prompte, plus efficace, plus généreuse et plus moralisante*. Paris: Cosse et Maréchal.

Botschaft des Bundesrates zur Änderung des Schweizerischen Strafgesetzbuches … vom 21. September 1998, *Bundesblatt* 1999, 1979.

Killias, M. and Biberstein, L. 2019. *Ersatzfreiheitsstrafen im Kanton Zürich*. Report to the Department of Justice and Home Affairs, Canton of Zurich.

Killias, M., Aebi, M. F. and Kuhn, A. 2019. *Précis de criminologie*. Bern: Stämpfli.

Killias, M., Markwalder, N., Kuhn, A. and Dongois, N. 2016. *Grundriss des Allgemeinen Teils des Schweizerischen Strafgesetzbuchs*. Bern: Stämpfli.

Schultz, H. 1987. *Bericht und Vorentwurf zur Revision des Allgemeinen Teils … des Schweizerischen Strafgesetzbuches*. Bern: Stämpfli.

Simmler, M. 2016. 'Sieben enttäuschte Hoffnungen? Zur statistischen Überprüfung der realen Folgen der AT-Revision', *Schweizerische Zeitschrift für Strafrecht* 134/1: 73–99.

Villettaz, P., Gilliéron, G. and Killias, M. 2014. *The Effects on Re-offending of Custodial versus Non-custodial Sanctions*. Stockholm: BRA. (Also published in the Campbell Library, www.campbellcollaboration.org.)

Von Liszt, F. 1883. 'Der Zweckgedanke im Strafrecht', *Zeitschrift für die gesamte Strafrechtswissenschaft* 3: 1–47.

17

Day Fines in Czech Republic

Jiří Kindl and Jan Kupčík

17.1 HISTORICAL DEVELOPMENT OF DAY FINES IN THE COUNTRY

Originally, the possibility to impose a fine as a punishment for a crime, however not in the form of a day fine, was included in the Czech (and Slovak) criminal justice system in 1950 by the Czechoslovakian Criminal Code (the 'Criminal Code 1950').[1] Fines could have been imposed only as a lump sum within a range specified by the Criminal Code 1950. Also the next Criminal Code (the 'Criminal Code 1961'), in force between 1962 and 2009,[2] included only provisions on a lump sum fine, whose range changed twice during the period.[3]

However, already in 2003, the Parliament passed a bill on liability of juveniles, which became the Juvenile Act[4] entering into force on 1 January 2004. The Juvenile Act was the first significant embodiment of the new trend of restorative justice after almost forty years of a criminal justice system being burdened with communist ideas. The Juvenile Act, inter alia, allowed for, besides a lump sum fine, a punishment in the form of a day fine.

Between 2004 and 2009, the Juvenile Act allowed criminal courts to impose a fine on a young offender (in general, a person committing an offence between his/her fifteenth and eighteenth birthday), if such an offender

---

[1] I.e. the Act No. 86/1950 Coll., the Criminal Code, entering into effect on 1 August 1950. Until the first Criminal Code was adapted in Czechoslovakia, the Czechoslovakian courts had applied (since the establishment of Czechoslovakia in 1918) the Act on Crimes, Misdemeanours and Administrative Offences enacted by a patent no. 117/1852 Coll.

[2] The Act. No. 140/1961 Coll., the Criminal Code.

[3] First, the range of a fine was set to CSK 500 – CSK 50,000 in the period between 1962 and 1990, then the range was increased to CSK 2,000 – CSK 1,000,000 in the period 1990–3 and finally, in the period from 1994 to 2009, the upper limit was increased to CZK 5,000,000 (approximately 189,000 euros in 2009).

[4] I.e. the Act No. 218/2003 Coll., on liability of juvenile for offences and on judiciary in juvenile matters (the 'Juvenile Act').

received an income from its employment or business activities.[5] Under such conditions, the court could have chosen between (i) a lump sum amount between CZK 1,000 (approximately 39 euros)[6] and CZK 500,000 (approximately 19,500 euros) and (ii) a day fine. Both forms of the fine could have been imposed individually as the only punishment, or as a supplement to another sanction (for example, imprisonment).

In the period between 2004 and 2009 the daily unit of the fine had to be between CZK 100 (approximately 3.90 euros) and CZK 1,000 (approximately 39 euros) and it had to be set with regard to the offender's daily income, while the number of days ranged between 5 and 500. Therefore, the provisions theoretically allowed the lowest fine of CZK 500 (approximately 19.50 euros), while the lump sum form had the lower limit set to CZK 1,000 (approximately 39 euros), but the upper limit was identical for both forms.

The Juvenile Act also empowered the courts to conditionally suspend the enforcement of the fine, if with regard to the character and circumstances of the offender and to circumstances of the case, the court had a reasonable belief that the enforcement of the sentence is not necessary for achieving its goals.

Hence in the period between 2004 and 2009, the Czech criminal justice system had known day fines only in cases of juvenile offenders. For the rest of the offenders, there was only a possibility of a lump sum fine.

Nevertheless, soon after the Juvenile Act was enacted it became clear that the theoretical foundations of restorative justice will also result in the new Criminal Code.[7] After many years of consultations and preparations, the new Criminal Code was passed in the Parliament and became Act No. 40/2009, the Criminal Code, effective from 1 January 2010 (the 'Criminal Code 2009' or the 'Criminal Code'). In the same legislative process, the Juvenile Act was amended in order to be compliant with the new Criminal Code.

Although the day fines specifically were not extensively discussed, one of the critical topics in the process of the preparation of the Criminal Code 2009 was alternative sanctions.[8] The previous criminal justice system was perceived as

---

[5]   Moreover, it was also possible to impose a fine, but only as a lump sum, if the offender's financial circumstances allowed a monetary form of a punishment.

[6]   The conversion rate as of 18 April 2019 of the Czech National Bank, i.e. of 25.68 CZK/EUR, is used herein.

[7]   Already in 2004, the government prepared a new criminal code and submitted it to the Parliament (see bill No. 744 in the election period 2002–06, available at: www.psp.cz/sqw/historie.sqw?O=4&T=744. In particular, see p. 186 of the explanatory memorandum to the bill. The bill was, however, rejected by the Senate and then abandoned by the Chamber of Deputies.

[8]   See, in particular, the explanatory memorandum to the Criminal Code 2009, pp. 181–6.

outdated with its focus on imprisonment.[9] The day fines were therefore discussed as a part of the new alternative sanctions system.

The reason for the new concept of setting fines was not explicitly declared. However, already in the course of the Juvenile Act adoption it was argued that the Czech criminal law needs better tools for individualisation of sanctions. The previous criminal legal regimes were burdened with a focus on imprisonment and the range and importance of alternative sanctions was rather negligible. The new Criminal Code was passed with the aim to widen the set of available alternative sanctions and make them more popular and more often used, as the ratio of imprisoned offenders per an inhabitant was generally seen to be too high.[10] More differentiated sanctions should have been ensured, inter alia, by the concept of day fines.

The preferability of alternative sanctions is, with respect to the sanctions against the offender's property, also emphasised in Section 39 (7) of the Criminal Code 2009. The group of the sanctions against property includes a day fine, a forfeiture of property (Section 66) and a forfeiture of an item or other assets (Section 70). The abovementioned Section 39 (7) orders the court to always impose such a sanction against property if the offender obtained or attempted to obtain a material benefit by the crime, unless his/her personal and financial circumstances preclude it.

Hence, since 2010 the only possibility to impose a fine as a criminal sentence in the Czech Republic has been as a day fine. Moreover, the new Legal Persons Liability Act[11] entered into force on 1 January 2012 and also provides for a punishment in the form of a day fine. Although the Juvenile Act's day fines are slightly different from the day fines in the Criminal Code (which are, by reference, applicable also for legal persons), the structure of day fines is similar throughout the Czech criminal justice system.

The specifics of the day fines pursuant to the Juvenile Act are the conditions of their application as well as their permitted range. The day fine may be imposed on a juvenile only if he/she receives an income from its employment or business activities or its financial circumstances allow for a monetary form of a punishment. These conditions are not included in the Criminal Code as it is less protective for the offenders, but even pursuant to the

---

[9]   *Ibid.*, p. 182.

[10] This is especially significant when compared to Western European countries. In 2008, before the new Criminal Act became effective, the ratio had been over 200 for 100,000 inhabitants.

[11] I.e. the Act No. 418/2011 Coll., on criminal liability of legal persons and proceedings against them (the 'Legal Persons Liability Act').

Criminal Code the court cannot impose the fine if it is evident that it would be unenforceable.[12]

Moreover, the Criminal Code, unlike the Juvenile Act, does not contain provisions on conditional suspension of the fine. The possibility was discussed during the preparation of the Criminal Code, but it was seen as inappropriate for adult offenders with regard to the conditions of imposing the day fine, while suspended custodial sentence or available forms of avoiding the criminal process in specific situations (via the institute of diversions) was found to be more effective.

Finally, the Juvenile Act sets, for logical reasons, the limits of both the daily unit and the number of days lower than the Criminal Code. As a result, the highest possible amount imposed pursuant to the Juvenile Act is twenty times lower than the highest fine pursuant to the Criminal Code. Furthermore, the Legal Persons Liability Act includes a special provision on the daily unit that effectively increases the highest possible fine for legal persons forty times as opposed to the fine pursuant to the Criminal Code.

For the sake of completeness, day fines are not, to our knowledge, imposed outside of the criminal justice system. The Administrative Offences Act,[13] as a general act for administrative law, does not prescribe the types of fines. However, most of the acts governing specific administrative offences and their sanctions set the fines as lump-sum and specify the range. There are also other ways of calculation of a fine, but none of these is as a day fine.[14] Therefore, the day fines are used solely in criminal law, *stricto sensu*. Other methods of setting fines are not used in criminal law.

17.2 THE LEGAL FRAMEWORK OF DAY FINES

The structure of the day fines for natural persons is based on the Sections 67 to 69 of the Criminal Code.[15] With certain exceptions, this structure is also

---

[12] Section 68 (6) of the Criminal Code states: 'A court cannot impose a monetary fine if it is obvious that it would be unenforceable'.

[13] *I.e.* Act No. 250/2016 Coll., on liability for administrative offences and proceedings about them (the 'Administrative Offences Act').

[14] For example, Act No. 143/2001 Coll., on competition, sets an alternative upper limit to 10 per cent of the offender's last year turnover for legal persons (Section 22(a)(2) of the Act). The same limit is applied by Act No. 395/2009 Coll., on significant market power (Section 8 (3) of the Act). Similarly, Act No. 254/2001 Coll., on waters, prescribes the highest possible amount of a fine for consumption of groundwater without a permission pursuant to cubic metres consumed. Act No. 526/1990 Coll., on prices, sets a fine for certain administrative offences as a multiplication of a material benefit (by a constant of one to five) achieved by them (Section 8 (4) of the Act).

[15] The Chapter reflects the legislation as of 1 January 2020, unless provided otherwise.

applicable within the framework of the Juvenile Act. First, in Section 67, the conditions for a day fine imposition are defined. The fine may be imposed if:

(1) the offender obtained or attempted to obtain for himself/herself or anyone else a material benefit by an intentional crime;

(2) the Criminal Code explicitly names the fine as a sanction with respect to the respective crime; or

(3) it is imposed for a misdemeanour[16] and with regard to the nature and relevance of the misdemeanour and the personality and circumstances of the offender no imprisonment is imposed.

The fine may solely be imposed if, with regard to the nature and gravity of the crime and the personality and circumstances of the offender, no other sanction is necessary, or in a combination with other sanctions prescribed by the Criminal Code.

When the court imposes the day fine, it also has to determine the specific substitute sanction of imprisonment that shall be served if the fine is not paid.[17] The Criminal Code does not prescribe any specific conversion ratio. The imprisonment period shall not exceed four years.[18] However, if the court imposes the imprisonment in combination with the day fine as a secondary sanction, the sum of potential imprisonment served can never exceed the upper limit set for the respective crime.[19] If the fine is not duly paid, the court may convert it into house arrest (if such a sanction is applicable) or into community service obligation.[20] Only subsequently the court may transform either of these sanctions into imprisonment under specific conditions.[21]

Different conditions are applied for legal persons (entities). The Legal Persons Liability Act constructs the day fine as a universal sanction, hence, regardless of the type of the crime and whether it was committed intentionally or negligently.[22] The only restrictive condition for the day fine imposed on legal persons is that it cannot be to the detriment of the victims of the crime. This follows the general principle of the legal persons criminal sanctions

---

[16] Please note that the Criminal Code divides crimes into felonies and misdemeanours. All negligence crimes and crimes with the upper limit of an imprisonment (as all crimes have the sanction of imprisonment set out) up to five years are misdemeanours, the other (more serious) crimes are felonies.

[17] Nevertheless, despite the determination of the substitute sanction in the judgment, the court still has to order an oral hearing when transforming the day fine into another sanction.

[18] Section 69 (1) of the Criminal Code.

[19] *Ibid.*

[20] *Ibid.*, Section 69 (2).

[21] *Ibid.*, Section 69 (3).

[22] Section 18 (1) of the Legal Persons Liability Act.

imposition, which requires always to consider legally protected interests of third parties, especially the victims.[23] Given that the day fine is a universal sanction for legal persons, it makes the sanction in practice one of the most often used as approximately 30 to 40 per cent of condemned legal persons are obligated to pay the fine.[24]

17.2.1 *The Number of Days*

The calculation of the fine is described in Section 68. It simply states that the fine is imposed in daily units. The range of the number of days is fixed between 20 and 730 days. However, since 2010, the Juvenile Act mitigates the range for juvenile offenders (below 18 years) to the range between 10 and 365 days.[25] The Legal Persons Liability Act does not have a specific provision regarding the daily units, hence the Criminal Code range applies. Sections 58 and 59 of the Criminal Code empower the court to reduce a criminal sanction below the bottom limit and to increase it above the maximum limit under specific circumstances. But those sections apply only to imprisonment; both the lower and the upper limit of the number of days must be observed.[26]

The number of days is set with regard to the nature and gravity of the crime.[27] Nevertheless, there is no legal connection between the number of days and the imprisonment range for the respective crime. The number of days is thus set by the court regardless of other potential forms of a punishment. Also, the Criminal Code does not allow a voluntary conversion of the day fine into any other form of a punishment. Before the Criminal Code was adopted, it was discussed whether it shall include a provision on a voluntary conversion[28] of the day fine into community service obligation (as it is possible in Germany whose criminal code stands as one of the main inspirations for the Criminal Code 2009). In the end it was concluded that this option will not be given to the offenders, both as the possibility of the community service sanction shall have the priority and thus is going to be considered by the court before contemplating an imposition of the day fine

---

[23] *Ibid.*, Section 14 (3).
[24] Jelínek, 'Koncepce trestní odpovědnosti právnických osob', 10.
[25] Section 27 (2) of the Juvenile Act.
[26] This was also previously confirmed by case law – see the judgment of the Supreme Court of 22 September 1966, No. 4/1967 of the criminal cases coll.
[27] Section 68 (3) of the Criminal Code.
[28] A conversion is voluntary if it is up to the offender's will whether he/she chooses to pay the fine or perform a determined number of community service hours. Conversely, the Czech system allows only a mandatory conversion ordered by a court if the fine is not fully paid.

and also as the conversion could be, according to the government, difficult if high fines were imposed.[29]

Hence, the courts are not bound by any strict legal guidelines how to set the number of days and they do not have to consider the potential length of the imprisonment or a number of community service hours that could have been imposed for the same crime. The court may, however, convert the day fine into alternative sanctions, namely house arrest or community service.[30] If none of these alternative sanctions may be effectively imposed, the court may also order to convert the day fine into imprisonment for the length previously determined.[31] Nevertheless, in neither of those cases the court is instructed to base the respective sanction on the number of days set previously for the purposes of the day fine. Therefore, hypothetically the court may convert any day fine into any number of days of house arrest, imprisonment or any number of community service hours within the ranges set for the respective crime. This lack of interconnection results in a minor importance of the determination of the number of days in practice, as will be further described in Section 17.3.

17.2.2 *The Daily Unit*

The daily unit may vary from CZK 100 (approximately 3.90 euros) to CZK 50,000 (approximately 1,950 euros) pursuant to the Criminal Code. Given the existence of the Juvenile Act and the Legal Persons Liability Act, this range effectively applies only to adult natural persons. The Juvenile Act, pursuing more educational and preventive goals, reduces the maximum daily unit limit to CZK 5,000 (approximately 195 euros) while keeping the lower limit of CZK 100.[32] However, the Legal Persons Liability Act, given that also large corporations may be subjected to it, increases both of the limits. Hence, a legal person's daily unit of a fine may vary between CZK 1,000 (approximately 39 euros) and CZK 2,000,000 (approximately 78,000 euros).[33]

The actual daily unit is determined with respect to the personal and financial circumstances of the offender. Generally, the court's assessment shall be based on the offender's average net daily income or the daily income

---

[29] See the explanatory memorandum of the government accompanying the Criminal Code 2009.

[30] Section 344 (2) of Act No. 141/1961 Coll., on the Criminal Proceedings, as amended (the 'Criminal Procedure Code').

[31] Section 344 (3) of the Criminal Procedure Code.

[32] Section 27 (3) of the Juvenile Act.

[33] Section 18 (2) of the Legal Persons Liability Act.

the offender would have,[34] should he/she invest reasonable effort. Although the primary condition for a day fine imposition is a material benefit or an attempt to obtain it, the specific daily unit is not linked to the amount of the benefit. Therefore, the final amount of the fine may exceed the benefit obtained. It is expected that the court gathers the information on the offender's income, his/her assets and relating profits in order to be able to properly establish the daily unit. Nevertheless, if the court is unable to gather the information, the respective daily unit may be determined on the basis of the court's estimate.

With respect to legal persons' crimes, the only facts to be taken into account when determining the daily unit are financial circumstances of the legal person in question. In other words, the court does not base its assessment on the daily income of the legal person as, in contrast to natural persons, it does not receive wage or other similar regular income, but when assessing the financial circumstances, the court shall take into account its assets, turnover, generated profit etc. Hence, in general, the court has a wider discretion as to the determination of the daily unit for legal persons.

17.2.3 *Access to Financial Information*

Since 2017, the Criminal Procedure Code contains a specific provision that enables the court to request information on the offender's financial circumstances, including the state of his/her assets, his/her income, existence of his/her accounts, etc. The information may be requested directly from the offender or a close person to him/her.[35] The person addressed by the court may refuse to provide the information on the basis of the same reasons as it may refuse to give a testimony.[36] Furthermore, the courts have a general authority to request information from state bodies as well as from legal and natural persons.[37] For the purposes of assessment of the offender's financial circumstances, the courts may also request information protected by the bank

---

[34] Section 68 (3) of the Criminal Code.

[35] Section 7(a) of the Criminal Procedure Code.

[36] The reasons are, pursuant to Section 100 of the Criminal Procedure Code, the following: (i) the person addressed is a direct relative, a sibling, a husband, a partner, an adopting or adopted person of the accused person, or (ii) the person addressed would have caused a risk of a criminal prosecution to his/her direct relative, sibling, husband, partner, a person adopted by him/her, adopting him/her or someone else, whose harm he/she would consider as his/her own. However, the person addressed may not refuse to give a testimony if it has a crime notification obligation (which is the case for specific, the most serious crimes).

[37] Section 8 (1) of the Criminal Procedure Code.

secret (for example, the existence and current state of the offender's accounts) and information from the registers of investment instruments and securities.[38]

Thus, the courts have quite wide powers in order to determine the decisive circumstances for the determination of the daily unit in each case. In practice, in the case of natural persons, the courts may summon the offender's employer and request the offender's average net daily income.[39] If the offender is an individual entrepreneur, the average income may be calculated from his/her tax returns, which may be requested from the Tax Offices. If the offender is not employed or self-employed, his/her income may be determined from data of the Czech Social Security Administration or from his/her bank accounts. As not only the income is decisive, the courts shall also focus on the offender's assets and the profit generated by such assets. To some extent, this can be also assessed from tax returns, but the court may also use any other evidence available, as well as the institute of witnesses' testimony. In the case of legal persons, the information on its financial circumstances is often publicly available (publication of the financial statements and the annual reports are obligatory for most of the legal persons). Moreover, their tax returns can be provided by the Tax Offices as well as data from their bank accounts may be obtained. If necessary, the court may appoint an expert to provide an opinion on the value of the company's assets.

Finally, if the evidence on the offender's daily income is not conclusive, the court has the possibility to estimate the offender's financial circumstances (both for the natural and legal persons). The estimation is a legal question,[40] hence the court shall be the one to provide the estimate, not an expert appointed by the court (nor other authorities active in the criminal proceedings) but, of course, in order to make the estimate correctly the court shall seek assistance of experts (e.g. when determining the value of assets as mentioned above).

Despite the court's powers, Drápal[41] found that in practice, the courts did not analyse the offender's daily income in detail. Due to the claimed lack of time,[42] the judges usually resort to the determination of the daily units on the basis of voluntary provided information by the offender to the police without verifying it. At most, they complement the findings on the basis of responses of the offender at

---

[38] *Ibid.*, Section 8 (2).

[39] The net income is then calculated pursuant to Sections 351 to 362 of Act No. 262/2006 Coll., the Labour Code, as amended (the 'Labour Code').

[40] Púry *et al.*, *Trestní zákoník (EVK)*, 2nd edn, p. 894.

[41] Drápal, 'Analýza ukládání peněžitých trestů v podobě denních pokut v České republice', 4–5. It shall be noted that the research was concluded before the abovementioned Section 7(a) of the Criminal Procedure Code was enacted.

[42] See Drápal, 'Day Fines: A European Comparison and Czech Malpractice', 469.

the oral hearing, but do not request evidence in that regard.[43] If the information is not provided voluntarily, the court exercises the possibility of estimating the income without attempting to obtain the information from other sources.

17.2.4 *Who Can Impose Day Fines?*

As currently the day fines in the Czech Republic may be imposed only within the scope of criminal proceedings, the court is the only authority that may impose it. The rules of criminal proceedings allow the public prosecutors to suggest the sanction in their closing speech, but the decision itself is solely within the authority of the court.

The court's judgment shall include the number of days and the daily unit. The principal rule is to obligate the offender to pay the fine at once, but if it cannot be expected with regard to the offender's personal and financial circumstances that he/she is able to pay it at once, the court may order the fine to be paid in monthly instalments. In such a case, the court may also decide that if one of the instalments is not duly paid, the offender loses the advantage of instalments and has to pay the fine at once in full.[44]

17.2.5 *The Institutions Involved in the Collection of Fines*

If the fine is imposed, it has to be paid to the court's account and the State is entitled to it.[45] Once the judgment becomes enforceable, the head of the court's senate summons the offender to pay the fine in fifteen days and notifies him/her of the consequences if the fine is not paid.[46] The head of the senate may approve the payment in instalments even if the judgment did not allow it, but only if there are serious reasons for it.[47] However, in this situation the instalments must be set in order to have the fine paid in one year from the date when the judgment became final. The court may also, if there are serious reasons, postpone the date on which the fine must be paid. The postponement shall not exceed three months from the date when the judgment became final.[48] The head of the court's senate may withdraw its decision on instalments or postponement if the serious reasons for it vanished.[49]

---

[43] *Supra* note 41, 4.
[44] Section 68 (5) of the Criminal Code.
[45] *Ibid.*, Section 68 (7).
[46] Section 341 of the Criminal Procedure Code.
[47] *Ibid.*, Section 342 (1)(b).
[48] *Ibid.*, Section 341 (1)(a).
[49] *Ibid.*, Section 341 (2).

If the fine is not paid within fifteen days from the court summoning or until the postponed deadline, the head of the court's senate orders the fine to be enforced.[50] As in certain situations the offender's assets may be seized during the proceedings, the Criminal Procedure Code states that such seized assets shall be primarily used for the payment enforcement.[51] The administration of the enforcement is entrusted to the court or a bailiff.[52]

Finally, the court may also pardon the payment of the fine or its remainder if the offender becomes unable to pay it long-term as a result of incidents outside his/her will or if the fulfilment of the offender's maintenance (nourishment) obligation would be jeopardised.[53]

17.3 THE PRACTICAL IMPLEMENTATION OF DAY FINES

The court cannot impose a day fine if it is evident that it would be unenforceable.[54] The case law of the Supreme Court[55] established the precedence of the offender's maintenance (nourishment) obligation[56] and the obligation to pay damages, hence the court must first assess whether after the fulfilment of those obligations the offender will be even able to pay the fine. Practically, in order to be able to impose the fine, the court must have the means to assess especially the financial circumstances of the offender in a reliable way (both by determining his/her income or by a sound estimation). Hence, if the court cannot estimate the income of the offender and his/her financial circumstances in general, the imposition of the fine is impossible.

17.3.1 *Categories of Offences Day Fines Can Be Used for De Jure and De Facto*

De jure, the day fine may be imposed on legal persons for all the crimes that the legal persons may commit.[57] The generality of the day fine with respect to

---

[50] *Ibid.*, Section 343 (1).

[51] *Ibid.*, Section 343 (2).

[52] Section 175 of the Act No. 280/2009 Coll., the Tax Procedure Code, as amended, referred in Section 343 (3) of the Criminal Procedure Code.

[53] Section 344 (1) of the Criminal Procedure Code.

[54] Section 68 (6) of the Criminal Code.

[55] Especially the judgment of the Supreme Court of 19 July 2017, ref. no. 7 Tdo 702/2017.

[56] With reference to Section 344 (1) of the Criminal Procedure Code.

[57] The Legal Persons Liability Act applies to all crimes in the Criminal Code except those listed in Section 7 of the Legal Persons Liability Act (for example, a manslaughter or a fight are excluded). This provision has been in force since 1 December 2016. Previously the Legal Persons Liability Act included an enumerative list of the crimes that could have been committed by a legal person.

the legal persons is confirmed by statistical facts as well. The distribution of the day fines as a sanction is quite uniform with regard to specific crimes committed by a legal person.[58] However, it must be emphasised that the number of the criminal proceedings with legal persons is quite low (tens of cases in a year). Therefore, the statistical facts may not be as informative as for natural persons. In 2016, the most pursued legal persons' crime was the crime of non-payment of taxes, social insurance or similar charges.[59] The second most pursued crime was the crime of fraud[60] and the third was the crime of tax evasion.[61] The same order was followed in numbers of imposed day fines for the respective crimes.

With respect to natural persons, the day fines may sanction only a limited group of crimes as specified in the Criminal Code (for more details see Section 17.2 above). In 2016, most of the day fines (both as a proportion to all sanctions and in absolute numbers) was imposed for crimes 'generally detrimental' (Chapter VII of the Criminal Code). The reason is that the chapter includes the crime of hazard due to intoxication (which includes some events of drunken driving), which was fined 1,826 times in 2016 out of 1,885 for the generally detrimental crimes and out of 3,358 day fines in total. Therefore, that crime stands for more than a half of the imposed day fines in total. The crime is most often committed by drunk driving. The second most fined chapter of crimes is Chapter X of the Criminal Code – crimes against public order. Accordingly, the second most-often fined crime is the crime of frustration of enforcement of a State authority's decision. The most prominent example of the crime is driving in a situation when it was prohibited to the offender (for example, when the driving licence was seized because of achievement of twelve penal points).[62] This crime was fined 547 times in 2016 which represents over 16 per cent of all day fines. The third most often fined crime is the crime of disorderly conduct (also included in Chapter X) which was fined 198 times in 2016. From the relative point of view (i.e. the most day fines imposed compared to all sanctions for the respective crime; the crimes fined ten times or less are excluded), the first five most fined crimes are the following (accompanied with the ratio of day fines among all cases and the absolute number of fines): (1) hazard due to intoxication – 17.6

---

[58] See Ministry of Justice, 'Annual Statistic Report of Crime', 15 and 17.
[59] Section 241 of the Criminal Code.
[60] *Ibid.*, Section 209.
[61] *Ibid.*, Section 240.
[62] The Czech system of traffic offences allows the driver to commit offences for up to twelve penal points (while the points are awarded to the offences pursuant to their gravity). When the twelfth point is achieved, driving is forbidden for a period of twelve months.

%, 1,826; (2) infringement of laws on labels and other marking of goods – 12.4 %, 12; (3) bodily harm of negligence – 10.9 %, 56; (4) false testimony and false expert opinion – 10.2 %, 17; and (5) frustration of enforcement of a State authority's decision – 7.9 %, 547.[63]

The preceding illustrates that day fines imposed on natural persons are by a large margin most often used for traffic offences.[64] The remaining day fines are distributed quite widely with respect to the crimes sanctioned, as the top ten most fined crimes (in absolute numbers) include crimes against health, freedom, property and public order.[65] The statistics, hence, confirm that the day fines are not intended only to be imposed for crimes causing financial benefits to the offender (or third parties).

Concerning the imposition of the day fines in comparison to other sanctions prescribed by the Criminal Code, day fines are with the sanction of prohibition of an activity the two most often used sanctions for legal persons. In 2015 and 2016, day fines were imposed to 52 legal persons and the prohibition of an activity to 54 legal persons out of 165 condemned in total.[66] No other sanctions were similarly popular. As the concept of criminal liability of legal persons was introduced in 2012, that is when the day fines were already the only way of a fine calculation in criminal law, it cannot be assessed what is the impact of the introduction of the day fines for legal persons sanctioning.

17.3.2 *Statistical Facts Regarding the Proportion of Day Fines in All Sanctions*

In the case of natural persons, the proportion of imposed fines (however not day fines, but lump sum fines) was increasing from the 1960s (when it accounted for approximately 1 per cent of all sanctions) to the 1980s, when it reached approximately 15 per cent. Then, since the beginning of 1990s, the proportion steadily decreased until 2006. After that, a short period of an increase occurred between 2006 and 2009,[67] which is explained by the amendment that criminalised driving without a licence.[68] However, with the new Criminal Code 2009, driving without a licence was decriminalised (there is still, however, the crime of frustration of enforcement of a State authority's decision, for example forbidding driving) and, at the same

---

[63] All data are from the Ministry of Justice, 'Annual Statistic Report of Crime', p. 603.

[64] This is also confirmed in a qualitative study *supra* note 44.

[65] See Ministry of Justice, 'Annual Statistic Report of Crime' (2016).

[66] *Ibid.*, for 2015 and 2016.

[67] Vicherek, 'Přeměna peněžitého trestu', 7.

[68] Válková *et al.*, 'Teoretické a trestněprávní aspekty reformy trestního práva v oblasti trestních sankcí', 20; Hulmáková and Rozum, 'Aktuální trendy sankční politiky v ČR', 256.

time, day fines were introduced.[69] The decriminalisation of the offence is believed to have caused the decreased imposition of day fines in 2010 of 2 per cent bringing it below the level of 5 per cent of all sanctions imposed. The proportion was then decreasing until 2013 when it reached 3.2 per cent. In absolute numbers, it kept decreasing until 2015. In 2016, the proportion returned to the level of 5 per cent. To put those figures into context, the most often used primary sanction in 2016 was suspended custodial sentence/ imprisonment (64 per cent), followed by immediate imprisonment (15 per cent) and punishment in the form of community service (12 per cent). Other types of sanctions (house arrest, prohibition of activities) were below the level of 1 per cent. Similarly, in less than 2 per cent of the cases the court awarded protective measure or refrained from imposing a sanction.[70]

Thus, a fine as a form of criminal sanction still plays a minor role, even after the introduction of day fines. It is generally believed that the introduction of day fines did not have any significant impact on the structure of the sanctions imposed by the courts.[71] The reasons for that lack of impact can be explained by the judges' reservation with the new system or potentially their voluntary disregard of it, as illustrated in a qualitative empirical study by Drápal.[72] The reluctance of the judges to impose day fines is also explained by the complexity of the process associated with their imposition as the judges have to collect and assess financial information and in the case of non-payment, they have to hold a hearing to transform the fine into another sanction.[73]

17.3.3 *Inability to Pay*

The day fines shall be aligned to the financial situation of the offender and the gravity of the crime. Thus, the day fine shall not be imposed on persons that are objectively unable to pay it.[74] That exclusion does not apply in situations when the offender is in a difficult financial situation, but there is a possibility that he/she would be able to pay the fine. Therefore, the day fines may be and are also imposed on low-income offenders. The empirical data even suggests that the practical implementation of the day fines is the harshest for the

---

[69] Except for juveniles, see Section 17.1 above.
[70] All data used are from the Ministry of Justice, 'Annual Statistic Report of Crime' for 2009 to 2016.
[71] *Supra* note 67; *supra* note 68, Válková *et al.*, 20.
[72] *Supra* note 42, 469.
[73] *Supra* note 68, Válková *et al.*, 27.
[74] Section 68 (6) of the Criminal Code.

poorest offenders.[75] The poorest offenders are more likely to rely on social benefits. There are four groups of social benefits in the Czech Republic. The first and the largest is the social security system, including retirement payments and other pensions. In addition, there are health security payments, social support payments and payments to persons in social needs. All the benefits intend to support mainly the poorest inhabitants, but do not have to be sufficient to cover increased expenses due to imposed day fines.

In 2017, the state awarded on average almost three million CZK of social benefits per month, that is approximately 0.28 benefit per inhabitant. The total amount of benefits in 2017 was approximately CZK 474 billion, which is approximately 37 per cent of state expenses in that year and approximately 9.4 per cent of the Czech HDP in 2017.[76] Therefore, the social benefit system is quite robust in the Czech Republic but is unlikely to ensure the full enforceability of day fines. First, certain social benefits (payments to persons in material emergency, housing allowances etc.) cannot be seized. Moreover, the law prescribes to every person a certain minimal amount that cannot be seized. Therefore, unless the offender pays the fines voluntarily, the full amount of the day fine (even in instalments, if set by the court) is unlikely to be enforced as the total income including social benefits will probably not significantly exceed the minimal threshold.

In addition to enforcement of fine payments, other measures to be taken in case of one's inability to pay depend on the reasons why the offender was unable to pay the fine. If the offender was unable to pay due to reasons beyond his/her will, the court shall forgive the sanction.[77] If the inability was due to the behaviour of the offender, the court shall decide on the conversion to house arrest or community service obligation (or, if that is not possible, to imprisonment).[78]

17.3.4 *Overview of Empirical Studies*

As illustrated above, most of the basic statistics can be derived from the annual statistic reports of the Ministry of Justice that collect information on all criminal proceedings. After two years of the new Criminal Code being effective, the Supreme Court of the Czech Republic (in connection with the Charles University and the Institute for Criminology and Social

---

[75] *Supra* note 42, 468.
[76] All data come from the Czech Statistical Office, 'Selected Data on Social Security – 2017'.
[77] Section 344 (1) of the Criminal Procedure Code.
[78] *Ibid.*, Sections 344 (2) and 344 (3).

Prevention)[79] performed an analysis of the criminal sanctions' effectivity. The data for 2010 and 2011 were collected at all district courts. The results are in general very diverse among the courts.[80] The prevailing output of the analysis is, however, rather negative as the courts did not properly use all the possibilities given to them by the new Criminal Code. It is believed that the courts should use day fines more often as an alternative to imprisonment, especially short-term imprisonment.[81] The courts also pointed out that the new obligatory enforcement of the day fines (by courts or bailiffs usually in a form of a property seizure) delays the potential conversions in comparison with the situation under the Criminal Code 1961 which did not prescribe the obligatory enforcement of the day fines.[82]

Furthermore, as a part of the project 'Theoretical and Political Aspects of Criminal Law Reform in the Area of Criminal Sanctions' led by Miroslav Scheinost and Helena Válková,[83] questionnaires were circulated among legal professionals in 2013. The questionnaires also concerned day fines. Judges and public prosecutors consider the Criminal Code 2009, as regards the provisions on fines, worse than the previous Criminal Code 1961.[84] This is apparently one of the reasons why they are reluctant to use it more and, hence, the idea that the new Criminal Code shall increase the overall percentage of alternative sanctions that has been unsuccessful with respect to fines. As the most controversial issue, the addressees of the questionnaire emphasised the conversion of the unenforced day fine into other sanctions (house arrest, community service obligation or imprisonment). Judges also criticised the concept of the conversion into house arrest and community service obligation itself as they argued that day fines do not have an educational potential. Offenders are aware that they are not directly threatened with imprisonment for non-payment of the fine, but the imprisonment may be imposed only subsequently when the house arrest or the community service has not been served. Moreover, it was complained that the obligatory enforcement of day fines is time-consuming and ineffective. Judges and public prosecutors prefer having a direct conversion of the day fine, if not duly paid, into imprisonment.[85]

---

[79] Within the scope of the project 'Theoretical and Political Aspects of Criminal Law Reform in Area of Criminal Sanctions'.

[80] See the opinion of the Supreme Court 'Zhodnocení praxe soudů v oblasti ukládání a výkonu vybraných trestních sankcí v letech 2010 a 2011' of 12 February 2014, No. R 9/2014 tr.

[81] See the opinion of the Supreme Court, part V.B.

[82] Ibid., part V.F.

[83] The results of the study are summarised in *supra* note 67, Válková *et al.*, 9–38.

[84] *Supra* note 68, Válková *et al.*, 27.

[85] Ibid.

The only study focusing on the day fines exclusively is the one by Jakub Drápal.[86] This study analyses all judgments imposing the day fines of two first instance courts in the Czech Republic – the District Court of Prague 2 and the District Court of Jeseník – between 2010 and June 2014. As the study includes only those two courts, it cannot be understood as a complete overview of the day fines imposition in the Czech Republic. However, this is not the aim of the study since its main value is in the qualitative analysis of the judgments and the judges' opinions. The results may be also distorted due to the choice of the courts. The District Court of Prague 2 is the court that deals with all Prague traffic offences, which, as was shown above, are by far the most fined crimes. The District Court in Jeseník is one of the smallest courts in the Czech Republic and also situated in one of its poorest parts. Therefore, the study is focused rather on the extremes than on the average.

The main result of the study is nevertheless quite conclusive both in the quantitative and the qualitative part. According to the study, judges do not, in fact, follow the rule of a calculation of the fines as day fines. There is no real difference from the way fines were imposed pursuant to the Criminal Code 1961 which worked with lump sum fines.[87] The individualisation of the fine is generally still based on the judges' opinion as to how high the overall fine should be. The judges expressed the view that the fine should be proportional rather to the infringing conduct (i.e. the crime itself), than to the culprit's income and assets.[88]

The views expressed by judges are confirmed by the analysis of their judgments. Although the study avoids the determination of the seriousness of the crimes, which is arguably quite difficult and likely subjective,[89] it finds a way to analyse the correlation between the number of days imposed and the seriousness of the crime. It compares the number of days imposed for the basic *actus reus* with the number of days imposed for a more severe *actus reus* of the same kind (as explicitly stated by law).[90] Should the sanction be properly individualised at least to the act itself, regardless of the offender, the less severe crimes would result into a smaller number of days of the fine. This was not the case in the study. The number of days imposed does not in any significant way correlate with the gravity of the crime.[91]

---

[86] *Supra* note 42, 461–80. The same study was also dealt with in *supra* note 41, 1–17.
[87] *Supra* note 41, 12.
[88] *Ibid.*, 13.
[89] *Ibid.*, 14.
[90] For example, it compares the number of days imposed for the crime of an injury by negligence and a crime of a gross injury by negligence.
[91] *Supra* note 41, 14.

The other element of the fine, the daily unit, does not correspond to the idea of 'distributive' justice as presented in the concept of day fines. It is true that more wealthy offenders do get higher daily units in absolute numbers. But the distribution in absolute numbers of the daily unit is not proportionate. Still, a tenth of the wealthiest offenders had 8.8 times higher income, but only a 1.5 times higher daily unit.[92] This disproportionality is only slightly modified if the total amount of the fine is compared to the offender's income. In the statistics, the ten wealthiest offenders received fines just 2.2 times higher than the ten poorest offenders.[93]

The data, therefore, show two major results. Judges do not comply with the concept of the day fines as they still begin with setting the overall amount of the fine that is then (rather arbitrarily) divided into the daily unit and the number of days. As a result, the total amount of the fine is not proportionate to the offender's income.

17. 4 PUBLIC PERCEPTION OF DAY FINES

As day fines are still rather marginal sanctions imposed on natural persons, there are no studies directly focused on the public perception of the day fines concept. However, as illustrated above, there are studies on the perception of day fines by legal professionals. First, the study by Scheinost and Válková included an analysis of the responses of judges, public prosecutors and heads of the Probation and Mediation Service.[94] As already mentioned above, the overall opinion in 2013 was rather negative. However, it shall be emphasised that the respondents considered the whole regime of fines in the Criminal Code 2009 as problematic, not only the day fines. The authors of the analysis did not mention any critics with respect to the change in the concept of the fines calculation, that is the turn into day fines. The core issues identified by the professionals were the conversion of the unenforced fine into another type of a sanction and the necessity of the obligatory enforcement of the fine.

The opinion of the Supreme Court[95] also touches the subject of the day fines perception by judges. Again, the criticism focuses on other elements of the fines imposition rather than on the concept of day fines itself. Judges express the view that there are not enough tools to motivate the offenders to duly pay the fine and, hence, they often postpone the payment without any

---

[92] *Ibid.*, 6.
[93] *Ibid.*, 7.
[94] *Supra* note 68, Válková *et al.*, 24.
[95] *I.e.* the opinion of the Supreme Court 'Zhodnocení praxe soudů v oblasti ukládání a výkonu vybraných trestních sankcí v letech 2010 a 2011' of 12 February 2014, No. R 9/2014 tr.

sanction as long as it is possible. It is also argued that the public prosecutors' conduct is unsatisfactory as well as they do not propose the imposition of the fines often enough and they do not participate in securing the assets in preparatory proceedings which they could do, as they are rested with powers to seize the property etc.[96] On the other hand, courts positively assessed the possibility to determine the offenders' income by estimation. The practice seems to be understandable and effective.[97]

Finally, the perception of day fines by selected courts' judges is evidenced in the study by Drápal. First, judges have certain concerns regarding whether the concept (the calculation) is just. As supported by statistical analysis, the distribution of the fines is not proportionate to the distribution of wealth.[98] Judges are reluctant to fine the rich offenders significantly more severely due to their higher income in comparison to the poor offenders.[99] It seems that there was an insufficient information campaign towards judges before and after the Criminal Code 2009 entered into effect and although the law directly prescribes that the offender's income shall be taken into account, judges do not consider it entirely fair. It stems from the responses that some of the judges have a certain absolute limit they refuse to exceed even if the fine would be relatively lower with respect to the offender's income (CZK 200,000 – which is approximately 7,800 euros – was mentioned as a limit by one judge).[100]

Another issue identified by judges was the questionability of the information on the offender's income. Judges expressed their distrust in the numbers provided by the offenders themselves, but they are quite unwilling to verify them due to time constraints. Neither do they put confidence in police's abilities to verify it.[101] Hence, when determining the fine, they may in fact hiddenly increase the estimated income in comparison to the number provided. The distrust is statistically embodied in the fact that the offenders that refuse to inform the court about their income (for whom there is a presumption that they consider to be better off without providing it, i.e. their income is above average) are fined with even lower amounts on average than those who provided the information.[102]

The study by Scheinost and Válková also partially focused on the public perception of the new system of criminal sanctions in the Criminal Code 2009

---

[96] See the opinion of the Supreme Court, part V.D.
[97] *Ibid.*, part V.E.
[98] *Supra* note 42, 467.
[99] *Ibid.*, 470.
[100] *Supra* note 41, 13.
[101] *Supra* note 42, 469.
[102] *Supra* note 41, 5.

and the media coverage of the topic. The study finds that the media significantly influence the public opinion.[103] The media coverage of the new Criminal Code was focused rather on particular selected issues (the increase of the imprisonment period limits for a murder, the new sanction of house arrest, the new crime of stalking etc.). The change of the fines concept was not discussed at all. A public survey, however, showed that a fine as criminal sanction is the most known alternative sanction.[104]

The media day-to-day coverage of the issues relating to the criminal system is strongly disproportionate to reality. The media focus mostly on violent crimes and often identify a criminal sanction with an imprisonment.[105] The public therefore still approaches criminal sanctions in a punitive way as the majority of people believe in the deterrent effect of sanctions. The knowledge of alternative sanctions overall and day fines in particular remains quite low.[106]

17.5 SPECIAL CHALLENGES

Day fines had already been introduced to the Czech criminal system in 2004, however, only as an option for sanctioning juveniles. Beginning in 2010, day fines became formally the sole form of imposing the pecuniary sanction (fine) in criminal law. Nevertheless, at least some judges keep working within the previous framework (mindset) of setting fines as an absolute lump sum amount. In practice, they first determine the overall amount and only divide it to the daily units and number of days in the judgments in order to formally meet the requirements of the Criminal Code. Moreover, the perception of the new system of the fines is negative among judges as they do not consider it effective. As the clear aim of the new Criminal Code was to improve the ratio of alternative sanctions, including day fines, the available studies suggest that it did not succeed.

It seems critical to convince judges about the fairness and effectiveness of day fines. Judges do have their entrenched habits and beliefs of the concept of fairness which is based on often many years of application of the previous Criminal Code 1961. As stated by one of the judges, their opinions cannot be changed overnight.[107] As suggested by Drápal, it would be helpful to promote the concept of day fines, provide the judges with criminology studies and organise educative events in order to change their opinion on the fairness

---

[103] *Supra* note 68, Válková *et al.*, 36.
[104] *Ibid.*, 34.
[105] *Ibid.*, 35.
[106] *Ibid.*, 36.
[107] *Supra* note 41, 12.

of day fines.[108] Unless the judges are convinced, the amount of imposed day fines will not increase.

Judges must also find day fines effective. The studies already suggested soft-law improvements and also amendments to the Criminal Code that, pursuant to legal professionals, shall improve the efficiency. In the first place, the police and public prosecutors should regularly collect the information on the alleged offenders' income in the preparatory proceedings. Moreover, if public prosecutors consider the imposition of day fines likely and complications with the later enforcement are foreseeable, they should use their powers to seize the alleged offenders' property. Second, guidelines for determining both the daily unit (especially with respect to self-employed or unemployed offenders) and the number of days could be published by the Ministry of Justice or the Supreme Court. We are also of the opinion that a uniform link (a conversion ratio) between the number of days and the length of the subsidiary sanction of an imprisonment could improve the efficiency of day fines. It may render it easier for judges to determine the number of days as they may convert it from the days of imprisonment, which is something they are better accustomed to. It also allows an automatic conversion of the day fine into imprisonment in case of payment default. Finally, it shall be considered whether the obligatory primary transformation into house arrest or community service obligation is effective. A direct conversion into an imprisonment, as prescribed by the Criminal Code 1961, could also improve the acceptancy of day fines by judges.

REFERENCES

Administrative Offences Act – Act No. 250/2016 Coll.
Criminal Code 1950 – Act No. 86/1950 Coll.
Criminal Code 1961 – Act. No. 140/1961 Coll.
Criminal Code 2009 or Criminal Code – Act No. 40/2009.
Criminal Procedure Code – Act No. 141/1961 Coll.
Drápal, J. 2016. 'Analýza ukládání peněžitých trestů v podobě denních pokut v České republice', *Česká kriminologie* 1: 1–17.
Drápal, J. 2018. 'Day Fines: A European Comparison and Czech Malpractice', *European Journal of Criminology* 15: 461–80.
Hulmáková, J. and Rozum, J. 2012. 'Aktuální trendy sankční politiky v ČR', *Trestněprávní revue* 11–12: 256–63.
Jelínek, J. 2017. 'Koncepce trestní odpovědnosti právnických osob', *Acta Universitatis Carolinae Iuridica* 63: 7–24.
Juvenile Act – Act No. 218/2003 Coll.

[108] Ibid., 16.

Labour Code – Act No. 262/2006 Coll.

Legal Persons Liability Act – Act No. 418/2011 Coll.

Ministry of Justice, 'Annual Statistic Report of Crime', 15 and 17.

Púry *et al.*, *Trestní zákoník (EVK)*, 2nd edn., p.894.

Válková, H. *et al.* 2016. *Teoretické a trestněprávní aspekty reformy trestního práva v oblasti trestních sankcí*. Fórum Sociální Práce.

Vicherek, R. 2017. 'Přeměna peněžitého trestu', *Trestněprávní revue* 1: 7–12.

18

Day Fines in Romania

Mihail Udroiu

18.1 HISTORICAL DEVELOPMENT OF DAY FINES IN ROMANIA

Understanding the system of day fines regulated by the Romanian Criminal Code requires prior clarification on the following: the context in which the legislative amendment occurred; the structure of the Criminal Code; the penalty system provided by the Criminal Code; the modifications introduced to the penalty of the fine; and the transitory situations requiring the application of the more favourable criminal law.

In 2009, the Romanian Parliament adopted the new Criminal Code (Law No. 286/2009), which entered into force five years later, on 1 February 2014.[1] The necessity to draft a new Criminal Code was outlined in the explanatory memorandum of the draft law[2] as a corollary of the economic and social evolution, as well as the Romanian doctrine and jurisprudence, in the context of profound political, social and economic transformations that occurred in the Romanian society for almost four decades since the adoption of the previous Criminal Code.[3]

The reform of the criminal legislation through the entry into force of Law No. 286/2009 focused on:

> Creating a coherent legislative framework in criminal matters, avoiding unnecessary duplication of existing rules in the Criminal Code and in special laws; the simplification of substantive law regulations, designed to facilitate

---

[1] It should be noted that this law repealed Law No. 301/2004, through which the Parliament adopted for the first time since 1969 a new Criminal Code. This law No. 301/2004 never entered into force. Therefore, the 1969 Criminal Code remained applicable in Romania (with amendments introduced over time) until 1 February 2014.

[2] The Explanatory Memorandum to the Criminal Code is available at www.cdep.ro/proiecte/2009/300/00/4/em304.pdf.

[3] This year we celebrate the five-year anniversary of the entry into force of the current Criminal Code and the fifty-year anniversary of the entry into force of the previous Criminal Code.

their uniform and rapid application in the work of judicial authorities; ensuring compliance with the requirements deriving from the fundamental principles of criminal law as stipulated in the Constitution and international human rights treaties to which Romania is a party; the transposition within national criminal law of the legislation adopted at EU level; the harmonisation of Romanian substantive criminal law with the systems of other Member States as a prerequisite for judicial cooperation in criminal matters based on mutual recognition and mutual trust.

The Romanian Criminal Code is structured in two parts. The general part of the Criminal Code contains the conditions and limits of the application of the criminal law, the essential features of the offence, the general conditions of criminal liability, the sanctions of criminal law, the rules applicable to juvenile offenders or legal persons, the causes that remove criminal liability or execution of the punishment. Thus, general rules are laid down, rules that apply to all offences provided in the special part of the Criminal Code or in the special laws.

The special part of the Criminal Code establishes the offences with the description of their constituent elements, qualifies the persons who can commit them, indicates when the attempt is also incriminated, the punishments that can be applied for each offence as well as the situations in which specific causes of non-punishment may apply, as well as causes that remove the unlawful character or the blameworthiness of the act.

In the general part of the Romanian Criminal Code penalties are defined as criminal law sanctions aiming to prevent the committing of new offences. For natural persons, Article 53 of the Criminal Code provides the following main penalties:[4] life imprisonment; imprisonment from fifteen days to thirty years and fine. For legal persons, the fine is the only main penalty that can be applied.[5]

---

[4] The main penalty is the penalty provided for by the law, which can be applied on its own, regardless of the application of other punishments. Alongside the main penalty, the natural person offender may also be sentenced to: (a) ancillary penalties consisting in the ban of the exercise of certain rights, military demotion, or publication of the final conviction judgment; (b) additional penalties: consisting in the ban of the exercise of one or more of the rights whose exercise was forbidden by the court as an ancillary penalty, from the moment the judgment remained final until the end of the serving of the main penalty, the total pardon or the pardon of the remaining of the penalty or after serving a sentence has come under the statute of limitations.

[5] In addition to the fine, Article 136 (3) of the Criminal Code provides that one or more ancillary penalties may be imposed on the legal person: (a) dissolution of the legal person; (b) suspension of the activity or of one of the activities performed by the legal person, for a term between three months and three years; (c) closure of working points of the legal person for a term between three months and three years; (d) prohibition to participate in public procurement procedures for a term between one and three years; (e) placement under judicial supervision; (f) display or publication of the conviction sentence.

The fine is defined in Article 61 (1) of the Criminal Code as the penalty that can be applied by the court to a natural or legal person for the commission of an offence, consisting of the amount of money the offender has to pay to the state. The most important element of novelty to the fine penalty regime[6] was the regulation of a calculation mechanism based on the day fine system, abandoning the classic system of setting the total amount of the fine. Thus, the new Criminal Code did not maintain the classical fine alongside the day fine, opting only for the latter mechanism for determining the amount of the fine.[7]

The introduction of the day fine system was anticipated, as five years prior to the adoption of the Criminal Code (Law No. 286/2009), the Parliament had provided in Law No. 301/2004 (which has never entered into force, as mentioned above) this method of determining the penalty. The aims pursued by the legislator by introducing the system of day fines was that the principle of equality before the law would be genuinely guaranteed and that the principle of proportionality would be applied more effectively when determining the number of days of the fine and setting the value of a day fine.

The introduction of the day fine system required transitional rules to ensure the correct application of the more favourable criminal law regime (*mitior lex*) in the case of fine penalties imposed by final judgments under the previous Criminal Code. Thus, according to Article 13 of Law No. 187/2012 implementing the Criminal Code, in the case of fines definitively established under the Criminal Code of 1969, the mandatory application of the more favourable criminal law is made by comparing the fine imposed with the amount resulting from the application of the new Criminal Code using the reference amount for a day fine of 150 lei (equivalent of 31 euros). For legal persons convicted by final judgments, the reference amount for a day fine, used for the application of the provisions of Article 137 (2) and (4) of the Criminal Code is 2,000 lei (equivalent of 425 euros).

---

[6] Other elements of novelty regarding the penalty of the fine, which were introduced in the Romanian criminal law by the new Criminal Code, are: (a) possibility to either increase the special limits of the fine or to apply the penalty cumulatively with the imprisonment penalty, when the offence committed was aimed at obtaining a patrimonial benefit; (b) execution of the fine penalty by performing community service.

[7] When drafting the new Criminal Code provisions regarding the day fine system, regulations from other legal systems such as Finland, Germany, Spain, France, Portugal, Switzerland and Sweden were taken into account.

18.2 THE LEGAL FRAMEWORK FOR DAY FINES

In this section, the following aspects related to day fines will be presented and analysed: the mechanism for determining the fine, indicating the judicial body competent to apply the penalty; the general and special limits of the day fines applicable to natural person offenders and legal person offenders, as well as the individualisation method of these fines; the method of determining the amount of a day fine. At the end of the chapter an example of how to apply the penalty based on the day fine system is provided.

In the case of a criminal offence committed by a legal person, or when for the offence committed by a natural person the law provides only the penalty of the fine or if the fine is provided as an alternative with the penalty of imprisonment and the court opts for the application of the fine, the penalty to be served will be determined through the following mechanism involving three steps: first, the court will determine the number of day fines; then the court will determine the amount of a day fine; and finally, the court will determine the amount of the fine to be paid by the defendant, which is reached by multiplying the number of day fines with the amount of a day fine. It follows that in the Romanian legal system the fine can only be imposed by the court and not by other judicial bodies (the prosecutor or the police) or by extrajudicial authorities.

As regards the first step of the mechanism for determining the penalty of the fine, it is necessary to analyse the limits of the day fines stipulated by the law, as well as the concrete manner of determining the number of days, as, considering the possibility of the court to set the amount of the penalty, the fine is a penalty relatively determined.[8] The number of days (of fine) is regulated in a distinct manner for natural and legal person offenders and there are general limits (set out in the General Part of the Code and entailing that the penalty of the fine cannot be less than the general minimum and not higher than the general maximum) and special limits (determined on the basis of the penalty stipulated in the special part of the Criminal Code or in the special laws for each individual offence). Thus, according to Article 61 (2) of the Criminal Code for natural person offenders the general limits of the day fines are between 30 and 400 day fines and the amount of a day fine is between 10 RON[9] (equivalent of 20 eurocents) and 500 RON (equivalent of 105 euros). Therefore, the general total limits of the fine penalty are between 300 RON

---

[8] The existence of any offence for which the law provides for an absolutely determined fine (fixed, with an a priori determined value) is not possible.

[9] RON means Romanian New Leu (Romanian currency).

(equivalent of 62 euros) and 200,000 RON (equivalent of 41,670 euros). Such limits cannot be exceeded irrespective of the number of causes of mitigation or aggravation of criminal liability applicable in a case.

In the case of legal person offenders, Article 137 (2) of the Criminal Code provides that the general limits of day fines are between 30 and 600 days and that the amount of a day fine is between 100 RON (equivalent of 20 euros) and 5,000 RON (equivalent of 1,040 euros). Therefore, the general total limits of the fine penalty are between 3,000 RON (equivalent of 625 euros) and 3,000,000 RON (equivalent of 625,000 euros). These limits cannot be exceeded irrespective of the number of cases of mitigation or aggravation of criminal liability that would be applicable.

The special limits of the day fines will be determined according to the punishment provided by the law.[10] Thus, according to Article 61 (4) of the Criminal Code, the special limits of the day fines are between: (a) 60 and 180 day fines, when the law provides only the fine penalty for the offence; (b) 120 and 240 day fines where the law provides for the fine penalty alternatively with the imprisonment penalty for not more than two years (less than or equal to two years); and (c) 180 and 300 day fines when the law provides for the fine penalty alternatively with the penalty of prison of more than two years.

Similarly, in the case of legal persons according to Article 137 (4) of the Criminal Code, the special limits of the day fines are between: (a) 60 and 180 day fines where the law provides only the fine as penalty for the offence; (b) 120 and 240 days fine where the law provides for a maximum five years' imprisonment penalty, on its own or alternative with the fine penalty; (c) 180 and 300 day fines where the law provides for the imprisonment penalty of no more than ten years; (d) 240 and 420 day fines where the law provides for the imprisonment penalty of up to twenty years; (e) 360 and 510 day fines when the law provides for the imprisonment penalty of more than twenty years' or life imprisonment.[11]

In the case of both natural and legal person offenders, when the court takes into consideration a cause for mitigation of the penalty (attempt or mitigating circumstances) or for aggravation of the penalty (continued offence, post-

[10] According to Article 187 of the Criminal Code by penalty provided by law it is construed the penalty stipulated in the text of the law that criminalises the act committed in the consumed form, without taking into consideration the causes of reduction or increase of the penalty.

[11] In the Romanian criminal law, for reasons of legislative technique, in the case of legal persons, penalties can be determined by reference to the penalties provided by the law for the natural persons. This is the reason why Article 137 (4) of the Criminal Code does not refer only to the penalty of the fine, but to other categories of penalties (such as imprisonment) depending on which the special limits of the day fines are determined.

penalty-serving reoffending, aggravating circumstances), the fractions established by the law to increase or decrease the penalty apply only to the special limits of the day fines, not to the amount of a day fine.[12]

In a similar manner, it should be noted that Article 79 (1) of the Criminal Code provides that when two or more provisions that have the effect of reducing the penalty are incidental, the special limits of the day fines prescribed by the law for the offence committed (not the amount of a day fine) are reduced through the successive application of provisions regarding attempt, mitigating circumstances and special cases of reduction of the penalty, in this order.

On the other hand, Article 79 (2) of the Criminal Code provides that when two or more provisions that have the effect of aggravating criminal liability are applicable, the special limits of the day fines prescribed by the law for the offence committed (not the amount of a day fine) are increased through the successive application of the provisions regarding post penalty service, aggravating circumstances, or continued offence.

As regards the concrete determination of the number of day fines to which the natural or legal person offender will be sentenced, the court will take into consideration for the individualisation of the penalty the principle of proportionality of the penalty in relation to the nature and the degree of danger of the committed act, taking into account the fundamental rights or freedoms or other protected social values that have been affected by committing the offence. The degree of involvement of the offender in the criminal activity should also be considered. The concrete determination of the number of day fines will be made according to the general criteria for the individualisation of the penalty provided by Article 74 of the Criminal Code.

Following the establishment of the number of day fines, the court will proceed to the second step of the mechanism for determining the fine penalty consisting of setting the amount of a day fine. In case of natural persons offenders Article 61 (3) of the Criminal Code provides for two general criteria according to which the court determines the amount of a day fine: the material situation of the defendant and the legal obligations of the defendant towards the persons in his/her care.

In order to determine the material situation of the natural person defendant, the court will take into consideration not only the net income of the defendant

---

[12] Thus, the special limits of the day fines will be reduced as follows: by half in the case of attempted offence and by one third in the case of mitigating circumstances, or will be increased by: one third in the case of the continued offence; by half in case of post-serving recidivism and at most one third in case of aggravating circumstances.

from his/her permanent activity, but also any other patrimonial elements that may lead to the determination of the patrimonial situation (for example, dividends or rents, buildings or vehicles owned, etc.). Even if the data provided by the tax authorities show that the defendant does not gain any income, the court is not prevented to set the amount of a day fine over the minimum special limit, by taking into account the financial situation of the defendant resulting from the evidence presented in the case, not having to relate to the minimum wage.

In this regard the legal doctrine[13] shows that Article 61 (3) of the Criminal Code does not refer directly to the income of the sentenced person but to his/her material situation. Per consequence, on the one hand, the income level is only an indicative element for the court, the main criterion being the material situation as a whole and on the other hand, the level of the recent expenses made by the defendant may also be taken into account, even if these do not correspond to the level of the declared income and proving a much better financial situation than the one resulting from the documents in the file. The authors also pointed out that

> even if, at the time of the trial, the person earns a small income according to the wage certificate submitted to the case file, the court will be able to determine the amount corresponding to a day fine at a higher level than that which would result from the reference to that salary, insofar as the assets owned by that person justify the measure. In turn, in the absence of an explicit text, a hypothetical level of income based on what the defendant would have earned if he/she had been employed, cannot be taken into consideration, even if the data in the file show that he or she did not take any steps to find employment.[14]

Information concerning the material situation of the defendant can be obtained by the judicial authorities either by requesting public authorities to communicate the defendant's income or taxable assets, or by using the PatrimVen service which provides public institutions access to available data regarding the patrimony and income of Romanian nationals (www.epatrim.anaf.ro). In judicial practice, this is the information most commonly used by the courts to determine the material situation of the defendant.[15]

---

[13] Streteanu and Nițu, *Criminal Law. General Part*, p. 303.

[14] *Ibid.*, p. 304.

[15] The requirement to collect such information through the available sources is mandatory for courts. From discussions I have had with judges and prosecutors, it seems that in practice such information is indeed collected to serve as the basis for the daily unit. The collection of information does not seem to lead to disproportionate delays in the procedure of sentencing. See also Udroiu, *Criminal Law. General Part*, p. 395.

It is also possible to present any other evidence to prove the patrimonial situation of the defendant (for example, statements of witnesses or documents showing the current expenses of the defendant, or the balance of the bank accounts held by the defendant or payments made by the defendant).

The defendant's statement regarding his/her material situation is sometimes used by the courts to determine the amount of a day fine in cases where no other evidence could be obtained in this regard, or when there is no other data on the defendant's income, although all necessary investigations have been taken.

The criterion of legal obligations towards persons supported by the defendant is aimed to avoid situations in which he/she is unable to perform his/her duties in respect of alimony, education and professional training of the persons towards whom he/she owes these obligations. Last but not least, the court has to individualise the amount of the day fine so as to avoid the risk that the defendant cannot afford the minimum necessary resources for daily living.

In the case of legal person offenders, the determination of the amount of a day fine is made according to the special criteria provided by Article 137 (3) of the Criminal Code, namely the turnover[16] (in the case of a for-profit legal person, it is determined annually and consists of the value of the goods and services invoiced), respectively the value of the patrimonial assets (in the case of non-profit legal persons), as well as the other obligations of the legal person.

In order to establish the penalty by reference to these criteria, it is necessary to take into account the documents presented in the case, consisting of the accounting documents of the company (for example, the balance sheet and the profit and loss account), company reports to tax authorities, etc.

Recently, in the Romanian legal literature[17] it was considered that in order to determine the amount of a day fine for a legal entity the following specific

---

[16] The doctrine (Lazăr, 'Determining the Penalty for Legal Persons', 34) shows that in the Romanian legal system, turnover represents all the goods and services sold by the legal person for profit or, in accounting terminology, the value of the goods and services invoiced. This criterion is useful in assessing the 'financial dimension' of the legal person, so that the fine imposed is sufficiently severe to prevent the repetition of the unlawful acts. At the same time, a reduced turnover will result in the application of a minimum penalty without endangering the commercial future of the legal person. The turnover criterion is relevant as it is calculated annually, so it represents the current financial status of the legal entity. Its use is particularly relevant when changes occur in the amount of turnover from the time the offence is committed until the penalty is sentenced, sometimes even due to the negative publicity generated by the media coverage of the offence committed. In this case, the competitive environment and the customers penalise by commercial means the legal person for the committed act, so that the turnover from the date of the ruling of the penalty ensures a balance between the criminal liability and the other economic consequences that the legal person has to bear.

[17] Lazăr, 'Determining the Penalty for Legal Persons', 36–40.

criteria should be taken into account for the individualisation of the penalty with regard to legal persons:

(a) the conduct of the governing bodies of the legal person assessed by reference to the duties laid down by law, government decision or regulation, articles of incorporation, job description or employment contract or accepted policies and practices or customs within the private or public law legal entity;

(b) the track record of the legal person: the existence of warnings or fines or other sanctions applied earlier by administrative bodies and the manner in which steps have been taken to ensure compliance with the breached provisions, as well as their effectiveness. Likewise, it was considered relevant to assess the existence of previous civil law litigations in order to see if there is a persistent attitude of the legal person in creating a risk;

(c) risk management: assessing the diligence of the legal person in identifying the risk and the measures taken to prevent it;

(d) audit: the existence or periodicity of the audit (internal or external), the completeness and depth of the verifications, the measures taken by the legal person if the audit has identified irregularities, are all considered relevant;

(e) professional assessment criteria: how a legal entity is classified under the safety and security criteria; the number of complaints registered by the competent authorities or even by its own department, etc.;

(f) recommendations of professional bodies and competent institutions: consideration will be given to compliance;

(g) compliance systems: the assessment of specific measures adopted to achieve the objectives, to combat uncertainty and to act with integrity in order to prevent the commission of criminal offences within the legal person.

For understanding the mechanism for the application of the day fines we present the following example. While in a public park, during day time, X (twenty-seven years old, without a criminal record) under the influence of alcoholic beverages steals a bicycle left unattended by its owner. Under these circumstances, X commits the offence of theft punishable according to Article 228 (1) of the Criminal Code with imprisonment from six months to three years or with fine.

In the process of judicial individualisation of the penalty, the court, which is the only competent body to apply criminal penalty for the offence of theft, first has to determine the penalty to be applied between the two alternative penalties provided by the law. Thus, considering the criteria set out in

Article 74 of the Criminal Code, let us presume that the court opts for the penalty of the fine considering the lack of criminal record as well as the state of intoxication of X. Then, the court will set the number of day fines.

Considering that according to Article 61 (4) c) of the Criminal Code, the special limits of the day fines are from 180 to 300 and assuming that the court wishes to show leniency towards X (considering his/her age, the fact that he/she is at his/her first contact with the criminal law and the circumstance of the offence being committed at the first contact with the criminal law), a fine of 180 days (the special minimum provided by law) can be established.

Once the number of day fines has been established, the court will determine the amount of a day fine. The limits are, according to Article 61 (2) of the Criminal Code, between 10 RON (equivalent to 20 eurocents) and 500 RON (equivalent to 105 euros). Given the material situation of X (suppose that he/she has an income of about 433 euros/month, equal to the minimum wage and does not own property, having a rented dwelling) and his/her legal obligations (suppose X pays an alimony pension of about 110 euros per month), the court may set an amount of 20 RON (about 4.15 euro) for a day fine.

Finally, the amount X will have to pay as a criminal fine is: 180 (day fines) X 20 RON (the amount of the day fine) = 4,000 RON (equivalent to 750 euros).

The court can rule to postpone the enforcement of the day fines[18] and set a time to be served on probation, but cannot impose a suspended fine.

18.3 THE PRACTICAL IMPLEMENTATION OF DAY FINES

This section presents the main categories of offences for which the fine penalty can be ordered; the deficiencies of the Romanian legal system regarding statistical analysis or the case studies regarding the effects of the introduction of the day fine system; as well as an outline on the evolution of income over the last five years in Romania in order to make some observations in relation to the special limits of the penalty. Furthermore, the methods for executing the fine penalty will be analysed, including the case when the court orders the execution of the fine through unpaid community work. Finally, cases when the

---

[18] The postponement of the enforcement of the day fines is a mean of individualising the punishment that can be ordered by the court if it considers that an offence has been committed, but considering the person of the defendant, their conduct before committing the offence, their efforts to remove or minimise the consequences of their offence and their likelihood of rehabilitation, the court feels that enforcing a penalty immediately is not necessary, but it is nevertheless mandatory to have their conduct supervised for a period of two years.

penalty of the fine may be replaced with the penalty of imprisonment will be addressed.

In the new Criminal Code, the penalty of the fine has a significantly extended scope, in comparison to the previous Criminal Code, resulting from the increase in the number of offences or their variants for which the fine can be applied as a penalty on its own, but also as an alternative penalty to the punishment of imprisonment (approximately 60 offences in the previous Criminal Code and 175 offences in the current Criminal Code).[19] Thus, the Romanian criminal law does not regulate any case in which the fine can be applied de facto, in the absence of an explicit incrimination provision.

The analysis of criminal law indicates the following categories of offences for which the fine may be imposed:

(a) offences for which the law provides only for the fine penalty: they are limited in number and as a rule, they are stipulated in certain special laws. In this case, the court may not impose a penalty other than the fine.

(b) small or medium-scale offences for which the law provides for the penalty of the fine as an alternative for the penalty of imprisonment. The special limits of the penalty of imprisonment alternative to the penalty of the fine are among the most diverse, in most cases the fine is provided by law alternatively with the penalty of imprisonment from six months to three years. Thus, the new Criminal Code provides for the penalty of the fine alternatively with the penalty of imprisonment:

   (i) from three to six months: for example harassment (Article 208 of the Criminal Code);

   (ii) from three months to one year: for example abandoning an individual in distress (Article 203 of the Criminal Code), or the threat (Article 206 of the Criminal Code);

   (iii) from three months to two years: for example trespassing (Article 224 of the Criminal Code), abuse of trust (Article 238 of the Criminal Code), or false statements (Article 326 of the Criminal Code);

   (iv) from three months to three years: for example the disclosure of professional secrecy (Article 227 of the Criminal Code), or disclosure of information classified as confidential or not public (Article 304 of the Criminal Code);

   (v) from six months to three years or with fine: for example theft (Article 228 of the Criminal Code), fraudulent crossing of the state border (Article 262 of the Criminal Code), misleading the

---

[19] Explanatory Memorandum to the Criminal Code (Law No. 286/2009).

judicial bodies (Article 268 of the Criminal Code), tampering with a technical record (Article 324 of the Criminal Code), false identity (Article 327 of the Criminal Code), or family abandonment (Article 378 of the Criminal Code);

(vi) imprisonment from six months to five years or fine: for example hitting or other violence when the traumatic injuries caused need up to ninety days of medical care (Article 193 of the Criminal Code), receipt and sale of stolen goods (Article 270 of the Criminal Code), or usurpations of office (Article 300 of the Criminal Code).

Unfortunately, so far no analysis has been published in Romania assessing the effectiveness of the system of day fines introduced by the new Criminal Code. Thus, over the last five years there has been no concern, neither at academic level, nor at judiciary level for the development of studies or analysis on the application or execution of the fine penalty in order to establish: (a) the extent of applied fines in relation to the other penalties decided by courts; (b) whether the number of convictions to imprisonment (in detention regime or with the suspended service of the sentence under supervision) has decreased following the increase in the number of offences for which the law provides for the imprisonment penalty alternatively with the fine penalty; (c) the categories of offences for which the courts have applied the sanction of the fine rather than that of imprisonment alternatively provided by the law, or the categories of offences for which courts have mainly applied the prison sentence, although they also had the possibility to impose the fine; (d) the specific circumstances envisaged by the courts for the determination of the number of day fines or the amount of a fine; (e) the situation of the execution of the fine penalty and the percentage of cases in which the fine was served through unpaid community service or replaced with imprisonment.

Given that one of the criteria laid down by the law for establishing day fines is the patrimonial situation of the offender,[20] in order to assess the effectiveness

---

[20] In the case of socially assisted persons, the level of income obtained from the state does not encourage the application of the fine. In Romania, social assistance is granted to single persons or families with legal residence in Romania if the net monthly wages of the single person or the family is lower than the minimum guaranteed income. The amount of social assistance is established as the difference between the levels of the minimum guaranteed income and the net monthly wages of the family or single person. Unfortunately, the monthly level of the minimum guaranteed income is very low: 142 RON (equivalent to 30 euros) for a single person, 255 RON (equivalent to 54 euros) for families consisting of two persons; 357 RON (equivalent to 75 euros) for families consisting of three persons; 442 RON for families consisting of four persons (equivalent to 89 euros); 527 RON for families consisting of five persons (equivalent to 111 euros).

of the enforcement and serving of the fine, the evolution of the income of Romanians from the entry into force of the new Criminal Code must also be taken into consideration, as follows: (a) if, in 2014, the total monthly average income per household was 2,500.70 RON (equivalent to 610 euro) and the total expenditure was on average 2,269.30 RON per month per household (equivalent to 553 euro), of which average consumption expenditures represented 72.2 per cent, in the last quarter of 2018 the total monthly average income was 4,608 RON per household (equivalent to 980 euros) and the total expenditures of the population were, on average, of 3,981 RON per month per household (equivalent to 865 euros) and accounted for 86.4 per cent of the total income; (b) if in 2014 the minimum net wages was 678 RON (equivalent to 142 euros), in 2019 it is 1,229 RON (equivalent to 258 euros); (c) if in 2014 the net average wages was 1,829 RON (equivalent to 446 euros), in 2019 it is 2,933 RON (equivalent to 611 euros).

By comparison, in the case of natural persons, the general total limits of the fine penalty are between 300 RON (equivalent to 62 euros) and 200,000 RON (equivalent to 41,670 euros), while the special limits are: (a) between 600 RON (equivalent to 125 euros) and 90,000 (equivalent to 18,750 euros), when the law provides only for the fine for the offence committed; (b) 1,200 RON (equivalent to 250 euros) and 120,000 RON (equivalent 25,000 euros), when the law provides for the penalty of the fine alternatively with imprisonment not exceeding two years and (c) 1,800 RON (equivalent to 375 euros) and 150,000 (equivalent to 31,250 euros), when the law provides for the fine penalty alternatively with the imprisonment penalty of more than two years.

One could note that the special limits between which the fine may be individualised are relatively high, including in relation to the average wages, given that in most cases the special maximum of the imprisonment penalty alternatively with the fine penalty is higher than two years.

As regards the execution of the fine penalty, it must be taken into account that the convicted natural or legal person is required to pay the full amount of the fine within three months from the date when the conviction becomes final and to communicate the proof of payment to the judge within fifteen days after it was made. Thus, the fine is deemed served by the submission of the full payment receipt.[21]

---

[21] Mention should be made that the legal person on which the criminal fine has been imposed cannot bring a regression civil action against the natural person (the governing body, the authorised person or the agent) who committed the act in its materiality for the recovery of the amount paid as a criminal penalty. For a detailed analysis of how to execute the fine, see *supra* note 15, pp. 392–4.

When the convicted natural or legal person is unable to pay the fine in full within three months from the date the judgment becomes final, he/she may request the judge entrusted with the enforcement to allow the execution of the payment of the fine in monthly instalments for a period not exceeding two years.

The judge entrusted with the enforcement, examining the request of the convicted person and the supporting documents proving the impossibility of full payment of the fine will issue an order which is not subject to any appeal. In the case of the instalments arrangement, the judicial order will include: the amount of the fine, the number of monthly instalments in equal amounts for which the fine is divided, as well as the payment deadline.

When the convicted legal person fails to observe the deadline for the full payment of the fine or of an instalment, the serving of the fine penalty will be made according to the provisions of Law No. 207/2015 on the Fiscal Procedure Code. Fiscal bailiffs are required to communicate to the judge entrusted with the enforcement the performance of payment, at the time of the full execution of the fine and to notify the judge of any circumstance that prevents its execution. In addition, it should be noted that in order to guarantee the execution of the fine penalty, the prosecutor, the preliminary chamber judge or the court can take provisional measures.

The new Criminal Code introduced a substitute method for the execution of the fine penalty, establishing for good faith insolvent natural persons the possibility to serve the penalty of the fine not by paying the sum of money, but by working for the benefit of the community.[22] Thus, the court has the obligation to order the serving of the fine through community service if the following three conditions are met cumulatively:

(a) the fine penalty imposed by final judgment cannot be served in whole or in part for reasons beyond the control of the convicted person. In order to determine the reasons for the non-execution of the fine, the court will request data on the material situation of the convict from the local public administration authority at his/her domicile and, if it deems it necessary, from the employer or tax authorities within the National Agency of Fiscal Administration, as well as other public authorities or institutions that have information on the patrimony of the convict.

(b) the consent of the convicted person. The court cannot order the sentenced person to perform unpaid community work without the person's

---

[22] For a detailed analysis of the modality of serving the penalty fine by means of providing unpaid community work, see *supra* note 15, pp. 398–401.

consent, since such a provision would amount to subjecting the sentenced person to forced labour.

(c) the convicted person must be medically fit to provide community service. The doctrine[23] showed that if the state of health of the sentenced person does not temporarily allow the performance of community work, the court will order the execution of the fine penalty by labour, the work being actually performed after recovery and if there is a permanent incapacity, the court will not be able to order the execution of the fine through work or replace the fine with imprisonment.

If the court orders the execution of the penalty through performing unpaid work for the benefit of the community, the system for determining the working days is the following: a day fine corresponds to a day of community service. Coordination of the performance of the community service obligation is done by the probation service.

The performance of community work must be carried out within a period of maximum two years from the final ruling of the judgment and shall cease on the date of the execution of the last working day determined by the court or by the payment of the fine corresponding to the remaining non-executed fine if the convicted person is no longer insolvent and no longer wants to continue working.

Replacing the penalty of the fine established by the court with imprisonment is possible in the following four cases.

(a) If the convicted person fails to execute, in whole or in part, in bad faith, the penalty of the fine. The term 'bad faith' means the situation in which the convicted person has sufficient financial means to pay the fine, but, for reasons attributable to him/her, does not make the payment and does not have any reasonable excuse. The 'bad faith' can be proved by any evidence. For this purpose the court can request public authorities to communicate the convicted person's income or taxable assets, or by using the PatrimVen service. It is also possible to use any other evidence (for example, statements of witnesses, or documents showing that the convicted person made no attempt to sell his/her property to pay the fine).

Replacement is mandatory, the court not being allowed to examine its usefulness, opportunity or proportionality to the intended purpose. In order to determine the reasons for non-execution of the fine, the court will request data on the convict's material situation from the local public administration authority at his/her domicile and, if deemed necessary, from the employer or

---

[23] *Supra* note 13, p. 319.

tax authorities within the National Agency of Fiscal Administration, as well as other public authorities or institutions that have information on the patrimony of the convict. Likewise, any relevant evidence to the analysis of good or bad faith in the non-execution of penalty may be presented. The new Criminal Code does not regulate the possibility for the court to individualise the prison penalty which replaces the fine, explicitly stipulating that the number of days of the unfulfilled fine is replaced by a corresponding number of days of imprisonment (a day fine corresponds to a day of imprisonment). The imprisonment penalty thus established will be executed only in detention, the postponement of the penalty or the suspension under supervision becoming impossible to be ordered.

For example, we will refer to the situation of X in the previous example, who was convicted to a fine of 3,600 RON (about 750 euros) for stealing the bicycle from the park, consisting of 180 day fines in the amount of 20 RON (equivalent to 4.15 euros). If X, although having financial resources, only pays 1,000 RON (equivalent to 208 euros) and refuses to pay the rest of the fine, the court will order the replacement of the fine penalty with the penalty of imprisonment. Thus, the court will consider that the remainder of the unpaid fine is 2,600 RON (equivalent to 542 euros) and as regards the amount of a day fine established by the conviction decision the convicted person would have to execute 130 days fine (2,600, the remainder of the non- executed fine : 20 RON, the amount of a day fine = 130 day fines). Considering that the replacement system presumes that an unpaid day fine is equivalent to a day of imprisonment, it follows that the court will order the replacement of the remainder of the unpaid fine of 2,600 RON (equivalent to 542 euros), in bad faith, with 130 days of imprisonment. If X, in bad faith, does not pay any amount of money from the penalty applied, the penalty of the fine of 3,600 RON will be replaced with the number of day fines set by the court (180 day fines).

> (b) Where the fine penalty cannot be executed (in whole or in part) for reasons beyond the control of the sentenced person and the person does not consent to the fine being served by unpaid community service.[24] Unlike the first case of replacement above, in this hypothesis the non-execution of the fine is not done in bad faith, but for reasons non-imputable to the convict. The number of non-executed day fines shall

---

[24] If the refusal to provide unpaid community service is determined by the existence of serious medical ground, which prevents the sentenced person from performing the community service, the replacement of the fine with imprisonment cannot be ordered.

be replaced by an appropriate number of days of imprisonment (a day fine corresponding to a day of imprisonment).

(c) If the convicted person does not perform the community service obligation under the conditions established by the court. The number of non-executed day fines shall be replaced by an appropriate number of days of imprisonment.

(d) Where the convicted person commits a new offence before the full serving of the community service obligation, for which a conviction is pronounced. The form of guilt with which the offence is committed is of no importance, the court having the obligation to impose the replacement of the penalty of the fine by imprisonment also in the case of unintentional acts. It is necessary that the new offence is committed and discovered before the last day of the community service, regardless of the moment when a judgment is issued on this act. The number of day fines not executed *through community work at the time of the final conviction for the new offence* is replaced by a corresponding number of days of imprisonment and added to the penalty (fine or imprisonment) for the new offence. Community working days in the execution of the fine, between the date when the new offence was committed and the date of the final conviction, will not be taken into account when determining the prison days the convicted person has to perform.

18.4 PUBLIC PERCEPTION OF DAY FINES

The introduction of the day fine system was intended to guarantee in an effective manner the principle of equality before the law and to ensure the more efficient application of the principle of proportionality when determining the number of day fines and establishing the value of a day fine.[25] Equally, another goal pursued by the increase of the number of offences for which the law imposes the penalty of the fine alternatively with the penalty of imprisonment was to avoid overcrowding of prisons.

Specialised studies published after the entry into force of the new Criminal Code did not reveal a position of the doctrine as rejecting this system of

---

[25]   It should also be borne in mind that the penalty of fine is provided in the new Criminal Code or in the special laws as an alternative penalty with the penalty of imprisonment for sanctioning minor or medium gravity offences. In addition, in many cases the law provides for such offences the possibility of amiably terminating the criminal conflict, by reconciling the offender and the victim, or by withdrawing the complaint formulated by the victim.

calculating the penalty of the fine. Similarly, there was no public or professional manifestation by which the effectiveness of this system was questioned.

The usefulness of this system was examined in case law in instances when the court found that the penalty of the criminal fine is much more effective for most members of the society than the imprisonment penalty. In that case the enforcement of the prison sanction is suspended or postponed.[26]

However, since the introduction in the Romanian criminal legislation of the day fine system, no studies have been published on public perception of safety and crime or on the level of acceptance of day fines among the general public. Similarly, no statistics on the ratio of the fine in the total criminal law sanctions applied are available in order to assess the level of acceptance of day fines by legal professionals.

However, it can easily be seen that both the monthly minimum net income and the average earnings are close to the special minimum of the fine penalty. Thus, the minimum net monthly wages for 2019 in the amount of 1,229 RON (equivalent to 258 euros) corresponds to the special minimum of the day fine when the penalty provided by the law is exclusively the fine (60 day fines) and of an amount of a day fine of 20 RON (equivalent to 4 euros), corresponds to the special minimum provided by law (10 RON, equivalent to 2 euros).

Also, the average wages of 2,933 RON (equivalent to 611 euros) corresponds to the special minimum of day fines when the penalty of the fine is provided alternatively with the imprisonment penalty of no more than two years (120 day fines) and the daily fine amount of 25 RON (equivalent to 5 euros), corresponds to the special minimum provided by the law (10 RON, equivalent to 2 euros), or, as the case may be, the equivalent of the special minimum day fines (180 day fines) when the fine penalty is provided alternatively with the imprisonment penalty of more than two years and a day fine of 16 RON (equivalent 3 euros), corresponds to the special minimum provided by the law.

Although the special limits between which the fine penalty may be individualised are relatively high, including in relation to the average wages, there have been no public manifestations and no public opinions stating that the system of day fines is perceived as an additional tax on the rich or that it would be rejected by the public.

18.5 SPECIAL CHALLENGES

The application of a newly introduced institution, the fine accompanying the prison penalty, has been a challenge for the judiciary. The new

---

[26] Oradea Court of Appeal, Criminal Division, Decision No. 365/2017, www.sintact.ro.

Criminal Code introduced new means of criminal coercion of the offender, which does not imply an increase in the length of the prison sentence. Thus, according to Article 62 (1) of the Criminal Code, the court may apply the penalty of the fine in addition to the imprisonment penalty set for the offence committed if the defendant has sought patrimonial benefit and the court considers that the imprisonment penalty is not sufficient to achieve its purpose. To apply this legal institution, it is not necessary for the material benefit to have actually been obtained by the offender, the law requiring only that the offender pursued this aim for personal or third party gain.

The analysis of Article 62 of the Criminal Code does not show any limitation regarding the scope of offences to which the penalty of the fine can be applied in addition to that of the prison penalty. Thus, the law allows the possibility to apply the fine penalty in addition to the imprisonment penalty not only for offences which, by their very nature, involve the pursuit of patrimonial benefit, but also for other offences (i.e. blackmail, deprivation of freedom, disclosure of professional secrecy).

I take the view that if the law provides as an aggravated form of the offence the situation in which the act is committed for patrimonial benefit, the higher sanctioning of the perpetrator's behaviour through increased limits of the applicable imprisonment penalty prevent the application of the fine penalty in addition to imprisonment.

If the court decides to impose the penalty of the fine together with the imprisonment penalty for sanctioning an offence aimed at obtaining a patrimonial benefit, the amount of a day fine is between 10 RON and 500 RON and the special limits of the day fine are: (a) 120 and 240 day fines where the imprisonment penalty established by the court is no more than two years; (b) 180 and 300 days fine, where the imprisonment penalty set by the court is of more than two years.

Unlike the situation when the fine is applied as a single penalty, there are two particularities: (i) in this particular case the special limits of the day fines are determined only on the basis of the imprisonment penalty actually imposed by the court for the offence committed and not depending on the penalty stipulated by the law for the offence committed, and (ii) the special limits of the aforementioned day fines cannot be decreased or increased due to causes of mitigation or aggravation of the penalty. Applying the fine in addition to the imprisonment penalty constitutes in itself an additional means of criminal coercion which, without leading to increased imprisonment penalty, aggravates criminal repression.

REFERENCES

Explanatory Memorandum to the Criminal Code (Law No. 286/2009).

Lazăr, G. A. 2018. 'Determining the Penalty for Legal Persons', *Legal Law Writings* 4: 34, 36–40.

Oradea Court of Appeal, Criminal Division, Decision No. 365/2017, www.sintact.ro.

Streteanu, F. and Nițu, D. 2018. *Criminal Law. General Part.* Bucharest: Universul Juridic.

Udroiu, M. 2019. *Criminal Law. General Part.* Bucharest: C.H. Beck.

19

Comparative Law and Economics Perspective on Day Fines

Elena Kantorowicz-Reznichenko and Michael Faure

19.1 INTRODUCTION

Not surprisingly all countries that were analysed in the previous chapters had a system of day fines, as that was exactly the criterion on the basis of which they were selected. But as the different chapters made clear, despite some convergence, countries also diverge on many aspects of the day fine model. The differences not only relate to the way in which the day fine system has been designed in the particular regulation, but also concerning the way in which it is implemented in practice. This final chapter will provide a comparison of the systems as they were presented in the country chapters in the light of the theoretical perspective on day fines, presented in Chapter 2. From a theoretical perspective, it was held that there are strong justifications for the introduction of a day fine system, based both on retribution as well as on deterrence arguments. The theoretical chapter equally sketched that the effectiveness of the day fine model to an important extent depends upon the specific design.

This comparative chapter will examine to what extent in the different countries day fines have been introduced according to the optimal day fine model.[1] We will sketch where the day fine model corresponds with the theoretical starting points, but also in which countries particular problems have arisen with respect to the application of day fines in practice. Focusing not only on 'successes', but equally on 'failures' may provide scope for mutual learning, potentially allowing the countries that already implement day fines to improve the institutional design, but also providing insights on best practices for countries that may wish to consider the introduction of day fines.

After this introduction we first provide a brief comparative view of the design of the day fine system in the various countries in a table and discuss

[1] Sketched above in Chapter 2, Section 2.3.

functionally where the main differences and similarities can be found (19.2); then we connect the theory chapter to the practical implementation in the countries discussed (19.3). Next, we discuss in further detail some successes or failures of the day fine system, focusing generally on whether the day fine system was able to reach the goals that were set by the policy-maker (19.4). Section 19.5 discusses policy recommendations and Section 19.6 concludes.

19.2 A COMPARATIVE VIEW

In this section, we will provide a comparison between the designs and the use of the day fine system in the various countries. We follow the order of the chapters, which was determined by the moment when the countries introduced the day fine system. We summarise the information in Table 19.1 and subsequently discuss similarities and differences, based on a functional comparative method,[2] as well as from a perspective of comparative Law and Economics.[3]

There is a striking uniformity/convergence as far as the rationales behind introducing day fines within the criminal legal framework are concerned. Most countries mention the necessity to have an equal burden of the fines on the rich and the poor; the reduction of short-term prison sentences; and sometimes also deterrence as reasons for the introduction of the day fine system. However, despite the belief in the advantages of day fines, most of the countries that introduced day fines still retain also a fixed fine system for petty or administrative offences. The range of offences to which day fines are applicable differ across the countries. In some jurisdictions the fixed fine system is part of the criminal code, alongside with day fines (e.g. Poland, Switzerland). In other systems fixed fines are excluded from the criminal code (e.g. Germany, Austria, Hungary), where only day fines are applicable. However, some of these systems have administrative offences, which are then punishable only by fixed fines. Therefore, this difference alone cannot serve to derive any conclusion with respect to the extent to which day fines are applicable. The same offence might be part of the criminal law in one country, and part of an administrative act in another.

There seems to be convergence to the extent that the day fine system can usually only be applied by the courts. Therefore, in countries where prosecutors can propose a so-called 'transaction', a payment that prevents further prosecution, this payment is often not imposed as a day fine. There is as

---

[2] See Zweigert and Kötz, *An Introduction to Comparative Law*, and Siems, *Comparative Law*.
[3] Mattei, *Comparative Law and Economics*.

TABLE 19.1 Summary of the Day Fine Models

Country	Year	Max. No. Days	Min. No. Days	Daily Unit limit (€)	Result of Default	Ratio Fines/ prison	Scope of Wealth	Reason of adoption
Finland	1921	120	1	6 –	Prison	3:1	Taxable income	Equal burden on rich and poor. Independent fine from inflation.
Sweden	1931	150	30	3 – 94	Prison	-	Wealth and income	Reducing the inequality between rich and poor. Decreasing the rate of short-term imprisonment sentences.
Denmark	(1930) 1933	60	1	0.27 -	Prison	1:1	Assets, income, financial obligations and other matters	Equal burden on rich and poor. Reducing fine defaulters. Alternative to short-term imprisonment.
Germany	1975	360	5	1 – 30,000	Prison	1:1	Net income	Equal treatment of poor and rich offenders. Decreasing the rate of short-term imprisonment sentences.
Austria	1975	720	2	4 – 5,000	Prison	2:1	Personal (actual and potential) income (including welfare benefits and income from assets)	Combating social inequality. Decreasing the rate of short-term imprisonment sentences.
Hungary	1978	540	30	3 – 1,500	Prison	1:1	Income and assets	An alternative to imprisonment sentences. To individualise sentences.
France	1983	360	1	- 1,000	Prison	1:1	Income	Alternative sanction to imprisonment sentence.
Portugal	(1982) 1983	360	10	5 – 500	Prison	1:1/3	Economic and financial conditions	Substitution to short-term imprisonment.

England & Wales	(1991) 1992	50 (week)	1 (week)	£4 – 100 (week)	Prison	~1:3.5	Income (financial circumstances)	Uniformity in fines across magistrate courts especially. Fairer fine and equal impact. Reduce imprisonment rates and especially the number of defaulters.
Slovenia	(1994) 1995	360	30	– 1,000	Prison	2:1	Income	Solving social injustice created by fixed fines. Effective replacement for short-term imprisonment sentences.
Spain	(1995) 1996	720	10	2 – 465	Prison	2:1	Financial situation incl. assets	Better deterrence. Reduction of imprisonment rates.
Poland	(1997) 1998	540	10	2 – 468	Prison	2:1	Actual and prospective income and assets	Reduction of imprisonment sentences. Equality before the law (equal burden irrespective of wealth).
Croatia	(1997) 1998	360	30	3 – 1,355	Prison	1:1	Income and assets (including potential income from e.g. unused property)	Harmonise the Croatian regulation of fine with modern legal systems. Correct the unfairness of fixed fines. Individualise the sentence to the circumstances of the offender. Increase the share of fines as a criminal punishment
Switzerland	2007	180	1	28 – 2,818	Prison	1:1	Any income	Alternative to short-term imprisonment sentences.

TABLE 19.1 (*continued*)

Country	Year	Max. No. Days	Min. No. Days	Daily Unit limit (€)	Result of Default	Ratio Fines/ prison	Scope of Wealth	Reason of adoption
Czech Republic[4]	(2009) 2010	730	20	4 – 1,950	Community service Home imprisonment Prison	-	Net (actual and potential) income (financial circumstances)	An alternative to imprisonment sentences.
Romania	(2009) 2014	400	30	0.20 – 105	Prison	1:1	Material situation	More equal and proportionate sanctioning system. Reduce prison overcrowding.

Source: own table based on preceding chapters.

Notes:

(1) the information in the table is correct for August 2019 and does not include later updates of the laws.

(2) In cases where there was a gap between the introduction year and the year when the day fine reform entered into force, the former is indicated in parentheses. It should be noted, that in some countries, day fines went through several significant reforms, e.g. in Croatia, even though day fines were first introduced in 1997, a completely new Criminal Code was enacted in 2011 which made significant changes to the day fines system. For sake of simplicity, the dates indicated in the table refer to the first time day fines were introduced in the country. However, the details about the system refer to the most updated legal provisions.

(3) In most systems a defaulting offender has the possibility to perform community service before resorting to conversion of the sentence to imprisonment.

[4]   In Czech Republic, day fines were first applied only to juveniles (since 2004) and only then introduced for adult offenders (in 2009). We mention the latter date in the table since this book is focusing on adult criminal justice systems.

such theoretically no clear justification why the day fine system should be limited to a financial penalty imposed by a judge and why it could not, for example, apply to either administrative fines or transactions proposed by the prosecutor as well. However, practical considerations might offer some explanation if the system of day fines entails significantly higher costs than the petty offences for which it is imposed.

Divergence could be noticed as far as the question is concerned whether the day fine system can also be applied to legal entities. Since it is only courts that can use the day fine system, this is to an important extent related to the question whether legal entities can be held criminally liable. In systems where there is no criminal liability of legal entities (like typically in Germany) there will not be a possibility to impose day fines on legal entities either. Also in Croatia and England and Wales, it was explicitly mentioned that the day fine cannot apply to legal entities. Some countries do have the possibility to apply day fines to legal entities as well. This is, for example, the case in Austria, the Czech Republic and in Romania.

Of course, there are, as the table also indicates, important differences between the countries concerning the minimum and maximum number of days that can be imposed. Many countries have a relatively low minimum (like one day in Finland, Denmark, France and Switzerland); others have relatively higher minima (like thirty days in Sweden, Hungary, Croatia and Romania) or are somewhere in the middle. Also as far as the maximum amount of days that can be imposed is concerned, there is substantial divergence with Finland (120), Sweden (150) and Denmark (60) being on the low end and Austria (720), Hungary (540), Spain (720), Poland (540) and the Czech Republic (730) being on the high end of the spectrum.

Divergence also relates to the limits on the amount of money which can be set as a daily unit. All countries mention a minimum amount for the daily unit (with the exception of France and Slovenia); most countries mention relatively low minimum amounts (like 0.27 euros in Denmark, 1 euro in Germany, 2 euros in Spain and Poland, 3 euros in Hungary and 4 euros in Austria). This seems to be in order to accommodate also fines for the low-income offenders. Almost all countries also have a financial limit on the maximum daily unit, which in some cases is relatively low (like 106 euros in Sweden and 105 euros in Romania); in other cases, the upper limit is substantially higher (like 30,000 euros in Germany). Only in Finland and Denmark there is no financial limit on the daily unit to be taken into account for calculating the day fine.

Differences also exist with respect to the question whether the judge can take into account the real net (i.e. after taxes) income of the individual concerned or whether particular basic costs should be deduced to allow a minimal subsistence level. Austria and Croatia indicate that basic costs for supporting the perpetrator and his or her family can be deduced, although the precise calculation of that amount is debated. Also in England and Wales, an 'appropriate expenditure level' was supposed to be deduced from the net income. In Germany as well, specific costs, more particularly maintenance payments due by the perpetrator would be deduced. And the same is the case in Hungary, Portugal and Slovenia, even though the formulations may differ.

A debated issue is what should be the scope of wealth which serves as the basis for the daily unit. On that point the solutions diverge between the legal systems. Some countries only refer to income which is stated in a tax report (Finland), whereas others refer more generally to 'wealth and income' (like, for example, Sweden, Hungary, Spain, Portugal, Croatia and Switzerland). Austria, Poland and the Czech Republic not only refer to actual, but also to potential income and in Hungary the court can account for the household income, rather than just the perpetrator's income when calculating the daily unit. But this is debated, given the principle that the penalty should only affect the perpetrator.

Substantial differences between the countries also exist as far as the question is concerned how the day fine is executed. In other words: what happens in case of a default (i.e. a non-payment of the day fine). It is in that respect striking that even though reducing short-term imprisonment was mentioned as one of the most important reasons for the introduction of the day fine system, the main alternative for the day fine system is still impris-onment. In fact, all countries mention that the default on the day fine can result in imprisonment although there are again differences between the countries as far as the precise procedure is concerned (in some cases the convergence to imprisonment in case of default is automatic; in others there is discretion of the court; finally in at least one country – Czech Republic – a day fine sentence cannot be converted to imprisonment until other options are exhausted); differences also exist as far as the conversion rate is concerned, that is the amount of days a perpetrator would have to serve in prison in case of a default on the day fine. In many countries the conversion is 1:1, meaning that one unpaid day fine leads to one day imprisonment (for example in Denmark, Germany, Hungary, France, Croatia, Switzerland and Romania), but in some countries two (Austria, Spain and Poland) or even three (Finland) days of unpaid days of fine lead to one day imprisonment. It is equally striking that not all countries mention the possibility of converting the unpaid day fine into community service (this is, for example, the case in Croatia, France, Germany, Poland, Romania and Slovenia). The way in which the conversion from a non-paid day fine to community service is calculated again largely differs between the countries.

The largest divergence between the countries probably concerns not so much the formal legal framework, but rather the application in practice. The day fine system seems to work well in countries like Germany, Austria and Finland, but is perceived very negatively (either by the public at large and/or the judiciary) in some countries where judges literally try to avoid applying the day fine or simply do not calculate the fine according to the prescribed procedure (like in Croatia, Spain, the Czech Republic, Denmark and Slovenia). In Portugal it is considered that the day fine system would impair deterrence and would lead to fines only having a symbolic value. The most striking case is of course the one of England and Wales, where the day fine system was even abolished less than seven months after its introduction. Judicial and public rejection of this penalty form was a crucial reason for the failure. It is in fact striking that a majority of the countries that apply the day fine system seem to suffer from such a negative perception that courts simply do not apply it. That of course merits a further inquiry into why the theoretical advantages of day fines (as explained in Chapter 2) can apparently not always be realised in practice (see, Section 19.4.4).

There are other important divergences with respect to access to financial information of the offender. However, the discussion on that is provided in the next section where practice is assessed in light of the theory.

19.3 THEORY VERSUS PRACTICE

In Chapter 2, we have discussed the main features of the day fine model which would optimise its effectiveness in the sense of enhanced deterrence and more adequate proportionality. In this section, we examine whether the existing models of day fines are in line with the optimal model.

In the optimal model, **the scope of wealth**, which is accounted for the daily unit, should be as broad as possible and preferably complete. In other words, as explained in Chapter 2, in order to achieve deterrence and proportionality of the punishment, the whole wealth needs to be considered. Anything less that this would under-deter offenders whose main income is outside the daily unit's scope. The countries' review demonstrates that at least de jure and consistently with the theory, the scope of wealth which needs to be considered for the daily unit is quite broad. Often when income is mentioned, it encompasses all forms of income rather than solely personal income from employment. Moreover, some criminal justice systems render even potential income as relevant, rather than merely actual (e.g. Austria and Poland). This practice may overcome the problem of a shadow economy. Nevertheless, it seems that in practice, in many countries, courts rely only on the offender's personal income to set the daily unit. Hence, in cases where the offender's main income is not from his or her employment, the optimal fine is not set.

Regarding the **limit on the daily unit**, this element is also important for theoretically increasing the effectiveness and the fairness of the fine. A cap, especially a low one, would create a similar problem to the fixed fine model. Those offenders receiving a higher income would not receive a fine which is truly tailored to their financial state. Consequently, they would potentially be under-deterred and the fine would not be proportionate in its broader sense. As the country chapters demonstrate, almost all countries have a cap on the daily unit. This is meant to avoid excessive fines, which is rendered as a more important argument than setting an optimal fine. The exceptions are Finland and Denmark. Interestingly, despite the several highly publicised cases of high fines for minor offences, those examples do not seem to harm the reputation of the fine in those countries. This is especially true in Finland.[5] Even though most countries do not follow the optimal model of day fines with respect to this feature, it is worth mentioning that the high caps set in some countries (e.g. 30,000 euro in Germany) might be sufficient in the majority of the cases.

Finally, full **access to financial information** is an important part of the optimal model of day fines. Without such access, the sentencer has no ability to calculate the income of the offender and is thus, unable to tailor the fine to the financial state of the offender. Without such access, a day fine becomes de facto a fixed fine, which solely or mainly depends on the severity of the offence. Consistently with the theoretical model, many legal systems provide courts (or other relevant authorities) with access to the offender's financial information. In some cases, very wide powers exist to access financial information (like in the Czech Republic, Hungary and Croatia where even banks can be asked to provide information or by accessing the database of the Ministry of Finance like in Poland). Nevertheless, not all countries have such access. Germany is the most extreme example where courts are not allowed to access the offender's financial information or to oblige the offender to provide such information him- or herself. Therefore, judges estimate the income based on profession and standard of living.

Despite the broad access to financial information in most countries, the country chapters demonstrate a surprising situation – most courts do not utilise this right or do not follow the obligation of fully collecting the financial

---

[5] Lappi-Seppälä, 'Crime Prevention and Community Sanctions in Scandinavia' at 29–30.

information about the offender before setting the fine. It seems that the main source of information is the offender him- or herself. Alternatively, judges use the average income to set the fine. In some systems, it even seems that judges calculate the fine backwards. Namely, they first determine for themselves the size of the fine based on the severity of the offence and then translate it to day fines terms (e.g. Denmark, Czech Republic). This practice inevitably deviates from the optimal model of day fines. As long as the information is not collected, the fine cannot be adequately tailored to each offender. The reason for this practice seems to be the complexity of collecting this information and often the lack of guidelines which information exactly should be considered.

19.4 BEST PRACTICES AND LIMITATIONS

Having discussed where the practice deviates from the theoretical model concerning the optimal application of the day fine, we will now focus in further detail on specific aspects of the day fine system in order to allow for an evaluation of particular aspects that might be considered either a success or a failure of the day fine system.

19.4.1 *The Role of Day Fines in the Sentencing System*

An important reason for most countries to introduce the day fine system was on the one hand distributional justice (proportionality of the fine) and the reduction of (especially short-term) imprisonment. The question therefore arises what role the (day) fine is playing in the entire sentencing system in the countries examined and what is its effect. That is obviously an empirical question and requires information on the relative number of day fines compared to other sanctions and especially compared to the situation before the day fine system was introduced. A general conclusion of the various chapters is that (although there are a few positive exceptions) the number of empirical studies (and generally data collection) is relatively limited. Some countries do provide data on the relative use of the day fine system, but more refined empirical studies, examining, for example, the effects of the introduction of the day fine system on the incidence of crime, are largely lacking.

A table in the chapter on Finland concerning the use of fines generally in Europe in 2006[6] shows that in Finland fines (both fixed and day fine) constitute 88 per cent of all convictions. Of all the sentences imposed by courts in that country, 61 per cent are day fines. In Sweden, 58 per cent of the total

---

[6] Table 3.5, Chapter 3 (Finland).

number of convictions in 2018 carried fines as the principal sanction. However, even though the day fine system is generally supported by legal practitioners, it is not considered sufficiently deterrent by the public at large.

In Denmark, for violations of the criminal code, in 44 per cent of the cases fines were imposed; in 46 per cent of the cases imprisonment was the sanction (in 2017). The day fine system could therefore be used to a larger extent than is presently the case in Denmark. Yet Danish courts have been reluctant to apply day fines.

In Germany, a priority rule (for fines) was introduced in 1969 resulting in fines constituting 80 per cent of all criminal penalties imposed. The introduction of the day fine system in 1975 did not change that relationship.

In Austria, it is striking that of all criminal sanctions imposed in 2017, 65.4 per cent were imprisonment and fines constituted only 28.3 per cent. But the introduction of the day fine system in 1975 led to a significant increase in the importance of fines in that country.

In Hungary the system of criminal sanctions still remains heavily tilted towards imprisonment. Only an average of 30 per cent of the sanctions are day fines. It is therefore concluded that in Hungary the day fine system is not used to its full potential.

In France in 2017, out of all convictions only in 4 per cent day fines were imposed. The importance of day fines in the total sanctioning system in France is therefore limited. Day fines are mostly used for traffic offences, simple thefts, narcotics and wilful violence.

In England and Wales, the introduction of the unit fines scheme (as day fines were referred to in England and Wales) led to an increase in the use of fines. The number of fines imposed relative to overall penalties rose to 48 per cent in 1993. But the abolition of the day fine system led to an overall reduction of the use of the fines: in 2017 fines constituted only 7.4 per cent of all sanctions imposed.

In Spain fines constituted 50 per cent of total sentences in 1975, but that percentage dropped to 14.1 per cent in 2002. In the twenty-first century, the imposition of fines increased compared to imprisonment.

In Poland, the day fine system is not used extensively. Increasing unemployment at the time and the impoverishment of the society can potentially explain the relatively small role day fines played in Poland. The burden the investigation and the calculation of the daily unit place on the judges are also mentioned. Day fines in Poland were, therefore, not able to replace more repressive sanctions like imprisonment, also because day fines remained relatively low.

Fines are not used to a large extent in Croatia. Only a small percentage of convicted individuals are sentenced to fines. Fines are de facto replaced by alternative sanctions (not necessarily imprisonment) and therefore do not play an important role in the overall sanctioning system. It is suggested that day fines have not been used to a large extent in Croatia, because of the importance of the shadow economy and an inefficient public administration. As a result, accurate financial information about the offenders' income is often not available.

The Czech Republic barely uses day fines. In recent years day fines were applied in between 3–5 per cent of all convictions. They therefore only play a minor role as a criminal sanction; judges impose a proportionate fine to the conduct rather than to the income of the offender. Judges also do not trust the information provided on the income of offenders and consider the calculations often as unfair.

This brief overview shows again a relatively diversified picture: in some countries (day) fines do play an important role in the overall penalty system, but there is also a considerable number of countries where, for a variety of reasons, day fines are not used to the full extent and de facto only in very few cases. As we will discuss in further detail below, in those countries where day fines are underused, it is often due either to a negative public perception or to the reluctance of the judiciary to apply the day fine system (often because they do not want to engage in a detailed research concerning the precise income) as a result of which they impose relatively low fines, leading in turn to the perception of weak deterrence of day fines.

19.4.2 Achievement of the Goals of Day Fines

As the table made clear, the most important reasons to adopt day fines were: (1) imposing an equal burden on the rich and the poor; (2) reducing the number of fine defaulters and (3) immediately related to that: reducing the short-term imprisonment. The previous subsection made clear that only in a few legal systems (such as Austria and Germany) day fines succeeded in playing an important role in the overall sanctioning system. In many of the other countries for a variety of reasons day fines remained underused. As a result, it is not surprising that many countries equally indicate that it was difficult to reach the policy goals of day fines, more particularly the reduction of fine defaulters and the reduction of the prison population. The experience of a few countries can be treated as an example to illustrate this.

Starting with the success story of Germany: the priority rule (whereby the fines were the default punishment when short-term imprisonment can be imposed) which was already introduced in the 1960s, led to a significant reduction of prison sentences. The introduction of the day fine system in

1975 was meant to compensate the unequal treatment of the poor and the rich offenders and to provide a more reliable alternative to a short-imprisonment sentence. Nowadays, day fines are broadly used and cover relatively serious offences, such as theft, fraud, forgery, drug offences, and even some forms of sex offences. Consequently, more than 80 per cent of sentences are day fines. The introduction of day fines in Germany did as such not affect the collection of the fines. The rate of fine defaulters is approximately 10 per cent in Germany and has doubled in the last forty years.

In England and Wales, following the abolishment of unit fines, the use of fines decreased (especially among unemployed offenders who now received conditional discharge) and the rate of default imprisonment for the unemployed increased. The problems that therefore led to the introduction of the unit fines (high imprisonment rates and many fine defaulters) came back after the abolishment of the system. In subsequent years those problems (notably of fine defaulters) were mitigated by using other alternative sanctions.

Also, for Poland it is reported that since the fines were not extensively used and since the amounts imposed were not high (as the investigation and calculation of the daily unit put a too high burden on the judges), day fines in that country were not able to reach the goal of the reduction of imprisonment sentences. The same was reported for Croatia (and for the other countries where day fines are not used to their full potential): for a variety of reasons, the day fine is heavily underused as a result of which the formal goal to increase the share of the fine as a criminal punishment could not be reached. Socio-economic reasons, low living standards, negative attitudes of judges, the complexity of calculating the fine (more particularly to calculate the income – the daily unit) and the lacking clarity of the provisions regulating the fine were all mentioned as reasons for not using the day fine to its full potential.

Finally, the experience of Switzerland stresses the problem of fine defaulters in particular. Despite very low unemployment rates in the country, roughly one half of prison entries concern fine defaulters. Nevertheless, one should keep in mind that quite uniquely, nine out of ten sentences of day fines in Switzerland are suspended. This leads to an especially large time gap between the day the size of the fine is set (at the time of the conviction) and the later execution date of the fine if the offender violated the conditions of the suspensions. Consequently, there is a high probability the financial state of the offender changed in the meantime. Furthermore, the high rate of default imprisonment includes also those sentenced to fixed fines, a sentence which is still extensively used in Switzerland.

Summarising, not surprisingly, in all systems where the day fine was not used to its full potential in the criminal penalty system (as indicated in Section

19.4.1), the formal goals that the day fine system was supposed to reach could not be fulfilled. This was partially due to difficulties judges had in collecting financial information and in a negative public and judicial perception of the system.

19.4.3 *Public and Judicial Perception of the System*

Public and judicial perception of day fines seems to be a crucial factor for its implementation and success. Given the novelty and complexity of this fine, lack of understanding might lead to antagonism towards this model while missing its advantages. In particular, the public might reject this model due to the potentially high amounts of fines in the rare cases where particularly wealthy offenders commit minor crimes. Judges on the other hand, may reject this fine system also due to the increased effort it requires from them in the form of collecting financial information and calculating the daily unit. This is the reason for discussing the perception of the system separately in the country chapters.

The most extreme case of negative reception of the fine model, both by judges and by the public, can be found in England and Wales. This negative perception in fact contributed to the abolition of this model all together. Day fines (or as they have been named in England and Wales – unit fines) were perceived by judges as rigid and unworkable; restrictive to their discretion and disproportionate to the offences. The difficulty to obtain information on the financial state of the offender also played a role in this negative perception. In addition to that there was never a campaign about this model of fines and the public was not informed on the way it works and its advantages. Consequently, fuelled by the media who reported in a sensational manner some extreme cases, this sanction was also rejected by the public.

Slovenia provides another example of the importance of judicial acceptance of this model. The system of day fines had to go through several reforms due to its initial rejection by judges.

In some cases, the system of day fines seems to be discussed in legal circles but the public awareness is insufficient. In addition, it seems that judges do not go through any special training before adopting this model. Consequently, as the experience of many countries demonstrates, judges do not collect financial information and do not set the daily unit as it is meant to be. For example, in Spain not only that fines are not tailored to the offender's financial information, but they are generally too low. Too low fines miss the goal of deterrence and retribution, as well as negatively affect public perception of pecuniary sanctions. As a result, its potential as an alternative sanction to imprisonment diminishes.

19.4.4 *Legal Transplants*

The day fine system originated in Finland in 1921, was taken over by Sweden in 1931 and subsequently by Denmark in 1933. It then took approximately forty years until Germany (1975) and Austria (1975) followed by Hungary (1978) and France (1983) introduced day fines, followed by the other countries, the last ones in the row being the Czech Republic (2009) and Romania (2009). The fact that the Scandinavian countries started with the day fine system provided an important example of a different way to calculate fines and provided an inspiration for other legal systems to follow it. The way in which day fines have been copied by other countries is a typical example of what is referred to in comparative law as a legal transplant: a mechanism whereby a host country receives a particular legal rule or instrument that is transplanted from a previous experience in a donor country.[7] Many of the country chapters make clear that their system was in fact copied from experiences in other countries. When Germany transformed the summary fine into a day fine system, it explicitly referred to the Scandinavian system and the same was true for Austria. Countries that later introduced the day fine system, such as Hungary, the Czech Republic, Portugal and Spain, all referred to the German system, whereas Slovenia referred to day fines in Finland.

Day fines therefore to a large extent constitute an example of a legal transplant (especially as far as the countries were concerned where it was introduced at a later stage). Whether it is also a successful legal transplant is yet another issue. As we indicated earlier, for some countries (mostly Germany and Finland) that may be the case, but in other countries the system is formally introduced, but remains largely a dead letter in practice. In that sense the legal transplant may not always have been successful. Literature both in law and development[8] and Law and Economics[9] warned that transplants may only work if they are based on local demand and ownership and if there is a large receptivity of the transplant within the existing legal culture in the host

---

[7] See further on legal transplants Siems, *supra* note 2; Watson, *Legal Transplants: An Approach to Comparative Law*.

[8] See, for example, Nader, 'Promise or Plunder? A Past and Future Look at Law and Development', 2.

[9] See, for example, Berkowitz, Pistor and Richard, 'Economic Development, Legality and the Transplant Effect', 173–4.

country as well as a familiarity of the host country with the transplanted rule.[10] If the institutional framework in the host country is different from that in the donor country from which the transplanted legal rule originates, there is a danger of a rejection of the transplant. That has in many countries apparently been the case, which underscores the need for an information campaign to explain the goals of the day fine system to both the public and practitioners in order to guarantee the receptivity of day fines in the host country with a different legal culture.

19.5 POLICY IMPLICATIONS

From the comparative remarks made earlier a few policy implications concerning the introduction of day fines in the penalty system can be deduced, some at a rather general level (Section 19.5.1), some at a more practical level (Section 19.5.2) related to the specific design of the day fine system. Despite the 'failure' of day fines in some jurisdictions, it in fact provides important insights how to improve the transplant of day fines and to increase its efficiency. It is our belief that addressing the causes of the identified problems may help better integrating day fines in the local sentencing system. Given the advantages of such a model of pecuniary sanctions, it seems worth analysing the methods to achieve it. This is the purpose of this section.

19.5.1 *General*

This book revealed that day fines are often underutilised and that courts in general impose too low fines. Such practice undermines the potential of day fines to replace some of the more repressive sanctions and to increase the fairness of the criminal sentencing system. The main two reasons for this 'failure', which were identified in this book, are the problem of negative perception of the fine and the complexity of the system due to its dependence on financial information of the offender. We suggest that these difficulties can be addressed as follows.

19.5.1.1 Perception of Day Fines

One important aspect, which seems to be overlooked in many countries, is the importance of raising the awareness, understanding and acceptance of day

---

[10] Faure, Goodwin and Weber, 'Bucking the Kuznets Curve: Designing Effective Environmental Regulation in Developing Countries', 125–44.

fines by the public and the sentencers before or shortly after its introduction. In terms of the public, given that day fines differ significantly from the more familiar model of fixed fines; an early campaign to explain how it functions and to stress its advantages might mitigate the resistance. Furthermore, once the public is well informed, sensational media news might have less of a negative effect. It should be noted that in the country with the most sensational examples of fines due to the lack of a limit on the daily unit – Finland – public opinion of day fines is quite positive. The majority of the people perceive this fine as fair.[11] This example simply illustrates that it is not the inherent problem of the fine model which creates the negative perception of it, but potentially the lack of understanding of this model.

An additional change, which can mitigate negative public perception, is the way the fine is communicated in the judgment (and later in the media). Instead of stating the total fine in their judgment, courts should state separately the number of days and the daily unit. This is the practice in Sweden, Austria and Switzerland. The number of days reflects the severity of the offence. Therefore, once the public understands how the fine works they can assess the proportionality of the fine in light of the number of days imposed rather than the total amount. Such system would avoid the potential outrage fuelled by the media as rare and extreme examples of high fines are reported. Furthermore, it increases the transparency of the sanctioning procedure.

With respect to judges, given that they are important players in this system, more attention should be paid to increasing their support of this model of fines. Before introducing day fines, it might be helpful to well inform the judges (and other sentencers if relevant) about the system and allow them to express their concerns. Such concerns can be addressed in early stages, thus improving the system based on the experience of judges, but also increasing their support. In a later stage, judges should receive training about day fines to learn about this model and how to apply it efficiently. Combined with proper guidelines, as will be discussed in the next part, such a change can have the potential to improve not only the acceptance but also the proper application of day fines. Training programmes can also relieve the feeling of judges that their discretionary power is being restricted. Even though day fines are more systematic than fixed fines, judges maintain their discretion to adjust the number of days to the severity of the offence and other relevant circumstances. Only the daily unit is the more systematic and 'fixed' element where the judge should not have discretion. This will in fact increase equality between

---

[11] *Supra* note 7.

offenders since different judges would impose similar daily units if offenders have the same level of wealth.

19.5.1.2 Financial Information

Investigation of the financial information and a proper calculation of the day fines appeared to be a major problem in many of the countries which apply day fines. Despite often having access to the different authorities, which hold such information, many judges do not use this power. The reason is often the complexity of doing so and the lack of clear guidelines.

We suggest two potential solutions for this problem. As a first step, clear guidelines need to be introduced stating what exactly should be accounted in the daily unit, which deductions should be made and which portion is the daily unit. As we have seen in this book, clear guidelines are missing in most systems. This inevitably makes the system uncertain and given the low amount of the fine, it might not worth for the judge to collect such information. To create a simpler system for implementation, besides clear guidelines, a computer programme can be created which requires only inserting information and receiving the respective amount. Unlike the number of days, which can depend not only on the severity of the offence, but also on some special circumstances of the crime the judge can take into account, the daily unit is straightforward. Therefore, it is possible to use an algorithm which provides the daily unit once all the information regarding income and deductions is inserted. With clear guidelines and such systematic manner of calculation, this task can also be performed by court clerks, releasing judges from the burden.

Due to the lack of time and limited resources of the judge, financial information can be collected by other authorities, potentially in earlier stages of investigation, for example by the police. The modern technology provides the possibility to collect financial information more efficiently. More and more information is stored digitally. Therefore, with clear guidelines and procedure, such information can be collected more easily. It should be noted, that already the tax authorities usually possess a wide range of financial information (such as personal income, assets, dividends, etc.). If the financial information would be available to the judge at the day of the sentencing and he or she will have a clear formula how to use it, the procedure of calculating the fine can become less complex. Consequently, more adequate fines can be imposed and eventually become a more reliable alternative for more repressive sanctions.

Alternatively, or complementary, the scope of wealth which should be part of the daily unit can be narrowed down. The theoretically optimal fine, as discussed in Chapter 2, should entail the entire wealth. However, there is a positive correlation between the scope of the accounted wealth and the costs of collecting information about it. Assuming that most offenders' main income is from employment, rather than from other sources, setting taxable income (as it appears in the tax report) as the scope for the daily unit might be an efficient compromise. This is the practice in Finland, which seems to work adequately. Reducing the costs of collecting information can then increase the number of cases in which judges use their power. Such fines will not be theoretically optimal, yet on average they will be more tailored to the offenders than fixed fines. Consequently, the level of deterrence, as well as retribution, can be enhanced. Such a solution does not provide an answer for countries where shadow economy plays a significant role. Nevertheless, there is no reason to assume that in such countries, fixed fines have a better potential of deterrence and retribution than day fines. Accounting also for a *potential* income, as done in some of the countries, might be a solution to this problem. Nevertheless, in light of the potential problems such solution raises (e.g. from a constitutional perspective), we do not discuss it here.

19.5.2 *Specific*

As far as the design of the day fine system is concerned, the comparative overview showed quite a few remarkable differences and divergences between the countries. In the light of Chapter 2, which discussed the theoretical justifications for the use of day fines, we argue that, provided that within a country generally the right legal climate and culture can be created to guarantee the receptivity of the day fine system, there are also possibilities to increase the use of day fines in the following ways.

- Open the possibility to allow the application of the day fine system for all offences. Currently many legal systems restrict the use of day fines to specific crimes and combine it still with a system of fixed fines that applies to other crimes. If the theoretical justifications for day fines are considered convincing, there is as such no reason to limit the day fine system just to particular crimes. That would hence be an argument to generalise the day fine system and make it applicable to all crimes. As such there would also not be reasons to exclude particular crimes (such as drugs-related offences) from the day fine system.
- Apply day fines to administrative offences as well. Again, from a principle perspective, there is no reason to restrict day fines only to courts. When administrative fines are imposed, that could in theory equally be

applied via a day fine system. This is of course conditioned on the possibility to reduce the administrative costs of collecting information on the financial state of the offender. But as we mentioned earlier, there are ample possibilities of improving the collection of information on income in an early stage (i.e. during the investigation), as a result of which also administrative authorities could be able to apply the day fine system.

- Permit applying day fines by other sentencers, such as prosecutors. For example, day fines could be part of the transaction (penal order) system, as it already is in some countries. Again, it would fit into an approach whereby the monetary sanction is always proportional to income and in that sense, distributionally fair and deterrent.

- Apply the day fine also to legal entities. The overview made clear that particular legal systems do allow the application of day fines to legal entities, but others do not. Again, also legal entities do have income that can relatively easily be calculated at an early stage of the investigation. The justifications to apply day fines towards natural persons apply to the same extent to legal entities. In fact, in some legal system that do not even apply day fines on natural persons, day fines are applied in case of firms.

- Make community service (or other sanctions such as house arrest) the alternative in case of default on the day fine. Day fines were originally introduced to reduce (especially short-term) imprisonment and generally to reduce the prison population. Still, in many legal systems when the day fine is not paid, the primary way of executing the day fine is to apply imprisonment. That may be a sign that the day fine has been wrongly calculated (as the offender is apparently not able to pay) and it also reflects a failure in the relation to the goals of the day fine system. In order to better meet the goal of reducing prison population, it would be desirable to set community service as the default for unpaid fines (if the offender can and is willing to perform community service). If for particular reasons community service would not be deemed an adequate replacement service, imprisonment would still be applied.

19.6 CONCLUDING REMARKS

The day fine system in Europe is definitely on the rise. For a long time, it was restricted to the Scandinavian countries and then taken over by Germany,

Austria and Hungary, but not seriously considered in other legal systems. However, in the 1990s a new wave of interest in the day fine system arose as a result of which a total of sixteen (including Liechtenstein) countries on the European continent have a day fine system. This rise of the day fine system is in line with the theoretical starting points arguing that the day fine system fits better a retributive interpretation of proportionality as well as the deterrent function of the fine.

Notwithstanding those theoretical advantages there still is a large reluctance among many countries to introduce day fines. Indeed, the fact that sixteen countries do have the day fine system equally implies that a probably equally large number does not. Moreover, the comparative overview showed that there are still considerable differences between the way the day fine system is regulated among the countries. Differences not only arise as far as the formal legal framework is concerned, but especially in legal practice. It is striking that in some countries the judges disregard the day fine system, do not apply it or only to a very limited extent and rather continue either with fixed fines or day fines which are simply based on estimates, which do not correspond to the real income of offenders.

To some extent the day fine system may have been a 'Fremdkörper', a legal transplant coming either from Scandinavia or Germany and imposed onto host countries that were apparently unfamiliar with this new concept, leading to major difficulties for the judiciary to apply the new system, but also difficulties among the public to accept it. That partial failure of the day fine system underscores the importance of an adequate communication that needs to accompany the introduction of a new legal instrument to the judiciary. Initial fears of the judiciary that they may face difficulties in applying this seemingly complex construct should be overcome by intensive training and capacity building programmes, facilitating the application of the day fine system by the judge. But it equally requires assistance of all partners in the enforcement chain. Investigators like the police or other authorities can play a crucial role in facilitating the application of the day fine system if they in an early stage would acquire complete and adequate information on the income of the perpetrator, as a result of which the judge does not have to engage him/herself in such an investigation but can simply apply the income information provided in the criminal file.

This book is the first of its kind, providing an overview of the legal structure and practical application of the day fine system in all countries in Europe that do have day fines. This overview demonstrates a mixed picture of successes and failures which can provide valuable insights to policy-makers. Countries that would consider the introduction of the day fine system can learn by studying the specific legal details that need adequate regulation (for example the necessity to regulate the collection of information concerning income) to guarantee an adequate application of the day fine system. The failures experienced in some countries may also stress for those candidate-countries the importance of investing in programmes teaching all partners in the enforcement chain, from police to the judiciary, how to effectively apply the day fine system. Countries that do already have the day fine system can equally learn from experiences in other countries which sometimes have a different design of the day fine system. This can give rise to mutual learning and exchange.[12] For those countries that currently still have limitations on the application of the day fine system, the comparison with other countries shows that there may be scope for a different design expanding the scope of the day fine system, for example to other crimes or to penalties not only imposed by the courts, but also by other entities.

As this is a first volume dealing with day fines in the various European countries, it may be clear that there is ample scope for further research. The country chapters in this volume made clear that there may be sufficient information on the legal-institutional design of the day fine system, but that empirical studies concerning the effective application of day fines within those countries are still lacking. As the theoretical perspectives predict that a correctly applied day fine system may be more deterrent than a fixed fine system, it would be important to examine empirically whether that assumption indeed holds. Of course, there may be difficulties in the empirical design of such a research (there may be a lack of data; additional legal changes at the same time, as a result of which it may not be clear which legal change caused a particular effect; an inability to randomise and the absence of a control group). But it is at least worthwhile to examine the possibilities of an empirical examination in further research.

As we hope that this volume already made clear: the day fine system is a fascinating penalty system, which can potentially have a highly important social function (of reducing the prison population and making the criminal sanctioning system fairer), which could at the same time potentially better

---

[12] It is a typical example of a positive competition between legal systems, providing scope for mutual learning resulting from the diversity of legal systems. For further details see Van den Bergh, 'Farewell Utopia?: Why the European Union Should Take the Economics of Federalism Seriously', 937–64; Van den Bergh, 'Subsidiarity As an Economic Demarcation Principle and the Emergence of European Private Law', 129–52; Van den Bergh, 'The Subsidiarity Principle in European Community Law: Some Insights from Law and Economics', 337–66.

serve both the retributive and deterrent functions of punishment. It therefore surely merits more research, not only given its academic, but also given its large societal importance.

REFERENCES

Berkowitz, D., Pistor, K. and Richard, J.-F. 2003. 'Economic Development, Legality and the Transplant Effect', *European Economic Review* 47: 165–95.

Faure, M., Goodwin, M. and Weber, F. 2010. 'Bucking the Kuznets Curve: Designing Effective Environmental Regulation in Developing Countries', *Virginia Journal of International Law* 51: 125–44.

Lappi-Seppälä, T. 2008. *Crime Prevention and Community Sanctions in Scandinavia.* Helsinki, Finland: National Research Institute of Legal Policy.

Mattei, H. 1998. *Comparative Law and Economics.* Ann Arbor: University of Michigan Press.

Nader, L. 2007. 'Promise or Plunder? A Past and Future Look at Law and Development', *Global Jurist Frontier* 7, 2: 1–24.

Siems, M. 2018. *Comparative Law.* Cambridge: Cambridge University Press.

Van den Bergh, R. 1994. 'The Subsidiarity Principle in European Community Law: Some Insights from Law and Economics', *Maastricht Journal of European and Comparative Law* 1(4): 337–66.

Van den Bergh, R. 1998. 'Subsidiarity As an Economic Demarcation Principle and the Emergence of European Private Law', *Maastricht Journal of European and Comparative Law* 5(2): 129–52.

Van den Bergh, R. 2016. 'Farewell Utopia?: Why the European Union Should Take the Economics of Federalism Seriously', *Maastricht Journal of European and Comparative Law* 23(6): 937–64.

Watson, A. 1974. *Legal Transplants: An Approach to Comparative Law.* Edinburgh: University of Georgia Press.

Zweigert, K. and Kötz, H. 1998. *An Introduction to Comparative Law.* Oxford: Oxford University Press.

Index

Printed in the United States
by Baker & Taylor Publisher Services